PUBIC PERSONNEL ADMINISTRATION

PUBLIC PERSONNEL ADMINISTRATION

Confronting the Challenges of Change

Don A. Cozzetto
University of North Dakota

Theodore B. Pedeliski
University of North Dakota

Terence J. Tipple
Virginia Polytechnic Institute and
 State University

PRENTICE HALL, Upper Saddle River, New Jersey 07458

Library of Congress Cataloging-in-Publication Data

Cozzetto, Don A.
   Public personnel administration : confronting the challenges of change / Don A. Cozzetto, Theodore B. Pedeliski, Terence J. Tipple.
     p.   cm.
   Includes bibliographical references and index.
   ISBN 0-13-009382-3
   1. Civil service—United States—Personnel management,
I. Pedeliski, Theodore B. II. Tipple, Terence J.
III. Title.
JK765.C68   1996
350.1'0973—dc20   95-37828
                                                                                          CIP

Acquisitions editor: Jennie Katsaros
Editorial/production supervision: Joseph Barron/P. M. Gordon Associates
Interior design: Terry O'Brien
Copy editor: Scott Filderman
Cover design: Wendy Alling Judy
Buyer: Bob Anderson

 © 1996 by Prentice-Hall, Inc.
Simon & Schuster/A Viacom Company
Upper Saddle River, New Jersey 07458

All rights reserved. No part of this book may
be reproduced, in any form or by any means,
without written permission from the publisher.

Printed in the United States of America
10 9 8 7 6 5 4 3 2 1

ISBN 0-13-009382-3

Prentice-Hall International (UK) Limited, *London*
Prentice-Hall of Australia Pty. Limited, *Sydney*
Prentice-Hall Canada Inc., *Toronto*
Prentice-Hall Hispanoamericana, S.A., *Mexico*
Prentice-Hall of India Private Limited, *New Delhi*
Prentice-Hall of Japan, Inc., *Tokyo*
Simon & Schuster Asia Pte. Ltd., *Singapore*
Editora Prentice-Hall do Brasil, Ltda., *Rio de Janeiro*

Contents

Preface xiii

MODULE I   THE REFORM DIMENSION

1. **Public Personnel Management in Perspective**   1
   Introduction   1
   Public Personnel Administration: A Framework   2
   Personnel Tensions   4
      Who's in Control?   4
      Bureaucracy as Neutral   5
      Role of the Judiciary   6
      Merit and Affirmative Action   7
      Changing Demographics and Representative Bureaucracy   7
      Private Sector Model   8
      Political Appointees Versus Careerists   9
      Rights of Public Servants   10
   Conclusion   10
   Overview of the Book   10
   Notes   12

2. **Development and Reform**   13
   Introduction   13
   Government by Aristocracy   13
   Spoils and Democracy   16
   Government by Merit   17
   Government by Principles   19
   Government by Professional Managers   21
   Government by the "Intendedly Rational"   23
   Government by Technocrats   23
   Government by Privatization   24
   Government by Boomers   26
   Conclusion   27
   Exercises   27
   Notes   28

3. **Recent Reforms**   30
   Introduction   30
   Human Resource Initiatives as Government Reform   31
   Earlier Reform Efforts   31
   National Performance Review (NPR)   33
      The Problem   33
      The Solution   34
      Cutting Red Tape   34
      Putting Customers First   35
      Empowering Employees to Get Results   36
      Cutting Back to Basics   36
      National Performance Review Summary   37
   Underpinning the NPR: Key Theory and Issues   37
   Total Quality Management (TQM)   38
      Basic Tenets   38
      TQM in Government   39
   Reengineering   40
      Three Key Elements   41
      The Lens of Work Processes   41
      Redefining the Roles and Relationships of Key Participants   42
      Integrating the Use of Modern Information Technology   42
      Future of Reengineering   43
   Conclusion   43
   Exercise   43
   Notes   43

MODULE II   THE TECHNICAL DIMENSION

4. **Position Management**   45
   Introduction   45

Position Descriptions   46
Quality-Oriented Position Management: A Practical
   Application   47
Position Classification   51
The Factor Classification Model   52
Classification: A Practical Example   54
Pay Systems: The Federal Example   55
Reform Initiatives   62
Restructuring the Traditional Workplace   63
College Recruitment Efforts   66
Conclusion   67
Exercises   68
Notes   71

5. **Performance Management**   73
   Introduction   73
   The Theoretical Framework   73
   Problems with the Traditional Approach   75
   Problems with the Rater   76
   Problems with the Appraisal Technique   77
   The Performance Management Model   80
      Performance Planning   80
      Managing Performance   81
      Achievements Review   82
   Problems in the Workplace   86
      Employee Discipline   86
      Employee Assistance Programs (EAPs)   87
      Employee Grievances   88
   Conclusion   89
   Exercises   89
   Notes   90

6. **Labor Management Relations**   92
   Introduction   92
   Historical Evolution   92
   The Private Versus Public Controversy   95
      The Private Sector Model   95
      The Public Sector Model   95
   Collective Bargaining   96
   The Process of Collective Bargaining   98
   Strikes   100
   LMR: A Systems Model   101
   Future Issues in Labor Management Relations   101
   LMR: A Practical Example   104

Conclusion **105**
Exercises **106**
Notes **106**

MODULE III   THE HUMAN DIMENSION

7. **Human Resources Development**   **108**
   Introduction   **108**
   Context   **108**
      Change, Change, and More Change   **108**
      Managing Change Through the Learning Organization   **110**
      Rethinking the Kinds of Work We Do   **111**
      Summary of the Work Context   **113**
   HRD in the Emerging Context   **113**
      Defining Human Resource Development   **113**
      Activity Areas within HRD   **115**
      Roles in HRD   **116**
      Key Issues in HRD   **117**
      Emerging HRD Areas   **118**
   Conclusion   **119**
   Exercises   **119**
   Notes   **120**

8. **Executive Development**   **121**
   Introduction   **121**
   What Is Executive Development?   **121**
   Growth of Executive Development Programs   **122**
   Executive Development Programs Emphasize Leadership   **123**
   Sample Executive Development Programs   **129**
      Senior Managers in Government   **129**
      Leadership Development Program   **131**
      Leadership for a Democratic Society   **132**
      Summary of Executive Development Programs   **133**
   Other Forms of Development   **133**
      Career Planning   **133**
      Rotational Assignments   **134**
      Continuing Education   **134**
   Avoiding Derailment   **135**
   Conclusion   **135**
   Exercise   **136**
   Notes   **136**

CONTENTS   ix

MODULE IV   THE LEGAL DIMENSION

9. **The Constitutional Dimensions of Employment Law**   138
   Procedural Due Process   140
   Constitutional Conditions: Free Speech in the Workplace   143
   Religious Free Exercise and Employment   148
   Conclusion   154
   Public Administrator Checklist: Applicable Personnel Law
      Questions   155
   Example of Employer Free Speech Policy   156
   Disclosure of Information by Employees   157
   Exercises   159
   Notes   159

10. **Public Employment and Privacy**   164
    Recruitment   165
    Lifestyle Issues in Employment   168
       Sexual Orientation   170
       Dress, Grooming, Personal Habits   173
    Workplace Searches   176
    Drug Testing   177
    Technological Surveillance   181
    Conclusion   183
    Checklist for Public Administrators: Personnel Law Questions   184
    Example of Substance Abuse Policy for Faculty and Staff   185
       Purpose   185
       Policy   185
       Conviction of Criminal Drug Statute Violation   186
       Aftercare   187
       Prescription Drugs   187
       Sale, Transfer, Possession of Illegal Drugs   187
    Exercises   187
    Notes   188

11. **Racial Discrimination in Employment**   193
    Title VII: Civil Rights Act of 1964 Applications   194
    Racial Harassment in the Workplace   198
    Reverse Discrimination   200
    Affirmative Action   200
       Quotas   201
       Thresholds for Violations   202
       Race-Norming   203
       Voluntary Affirmative Action   205
       The Future of Affirmative Action   210

Conclusion 211
Public Administrator Checklist 211
Equal Opportunity/Affirmative Action Policy Statement 213
Exercises 213
Notes 214

12. **Gender Discrimination in Employment** 219
    Affirmative Action 225
    Sexual Harassment 227
    Sex-Linked Discrimination 235
    Conclusion 238
    Public Administrator Checklist 238
    Example of Sexual Harassment Policy 239
    Ten Top Questions to Ask When Investigating Sexual Harassment Complaints 240
    Exercises 240
    Notes 241

13. **Discrimination Based on Age and Disability: Accommodation and Adjustment** 246
    Employment Discrimination: Disability and Handicaps 250
    The Family and Medical Leave Act 264
    Conclusion 265
    Public Administrator Checklist 265
    Example Policy: Discrimination Against the Disabled 266
    Exercises 267
    Notes 267

14. **Appraisal, Discipline, Employer Sanctions** 273
    Adverse Actions for Unsatisfactory Performance 275
    Adverse Actions for Misconduct 278
    Conclusion 284
    Checklist for Personnel Administrators (Based on Federal Model) 284
    Exercises 286
    Notes 287

15. **Future Issues in Personnel** 290
    Introduction 290
    Resources 291
    Workforce Diversity 293
    Labor Management Relations 294
    Role of the Courts 295
    Benefits 296
    Technology 296

Human Resource Development   **297**
An Epilogue for Public Managers   **298**
Notes   **298**

Appendix: Personnel Law Grievances   300
Glossary   322
Bibliography   328
Case Citations   339
Index   345

Preface

The 1990s have brought about a transformation in the manner in which government conducts the public's business. In 1992, Bill Clinton was elected to the presidency on a platform of change. Vice President Gore's 1993 *Report of the National Performance Review* recommended a comprehensive "reengineering" of the national government. The midterm elections of 1994 placed Republicans in firm control of the House of Representatives and the Senate and set the stage for the implementation of the change initiatives contained in the "Contract with America."

These changes will affect all aspects of what government does, the programs that it delivers, and the clients that it serves. These changes will also have a dramatic impact on human resource management in government. When federal regional agriculture offices are closed, people lose their jobs and businesses in the community lose customers. When program responsibilities are transferred from the national to sub-national governments, the latter need to develop human resource management plans to ensure that they have the capacity to deliver these new services. As governments adapt to a world of rapidly changing technology, major investments will be needed to train public servants to be technologically competent.

Students pursuing degrees in professional programs in public administration and public policy need to be prepared to meet the human resource management challenges presented by these reforms. This book aims to help them do that. It differs from its competitors in three important ways. First, it discusses the ramifications for public managers of the current reform efforts. Second, it provides a technical framework to improve agency productivity and employee development. Third, it provides a comprehensive overview of personnel law to guide managers and personnel specialists in dealing with the constitutional and legal challenges facing public agencies.

There are a number of individuals to whom we are indebted for the assistance they provided in the completion of this project. We thank our graduate teaching assistants, Jason Fisher, Valerie Trader, and George Waller for their library work and for undertaking the tedious task of compiling the bibliography, glossary, and index. We also thank Karen Bowles, the secretary in the Department of Political Science and Public Administration at the University of North Dakota, for her invaluable assistance. The comprehensive suggestions provided by our reviewers very much improved the book. We thank James C. Harvey of Jackson State University and David S. Callahan of Longwood College. Three other individuals provided extensive feedback during the development of the manuscript: Marcia O'Kelly, Professor of Civil Rights Law at the University of North Dakota School of Law; Sally Page, Affirmative Action Officer at the University of North Dakota School of Law; and Melissa Nething, Human Resource Officer at the Weyerhauser Corporation.

We extend appreciation to the people at Prentice-Hall for their dedication and professionalism. Finally, we thank our wives, Helen, Virginia, and Cynda, for their support and encouragement.

PUBIC PERSONNEL
ADMINISTRATION

MODULE I The Reform Dimension

1

Public Personnel Management in Perspective

INTRODUCTION

Government is the largest enterprise in American society. The federal government spends $1.6 trillion annually in the delivery of public goods and services such as health, education, defense, and transportation. No private sector entity comes close. As incredible as it may seem, there are some eighty thousand state and local government units in the United States. They, in turn, have equally avaricious appetites for resources, both human and capital.

Some nineteen million Americans are employed in the public sector. This represents one out of every six jobs in this country! Table 1–1 shows the changes in public sector employment at the national and subnational levels of government since 1960. Despite the fact that total government employment continues to increase, federal employment, both as a percentage of total government employment and in real terms, is declining.

The enormous secondary economic spin-off generated in the private sector as a result of government expenditures, in areas such as defense, is impossible to estimate accurately. Wildavsky points out, for example, that defense department officials alone sign over 52,000 contract actions each and every day.[1]

Politicians, business leaders, interest groups, and even some public sector bureaucrats continually call for more efficient government. This effi-

TABLE 1-1. Total Government Employment By Jurisdiction

YEAR	FEDERAL	STATE	LOCAL	TOTAL
1960	2.4	1.5	4.9	8.8
1970	2.9	2.8	7.4	13.1
1980	2.9	3.8	9.6	16.3
1988	3.1	4.2	10.2	17.5
1992	3.0	4.6	11.1	18.7

Source: *Public Employment in 1992*, U.S. Bureau of the Census (Washington, D.C.: U.S. Government Printing Office, 1993).

ciency argument is such a deep-rooted part of American public administration that it has been the backbone of several presidential campaigns. Presidents Nixon and Carter vowed to control the bureaucracy and President Reagan promised to "get government off the backs of the people." President Clinton continues the tradition when he asserts that we need to change in a fundamental manner the way government delivers programs to the public. Vice President Albert Gore's *Report of the National Performance Review* offers a series of specific proposals to create a more "effective, efficient, and responsive government."[2] The report notes:

> To create an effective federal government, we must reform virtually the entire personnel system: recruitment, hiring, classification, promotion, pay, and reward systems. We must make it easier for federal managers to hire the workers they need, to reward those who do good work, and to fire those who do not. . . . We must enable all managers to pursue their missions, free from the cumbersome red tape of current personnel rules.[3]

An important point that requires emphasis is that personnel reform is linked directly to *creating an effective federal government*.

No one would argue with the spirit of efficient delivery of public programs. However, a critical component of efficiency concerns the people who work day to day in public sector agencies. How we treat them, the type of working environment that we provide, how we invest in their training and professional development, and the type of leadership that we provide to enable public servants to tackle new problems are important factors in our attempt to improve public services. In other words, people are the most important resource in any organization.

PUBLIC PERSONNEL ADMINISTRATION: A FRAMEWORK

Public personnel administration is about managing people. Personnel specialists are responsible for establishing personnel policies and procedures in areas such as recruitment, compensation, and employee benefits. Agency supervisors also share an important role in managing people. These supervisors must implement on a daily basis the agency personnel policies. Sometimes this can be a difficult task. For example, the supervisor may have an employee who is not performing in a satisfactory manner. Another employee has recently filed a grievance alleging sexual harassment. A third employee has a substance abuse problem that is affecting job performance. Although these examples may be extreme, they do point to the fact that supervisors at all levels of government confront problems similar to these on a regular basis. Moreover, these supervisors are expected to know how to handle personnel matters in a competent, professional manner.

The best way to understand the components and dynamics of public personnel is to view personnel administration as a management system. The public personnel framework presented in Figure 1–1 is such a system. This framework places the agency mission at the core. All other functions in the outer rings can either enhance the agency mission or detract from it, depending upon how the human resource function is managed.

Recruitment, selection, retention, and promotion represent the acquisition function of personnel. How effective public agencies are in attracting, retaining, and promoting qualified candidates has an obvious impact on the

FIGURE 1–1 Public Personnel Framework

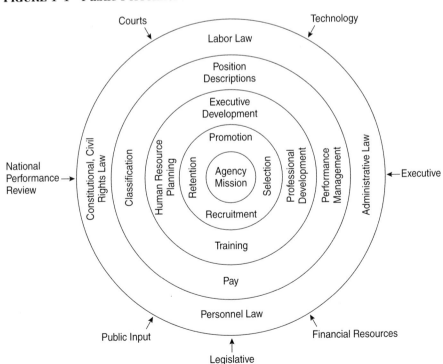

successful implementation of the agency mission. Training, professional development, executive development, and human resource planning relate to how the agency prepares its employees to adapt to changes in the workplace. This requires public employers to invest heavily in new technologies and implement innovative management strategies to avoid obsolescence. The design and implementation of effective personnel systems in areas such as position descriptions, compensation, and performance management represent the "nuts and bolts" of personnel. The outer ring in the framework depicts the constitutional and legal dimensions of public personnel. In recent years, the increase in the amount of litigation in the field has begun to reshape the content of public personnel courses. Much more time is being devoted to training personnel specialists and agency supervisors in the complexities of personnel law.

A number of factors external to the personnel system also impact the framework. These factors, such as changing technology, court decisions, and national change initiatives such as the National Performance Review, exert pressure on the personnel functions to adapt to a changing environment. The ability of the system to adapt and respond to these pressures affects the degree of success that any individual agency will achieve in accomplishing its mission. All the components that comprise this framework will be discussed in detail. Keeping the framework in the back of one's mind as the specifics are developed should provide assistance in understanding the complexities of public personnel.

PERSONNEL TENSIONS

Before one can begin to study the substance of personnel administration, a solid knowledge of a number of tensions or conflicts that constantly impact personnel management needs to be developed. These tensions, in turn, are translated into competing demands that carry with them political, economic, and social overtones. Throughout this book, these tensions constantly resurface and directly affect personnel practices. How managers accommodate these tensions determines their ability to successfully accomplish the mission of their organization.

Who's in Control?

The first tension that impacts government in general and public personnel in particular relates to the model of separation of powers embodied in the U.S. Constitution. Many Americans mistakenly believe that the executive, legislative, and judicial powers enumerated in the Constitution are separate. In fact, one simply needs to examine the powers of the Senate to discover that this body exercises all three functions, and is constitutionally mandated to do so. The Senate's obvious function is legislative, in working with the House to pass the laws of the land. The Senate exercises executive authority in approving treaties with other countries and in its role of providing advice and consent in the appointment of senior federal officials. The Senate acts in a judicial capacity when it tries impeachments.[4]

This intermixture of powers makes the federal bureaucracy servant to many masters. Is the bureaucracy responsible to the chief executive officer, the President? Or must the bureaucracy follow the legislative intent of Congress? The answer is: both. Yet, in introductory management courses professors espouse the great principle of unity of command. Students learn that having more than one boss is inefficient. In the public sector, at least, the inefficiencies are built in.

Being servant to many competing interests has profound consequences for personnel management in government bureaucracies. For example, does a central personnel agency such as the Office of Personnel Management, which is responsive to the president, provide the most effective management of human resources? Should the personnel agency be independent, or should the personnel function be decentralized to the agency level? What role if any does Congress have in capping the number of positions within specific agencies? As the reader will discover in the next chapter, these and other questions concerning who is in control have embroiled presidents and Congress in many battles over the personnel function. President Nixon impounded $15 billion in appropriated funds in an effort to control what he perceived to be an unresponsive bureaucracy that was meddling in policy matters that should be reserved for elected officials. Congress reacted by passing the 1974 Budget and Impoundment Control Act, which strictly limited the president's discretion in refusing to spend money legally appropriated by Congress. In a similar vein, Fred Malek, head of the White House personnel office under Nixon, produced the *Federal Political Personnel Manual*, commonly referred to as the Malek Manual. Many claim that it was an overt attempt at a Machiavellian rape of the merit system by advocating hiring or dismissing individuals based upon party affiliation and personal relationships so as to control the bureaucracies. The bottom line in all of these examples is that legislators and chief executives often fight for control over public bureaucracies. This ability to command and utilize large cadres of professional civil servants tilts the balance of power toward one branch of government or the other.

Bureaucracy as Neutral

A related tension impacting human resource management is a popular notion throughout the public administration literature that public sector bureaucracies are neutral, value-free instruments of implementation. In his famous 1887 essay, Woodrow Wilson advocated the politics/administration dichotomy.[5] His thesis was that the elected representatives formulated public policies and the professional bureaucrats simply followed the desires of the regime in power. Max Weber's ideal bureaucratic model also stressed the desirability of a technical, professional cadre of bureaucrats.[6] Wilson was wrong in 1887, and few individuals in the 1990s would agree that bureaucrats are neutral. In fact, bureaucrats are very proactively involved in formulating public policy, implementing policy, and adjudicating an elaborate administrative appeals process. These powers, and specifically those exercised by regulatory agencies, prompted Peter Woll to pronounce that the bureaucracy was the most powerful fourth branch of government—more powerful than the president, Congress, and the courts.[7] Woll goes on to argue that these powers exercised by nonelected public servants destroy the intent of the separation of powers doctrine that occupied so much time during the founding debates.

Role of the Judiciary

Many Americans erroneously believe that the judicial system in general and the Supreme Court in particular provide direction to line and staff managers as the latter struggle on a daily basis with the constitutional and other legal factors affecting discrimination, affirmative action, drug testing, and sexual harassment. Sometimes the courts are anything but a beacon of guidance. Their opinions can confuse rather than clarify the meaning of individual rights as they are applied in the area of personnel. This confusion makes it very difficult for personnel specialists and agency managers to understand the substance of personnel law. A few cases in the area of the constitutionality of drug testing will serve to reinforce this point. The major constitutional issue in these cases contrasts the government's right to maintain a safe and drug-free working environment with the employee's right to privacy and undue search and seizure.

On October 19, 1990, the U.S. District Court for the Northern District of Georgia, in the case of *Georgia Association of Educators v Harris*, declared unconstitutional the Georgia Applicant Drug Screening Act because it violated Fourth Amendment rights.[8] On November 16 of the same year, in the case of *National Treasury Employees Union v Clayton Yeutter, Secretary of Agriculture*, the U.S. District Court of Appeals for the District of Columbia struck down a Department of Agriculture drug-testing policy because it was based on off-duty use.[9] The court reasoned that this violated Fourth Amendment rights. Yet, on March 29, 1991, in the case of *Willner v Thornburgh*, the U.S. District Court of Appeals for the District of Columbia ruled that attorneys applying for positions within the Justice Department *could* be tested for drugs *without* violation of their rights under the Fourth Amendment.[10] On April 12, 1991, in *Catherine Tanks v Greater Cleveland Regional Transit Authority*, the Sixth Circuit Court of Appeals upheld the dismissal of a bus driver following an accident who tested positive for cocaine.[11] In the *Willner* and *Yeutter* cases, the rulings came from the same court, yet they were contradictory. The question becomes: how is the personnel specialist supposed to take guidance from this seemingly contradictory assessment of the constitutionality of testing employees for substance abuse? Module 4 of this book provides a detailed analysis and a framework for public managers to help them understand and apply the principles that are derived from the Constitution, statutory law, and case law.

Merit and Affirmative Action

Human resource specialists at all three levels of government take pride in the fact that the majority of positions filled in the public sector are based upon a merit system. The names of the three most qualified applicants (called the rule of three) are forwarded to the agency filling the position. The supervisor can then select any one of the three applicants. In some instances, however, applications of white males with equal or greater qualifications are not forwarded because of affirmative action policies. If an individual is selected for a position or promotion at least in part on the basis of racial or ethnic origin or gender, some qualified white males respond angrily or allege reverse discrimination when they discover that a job for which they applied was awarded to a female or a Native American because the agency allocated "affirmative action points" to applicant rankings. If agencies can allocate these points based upon gender, ethnic origin, disability, and veteran's service, can the agency simply establish quotas as remedies for specific societal groups that have suffered from historic discriminatory practices? In 1990, President Bush vetoed civil rights legislation because he claimed that it would result in a quota system.

Affirmative action policies are likely to surface as a topic in the 1996 elections. Voters in California may decide on an amendment to the state constitution, prohibiting preferential treatment based upon race, gender, or disability. Senator Phil Gramm from Texas has publicly announced that if elected president, he will issue an executive order countermanding all previous federal preferential treatment policies.

Affirmative action is a contentious issue. The specific court cases that address this issue are discussed in greater detail in module 4. What the reader needs to remember is that these are complex matters involving human emotion, politics and values, and individuals' constitutional or other legal rights.

Changing Demographics and Representative Bureaucracy

The tensions are exacerbated when we consider the notion of a representative bureaucracy. One concept of a representative bureaucracy is one that mirrors the demographics of society. In America today, white males account for 45 percent of the national workforce. Women, Blacks, and Hispanics are in the majority in the population yet occupy lower percentages of civil service managerial jobs compared to their white male counterparts. Proponents of a demographically representative bureaucracy argue that this is discrimination. If Blacks represent 12 percent of the population, they should occupy 12 percent of the federal jobs at all levels, including the senior management levels.

A major issue related to this model of representative bureaucracy concerns the argument presented by many people that it results in a lower-quality service to the client—in this case, the public. An example from another country illustrates this argument. In Canada, for the past three decades the federal government has gradually institutionalized a policy of representative bureaucracy that reflects the unique attributes of French-speaking and English-speaking Canada. The national government allocated enormous financial resources to bring French Canadians into the federal service. Financial incentives and training programs targeted at "fast tracking" potential senior managers were implemented. In fact, bilingual bonuses are still paid today. The government achieved its desired goals because the number of Francophone civil servants has grown exponentially at all managerial and administrative levels. Civil servants are told that unless they are fluent in French, the probability of promotion into senior management is low. This upsets many Anglophone Canadians, particularly those in western Canada. This example highlights the fact that government's role in balancing individual and societal needs with demographic equity and fairness oftentimes conflicts with regional, ethnic, and cultural interests.

Private Sector Model

In many facets of government in general and personnel in particular, we see private sector managerial principles and concepts applied in an effort to run government more efficiently. A recent case in point at the national level is Vice President Gore's National Performance Review. The recommendations found in the report claim to represent historic change in the way government conducts the public's business: improved efficiency and reduction in red tape. One problem with implementing recommendations contained in such proposals lies in the fact that although some management principles are generic to both business and government, the unique attributes of managing in the public sector make it difficult to apply business principles such as increased productivity and efficiency. In the area of labor-management relations, for example, the neat private sector model tends to fall apart when applied in the public sector. At the federal level, collective bargaining is not a process of unfettered debate where both management and labor articulate their respective positions in an effort to attain consensus. Government defines what is fit for negotiation by its employees. In the private sector, if consensus cannot be reached, one dispute resolution mechanism is the strike. Many public sector employees are prohibited from striking. The case in point is President Reagan's 1981 firing of striking members of the Professional Air Traffic Controllers Organization, the union representing them.

The second and obvious difficulty in making government more efficient and effective is that oftentimes efficiency and effectiveness are in direct conflict with public demand for services. We ask our students how many think that the U.S. Postal Service should be more efficient and effective, perhaps modeled after UPS. Most of them raise their hands in support. We then point out that unlike the U.S. Postal Service, UPS is not expected to have offices in every community across the country regardless of size. When the Postal Service tries to close an outlet in a small town because it is losing money, those very advocates of efficiency and effectiveness and making government more businesslike lobby their congressional delegation to keep the office open. Government must consider what is in the public interest; sometimes efficiency takes a back seat to providing the public the services it desires.

There are also some notable differences between senior managers in government and corporate executives in the private sector. First, corporate executives receive financial compensation that is substantially greater than that which their public sector counterparts receive. The private sector can lure competent public managers away from their agencies with larger salaries, benefits, and other financial incentives. Second, the Senior Executive Service at the federal level was faced with a 40 percent turnover during its first four years of operation (1979–1983). What private sector agency could lose that many senior executives and still operate effectively?

Political Appointees Versus Careerists

Over the course of American history, a recurring debate has focused on the number of political appointees that should be involved in administering the affairs of public bureaucracies. As we shall discover in chapter 2, the problem was so acute in the late 1880s that a president was assassinated by a disgruntled office-seeker demanding a low-level patronage appointment. Political appointees often are in conflict with the career public administrators over whom they exercise authority. Moreover, many political appointees do not possess the requisite qualifications to undertake the senior management responsibilities assigned to them. When a new regime is elected, the newly appointed cadre of politicos often enters government with a platform premised upon bureaucrat-bashing. Many political appointees stay in their positions for only eighteen to twenty-four months. They tend to want quick results that will both provide political brownie points and win them favor in the eyes of the politicians who appointed them. The tensions between the patronage appointees and the careerists intensify and subside depending upon the administration in power and the political issues of the day.

Rights of Public Servants

Career civil servants have different rights than ordinary Americans. Restrictions on the right to strike has been mentioned. It is important to note that fundamental freedoms such as speech, association, and privacy have a more limited meaning when applied to public servants, although it can be argued that a public servant has much more latitude in criticizing public policy than a business executive does in questioning company policy. Should a career employee in the state government of Minnesota have the right to go to work during an election campaign and openly advocate a certain political party? Perhaps this person even wears campaign pins on her suit jacket. Can this same individual remark to her office colleagues that the current governor is "incompetent, unethical, and irresponsible?" Certainly, ordinary Americans are free to campaign for the candidate of their choice, and we often hear cries from citizens that politicians are incompetent, unethical, and irresponsible. In module 4, the reader will discover that the Constitutional rights of civil servants are governed by many political factors, including the contention by some that government is sovereign and therefore public servants hold their positions at the will of the elected representatives of the people.

CONCLUSION

One can probably think of some additional tensions or conflicts that impact personnel management in the public sector. The important message is that without a solid understanding of the complex and sometimes turbulent environment in which personnel decisions are made, students cannot comprehend the complexities surrounding public personnel administration in the 1990s. This book seeks to provide students with a theoretical and practical framework to facilitate this understanding.

This book emphasizes the major components of public personnel management that managers must understand as we approach the next century—personnel law; the technical application of managerial and personnel-specific techniques; and training, motivation, and executive development. The exercises and cases at the end of the chapters serve to reinforce the important concepts raised in each area of personnel management.

OVERVIEW OF THE BOOK

The book is divided into four modules, the reform dimension, the technical dimension, the human dimension, and the legal dimension. Instructors and students should note that the book is designed in such a way that the ordering of the modules is flexible. They can be read in or out of sequence. A course emphasizing personnel law, for example, would concentrate on module 4, and the students could be asked to read that section first. Similar logic applies to the other modules.

Module 1 provides an introduction and an overview of the history of civil service reform and a discussion of the most recent reforms contained in Vice President Gore's National Performance Review. Chapter 2 examines key political and institutional reforms. Personnel management moved from a model of "government by the elite," through the spoils era of Jackson and his successors, to the first major institutional reform, the 1883 Pendleton Act. The chapter also covers Wilson's politics/administration dichotomy, the scientific management movement and the various rational personnel tools, the 1978 Civil Service Reform Act, bureaucrat bashing, the Volcker Commission Report, and the National Performance Review. Chapter 3 explores how innovative human resource management strategies can enhance government initiatives to reform the manner in which it conducts the public's business. The chapter discusses the implications for public personnel management of the key reform initiatives contained in the National Performance Review.

Module 2 covers the technical application of personnel procedures: what managers need to do as part of the routine personnel function. In chapter 4, students are given hands-on experience through the use of exercises in developing a quality-oriented position description. They learn the importance of critical elements and how the position description can be the key to classification, pay, and performance management. Varieties of job classification systems and pay scales are also introduced. Chapter 5 discusses performance management and how the performance appraisal process can be used to improve employee motivation and productivity. Chapter 6 highlights the complexities of labor-management relations in the public sector.

Module 3 moves from the technical components of public personnel to the human dimension, focusing on human resource development, executive development, and developing a quality workforce. Chapter 7 provides an overview of human resource development and how planned change can help government agencies adapt to the growing number of challenges that confront them. Chapter 8 expands this discussion and reviews several executive development programs that are designed to enhance the leadership capabilities of senior public sector managers.

Module 4 of the book addresses personnel law in detail. It is our contention that the constitutional and legal environment of public personnel is now one of the dominant components of human resource management. Some managers and instructors may find the discussion of the constitutional and legal principles detailed and in some instances difficult. Recognizing that this may be the case, the chapters in this section are very comprehensive and provide important analysis of the historical progression of judicial opinion in order to assist the reader in understanding the current application of the principles. At the end of each chapter a checklist is provided as a practical guide for managers as they confront the myriad of personnel law questions impacting public employment. Chapter 9 examines a number of cases that involve freedom of speech, freedom of association, privacy, political neutrality, equal protection, discrimination, liberty, and due process and relates these to personnel administration. This chapter lays the foundation for the specific treatment of affirmative action, sexual harassment, substance abuse, and so forth, that are addressed in subsequent chapters.

Chapter 10 provides detailed analysis of the issues concerning public employment and privacy. Chapter 11 deals with racial discrimination and affirmative action. Chapter 12 explores gender discrimination. Chapter 13 concerns age discrimination. Chapter 14 provides a legal framework for performance appraisal and employee sanction. In examining the constitutional and other legal factors that affect public sector personnel, the discussion is a distillation of pertinent judicial opinion. Examples of agency policies are also included as a managerial guide. Chapter 15 discusses future personnel issues within the context of the National Performance Review. The series of hypotheticals that appear in appendix A challenges the reader with some very interesting and complex personnel law issues.

Notes

1. For an excellent discussion on the implications of the defense budget, see Aaron Wildavsky, *The New Politics of the Budgetary Process*, 2d ed. (New York: Harper Collins Publishers, 1992), chap. 9.
2. Al Gore, *From Red Tape to Results: Creating a Government That Works Better and Costs Less: Report of the National Performance Review* (Washington, D.C.: U.S. Government Printing Office, 1993), p. i.
3. Ibid., p. 22.
4. See U.S. Constitution, art. 1 and art. 2, sec. 2. For a detailed treatment of the intermixture of powers see John A. Rohr, *To Run A Constitution: The Legitimacy of the Administrative State* (Lawrence, Kans.: University of Kansas Press, 1986).
5. Woodrow Wilson, "The Study of Administration," *Political Science Quarterly* 2 (June 1987).
6. Max Weber, "Bureaucracy," in *From Max Weber: Essays in Sociology*, ed. H. Gerth and C. Wright Mills (Oxford: Oxford University Press, 1946).
7. Peter Woll, *American Bureaucracy*, 2d ed. (New York: W. W. Norton & Company, 1977).
8. *Georgia Association of Educators v Harris*, 749 F Supp 1110 (N.D.Ga., 1990).
9. *National Treasury Employees Union v Clayton Yeutter, Secretary of Agriculture*, 733 F Supp 403, 918 F2d 968 (D.C. Cir 1990).
10. *Willner v Thornburgh*, 928 F2d 1185 (D.C. Cir 1991).
11. *Catherine Tanks v Greater Cleveland Regional Transit Authority*, 930 F 2d 475 (6th Cir 1991).

2

Development and Reform

INTRODUCTION

In the preceding chapter a personnel framework was presented and a number of tensions were introduced that continually constrain efforts at more effective management of human resources in the public sector. In this chapter the reader will understand that these tensions did not come about by chance. Rather, they emerged over the course of the last two centuries as a result of the political and administrative evolution of the country. Great public debates were staged over what role government should play in the lives of the American people. These debates, in turn, led to a series of important political and institutional reforms in the area of personnel. These reform efforts are important because they helped mold the personnel systems that we have today at all three levels of government. The ability to comprehend the complex personnel issues of today is predicated upon having a grasp of the political and institutional changes that have taken place over time. These reforms are the subject of this chapter.

GOVERNMENT BY ARISTOCRACY[1]

During the early years of the republic and even during the decade of government by the states under the Articles of Confederation, there was a public administration infrastructure. It was rather small by today's standards but important nonetheless. The leaders of the new republic needed to maintain a military, debts incurred by the confederate states needed to be repaid, a postal service was needed so that individuals could communicate, and some system of revenue collection was needed to fund the continued operation of government.

Occupying a position in the public sector in the early years brought with it esteem, high social status, and community recognition. Public sector employment was not considered pejorative as many in the United States view it today. In fact, the first secretary of the treasury was one of the most prominent Americans of all time, Alexander Hamilton. Senior positions in government were occupied by an elite gentry, and the practice of bestowing government office upon one's political supporters was a common, accepted practice. Van Riper comments that "the government of our early days was a government led by the well-educated, the well-born, the prosperous, and their adherents. In short, it was a government by the upper classes."[2] Despite patronage and elitist government, public administration in the early years of the republic was very efficient and was the envy of many European nations.[3] How times have changed!

Over two hundred years ago, President Washington found himself in the unique position of nation-building. Leonard White's treatise on the Federalists notes that these were particularly difficult times for the nation. The new Constitution was adopted by a narrow margin, and the general population feared another government that had the power to levy additional taxes on them.[4] As Cayer points out:

> A significant requirement for public service employment under Washington was support of the new federal political system. Although support for the political system does not seem particularly radical today, it was a controversial issue at the time, as many people hoped that the new system would fail. Thus, oddly enough, a political position with which many citizens strongly disagreed was a requirement for holding a public job.[5]

Because many people believed that the national government would usurp the powers of the states, Washington needed to assure the public that local interests would not be compromised. He wanted community input into the decisions of government and believed that the best vehicle for attaining this was a representative civil service, a concept that we call representative bureaucracy today. Cayer writes:

> President Washington wanted to ensure that local programs would be administered by the members of each community and that all regions of the country would be represented in the high echelons of the public service. He thereby hoped to gain nationwide support for and identification with the new political system.[6]

Washington also needed to appease those army officers who fought in the Revolution. He thus created a system of veterans' preference, a concept that forms a fundamental component of affirmative action plans in the 1990s.

Washington was an astute politician. He once said that appointments to the government sector constituted "one of the most difficult and delicate parts of the duty of my Office." He went to great lengths in consulting with members of Congress before making appointments to ensure a degree of regional equality. Van Riper explains that Washington "paid deference to a desirable geographical distribution of appointments as well as to the opinions of senators, congressmen, and governors. . . ."[7] He valued integrity, honor, and a strong character. In looking back on Washington's terms in office, reformers in later years judged him as an individual who cared deeply about the efficient operation of the new republic and who stressed competent management over political considerations.[8]

The second president, John Adams, while continuing to subscribe to the philosophy of a government by the elite, went one step further by implementing an appointment ideology based upon patronage. Aronson writes that "John Adams felt that appointments should be given only to persons who subscribed to his own political views."[9] Other presidents, including Jefferson, also based appointments upon patronage.[10] Moreover, Jefferson purged the federal personnel system because he believed it had become too partisan in favor of the Federalists. In describing Jefferson's appointment ideology, Aronson notes that his appointment of Republicans to public offices and his refusal to consider requests from his own supporters to appoint at least some Federalists caused some internal turmoil for the party.[11]

In 1811, a Congress alarmed at the increasing use of patronage appointments formally proposed a constitutional amendment prohibiting access to government positions by any member of Congress who served during that president's term of office. Members felt, and probably with some justification, that the president would be able to subsume the legislative powers of Congress by dangling the carrot of a secure government position in the faces of congressmen. For example, Jefferson appointed twenty ex-members of Congress and Madison twenty-nine to public service positions. Adams once remarked that half the members of Congress were actively soliciting appointments for their relatives and the other half for themselves. In any case, the amendment did not receive the necessary two-thirds support, although many members of Congress supported it.[12]

Although the early presidents intuitively recognized the practical and political need to allow participation by the masses, government continued for many years to be operated by an elite group of prominent, well-educated, and influential individuals: the cream of society; hence the term in the heading to this section—aristocracy. One of the reasons for the Revolution was a belief in the colonies that governments run by the elite were not representative of the people.

SPOILS AND DEMOCRACY

Andrew Jackson forever changed personnel management in government. With the adoption of nine new states into the Union and with the extension of the franchise to the middle and lower classes, the political landscape of the United States had changed radically prior to the election of 1828. Jackson was elected on a grass-roots, throw-the-old-boys-out platform. His election was the culmination of what Mosher calls the triumph of the common man.[13]

Jackson is associated with the advent of the "spoils system."[14] Leonard White cautions, however, that Jackson has been blamed unjustly for introducing the spoils system. White writes:

> The deterioration is often charged against Jackson, as the originator of the spoils system. Such a conclusion would be unjust. Jackson did introduce rotation . . . he did not introduce the spoils system.[15]

Although several of his predecessors turned out as many civil servants as Jackson, the latter was more vocal in linking spoils to democratic principle. Crenson explains that Jackson had barely settled into the executive chair in the oval office when the building was overrun with political allies seeking appointments to prestigious government positions.[16] "Old Hickory" believed that because he was popularly elected, it was a fundamental tenet of democracy to appoint those individuals who provided support. In other words, to refute the president's ability to appoint public servants on the basis of political partisanship was tantamount to being antidemocratic. Freedman explains that "it remained for Jackson to elevate rotation in office into a principle of democratic government."[17] This is an important point because, as we shall discover later on, the spoils/democracy argument had to be refuted before reformers could pave the way for a merit-based personnel system. Jackson also believed that public service jobs did not require any special skills, talent, or education beyond literacy and that any "common man" could undertake the task.

Jackson's successors, including Fillmore, Buchanan, and Lincoln, continued with the practice of patronage. Not surprisingly, this practice of turning out civil servants every four years began having dramatic negative effects on the operations of government. As America was beginning to become a force both politically and economically, and as the Union was expanding, the public administration infrastructure struggled to keep up. Agencies such as the postal service and the customs department were both corrupt and inefficient. Business leaders, scholars, and forces in subnational governments began to call for reform, placing the blame for the county's problems squarely at the feet of the spoils system.

By the end of the Civil War, the federal government was the largest employer in the nation; it comprised seven departments employing thirty thousand workers with an annual payroll of $53 million. The qualifications of the majority of those employed in the public sector were questionable. As Hoogenboom points out, the 282 employees within the Treasury Department were indeed a motley crew: they included 1 detective, 2 druggists, 1 editor, 5 farmers, 1 hackdriver, 1 sculptor, 24 teachers, 1 minister, 1 page, 1 waiter, 1 housekeeper, and 1 washerwoman. The department employed only 7 accountants![18]

Lincoln's successor, Andrew Johnson, became embroiled in a battle with Congress over control of the personnel function. The fight was so intense that it led to impeachment proceedings against the president. The issue concerned the passage of the 1867 Tenure of Office Act. The act curbed the president's patronage powers by prohibiting him from dismissing senior government officers without the approval of Congress. Johnson's refusal to comply with the act led to the impeachment proceedings. Although the president survived by a single vote, Congress made clear its intention to have a say in personnel matters.

One early attempt at civil service reform came during the Grant administration. In 1871 the Civil Service Act became law. This empowered the president to implement personnel rules and guidelines for public service employees and to establish an administrative framework to ensure compliance with the procedures. Grant created the first civil service commission to carry out this mandate. Fearing an erosion of its control over personnel, Congress refused to fund the commission. Despite the fact that these initial reform efforts were short-lived, they did form the basis for a movement toward a merit-based model of personnel in the next decade.[19]

GOVERNMENT BY MERIT

The assassination of President Garfield in 1881 sounded the death knell for the spoils system. Cayer explains:

> The assassination of President James A. Garfield became a dramatic symbol of the evils of spoils—it could even lead to murder. The fact that Charles Guiteau, Garfield's assassin, was an unsuccessful seeker of patronage employment gave the reformers the impetus they needed, and that Garfield was a supporter of reform only added to their sense of urgency.[20]

As Hoogenboom reveals, "Garfield dead proved more valuable to reformers than Garfield alive."[21]

In 1883, Congress passed the Pendleton Act, named after a Democratic Senator from Ohio, which institutionalized the reform agenda. Other key members of the reform movement, including George Curtis, Charles Bonaparte, and Dorman Eaton, viewed the introduction of a merit system as "the most essential governmental reform."[22] Following similar efforts in Great Britain, the act defined a number of specific reforms:

1. A merit-based system was introduced.
2. Protections were incorporated against patronage removals.
3. The United States Civil Service Commission was created. It comprised three commissioners appointed by the president, with the advice and consent of the Senate. No more than two commissioners could be from the same political party. In other words, it was a bipartisan commission.
4. A system of open, competitive examinations was introduced.
5. A probation period of six months was now required.
6. The act stipulated that no members of the civil service could be coerced into identifying their political ideology, nor could they be forced to contribute financially to any political party.

Van Riper sums up rather succinctly the political and administrative impact of the act:

> We can conclude, then, that the American legislation of 1883 stimulated the development in the United States of a *merit system* founded on British precedents: That is, a system of civil service recruitment and organization based on (1) competitive examinations, (2) relative security of tenure, and (3) political neutrality. On the other hand, the new act also reflected peculiar patterns of American thought and action. . . . We thoroughly adapted it to the American political and social climate.[23]

The Pendleton Act was also a catalyst for reform at the state level. Although New York and Massachusetts passed personnel reform legislation in 1883 and 1884, respectively, Aronson points out that it was not until 1905 that Wisconsin and Illinois passed comprehensive merit reform.[24]

Initially, only about 10 percent of the federal service came under the merit system. As Van Riper explains, the new act was purposely designed with a fair degree of flexibility because there were a number of questions that remained unanswered. First, a constitutional question was raised: if personnel administration came under the responsibility of a commission, did this usurp the powers of the president and Congress to manage the federal government? Second, instituting a comprehensive merit system takes time. The commission needed an administrative support staff, designing and administering competitive examinations takes time, and so forth. Finally, the flexibility built into the legislation allowed the president to espouse reform efforts and retain a significant role in patronage—it was clearly a win-win situation.[25] In subsequent years, the merit system was extended through the use of executive orders that "blanketed in" those individuals previously not covered.

Now that a merit system had been accepted and partially implemented at the national level, the question turned to the argument presented by the proponents of spoils. Did a merit system violate democratic principle? Recall that Jackson was adamant that appointments to the public service by the popularly elected President enhanced democracy, the implication being that merit was undemocratic.

Woodrow Wilson and Frank Goodnow, two scholars who built upon the earlier reform efforts discussed above, addressed the question. Wilson, who later became president, was a political scientist and scholar in the area of public administration. Goodnow, also a political scientist, was the first president of the American Political Science Association. In "The Study of Administration," Wilson developed the politics/administration dichotomy that had been espoused earlier by reformers such as Curtis and Eaton. The dichotomy implied that administrators in a merit-based system were professional, competent, and neutral. They simply carried out the wishes of the elected representatives *irrespective* of what party was in power. Wilson wrote:

> The field of administration is a field of business. It is removed from the hurry and strife of politics; it at most points stands apart even from the debatable ground of constitutional study.[26]

There was, therefore, no threat to the president or to democracy. Goodnow supported Wilson's dichotomy by referring to the two functions of government as politics and administration. The former was the expression of the state's will; the latter the execution of that will.[27] The work of these two scholars, therefore, provided a theoretical foundation for merit-based systems.

GOVERNMENT BY PRINCIPLES

With the democracy/merit issue settled for the time being, public personnel management embarked upon a new era. First, Frederick Taylor's theory of scientific management had enhanced productivity and efficiency in the private sector. Taylor explained his four principles to the House of Representatives committee in January, 1912. His time and motion studies sought the one best way to accomplish a task. The first principle was make production efficient, or maximize input versus outputs. Second, arrange work in the most rational manner to attain organizational goals within a specific task environment. Third, maximize productivity. Fourth, maximize profits. Congress was interested in learning how Taylor's "magic" could be applied in government because the nation's public sector had been unable to cope with the demands placed upon it by the rapidly evolving industrial economy.

Taylor had a rather dehumanizing perspective of workers. He believed that they were lazy and unmotivated. Management's role was to break work down into specific technical units and to select workers according to physical and intellectual attributes. Once the task environment was defined scientifically, the worker would be paid on a "piece-meal" basis, according to the quantity produced. By studying workers in a scientific manner (that is, by analyzing and quantifying every aspect of production), management then assumed the production knowledge-base traditionally controlled by the workers.

Taylor was famous for his explanations concerning the one best way to move coal. Through careful empirical study, he determined that the optimum level of production for moving coal with a shovel was in loads weighing twenty-one pounds. Anything less would be inefficient, and weights in excess of the optimum would tire the worker prior to the completion of the shift. Once the optimum production level was determined scientifically, this would be applied uniformly across all similar task environments, a process that today is called standardization.

Taylor's scientifically derived principles of workforce and task management directly influenced personnel management at the turn of the century and continue to do so today. The high degree of specialization in many public sector agencies has many of today's critics complaining of government by technocrats. It seems that the process sometimes becomes more important than the needs of the client. Other examples of Taylorism include pay for performance and bonus systems, rigid classification systems, position descriptions that quantify in precise detail the duties of the employee, computer-based assessment centers, depersonalizing the workplace by writing memoranda to the position instead of the person, and even certain elements of Total Quality Management, the statistical quality controls advocated by W. Edwards Deming. Although these types of personnel procedures are intended to standardize the process to ensure consistency and fairness in application, their rigidity can in fact stifle innovation in personnel management.

The second foundation of the scientific approach was the pioneering work of German sociologist Max Weber. His ideal bureaucratic model meshed nicely with Taylor's principles. Weber's model contained attributes of both the organization and the individual official. From the organizational perspective, the ideal model was hierarchical, with clearly established superior-subordinate relationships. There was a distinct division of labor and a clearly delineated span of control. Management was based upon specific rules, procedures, and laws. The official was appointed based upon professional and technical competence, and the appointment was usually for life.

Application of the scientific method in the public sector was popularized by Leonard D. White. His 1926 classic, *Introduction to the Study of Public Administration,* was the first textbook in the field of public administration. Acknowledging that the administration of the American state had been neglected for the past century, White called for a refocusing on the "business side" of government. The goal of administrators was to expedite the public business by utilizing the most efficient and economical means available.[28] The debate whether management principles in business and government are similar or different continues today. When politicians and citizens call for a government that is more businesslike, they are in essence resurrecting similar arguments that were developed seventy years earlier.

In terms of the personnel functions, the efficiency/scientific principles movement led to standardized personnel procedures, today called standard operating procedures. The use of position descriptions to define specific tasks and to standardize jobs across similar task environments are examples. Sophisticated classification systems were later developed to assign pay scales to positions. Again, there was an attempt to standardize the process of matching work and compensation for work in a variety of environments. For example, all Engineer IIs fall in the same pay range whether the individual is employed in a public works agency or in a research agency. Performance appraisal systems also have their roots in the scientific management model. Individual performance is evaluated through a standardized process, and this is used as a basis for reward, promotion, and sanction. Finally, the efficiency movement strongly emphasized the use of competitive examinations.

GOVERNMENT BY PROFESSIONAL MANAGERS

Thanks to the reform movement, when Franklin D. Roosevelt became president the federal bureaucracy was once again staffed by a cadre of professional, competent individuals. The high quality of midlevel personnel was instrumental in the successful implementation of the myriad of public programs initiated under the New Deal. The 1937 Brownlow Committee Report had a significant impact on human resource management in the federal government, although most of the report was never adopted by Congress.[29] In fact, it characterized the personnel function as the core of administrative management.

The management focus under the New Deal administration is best explained by referring to the *theoretical* management framework developed by Gulick and Urwick. The term theoretical is figurative because Gulick, Urwick, and other New Deal leaders focused on the philosophical foundation for public management and were not the technocrats that some would believe. In their work, *Papers on the Science of Administration,* POSDCORB was proclaimed as the essence of what effective managers actually do. The initials translate into the following:

Planning:	This is a systematic effort by the executive to develop macro-level agendas and to specify appropriate methodologies for implementation.
Organizing:	This is the formal authority structure. Sub-units within the organization are defined, and the specific task structure is identified.
Staffing:	This is personnel, including staffing, training, and development.
Directing:	This involves the direction of subordinates.
Coordinating:	This is where the manager is able to integrate the various units within the task environment in order to achieve organizational goals.

Reporting: This is the process of communication where both superiors and subordinates are kept informed as to the successes and problems within the task environment. Formal records are maintained.

Budgeting: This is the formal process of resource allocation, accounting, and audit.[30]

During the early years of the Roosevelt administration, personnel received considerable attention. The President's Keynesian fiscal policy agenda of using government expenditures as a proactive tool in managing the economy led to a proliferation of government agencies—the Tennessee Valley Authority, The National Industrial Recovery Administration, and the Public Works Administration are examples. These agencies, in turn, needed to compile position descriptions and recruit qualified candidates. This led to a debate on the appropriate structure and role of the Civil Service Commission. The major issue of whether personnel management should be a centralized function or decentralized to the agency level occupied considerable time on the administration's agenda. In the end, Roosevelt opted for the latter. Accordingly, the role of the Civil Service Commission was altered, and many of the "nuts and bolts" personnel functions were transferred or delegated to specific agencies. Each agency now had under its employ professional personnel administrators.

Long after the Roosevelt administration, the debate about professionalization took a new turn. The heart of the question was whether top administrative posts should be occupied by "substantive area professionals" or by general career-type management experts. In some circles, this argument continues. For example, does a senior administrator in an engineering agency have to be a professional engineer, or can a general management specialist do an equally effective job of running the agency?

Another significant event for personnel management occurred under the Eisenhower administration. Former President Hoover headed the Hoover Commission, known formally as the Commission on Organization of the Executive Branch of the Government. An important component of the second Hoover Commission report was that for the first time the relationship between political appointees and career civil servants received attention. One of the recommendations in the report was that a Senior Career Service of about three thousand senior managers be established.[31] This cadre of "super bureaucrats" would be the nexus between the political appointees and middle managers. Although the recommendation was never formally adopted, it formed the basis for the creation of the Senior Executive Service in 1978. During the Commission's work, Hoover was asked which of the Commission's 314 recommendations was most important. His response was: "I would pick the recommendation for the setting up of a senior civil service."

At that time the U.S. government had 2.3 million personnel with an annual payroll in excess of $9 billion. Hoover went on to comment that government's high turnover of 25 percent per year and its inability to attract and retain quality people was one of the biggest problems facing government.[32] Many argue that his words continue to ring true in the 1990s.

GOVERNMENT BY THE "INTENDEDLY RATIONAL"

In the mid-1940s and early 1950s public administration came under attack from scholars such as Dwight Waldo, Robert Dahl, and Herbert Simon. Much of their research and writings were academic in nature as contrasted with the practical focus of government, but their work had an important impact on the field of public administration. All three contended that it was impossible to develop and implement a series of administrative principles. Waldo's *The Administrative State* challenged the contention that these principles constituted science.[33] Dahl's "The Science of Public Administration: Three Problems" challenged the universality of administrative principles in organizations because rational administrative behavior was tempered by individual personalities, values, and the culture of the organization.[34] The most vocal opponent of the principles approach was Simon. His work demonstrated that for every administrative principle there was a counterprinciple. For example, the principle of span of control dictated that managers should have a narrow span of control in order to be most effective—perhaps they should directly supervise no more than five employees. Another principle argued that in order to maximize efficiency, communication was important. Effective communication meant limiting the layers in the bureaucracy. This obviously flies in the face of span of control. One principle supports the notion of a tall hierarchy, the other a flat structure. Simon was able to demonstrate that for each principle there was a contradictory principle.

Simon went on further to state that although managers wanted to act rationally—in other words, to consider all of the variables and options related to any decision—they were unable to do so. There were technological limits, limits in the abilities of the individual decisionmakers and, in the public sector, the major limitation of politics. The best that managers could hope for was to be intendedly rational or to satisfice.[35] Simon's view of individual behavior supported the thesis constructed earlier by Weber and Taylor. The role of the organization, therefore, was to control the inefficiencies associated with individual behaviors. All organizational goals are established by management and a series of subgoals are communicated to each level in the organization. Workers accept these goals because the organization has the capability to force acceptance.

GOVERNMENT BY TECHNOCRATS

With the increasing complexity of the national government and the more demanding role it played in dealing with the social, economic, and political issues impacting the nation both domestically and abroad, there came a need to develop highly trained, specialized public administrators. Beginning in the 1950s graduate schools in the social sciences, planning, public administration, and business administration began cranking out professionals highly trained in the application of sophisticated quantitative and computer skills. As Mosher points out, by 1978, 40 percent of all government jobs were labeled as "professional." The private sector, on the other hand, employed professionals in only 11 percent of the total workforce.[36]

A professional is normally defined as an individual with four or more years of college education and who purports to be a specialist in some field—lawyer, engineer, scientist. Many of these individuals belong to professional organizations—the American Society of Public Administration, International Personnel Managers Association, the International City Management Association, and so forth.

The November/December 1977 and the March/April 1978 editions of *Public Administration Review* were devoted to professions in the public sector. The articles quantified actual numbers of professionals on an agency basis and attempted to determine the affect that these groups have on the operations of government. This debate continues today.

The civil service is becoming even more professionalized and specialized than it was only two short decades ago. There are tens of thousands of engineers, lawyers, computer specialists, economists, accountants, and so on, employed by government agencies. The concern raised by many analysts is that this emphasis on technical, professional personnel can contribute to a lack of innovation and the ability to think critically beyond the narrow focus of individual expertise. Even though the public service at all levels has become increasingly technocratic in the last four decades, some argue that government has not had a good track record in the area of effective delivery of public services. Perhaps there is some truth to the contention that generalists make better managers or that the education system is not providing the training necessary to allow professionals to consider innovative strategies in the day-to-day management of public agencies. In any event, there are serious long-term personnel implications in transforming policy and decision making into highly specialized, mechanized exercises that focus primarily on the quantitative dimensions of public policy and in so doing ignore many of the important qualitative factors.

GOVERNMENT BY PRIVATIZATION

Ronald Reagan's election in 1980 spawned a new era in public administration in general and public personnel management in particular. Early on in his presidency, Reagan did two things. First, he asked that a comprehensive evaluation be conducted on *all* federal programs in an effort to make government more business-like. Second, OMB (Office of Management and Budget)

Circular A-76 was revised to determine where these programs could be more effectively delivered by the private sector through outright privatization or through contracting out. Outright privatization involves turning an entire operation over to the private sector. The government no longer participates or provides funding. In Britain, former Prime Minister Thatcher's sale of British Airways is an example. Contracting out, on the other hand, involves providing service contracts to the private sector to provide services previously delivered "in house" by government. In this case, the government still pays the bill. Examples include janitorial services in government office buildings and refuse collection in municipalities.

The President's Private Sector Survey on Cost Control (the Grace Commission) consisted almost solely of business leaders—161 in total. Its massive evaluation of government programs was made public in 1984. The Commission provided the president with almost 2,500 recommendations to make government more efficient and claimed that in just three years the savings to the American taxpayer would amount to $500 billion dollars! The Commission report came under severe attack for ignoring a number of factors unique to the public sector, the most important of which was politics.

The fact that many of the Commission's recommendations had already been implemented long before it reported and the fact that many other recommendations were unrealistic is not the issue. The important aspect of the Commission report is the effect it had in the area of personnel. The commissioners, through their public proclamations of how poorly government was run, lent credibility to Reagan's platform of bureaucrat-bashing and reducing government's involvement by "getting government off the people's backs." Morale in the career ranks soon hit an all-time low, and disgruntled employees either left the service or became less productive because employee motivation had been negatively affected. Although all levels of management were affected, the one hardest hit was the Senior Executive Service, where turnover from 1978 to 1983 was in the range of 50 percent (2,000 top administrators).

Originally issued in 1966, OMB Circular A-76 mandated that detailed cost comparisons be undertaken on all in-house projects to determine if they could be delivered more effectively by the private sector. The Reagan administration used this directive as a vehicle to implement an extensive series of contracting-out initiatives. Agencies were required to demonstrate to the satisfaction of the Office of Management and Budget that any programs that were delivered in-house were more cost-effective than similar programs delivered by the private sector. Otherwise, the program or service was to be delivered by the latter. The jury is still out as to how effective the contracting-out efforts were under the Reagan administration. One outcome is clear, however. The push for privatization further exacerbated the resentment within the federal civil service toward the employer. Employees were RIFed (reduction-in-force), turnover increased, and morale and motivation in the federal workforce continued to decline.

GOVERNMENT BY A BUREAUCRAT

President Bush neither advocated nor implemented any critical policies in the area of federal human resource management. He also didn't disturb the bureaucracy. His administration survived four years without any major battles over civil service issues. The president made some astute appointments to key government positions and signed a pay raise for civil servants in 1990. Most important, Bush made a point of praising the work of public servants, departing significantly from the bureaucrat-bashing of his predecessor, Ronald Reagan.

Bush had a certain sensitivity to, perhaps even an affinity for, bureaucrats. After all, the president was probably the bureaucrat's bureaucrat. Besides being elected to Congress, the vice presidency, and the presidency, Bush had held a number of positions within the bureaucracy, such as the CIA and the foreign service. He understood that the success of government programs is largely the result of the efforts of a professional, competent civil service. Bush seemed intent on working with the bureaucracy as opposed to controlling the executive branch of government. This collaborative approach, different from the combative atmosphere of Nixon and Reagan, stemmed from both the president's length and diversity of his career in public service.

GOVERNMENT BY BOOMERS

The Clinton administration was elected on a platform of change. Although the public and media were preoccupied with health reform and deficit reduction, several personnel issues also rose to national prominence during 1993 and early 1994. Immediately after taking office, the new administration became embroiled in a controversy over the policy of lifting the ban on employing gays and lesbians in the military. Several of the president's cabinet-level nominees became the subject of public ridicule and were forced to withdraw from the process, and several of the administration's key policy personnel resigned. As part of the plan to reinvent government and manage the deficit, the new administration proposed a reduction in the federal workforce of 250,000 employees and further reductions in military personnel.

In 1993, vice president Albert Gore's *Report of the National Performance Review* was completed. The report was a comprehensive evaluation of how the federal government conducted the public's business. Citing polls that show that the American people's confidence in the federal government is at an all-time low, the report offers a series of comprehensive recommendations to improve the delivery of government services. In the area of personnel, the Office of Personnel Management is asked to deregulate personnel policy by reducing or eliminating thousands of pages of rules and regulations governing federal agencies. In areas such as recruitment, the report indicates a need to decentralize to the agency level the authority to recruit quality employees. Classification categories and pay scales would also be collapsed to allow agency managers additional flexibility, and performance evaluation systems would be revamped to focus on customer service and the empowerment of employees.[37]

The 1994 midterm elections witnessed further demands by the American people for change. One of the most interesting issues that has the potential to have a dramatic effect on personnel management in all sectors concerns the anti-affirmative action sentiment that appears to be gaining momentum across the country. There is a constitutional amendment initiative in California that has the support of Governor Pete Wilson, and several key Republican members of Congress support changes in affirmative action policies at the national level. Proponents of the changes want to eliminate preferential treatment for minorities, women, and the disabled in the hiring and promotion of employees.

CONCLUSION

This chapter is intended to provide the student of public sector personnel management with a historical perspective of the efforts over the past two hundred years in political and institutional reform of human resource management. Many of the issues currently on the public personnel agenda have a direct connection to past reform initiatives. The development of merit systems, the development and application of scientific management principles, the increased professionalization of the civil service, the academic debates concerning how government programs can be managed in a more effective and efficient manner, and the present dialogue concerning affirmative action programs all have one thing in common. They seek to improve personnel management and thereby improve the quality of service to the public.

Exercises

2.1 Contact a government agency or your local university. Determine what functions are provided in-house and what functions are contracted out to private firms. Is there any way that the current policies can be improved toward increasing efficiency? What are the political ramifications of altering the current practices?

2.2 Obtain a copy of the *Report of the National Performance Review* from the library. Examine some of the recommendations in the area of personnel. Prepare a memorandum discussing how these changes might be implemented in your state government.

Notes

1. The subheadings used in this chapter are adapted from Paul P. Van Riper, *History of the United States Civil Service* (White Plains, N.Y.: Row, Peterson and Company, 1958) and Frederick C. Mosher, *Democracy and the Public Service*, 2d. ed. (Oxford: Oxford University Press, 1982), chap. 3.
2. Van Riper, *History of the United States Civil Service*, pp. 17–18.
3. Ibid., chap. 2.
4. For an excellent discussion of government during the Federalist era, see Leonard D. White, *The Federalists* (New York: The Macmillan Company, 1948).
5. N. Joseph Cayer, *Public Personnel Administration in the United States*, 2d. ed. (New York: St. Martin's, 1986), p. 18.
6. Ibid., p. 18.
7. Van Riper, *History of the United States Civil Service*, p. 18.
8. Herbert Kaufman, "The Growth of the Federal Personnel System: A Profile of the Federal Civil Service," in *The Federal Government Service*, ed. Wallace S. Sayre, 2d. ed. (Englewood Cliffs, N.J.: Prentice-Hall, Inc., 1965).
9. Sidney H. Aronson, *Status and Kinship in the Higher Civil Service: Standards of Selection in the Administrations of John Adams, Thomas Jefferson, and Andrew Jackson* (Cambridge, Mass.: Harvard University Press, 1964), p. 6.
10. For a comprehensive discussion of the Jeffersonians, see Leonard D. White, *The Jeffersonians: A Study in Administrative History* (New York: The Macmillan Company, 1951).
11. Ibid., pp. 7–13.
12. Ibid.
13. Mosher, *Democracy and the Public Service*.
14. It should be noted that the statement "to the victor belongs the spoils" was made in an 1832 Senate debate by William Marcy.
15. Leonard D. White, *The Jacksonians: A Study in Administrative History 1829–1861* (New York: The Macmillan Company, 1954), pp. 4–5.
16. Matthew A. Crenson, *The Federal Machine: Beginnings of Bureaucracy in Jacksonian America* (Baltimore: The Johns Hopkins University Press, 1975).
17. Anne Freedman, *Patronage: An American Tradition* (Chicago: Nelson-Hall Publishers, 1994), p. 11.
18. Ari Hoogenboom, *Outlawing the Spoils: A History of the Civil Service Reform Movement 1865–1883* (Urbana: University of Illinois press, 1961).
19. Cayer, *Democracy and the Public Service*.
20. Ibid., p. 24.
21. Hoogenboom, *Outlawing the Spoils*, p. 212.
22. Van Riper, *History of the United States Civil Service*, p. 83.
23. Ibid., p. 100.
24. A. H. Aronson, *State and Local Personnel Administration: Biography of An Idea*. United States Civil Service Commission (Washington, D.C.: U.S. Government Printing Office, 1974).

25. Van Riper, *History of the United States Civil Service*, pp. 103–109.
26. Woodrow Wilson, "The Study of Administration," *Political Science Quarterly* 2 (June 1887), pp. 197–212.
27. Frank J. Goodnow, *Politics and Administration: A Study In Government* (New York: Russel and Russel, 1900).
28. Leonard D. White, *Introduction to the Study of Public Administration* (New York: Macmillan Publishing Company, 1926).
29. The formal title of the committee was The President's Committee on Administrative Management. It comprised three members: Louis Brownlow, chair; Luther Gulick; and Charles Merriam.
30. Adapted from *Papers on the Science of Administration*, ed. Luther Gulick and Lyndall Urwick (New York: Institute of Public Administration, 1937).
31. The first Hoover Commission reported to President Truman in 1949. The second report was a follow-up study that ultimately made 314 recommendations concerning the reorganization of government.
32. An excellent discussion of the Commission is found in Neil Macneil and Harold W. Mietz, *The Hoover Report 1953–1955: What it Means to You as Citizen and Taxpayer* (New York: The Macmillan Company, 1956).
33. Dwight Waldo, *The Administrative State: A Study of the Political Theory of American Public Administration* (New York: The Ronald Press, 1948).
34. Robert A. Dahl, "The Science of Public Administration: Three Problems," *Public Administration Review* 7 (1947).
35. Herbert A. Simon, *Administrative Behavior: The New Science of Management Decision* (New York: Harper and Row, 1960); Idem, "The Proverbs of Administration," *Public Administration Review* 6 (winter 1946).
36. Mosher, *Democracy and the Public Service*, p. 113.
37. Albert Gore, From Red Tape to Results: Creating a Government that Works Better and Costs Less: Report of the National Performance Review (Washington, D.C.: U.S. Government Printing Office, 1993).

3

Recent Reforms

INTRODUCTION

From Red Tape to Results: Creating A Government That Works Better and Costs Less is the title of a report authored by Vice President Al Gore as part of the Clinton administration's National Performance Review of the federal government. In many ways that title sums up many of the efforts to improve government through more effective use of its most valuable resource: the human resource. This chapter explores many of those efforts, past and present, as public administrators at all levels of government have attempted to improve public service through effective human resource management. A special premium is also placed in this chapter on exploring the theoretical foundations upon which these efforts are based.

Public administrators are not alone in their pursuit of more effective organizations. Their business counterparts are also looking to achieve competitive advantage for their organizations through effective human resource management. In fact, since the early 1980s when Peters and Waterman wrote *In Search of Excellence*,[1] much attention has been paid to improving long-term profitability through effective deployment of human resources. Phrases such as "Our employees are our most valuable resource" and "Effective use of the human capacity is the only sustainable competitive advantage" have become commonplace in company communications such as vision statements and annual reports. Companies now spend unprecedented amounts of money hiring consultants to help them with human resource management initiatives, such as Total Quality Management (TQM) and Reengineering.[2]

HUMAN RESOURCE INITIATIVES AS GOVERNMENT REFORM

Unlike business where the objective of human resource management initiatives may simply be enhanced profitability, similar efforts in public organizations often bring with them an ideological component that promotes an agenda that goes beyond improving the efficiency of government operations. Since government has no universally agreed-upon "bottom line," government effectiveness is often in the eye of the beholder. One key aspect of this is explained by DiLulio et al. when they write:

> First, it is attempting to confuse disagreement over what government ought to do with how well it does it. There is a common presumption that government programs are larded with too much bureaucracy and wasteful spending. But what critics call waste, fraud, and abuse often are programs managed well but managed according to values different from the critics' own. Many of the potential savings identified by the Grace Commission, for example, would have resulted from eliminating programs with which commission members disagreed. The programs might have indeed been wasteful by some definitions, but they represented the legitimate product of the American democratic process. The danger here is that solutions billed as administrative, managerial, or technical may disguise underlying differences of policy or significant competition among disparate interests.[3]

Hence the political element, which is ever-present in public administration, is very relevant to our discussion of government reform and human resource initiatives. As the quote implies, questions about government performance and utilization of human resources bring with them a subjective aspect that guarantees a lively debate about any proposed changes to the existing system.

EARLIER REFORM EFFORTS

Before examining the Clinton administration's National Performance Review and other current initiatives such as TQM and Reengineering, it is necessary to pause and recognize that a number of other reform efforts were initiated earlier at the federal level. Additionally, state and local governments have also been actively engaged in attempting to improve performance through various strategies and programs that center around more effective use of human resources. Scholars such as Goodsell, Moe, and DiLulio help chronicle some of the efforts to date at the federal level.[4] A summary of Moe's chronology, as reported by DiLulio, is shown in Table 3–1. A cursory look shows that the twentieth century has seen no shortage of high-level commissions address the issue of government performance and the deployment of human resources. Yet, notice that their prescriptions include a wide array of recommendations that address issues as broad as:

The balance of power among the branches of government. Government reform often addresses the power and authority of the three branches and arrives at recommendations such as the one to strengthen the executive branch, made by the President's Committee on Administrative Management (1936–1937), often called the Brownlow Committee.

Reorganizing the executive branch. Many reform proposals see reorganization as a key part of reforming the executive branch, such as proposed by the Ash Council (1969–1971) and the Carter reorganization effort (1977–1979).[5]

TABLE 3–1. Major Commissions to Improve the Executive Branch, 1905–93

Keep commission (1905–09)
Personnel management, government contracting, information management
President's Commission on Economy and Efficiency (1910–13)
The case for a national executive budget
Joint Committee on Reorganization (1921–24)
Methods of redistributing executive functions among the departments
President's Committee on Administrative Management (1936–37)
Recommended creation of the Executive Office of the President; study founded on substantial academic theory
First Hoover commission (1947–49)
Comprehensive review of the organization and function of the executive branch; built on task force reports
Second Hoover commission (1953–55)
Follow-on to the first Hoover commission; focused more on policy problems than organizational structure
Study commissions on executive reorganization (1953–68)
Series of low-key reforms that produced quiet but important changes
Ash council (1969–71)
Proposals for a fundamental restructuring of the executive branch, including creation of four new super departments to encompass existing departments
Carter reorganization effort (1977–79)
Bottom-up, process-based effort to reorganize government that mostly ended in failure; new cabinet departments created independently of effort
Grace commission (1982–84)
Large-scale effort to determine how government could be operated for less money
National Performance Review (1993)
Attempt to "reinvent" government to improve its performance

Source: Ronald C. Moe, *Reorganizing the Executive Branch in the Twentieth Century: Landmark Commissions*, report 92-293 GOV (Congressional Research Service, March 1992).

Eliminating unnecessary programs and functions. One common reform approach is to propose to stop funding and managing programs that are no longer needed or are not appropriate areas for the government to be managing. For example, the Grace Commission (1982–1984) proposed eliminating the Rural Electrification Program. The "Contract With America," offered by the Republicans in the 1994 election, contains much of this type of language.

Numerous other specific reform measures are constantly being proposed. Yet, many are not based as strongly on human resource initiatives. For example, much attention has been paid to improving the budget process through implementing such legislation as The Budget and Impoundment Control Act of 1974 and proposals to move to a biennial budget rather than the current one-year budget that many government organizations follow. Similar efforts have addressed other management processes such as planning, procurement, and information processing. Our focus in this chapter will be on human resource-based improvement efforts and their underlying theoretical approaches.

NATIONAL PERFORMANCE REVIEW (NPR)

One of the first major initiatives of the Clinton administration was to undertake the NPR with the objective of "reinventing" the federal government. The NPR's report, cited in the first sentence of this chapter, contains the latest set of prescriptions for improving the performance of government. The human resource deployment and management aspects of the report are significant. This is not merely a call for reorganization or improved management processes, though it does contain some recommendations in those areas. Rather, it examines the relationships of a government with the people it serves and the people it employs. Public service and public employment are reexamined in this latest reform initiative.

The Problem

The NPR's framing of the performance problem of the federal government is interesting. Rather than blaming the usual suspects (such as entrenched bureaucrats, public unions, poor leadership, legislative gridlock) the Clinton administration chose to focus on the inappropriateness of the organization structures, work processes, and environments that characterize the federal government. The report claims that the root problem is "Industrial-Era Bureaucracies in an Information Age."

> Is government inherently incompetent? Absolutely not. Are federal agencies filled with incompetent people? No. . . . From the 1930's through the 1960's we built large top down, centralized bureaucracies to do the public's business.

They were patterned after the corporate structures of the age: hierarchical bureaucracies in which tasks were broken into simple parts, each the responsibility of a different layer of employees, each defined by specific rules and regulations. With their rigid preoccupation with standard operating procedure, their vertical chains of command, and their standardized services, these bureaucracies were steady—but slow and cumbersome. And in today's world of rapid change, lightning quick information technologies, tough global competition, and demanding customers, large top-down bureaucracies—public or private—don't work very well. Saturn isn't run the way General Motors was. Intel isn't run the way IBM was.[6]

The Solution

The NPR's solution to the performance problem is to create "entrepreneurial organizations," which are described as being better suited to the challenges of today. Specifically they are thought to be more efficient, adaptive, and responsive to quickly changing conditions. The report says that four principles will characterize the journey to creating these successful public organizations of the future. They are cutting red tape, putting customers first, empowering employees to get results, and getting back to basics: producing better government for less.

By boldly pursuing these four principles, the report argues that government truly can be "reinvented" to "work better and cost less." First we will examine what actions lie behind these four principles. Then we will look at the theoretical work and controversial issues that accompany this latest reform proposal.

Cutting Red Tape

In America, when one hears the term government or bureaucracy it is often in the context of some frustrating experience someone has had with the rules, regulations, and paperwork associated with "doing business" with a government agency. The red tape, as it is known, is often frustrating to the person trying to get a driver's license, pay taxes, or bid on a government contract. The NPR found red tape to be overwhelming not only to those outside of government trying to cope with it but also to government employees whose workdays are gobbled up trying to comply with red-tape requirements. The report states:

> Counting all personnel, budget, procurement, accounting, auditing, and headquarters staff, plus supervisory personnel in field offices, there are roughly 700,000 federal employees whose job it is to manage, control, check up on or audit others. This is one third of all federal civilian employees.[7]

Thus, red tape is seen as a major villain and as anathema to the entrepreneurial organization. Toward cutting the red tape, the NPR suggests six areas of focus, including streamlining and simplifying the budget, personnel, and procurement processes; enlisting the support of agency inspectors general to help lead the reform; deregulating federal employees; and empowering state and local governments. Though many of these suggestions have been made before, together they do send a strong message of setting an environment that is more trusting of government employees and of recipients of federal funding (i.e., state and local governments) to make wise decisions about the management of that money. For example, the report calls for decentralizing the personnel process so that managers at an actual job site can make the critical personnel decisions, such as hiring a new employee, rather than having to wait for authority to hire to come from a central personnel office miles away.

Putting Customers First

Borrowing from the recent successes of businesses that have improved themselves by becoming "customer driven," the report calls on government agencies to begin considering the applicant for a driver's license, the person paying taxes, and the businessperson bidding on a government contract as "customers" and to reorient their work processes to serve those customers. Borrowing a key tenet of Total Quality Management (TQM) (which is discussed later in this chapter), customer needs must be the focus of work. Otherwise processes and procedures are developed for the sake of the bureaucracy, and a disproportionate amount of resources go into satisfying internal processes while the customers receive less than satisfactory service. The report notes:

> We can create an environment that commits federal managers to the same struggle to cut costs and improve customer service that compels private managers. We can imbue the federal government—from top to bottom—with a driving sense of accountability.[8]

Describing the American people as customers frames the relationship between a government and the people it serves in a very business/market-like way. Hence it shouldn't be surprising that the NPR emphasizes these mechanisms to help put the customer first. Specifically, it recommends four: setting customer service standards, making service organizations compete, using market mechanisms to solve problems, and creating market dynamics. This series of recommendations is based on the notion that, where appropriate, the market forces of competition should be allowed to work. The result would be that parts of government organizations, such as the nation's air traffic control system, would be restructured as corporations, and other internal service providers, such as the Government Printing Office, would be forced to compete for business with the private sector. Making government more business-like is an attempt to rein in the cost of government and continues a theme brought out in the Reagan administration, through the Grace Commission, and carried on in the "Contract With America."

Empowering Employees to Get Results

This third major area speaks to changing the organization culture associated with public bureaucracy. As noted earlier, the top-down, hierarchical, industrial-style bureaucracy was diagnosed as a major part of the problem. The report states that these organizational structures and the cultures that accompany them are both inappropriate for serving the American people in today's fast-paced world and they have a negative effect on the employees working in them. Empowerment of workers generally refers to getting unnecessary administrative barriers (red tape) out of the way of employees so that they can focus on the important parts of their jobs (serving customers). It is being pursued vigorously in business as a means to improve competitiveness and as the modern way to manage a workforce in the information era.

> Our long term goal is to change the very culture of the federal government. . . . A government that puts people first, puts its employees first, too. It empowers them, freeing them from mind-numbing rules and regulations. It delegates authority and responsibility. And it provides them a clear sense of mission.[9]

Changing organizational culture and empowering employees are no easy tasks, as innumerable forces are in place to resist change.[10] The NPR proposes a six-step strategy to bring about these changes. The strategy includes decentralizing decision making power; holding organizations and employees accountable for results; providing training, information systems, and other tools to workers to get the job done; forming labor-management partnerships; and exerting leadership. Such efforts would represent changes in the relationship between the government and its employees in at least two significant areas. First, by decentralizing decision making power, the level of responsibility for lower- and middle-level managers goes up, as their work presumably would receive less review from personnel at higher levels. Second, labor-management partnerships would represent a shift from the traditionally adversarial relationship those two parties have been a part of since the unions were formed.

Cutting Back to Basics

This fourth area makes the well-known case that the government is much better at starting programs than ending them and that the expenditures for programs, facilities, and services that are of questionable value take away from resources that should be available for continually improving the efficiency of delivery of the more important endeavors of government. The result is that resources (human and financial) are spread too thinly across the government landscape and facilities that should be closed and sold remain open while crucial aspects such as core computer systems become obsolete because of lack of investment. This area in particular reminds us that government is not a business and because there is no bottom line, one person's wasteful program is another's top government priority.

> After a decade of tight budget talk, for example, federal budget expert Allen Schick says he can identify just three major nondefense programs eliminated since 1980. . . . Why is it so difficult to close unneeded programs? Because those who benefit from them fight to keep them alive. While the savings from killing a program may be large, they are spread over many taxpayers. In contrast, the benefits of keeping the program are concentrated in a few hands. So special interests often prevail over the general interest.[11]

The NPR, in this last area, focuses on some of the challenges that are truly unique to public administrators. Toward cutting back, the recommendations include eliminating obsolete, redundant, and special-interest portions of the government; collecting more revenues; and investing in greater productivity and Reengineering programs to cut costs. Many of the recommendations (e.g., eliminating subsidies and closing facilities) will be heavily dependent on the cooperation of Congress. Others, such as investing in technology to enhance productivity and Reengineering (which is discussed later in this chapter), would seem to be less dependent on the approval of Congress to implement.

National Performance Review Summary

In summary, the NPR represents the latest government reform proposal that emphasizes changes in the deployment and management of human resources. The four areas described above are noteworthy here for three reasons:

1. The relationship between government and the people is reframed as one between a business and its customers.
2. The relationship between the government and its employees is shifted to one of empowerment and accountability.
3. Major human resource based strategies such as TQM and Reengineering are to be used to improve government's performance.

All of these proposals have a theoretical base, and virtually all have their proponents and detractors. In the remainder of this chapter we will explore some of the key theoretical underpinnings and some of the arguments they engender.

UNDERPINNING THE NPR: KEY THEORY AND ISSUES

Clearly, the written work of Osborne and Gaebler, most notably *Reinventing Government: How the Entrepreneurial Spirit is Transforming the Public Sector*,[12] had significant influence on the NPR. Osborne and Gaebler utilize many "success stories" taken mainly from state and local governments to build their case for entrepreneurial government. These cases, blended with a preference for market-generated solutions such as contracting-out, combine to provide the perfect primer for the NPR. Even some of the phrases could be used interchangeably. For example Osborne and Gaebler promote "customer driven government,"[13] "competitive government,"[14] and "community-owned government: empowering rather than serving,"[15] all terms that could fit nicely in the NPR report. Additionally, the influence of some current business management theorists such as Tom Peters is evident in the report.

The NPR and its theoretical underpinning are not without critics. At the highest level of critique is the argument that the authors have forgotten what an early public administration scholar said years ago, that government is different.[16] By that he meant that because of the political element of government, pure business administration approaches to government will not work. More specifically, some of the values associated with entrepreneurial government (autonomy, a personal vision of the future, secrecy, and risk-taking behavior) could potentially be at odds with some values associated with our democratic form of government (accountability, citizen participation, open policymaking processes, and "stewardship" behavior).[17] In other words, some critics claim that this latest wave of performance proposals overemphasize values associated with businesslike efficiency and minimize values associated with our political system such as responsiveness and inclusion of minority interests.[18]

TOTAL QUALITY MANAGEMENT (TQM)

TQM is a process-oriented approach to improving organizations. It influenced not only the NPR but also countless other organizational improvement efforts in the 1980s and 1990s. It is often associated with some of its early pioneers such as W. Edwards Deming, Joseph Juran, and Philip Crosby. TQM initiatives can be found in virtually all types of organizations (business, government, not for profit) around the world. TQM has been credited with playing a major role in turning the Japanese manufacturing sector into a major success story of the 1970s and 1980s.[19]

Basic Tenets

In discussing TQM's applicability to government, Swiss notes that TQM has seven basic tenets.[20] First and foremost, the customer is the ultimate determiner of quality. In most TQM literature, there is no equivocation on this matter. If the customer is not satisfied, then the quality is inadequate. Pleasing or "delighting" the customer should be the overarching goal of the organization.

Second, quality should be built into the product early in the production process (upstream) rather than being added on at the end (downstream). "Do it right the first time" is a common phrase in TQM literature and training classes. It is used to show how much more efficient it is to produce a good or service properly from the very beginning than it is to send it back for "fixing" after errors or defects are found by quality control personnel at the end of the line. Doing it right the first time reduces rework and the need for quality control/inspection personnel.

Third, preventing variability is the key to producing high quality. TQM advocates firmly believe that "if you can't measure it, you can't manage it." Hence, one of the key areas of emphasis in TQM is to identify measurable performance standards and utilize statistical techniques to measure and chart progress.

Fourth, quality results from people working within systems, not individual efforts. This is one of TQM's more contentious points in the United States, where individual rights and individual superstars receive so much attention. In fact, Deming argues that individual performance appraisals, a standard part of most public personnel systems, should be abolished. TQM is team-based and stresses team performance, not individual performance.

Fifth, quality requires continuous improvement of inputs and processes. This tenet emphasizes that quality (customer satisfaction) is not static. Organizations must continuously improve if they are to stay competitive and keep meeting customer expectations. Managers should focus on inputs and internal processes, as those are the elements over which they have control.

Sixth, quality improvement requires strong worker participation. Theorists such as Deming believe that process improvements are best made by the very people responsible for the work. They should work in teams to solve process problems. Teams should consist of workers of various functions and levels in the organization and should work in an open, nonthreatening environment. Teams should be aware of the principles of group dynamics and utilize group problem-solving techniques.[21]

Seventh, quality requires total organizational commitment. TQM proponents bristle at the mention of "TQM programs" because they believe that the pursuit of quality requires a total organizational commitment. This means that the organizational culture must change to embrace the quality approach. Hence, the idea of TQM being a program implies that it is to be placed alongside all the other programs such as employee assistance programs, safety programs, and the like. The TQM advocates argue that TQM must be bigger than just another program and must involve the total organization culture.

TQM in Government

Of critical importance to the public administrator is the applicability of TQM to government. Clearly the NPR draws on the TQM approach in describing entrepreneurial government organizations. Especially clear are the linkages of putting customers first and giving workers the tools they need to do their jobs. Additionally, President Clinton frequently speaks of his positive experience with TQM at the state level in Arkansas. Numerous other government organizations have adopted TQM approaches in varying degrees. Hence, at the practical level, government organizations are significantly involved in TQM.

At the theoretical level, many have raised questions about the applicability of TQM to government organizations. Two of the more significant arguments in this regard have to do with the nature of the work and the presence of many stakeholders. First, on the nature of the work, TQM was developed in a manufacturing environment, where processes are repetitive and outputs are easily measured. Government work has a high percentage of service work with highly variable outputs, making routine processes and uniformed measuring more difficult. How can the principles of TQM be applied, for example, to a city manager's office or to a police department?

Second, many find the notion of "customer" in government problematic. At the grandest level, one could easily argue that the American people are not customers of government, they are the owners. Also, because of the many stakeholders involved in government work, it can be difficult to identify the customers. For example, should the federal government strive to "delight" the oil and timber companies who purchase oil, gas, and timber from public lands? Isn't the recreationist who wants to use those same lands a customer? How about a person living miles away who is a taxpayer and just wants to know that the lands are managed professionally and in the public interest? What about future generations of Americans who will want to enjoy those lands? Are they customers, too?

Clearly, the pure TQM theory does not work as well for some government work as it does for product manufacturing in the private sector. Yet, at the same time, government managers at all levels appear to be finding value in the TQM process improvement approach. At the federal level the potential benefits of TQM were thought to be of such significance that the Federal Quality Institute was established and has been providing quality-related information and training since the late 1980s. Many states, often in combination with universities, have established similar organizations, and numerous government organizations have integrated TQM principles into their daily operations.

REENGINEERING

The last performance improvement approach discussed in this chapter is Reengineering. Made prominent by the book *Reengineering the Corporation: A Manifesto for Business Revolution*,[22] many managers are looking to Reengineering as a way to better structure the organization's work efforts. Again, drawn by successes from the business world, public administrators are looking for similar improvements in government.

Whereas TQM represents a process of making many small incremental changes to existing processes, which will result in overall large increases in quality, Reengineering stands for making major changes in the way work is done and looking for significant improvements immediately. To use a baseball metaphor, TQM is about hitting singles and Reengineering looks to hit home runs.

> When someone asks us for a quick definition of business reengineering, we say it means "starting over." It *doesn't* mean tinkering with what already exists or making incremental changes that leave basic structures intact. It isn't about making patchwork fixes—jury-rigging existing systems so that they work better. It does mean abandoning long-established procedures and looking afresh at the work required to create a company's product or service or deliver value to the customer. It means asking this question: "If I were re-creating this company today, given what I know and given current technology, what would it look like?" Reengineering a company means tossing aside old systems and starting over. It involves going back to the beginning and inventing a better way of doing work.[23]

Three Key Elements

"Starting over" and "looking afresh" sound inviting, but perhaps a little overwhelming. Where would one get started with Reengineering? And why should the results be any different this time? Reengineering offers two elements that seem to differentiate it as an approach to organizational improvement through more effective utilization of human resources. Its proponents look at the organization through the lens of work processes, redefining the roles and relationships of key participants and integrating the use of modern information technology. These factors taken as a whole provide the potential to truly redefine how an organization conducts its business and organizes and deploys its human resources.

The Lens of Work Processes

A cornerstone of Reengineering is that work is defined by processes and not by the usual measures of tasks or functions.

> Most business people are not "process oriented"; they are focused on tasks, on jobs, on people, on structures, but not on work processes. We define a business process as a collection of activities that takes one or more kinds of input and creates an output that is of value to the customer.[24]

An example often given is that of lending at a bank or at a government agency, where the work can easily involve the following steps (each possibly taking place in its own department): sales/customer service, credit check, business practices to customize the loan, pricing, and clerical support for final packaging. The example cited by Hammer and Champy took six to seven days to complete. After looking at this through the lens of "the loan approval process" they found that the actual work took only ninety minutes. The remainder went to passing the work from department to department and to having systems designed for the very rare, complex exception rather than for the majority of loan applications.[25] Hence, the lens of work processes helps to analyze work in a new and creative way.

Redefining the Roles and Relationships of Key Participants

Reengineering encourages organizations to rethink who does what. A business example that brings this point home is the huge retail chain Wal-Mart reaching an agreement with Procter & Gamble (P&G) that says Wal-Mart will buy all of its Pampers from P&G if P&G will manage Wal-Mart's inventory and storage of Pampers. P&G gets an exclusive contract, and Wal-Mart is relieved of having to provide warehouse storage and worry about inventory management.[26] This agreement changes the traditional roles and relationships of supplier (P&G) and customer (Wal-Mart) by integrating their work to an unprecedented level. This line of thinking allows exploration of all kinds of creative options and provides opportunity to deploy resources in a far greater number of ways. We are already starting to see this kind of creativity in government between agencies and private-sector and not for profit organization partners, between agencies and volunteers, and agencies and their own employees.

Integrating the Use of Modern Information Technology

Reengineering is a process that consciously attempts to take advantage of the productivity enhancement of information technology. Today's (and tomorrow's) technological capabilities greatly facilitate the redeployment of human and financial resources. Each of the examples cited above was aided by the use of sophisticated information technology. The loan approval process can now be completed by far fewer people in part because more comprehensive, integrated information services are more readily accessible. P&G can successfully provide just-in-time delivery to Wal-Mart in part because of its linked, sophisticated computer system that allows P&G to track sales store by store. But the point to remember here is that the advanced information technology only assists the Reengineering process. It alone, without the lens of work processes and the redefinition of roles and responsibilities, will not bring about the major changes sought by Reengineering.

Future of Reengineering

Though the NPR calls for Reengineering, government is just beginning to explore this new improvement strategy, but the possibilities are many. No doubt value concerns like those expressed about TQM will be voiced such as that government is built on a notion of stability and incremental change and that Reengineering is oriented around dramatic change. Another concern could be that Reengineering argues for new roles and relationships, yet it has taken us two hundred years to establish how this government interacts with its people and various interest groups. Hearing those cautions, one also hears the constant call, as is articulated in the NPR, for a government that is more effective and efficient. It will be interesting to see what role Reengineering will play in moving government forward.

CONCLUSION

This chapter has explored government reform efforts that emphasize human resource management. All such government reform proposals, including the National Performance Review, are controversial because they propose to disrupt the current balance of interests. There are political aspects to all "administrative" reform efforts. Total Quality Management and Reengineering, two process improvement approaches borrowed from experiences in business, serve as the foundation for many reform initiatives today. As expected, they, too, are controversial. Though considerable energy is being expended on incorporating TQM and Reengineering into government, only time will show their true impact.

Exercise

3.1 Obtain a copy of the *Report of the National Performance Review*. Examine the specific recommendations that impact personnel. Discuss the strengths and limitations of the proposals and how agencies might go about implementing them.

Notes

1. Thomas J. Peters and Robert H. Waterman, Jr., *In Search of Excellence* (New York: Harper and Row, 1982).
2. John A. Byrne, "The Craze for Consultants," *Business Week,* July 25, 1994.
3. John J. DiLulio, Jr., Gerald Garvey, and Donald F. Kettl, *Improving Government Performance: An Owner's Manual* (Washington, D.C.: Brookings Institution, 1993), p. 9.

4. Ibid.
5. For a complete discussion of reorganization in the federal government, see Harold Seidman and Robert Gilmour, *Politics, Position, and Power*, 4th ed. (New York: Oxford University Press, 1986).
6. Al Gore, *From Red Tape to Results: Creating a Government That Works Better and Costs Less: Report of the National Performance Review* (Washington, D.C.: U.S. Government Printing Office, 1993), p. 5.
7. Ibid., pp. 13–14.
8. Ibid., p. 43.
9. Ibid., p. 66.
10. See note 3 above.
11. Gore, *Report of the National Performance Review*, p. 93.
12. David Osborne and Ted Gaebler, *Reinventing Government: How the Entrepreneurial Spirit is Transforming the Public Sector* (Reading, Mass.: Addison Wesley, 1992).
13. Ibid., pp. 166–94.
14. Ibid., pp. 76–107.
15. Ibid., pp. 49–75.
16. Paul Appleby, "Government is Different," in Jay M. Shafritz and Albert C. Hyde, *Classics of Public Administration*, 3d ed. (Pacific Grove, Calif.: Brooks Cole, 1992).
17. Carl J. Bellone and George Fredrick Goerl, "Reconciling Public Entrepreneurship and Democracy," *Public Administration Review* 52, no. 2 (March/April 1992).
18. See, for example, Ronald C. Moe, "The 'Reinventing Government' Exercise: Misinterpreting the Problem, Misjudging the Consequences," *Public Administration Review* 54, no. 2 (March/April 1994).
19. See, for example, Peter R. Scholtes, *The Team Handbook* (Madison, Wis.: Joiner Associates, 1992); Philip Crosby, *Quality is Free* (New York: New American Library, 1979); Joseph Juran, *Juran on Leadership for Quality* (New York: Free Press, 1989); Mary Walton, *The Deming Method* (New York: Praeger, 1986); Albert C. Hyde, "Rescuing Quality Measurement from TQM," *The Bureaucrat* 19 (winter 1991).
20. James E. Swiss, "Adapting Total Quality Management (TQM) to Government," *Public Administration Review* 52, no. 4 (July/August 1992).
21. Scholtes, note 19 supra.
22. Michael Hammer and James Champy, *Reengineering the Corporation: A Manifesto for Business Revolution* (New York: Harper Collins, 1993).
23. Ibid., p. 31.
24. Ibid., p. 35.
25. Ibid., p. 37.
26. Ibid., pp. 60–62.

MODULE II The Technical Dimension

4

Position Management

INTRODUCTION

Many students of public administration and management misunderstand the importance of position descriptions, classification methodologies, and pay scales. For some, the topic connotes a rote, mundane image of dull bureaucrats whose sole *raison d'être* is to fill out these horrible forms in an environment where the rule becomes the end rather than a means toward the attainment of some desired outcome. The subject is viewed as very technical, with little practical applicability beyond the realm of the personnel department.

This chapter seeks to dispel this commonly held belief that the "nuts and bolts" of personnel are of little interest to line managers already overburdened with the daily management of their agencies. Moreover, we argue that paying serious attention to these so-called technical issues is one of the most important personnel functions that managers undertake. Understanding them is the precursor to effective position management, recruitment, and performance management, and it even impacts decisions concerning the training and professional development of employees. The flip side of the coin is that a frivolous, cavalier attitude on the part of a manager toward these essential personnel functions can lead to numerous difficulties. Indeed, a retrospective analysis conducted by many public sector managers, including two of the authors of this book, reveals that paying closer attention to the process at the outset reaps major rewards.[1] With this in mind, we move on to discuss the application of position descriptions, classification mechanisms, and pay scales.

POSITION DESCRIPTIONS

There are two basic types of position descriptions, the traditional job description and what we call a quality-oriented position management system(QOPMS). The former had its beginnings in the scientific management approach of Frederick Taylor.[2] As noted in chapter 2, Taylor popularized the notion that managers needed to standardize operating procedures and that employees required carefully delineated tasks in order to perform effectively. QOPMS, on the other hand, is premised upon the Total Quality Management(TQM) doctrine of W. Edwards Deming[3] and the work of the human relations school.[4] Both believe that people are the most important component of any organization and that when the organization's goals are congruent with the goals of the employee, the organization is productive and the employee is motivated to perform.

An example of a traditional position description is found in Figure 4–1. The job is a forestry foreman position in a municipal park district. Most traditional approaches incorporate similar methods. There is normally some sort of a statement of purpose, a list of duties, and a statement of qualifications.

Managers who use these types of traditional position descriptions cause themselves all kinds of difficulty. Because the tasks and qualifications for the

---

FIGURE 4–1. Forestry Foreman

Supervisor: Forestry Superintendent
Location: Headquarters
Classification: TEMN III
Pay Level: 12E

Job Objective:
This position supervises the daily activities of the Forestry Department in performing a variety of tasks that are essential to the maintenance and delivery of services to the public.

Primary Duties:
Workers at this position will perform job tasks that will include, but are not restricted to, the following:

1. Supervise forestry crews
2. Plant trees
3. Operate forestry equipment
4. Oversee tree pruning
5. Supervise chemical and pesticide application
6. Other related duties

forestry foreman are vague, the probability is high that the classification assigned to the position by the personnel department will be lower than the manager anticipated.[5] This constrains the ability to offer a competitive salary during recruitment. The traditional method also makes it very difficult to correct work that is deficient or to offer training to enhance the employee's productivity. This is so because specific performance standards are not defined for each duty. For example, one of the duties for this position is to "supervise chemical and pesticide application." What qualifications does this person need to oversee such an operation? What if an employee who is applying these toxic substances contaminates a stream or exposes children playing in a park? Who would be liable? Upon what basis could the employee's supervisor reprimand the employee when there are no guidelines in the position description indicating what constitutes satisfactory performance? The employee may be justified in arguing that he did not know what was expected of him. If the manager takes disciplinary action against the employee and the employee files a grievance, an independent adjudicator could easily decide in favor of the employee simply because the documentation was not sufficient to justify the manager's actions.

There are additional problems with this position description. The objectives of the position are unclear, there are no standards associated with the duties, and the number and types of positions supervised are not identified. Under duties, phrases such as "other related duties" should be eliminated. All tasks for which an employee is going to be evaluated should be listed. The catch-all phrase, "other related duties," is not a justification to expect employees to complete any assignment that they are instructed to carry out by the supervisor.

QUALITY-ORIENTED POSITION MANAGEMENT: A PRACTICAL APPLICATION

A QOPMS eliminates many of the problems inherent in the traditional approach to position management. Its orientation is quality improvement and the training and professional development of employees. An example of a quality-oriented position description (QOPD) adapted from a state transportation agency is shown in Figure 4–2. (A completed QOPD is found as part of exercise 4.1 at the end of the chapter.) Part A provides basic background information on the position. The next section is a detailed explanation of the *critical tasks* associated with the job. Each position must have at least one critical task, although most jobs have several, depending upon the level of the job. Notice that in Part B of the form each critical task also has a specific performance standard. This communicates to the employee what standards must be achieved in completing the task to receive a satisfactory or outstanding performance evaluation. Part C details the qualifications that are required to fulfill the responsibilities of the position. An example might be an

QUALITY ORIENTED POSITION DESCRIPTION

Position:
Position #:
Position Category:
Classification:
Department:
Supervisor:
Incumbent:

A: Statement of Purpose

B: Duties/Responsibilities/Standards

Critical Element #1

Responsibility:

Standard:

FIGURE 4-2

B: Duties/Responsibilities/Standards

Critical Element #2

Responsibility:

Standard:

Critical Element #3

Responsibility:

Standard:

FIGURE 4–2, *continued*

50 POSITION MANAGEMENT

C: Knowledge/Skills/Abilities

D: Supervisory

E: Contacts

F: Consequences of Errors

G: Working Environment

Supervisor   Employee

FIGURE 4–2, *continued*

undergraduate degree in engineering from an accredited institution and eligibility for membership in the national association of professional engineers.

Part C also provides additional specific details concerning the required technical knowledge, skills, and abilities (KSA), which relate directly to Part G, the working environment. This component is particularly important in highly specialized task environments. The working environment of a law enforcement officer in a major U.S. city obviously involves the handling of delicate and often dangerous situations. The position also requires that the officer be proficient at handling a weapon, an obvious technical requirement of the job.

Part C is useful when circumstances dictate that an existing position description be amended to reflect a change in duties or responsibilities. This is important because when the duties change the position needs to be reclassified. If additional responsibilities or KSAs are added, the classification should be higher. Conversely, when the overall level of the job declines, the classification should go down.

We purposely avoid spending a great deal of time discussing the format of the QOPMS. The example described above is rather straightforward and the exercise at the end of the chapter provides an opportunity to develop your own documentation. In addition, a number of excellent computer programs are available, complete with large databases and sample position descriptions, to assist the manager. It is important, however, that several key points be reinforced: (1) paying special attention at the outset to the QOPMS saves many headaches later with position classification, recruitment, and performance management; (2) *always* seek guidance from a personnel specialist in preparing the QOPMS; and (3) take advantage of the computer software packages.[7] Once the QOPMS has been completed, it is forwarded to the personnel department for classification.

POSITION CLASSIFICATION

Classification systems are used by government agencies for two primary reasons: to assign pay levels for each position and to standardize remuneration practices. In this section, the basic model is explained in some detail and an example of a system that is currently in use in a state government is provided.

Normally, the classification analysis is conducted by the personnel department. Most agencies utilize a *factor classification system*. Factors that are assessed include knowledge and skills required for the position, supervisory responsibilities, nature of decisions and consequences of errors, the authority to commit and to approve the expenditure of funds, and so forth. The point factor method is a means whereby all classes within the particular service delivery system are compared in quantifiable terms.[8] The comparison utilizes a consistent numbering pattern that determines the point value for the work assigned to each class.

The ratings established through the consistent application of the point factor system provide for definitive, comprehensible relationships between classes. Once established, the points can only be modified if the position description reflects a demonstrable change in the work assigned.

The classification systems that exist today have their roots in the reform debates that took place prior to the passage of the Pendleton Act in 1883. Under the spoils/patronage model of personnel, salaries were established by legislative mandate or executive order. More often than not there was little correlation between duties and the compensation received for the performance of those duties. Pay was based on political affiliation or who one knew and there was no consistency in the application of the standards for setting pay and benefits. The reformers sought to make this process more equitable through the standardization of pay scales. As Cayer points out, along with standardized position descriptions, position classification was the cornerstone to traditional personnel management.[9]

THE FACTOR CLASSIFICATION MODEL

Tables 4–1 and 4–2 provide an example of a classification for an engineering technician in a public works department. The classification category is Technical/Architectural/ Engineering (TKAE). All positions that are part of this group are classified utilizing the same method. There are four possible classifications:

TABLE 4–1. Classification Points

CATEGORY	POINTS
TKAE I	200–399
TKAE II	400–599
TKAE III	600–749
TKAE IV	750–1000

The maximum number of points available under the TKAE category is 1,000. All position descriptions in this category are evaluated based upon the following five factors, each with a maximum number of factor points:

TABLE 4–2. Classification Factors

CATEGORY	POINTS
Knowledge	200–400
Supervisory	0–100
Contacts	40–100
Nature of Decisions	50–200
Consequence/Errors	50–200

The point intervals are established by the personnel department utilizing factors pertinent to the architectural/engineering industry and market indicators.

The process works as follows. Assume that a QOPD for an engineering technician is forwarded to personnel for classification. In some instances, personnel departments require the use of classification committees consisting of trained evaluators in order to avoid single-evaluator bias. Representation from the agency or incorporating the expertise of subject matter professionals is also encouraged. The position description is then evaluated, and "factor plotting," a process of determining both the category in which the position will be placed (TKAE) and the numerical values assigned to each factor, is used to arrive at the final classification of the position.

Knowledge. The position description for the engineering technician requires an undergraduate degree in civil engineering and membership in the national professional engineering society. This does not mean that if the incumbent has a master's degree in engineering that a higher number of points will be assigned in determining the pay scale. The classification is based upon the qualifications stipulated in the position description and not on the attributes of the incumbent or the applicant.

Supervisory. The engineering technician supervises two engineering technologists. Supervisory responsibility is determined by who conducts the performance evaluation. Although the technician may provide professional counsel and direction to other individuals within the public works department, in this instance no points are awarded for supervision because the technician does not personally conduct the performance review of those individuals to whom the advice is provided.

Contacts. This factor refers to the nature and type of contact this position has with others. For example, the contacts may be primarily with peers within the agency. Conversely, much of the interaction within the work environment may be with senior managers, perhaps elected officials, members of the public, or private sector consultants. In this case, the technician interacts primarily with other professionals within the agency.

Nature of decisions. This factor concerns the amount of responsibility associated with this position. The evaluation team will determine the amount of supervision that the position requires in the discharge of daily responsibilities. This factor can range from "subject to frequent supervision" to "working in a semi-autonomous manner." The nature and amount of financial signing authority is also a determinant of job responsibility. Financial signing authority is the amount of agency money this position can commit at any one time. Examples might be issuing contracts for services or issuing purchase orders for the delivery of goods or services. The technician is primarily re-

54 POSITION MANAGEMENT

sponsible for technical decisions within the specific task environment of the unit with all other decisions being referred to the supervisor. The position has a $2,000 per-item limit signing authority for the purchase of supplies and the issuance of small service contracts.

Errors. The nature and consequences of errors made in judgment is the final factor evaluated in the classification of this position. The question is: what happens if the technician makes a mistake? Is the engineering unit affected? Is the department liable? Are government operations affected? What are the political consequences of errors? In the case of the engineering technician, errors in judgment affect the unit and can have serious consequences for the public if mistakes are made in the design and engineering of public works projects. An example would be if a pedestrian bridge designed by this technician collapsed and injured several members of the public.

Once the position description is analyzed the evaluation team assigns the following factor loadings or points:

TABLE 4–3. The Final Classification

FACTOR	MAXIMUM	ACTUAL
Knowledge	400	400
Supervisory	100	60
Contacts	200	50
Decisions	200	100
Errors	200	100
Total	1,000	710

The total number of points assigned to this position is 710. This means that the classification is a TKAE III (see Table 4–1). The salary range is then determined by this classification. The salary, in turn, dictates how successful the agency will be in recruiting a person to fill the position if it is a new position or when the incumbent leaves. If proper care was not exercised in completing the position description, the salary may not be competitive and may constrain the ability to recruit an excellent engineer. The personnel department takes a very dim view of managers who try to redo the position description after the fact in an attempt to confer a higher classification. The point here is that a quality-oriented approach to position analysis is the precursor to effective position classification and ultimately, as we shall see in the next chapter, effective performance management.

CLASSIFICATION: A PRACTICAL EXAMPLE

The following is a classification system used in a state government.[10] The system is based on eight elements grouped into three factors as shown in Table 4–4.

TABLE 4-4. A State Classification Model

Primary Factors	KNOWLEDGE SKILLS	COMPLEXITY	ACCOUNTABILITY
Elements	Technical knowledge Managerial breadth Interpersonal skills	Guidelines Mental challenge	Independence of action Effect of decisions Budget authority

Every position in the state system has one or more of these factors and elements. It should be obvious that the more factors present in the position description, the more responsibility assigned to the position, and the higher the classification and the level of compensation.

The central personnel division has developed three factor charts that include the respective elements and the factor loadings that have been assigned for each factor. Figures 4-3, 4-4, and 4-5 explain the various levels and degrees for each element within the factor and the loadings.

A position that requires a technical knowledge level of 6, managerial breadth of degree C, and interpersonal skills at degree 2 would fall within a numerical range of 202-268 for this factor. This range is designed to allow flexibility in recruiting an outstanding candidate or for allowing extra points for longevity if an incumbent employee is being promoted to a higher classification. Figure 4-5 is interpreted in much the same manner. The percentage is multiplied by the numerical value computed above.

For example, level 5 and degree C yield a percentage of either 33 or 38. Assume the lowest value for the technical knowledge factor (202) and 33 percent for the complexity factor are used. The computed factor for complexity is $202 \times .33 = 66$. In considering the first two factors, a total of 268 points have been assigned (202 + 66). The final component in this classification is to include factor loadings for accountability. A position that has budget-signing authority for a value of up to $500,000, general supervision, and specific decisionmaking authority receives a numerical score of 38. The total points awarded for this position is 306 (202 + 66 + 38). The total points are then converted into a salary range.

The above example shows that some classification systems can indeed be complex and arguably may result in quantification for the sake of quantification. These types of models also may leave the impression that classification is a value-free, apolitical personnel technique. In fact, classification can be extremely political. Managers play games in attempting to get higher classifications, and in many instances disagreements between personnel specialists and agency managers culminate in outright antagonism.

PAY SYSTEMS: THE FEDERAL EXAMPLE

Given that we used a municipal and a state example in our discussion of position descriptions and classification, it seems appropriate to use the federal government to illustrate the application of pay scales. The U.S. government

FACTOR CHART 1 -- KNOWLEDGES & SKILLS

TECHNICAL KNOWLEDGE

LEVEL 1: Knowledge of the processes, procedures, and methods needed to perform duties involving routine or repetitive occurrences requiring KSA's generally acquired and developed through OJT with little or no previous experience.

LEVEL 2: Knowledge of the processes, procedures, and methods needed to perform duties involving some routine or repetitive occurrences requiring KSA's generally acquired and developed through some formal education, training, and/or relevant work experience.

LEVEL 3: Knowledge of the processes, procedures, and methods needed to perform duties requiring some specialized KSA's generally acquired and developed through formal education, training, and/or relevant work experience in duties very similar in type and complexity.

LEVEL 4: Knowledge of the processes, procedures, and methods needed to perform duties requiring considerable specialized KSA's generally acquired and developed through formal education, training, and/or relevant work experience in duties very similar in type and complexity.

LEVEL 5: Knowledge of the principles, concepts, and methodology needed to perform and/or direct duties and with KSA's generally acquired and developed through formal education resulting in an undergraduate degree, extensive training, and/or relevant experience in work of an equivalent type and complexity.

LEVEL 6: Knowledge of the principles, concepts, and methodology needed to perform and/or direct duties and with KSA's generally acquired and developed through formal education resulting in a graduate degree, extensive training, and relevant experience in work of an equivalent type and complexity.

LEVEL 7: Knowledge of the principles, concepts, and methodology needed to perform and/or direct duties and with KSA's generally acquired and developed through formal education resulting in a postgraduate degree, extensive training, and relevant experience in work of an equivalent type and complexity.

MANAGERIAL BREADTH

DEGREE A: Management does not exist or is limited in scope.

DEGREE B: Management of persons involved in activities of the same or a similar nature seeking fulfillment of a single objective.

DEGREE C: Management of persons involved in activities of diversified functions seeking fulfillment of a single or closely related objective(s).

DEGREE D: Management of persons involved in diversified functions seeking fulfillment of multiple objectives.

NOTE: Management is narrowly defined as management of people not programs or functions. For further explanation, see Chapter 3 of the North Dakota Class Evaluation System Manual.

INTERPERSONAL SKILLS

DEGREE 1: COMMON COURTESY – No need to influence others in carrying out assignments.

DEGREE 2: MODERATE DEGREE – Involves interplay where common courtesy and effectiveness in dealing with people is not sufficient to satisfactorily perform the job.

DEGREE 3: HIGH DEGREE – Ability to motivate, persuade, or convince others and/or change own behavior.

INTERPERS SK'LS	MANAGERIAL BREADTH														
	A			B			C			D			E		
	1	2	3	1	2	3	1	2	3	1	2	3	1	2	3
LEVEL 1	25	29	33	33	38	43	43	50	57	57	66	76	76	87	101
	29	33	38	38	43	50	50	57	66	66	76	87	87	101	116
	33	38	43	43	50	57	57	66	76	76	87	101	101	116	133
LEVEL 2	33	38	43	43	50	57	57	66	76	76	87	101	101	116	133
	38	43	50	50	57	66	66	76	87	87	101	116	116	133	153
	43	50	57	57	66	76	76	87	101	101	116	133	133	153	176
LEVEL 3	43	50	57	57	66	76	76	87	101	101	116	133	133	153	176
	50	57	66	66	76	87	87	101	116	116	133	153	153	176	202
	57	66	76	76	87	101	101	116	133	133	153	176	176	202	233
LEVEL 4	57	66	76	76	87	101	101	116	133	133	153	176	176	202	233
	66	76	87	87	101	116	116	133	153	153	176	202	202	233	268
	76	87	101	101	116	133	133	153	176	176	202	233	233	268	308
LEVEL 5	76	87	101	101	116	133	133	153	176	176	202	233	233	268	308
	87	101	116	116	133	153	153	176	202	202	233	268	268	308	354
	101	116	133	133	153	176	176	202	233	233	268	308	308	354	407
LEVEL 6	101	116	133	133	153	176	176	202	233	233	268	308	308	354	407
	116	133	153	153	176	202	202	233	268	268	308	354	354	407	468
	133	153	176	176	202	233	233	268	308	308	354	407	407	468	539
LEVEL 7	133	153	176	176	202	233	233	268	308	308	354	407	407	468	539
	153	176	202	202	233	268	268	308	354	354	407	468	468	539	620
	176	202	233	233	268	308	308	354	407	407	468	539	539	620	712
LEVEL 8	176	202	233	233	268	308	308	354	407	407	468	539	539	620	712
	202	233	268	268	308	354	354	407	468	468	539	620	620	712	819
	233	268	308	308	354	407	407	468	539	539	620	712	712	819	942

FIGURE 4–3

Source: North Dakota Central Personnel Division

FACTOR CHART 2 -- COMPLEXITY

GUIDELINES	MENTAL CHALLENGE
LEVEL 1: Guidelines exist, are pre-designated for all situations, worded in specific terms, with little or no change when tasks are repeated.	DEGREE A: The work consists of tasks that are clear – cut, repetitive and directly related. There is little or no choice in deciding what needs to be done.
LEVEL 2: Guidelines exist, are pre-designated for most situations, worded in general terms requiring some interpretation, with little or no change when tasks are repeated.	DEGREE B: The work consists of duties that involve various related steps, processes, or methods. Decisions involve the selection of tasks to be performed and the procedures, processes, or methods to be used from among available choices.
LEVEL 3: Guidelines exist, are pre-designated for most situations, worded in general terms requiring some interpretation which may change because of varying circumstances when task is repeated.	DEGREE C: Work involves various duties of different and unrelated processes and methods. The decision regarding what needs to be done involves the analysis of the subject or issues involved and selecting among a variety of approaches.
LEVEL 4: Guidelines exist, are not pre-designated requiring judgement in selecting those most appropriate to a given situation, are worded in general terms requiring some interpretation which may change because of varying circumstances when task is repeated.	DEGREE D: Work involves varied duties requiring many different and unrelated processes and methods applied to a broad range of activities or substantial depth of analysis typically for an administrative or professional field.
LEVEL 5: Guidelines exist, are not pre-designated requiring judgement in selecting those most appropriate to a given situation, are worded in general terms requiring some interpretation which may change because of varying situations and are seldom, if ever, repeated.	DEGREE E: Work consists of broad functions and processes of an administrative or professional field which requires continuing efforts to establish concepts or theories or to resolve unyielding problems.
LEVEL 6: Guidelines may not exist for all situations requiring judgement in selecting or establishing those most appropriate to a given situation, and requiring extensive interpretation of circumstances to apply guidelines to a variety of situations.	
LEVEL 7: Guidelines do not exist in most situations requiring judgement in selecting or establishing those most appropriate to a given situation, and requiring extensive interpretation of circumstances to apply guidelines.	
LEVEL 8: Guidelines do not exist beyond indications of legislative intent, socially or morally accepted practice, broadly stated philosophy, etc.	

	MENTAL CHALLENGE				
GUIDELINES	A	B	C	D	E
LEVEL 1	10%	14%	19%	25%	33%
	12%	16%	22%	29%	38%
LEVEL 2	12%	16%	22%	29%	38%
	14%	19%	25%	33%	43%
LEVEL 3	14%	19%	25%	33%	43%
	16%	22%	29%	38%	50%
LEVEL 4	16%	22%	29%	38%	50%
	19%	25%	33%	43%	57%
LEVEL 5	19%	25%	33%	43%	57%
	22%	29%	38%	50%	66%
LEVEL 6	22%	29%	38%	50%	66%
	25%	33%	43%	57%	76%
LEVEL 7	25%	33%	43%	57%	76%
	29%	38%	50%	66%	87%
LEVEL 8	29%	38%	50%	66%	87%
	33%	43%	57%	76%	100%

FIGURE 4-4

Source: North Dakota Central Personnel Division

FACTOR CHART 3 -- ACCOUNTABILITY

INDEPENDENCE OF ACTION	EFFECT ON DECISIONS
LEVEL 1: The position works as instructed and consults with the supervisor as needed on all matters not specifically covered in the original instructions. Immediate Supervision	DEGREE 1: LIMITED – Activities consist of duties that produce a standard product or provide a routine service used by others in making decisions.
LEVEL 2: The work involves the performance of specific, routine operations that include a few separate tasks and procedures. Immediate Supervision	DEGREE 2: INDIRECT – Activities consist of duties that produce an analysis, recommendation, or provide significant advice used by others in making decisions.
LEVEL 3: The position uses initiative in carrying out recurring assignments independently without specific instructions, but refers deviations, problems, and unfamiliar situations not covered by instructions to the supervisor for decisions or help. Close Supervision	DEGREE 3: SPECIFIC – Activities consist of duties that produce significant portions of decisions made in conjunction with others.
	DEGREE 4: MAJOR – Activities consist of duties that produce decisions and provide control of outcome of decisions.
LEVEL 4: The position plans and carries out the successive steps and handles problems and deviations in the work assignments in accordance with guidelines, previous training, or accepted practice in the occupation. General Supervision	CONTROL OF BUDGETED DOLLARS (BIENNIUM)
LEVEL 5: The position is responsible for planning and carrying out the assignment, resolving most of the conflicts which arise, coordinating the work of others as necessary and interpreting policy on own initiative in terms of established objectives. Guidance and Direction	A Up to $500,000
	B $500,000 to $10 million
LEVEL 6: Position receives administrative directions with assignments in terms of broadly defined missions or functions. General Guidance and Direction	C $10 million to $100 million
	D $100 million to $1 billion
LEVEL 7: The position represents the agency on questions fundamental to the major purposes and policies limited only by laws, court decisions, and executive orders. Broad Policy Guidance and Direction	E Over $1 billion
LEVEL 8: Chief Executive Officer	

EFF ON DECIS'NS		CONTROL OF BUDGETED DOLLARS																		
		A				B				C				D				E			
		1	2	3	4	1	2	3	4	1	2	3	4	1	2	3	4	1	2	3	4
I N D E P	LEVEL 1	5	7	9	12	7	9	12	16	9	12	16	22	12	16	22	29	16	22	29	38
		6	8	11	14	8	11	14	19	11	14	19	25	14	19	25	33	19	25	33	43
		7	9	12	16	9	12	16	22	12	16	22	29	16	22	29	38	22	29	38	50
E N D	LEVEL 2	8	11	14	19	11	14	19	25	14	19	25	33	19	25	33	43	25	33	43	57
		9	12	16	22	12	16	22	29	16	22	29	38	22	29	38	50	29	38	50	66
		11	14	19	25	14	19	25	33	19	25	33	43	25	33	43	57	33	43	57	76
E N D	LEVEL 3	12	16	22	29	16	22	29	38	22	29	38	50	29	38	50	66	38	50	66	87
		14	19	25	33	19	25	33	43	25	33	43	57	33	43	57	76	43	57	76	101
		16	22	29	38	22	29	38	50	29	38	50	66	38	50	66	87	50	66	87	116
E N C E	LEVEL 4	19	25	33	43	25	33	43	57	33	43	57	76	43	57	76	101	57	76	101	133
		22	29	38	50	29	38	50	66	38	50	66	87	50	66	87	116	66	87	116	153
		25	33	43	57	33	43	57	76	43	57	76	101	57	76	101	133	76	101	133	176
	LEVEL 5	29	38	50	66	38	50	66	87	50	66	87	116	66	87	116	153	87	116	153	202
O F		33	43	57	76	43	57	76	101	57	76	101	133	76	101	133	176	101	133	176	233
		38	50	66	87	50	66	87	116	66	87	116	153	87	116	153	202	116	153	202	268
A C T I O N	LEVEL 6	43	57	76	101	57	76	101	133	76	101	133	176	101	133	176	233	133	176	233	308
		50	66	87	116	66	87	116	153	87	116	153	202	116	153	202	268	153	202	268	354
		57	76	101	133	76	101	133	176	101	133	176	233	133	176	233	308	176	233	308	407
	LEVEL 7	66	87	116	153	87	116	153	202	116	153	202	268	153	202	268	354	202	268	354	468
		76	101	133	176	101	133	176	233	133	176	233	308	176	233	308	407	233	308	407	539
		87	116	153	202	116	153	202	268	153	202	268	354	202	268	354	468	268	354	468	620
	LEVEL 8	101	133	176	233	133	176	233	308	176	233	308	407	233	308	407	539	308	407	539	712
		116	153	202	268	153	202	268	354	202	268	354	468	268	354	468	620	354	468	620	819
		133	176	233	308	176	233	308	407	233	308	407	539	308	407	539	712	407	539	712	942

FIGURE 4–5

Source: North Dakota Central Personnel Division

has approximately three dozen pay systems. The five major pay systems are the General Schedule, the Executive and Administrative Schedule, the Foreign Service Schedule, the U.S. Postal Service Schedule, and the Federal Wage System.[11] In addition, the federal system provides for income adjustments based upon the cost of living in specific geographic locations. For example, the cost of living in such large metropolitan centers as Washington, D.C., and Los Angeles dictates higher compensation rates for federal employees in these areas as compared to their counterparts in other parts of the country. The current General Schedule, the Geographic Adjustment Schedule, and the Foreign Service Schedule are presented in Figure 4–6.

A junior air traffic controller with the Federal Aviation Administration begins at GS level 9. Notice that each level has ten increments. Most new hires begin at the first step, in this case $26,798. During the annual performance review the employee can be awarded a merit increase allowing the individual to move to the second step, and so forth. Once the employee reaches step 10 no additional merit increases can be granted. However, with the example of the controller, if the employee performs in a satisfactory manner the individual can be promoted to a controller II. The added responsibilities of this position dictate a classification at GS-11. Eventually, this individual could be promoted to a management position at one of the nation's airports and be classified as a GS-13. This same kind of logic applies to most other civilian positions in the federal government.

The Executive Salary Schedule (not shown) applies to members of the Senior Executive Service. These are the "super bureaucrats" within the federal system, those individuals who manage government agencies. They are the equivalent of senior corporate executives in the private sector.

REFORM INITIATIVES

Despite our best efforts, position analysis, classification systems, and salary policies as they are currently constituted constrain our ability to improve how public sector agencies are managed. The focus of traditional position management is on standardization and therefore little autonomy or discretionary authority is tolerated in the application of these instruments. In fact, one function of a central personnel department is to ensure that the standards are uniformly applied across all jurisdictions. On the one hand, standard operating procedures are important to ensure fairness and consistency in the application of personnel policies. On the other hand, the rigidity inherent in the application of these procedures stifles innovation and promotes risk aversion within the public sector. Three-quarters of all federal managers surveyed identified complexity and rigidity as the major cause of their personnel problems.[12]

An example from the Gore task force on reinventing government highlights the nature of the problem. There are 850 pages of federal personnel law, 1,300 pages of Office of Personnel Management regulations including elaborate details as to how these regulations are to be implemented, and 10,000 pages of guidelines in the *Federal Personnel Manual*. Fifty-four thousand federal employees work in the area of personnel, and all the different personnel forms used within the federal system stacked on top of each other would create a pile 3,100 feet tall![13]

Several specific initiatives have formed part of the reform debate, and some have been implemented in various government agencies on an experimental basis. Some of these initiatives are discussed in the following section.

RESTRUCTURING THE TRADITIONAL WORKPLACE

One area that is particularly troublesome for government agencies concerns the recruitment and retention of women in the managerial ranks. Part of the problem relates to the fact that many women are precluded from participating in the workforce because of family demands in general and caring for young children in particular. A U.S. Merit Systems Protection Board report captures the essence of the problem:

> In order for the Federal Government to efficiently and effectively fulfill its many responsibilities on behalf of the Nation, it is imperative that it attract, motivate, and retain a highly qualified workforce. . . . One particular area receiving increased attention is the change in workers' needs and expectations regarding the balancing of their work and personal lives. If the Federal Government fails to adequately respond to these changes, it will be at a competitive disadvantage compared to other major employers.[14]

Alternative work scheduling (AWS) is one way of providing the balance between work and familial responsibilities, whether it be in the area of day care for infants, elder care, or dealing with personal tragedy. The philosophy underlying AWS is that employees require flexibility in how they schedule their work. Computer technology and sophisticated telecommunications networks no longer require that managers be in their offices eight hours a day, forty hours a week. AWS allows people two options: *flextime* and *compressed work scheduling*. The former permits the employee significant latitude in structuring work hours while the latter permits compressing the schedule perhaps into four ten-hour days instead of five eight-hour days. Both approaches recognize that completing the work in a timely and competent manner is important. How or where one completes it is of little consequence.

A second, related component concerning this debate is the actual provision of child care services by public sector employers. Many parents who work full time, especially in those households headed by a single parent, need someone to provide adequate day care for their children. In these instances AWS does not meet the needs of many individuals. A number of options for

GENERAL SCHEDULE
Base Annual Salaries — January 1995

Longevity Steps	1	2	3	4	5	6	7	8	9	10
Grade GS 1	$12,141	$12,546	$12,949	$13,352	$13,757	$13,994	$14,391	$14,793	$14,811	$15,183
2	13,650	13,975	14,428	14,811	14,974	15,414	15,854	16,294	16,734	17,174
3	14,895	15,392	15,889	16,386	16,883	17,380	17,877	18,374	18,871	19,368
4	16,721	17,278	17,835	18,392	18,949	19,506	20,063	20,620	21,177	21,734
5	18,707	19,331	19,955	20,579	21,203	21,827	22,451	23,075	23,699	24,323
6	20,852	21,547	22,242	22,937	23,632	24,327	25,022	25,717	26,412	27,107
7	23,171	23,943	24,715	25,487	26,259	27,031	27,803	28,575	29,347	30,119
8	25,662	26,517	27,372	28,227	29,082	29,937	30,792	31,647	32,502	33,357
9	28,345	29,290	30,235	31,180	32,125	33,070	34,015	34,960	35,905	36,850
10	31,215	32,256	33,297	34,338	35,379	36,420	37,461	38,502	39,543	40,584
11	34,295	35,438	36,581	37,724	38,867	40,010	41,153	42,296	43,439	44,582
12	41,104	42,474	43,844	45,214	46,584	47,954	49,324	50,694	52,064	53,434
13	48,878	50,507	52,136	53,765	55,394	57,023	58,652	60,281	61,910	63,539
14	57,760	59,685	61,610	63,535	65,460	67,385	69,310	71,235	73,160	75,085
15	67,941	70,206	72,471	74,736	77,001	79,266	81,531	83,796	86,061	88,326

GENERAL SCHEDULE — 8 PERCENT
INTERIM GEOGRAPHIC ADJUSTMENT (IGA) SCHEDULE
Base Annual Salaries — January 1995

Longevity Steps	1	2	3	4	5	6	7	8	9	10
Grade GS-1	$13,112	$13,550	$13,985	$14,420	$14,858	$15,114	$15,542	$15,976	$15,996	$16,398
2	14,742	15,093	15,582	15,996	16,172	16,647	17,122	17,598	18,073	18,548
3	16,087	16,623	17,160	17,697	18,234	18,770	19,307	19,844	20,381	20,917
4	18,059	18,660	19,262	19,863	20,465	21,066	21,668	22,270	22,871	23,473
5	20,204	20,877	21,551	22,225	22,899	23,573	24,247	24,921	25,595	26,269

Step										
6	22,520	23,271	24,021	24,772	25,523	26,273	27,024	27,774	28,525	29,276
7	25,025	25,858	26,692	27,526	28,360	29,193	30,027	30,861	31,695	32,529
8	27,715	28,638	29,562	30,485	31,409	32,332	33,255	34,179	35,102	36,026
9	30,613	31,633	32,654	33,674	34,695	35,716	36,736	37,757	38,777	39,798
10	33,712	34,836	35,961	37,085	38,209	39,334	40,458	41,582	42,706	43,831
11	37,039	38,273	39,507	40,742	41,976	43,211	44,445	45,680	46,914	48,149
12	44,392	45,872	47,352	48,831	50,311	51,790	53,270	54,750	56,229	57,709
13	52,788	54,548	56,307	58,066	59,826	61,585	63,344	65,103	66,863	68,622
14	62,381	64,460	66,539	68,618	70,697	72,776	74,855	76,934	79,013	81,092
15	73,376	75,822	78,269	80,715	83,161	85,607	88,053	90,500	92,946	95,392

NOTE: The adjusted annual rates of pay shown on this schedule are applicable only to General Schedule employees in the following Consolidated Metropolitan Statistical Areas: New York-Northern New Jersey-Long Island, NY-NJ-CT, PA; and Los Angeles-Riverside, CA. These adjusted rates are considered basic pay for retirement, life insurance, premium pay, severance pay, and workers' compensation purposes and for advances in pay. They are **not** considered basic pay for any other administration purposes.

FOREIGN SERVICE SCHEDULE — Base Annual Salaries — January 1995

Step	Class 1	Class 2	Class 3	Class 4	Class 5	Class 6	Class 7	Class 8	Class 9
1	$67,941	$55,053	$44,609	$36,147	$29,290	$26,184	$23,408	$20,926	$18,707
2	69,979	56,705	45,947	37,231	30,169	26,970	24,110	21,554	19,268
3	72,079	58,406	47,326	38,348	31,074	27,779	24,834	22,200	19,846
4	74,241	60,158	48,745	39,499	32,006	28,612	25,579	22,866	20,442
5	76,468	61,963	50,208	40,684	32,966	29,470	26,346	23,552	21,055
6	78,762	63,822	51,714	41,904	33,955	30,354	27,136	24,259	21,687
7	81,125	65,736	53,265	43,161	34,974	31,265	27,950	24,987	22,337
8	83,559	67,708	54,863	44,456	36,023	32,203	28,789	25,736	23,007
9	86,066	69,739	56,509	46,790	37,104	33,169	29,653	26,508	23,697
10	88,326	71,832	58,205	47,164	38,217	34,164	30,542	27,304	24,408
11	88,326	73,987	59,951	48,579	39,363	35,189	31,458	28,123	25,141
12	88,326	76,206	61,749	50,036	40,544	36,245	32,402	28,966	25,895
13	88,326	78,492	63,602	51,537	41,761	37,332	33,374	29,835	26,572
14	88,326	80,847	65,510	53,083	43,013	38,452	34,375	30,731	27,472

FIGURE 4–6

Source: Federal Personnel Guide, 1995 edition.

the provision of child care have been explored by government agencies. The Department of Defense, for example, provides on-site child care facilities for military and civilian personnel. Other government entities choose to provide direct financial subsidies in the form of cash or vouchers that can be used to secure private child care services.

A third dimension of seeking a compromise between personal responsibilities and work commitments relates to employer-provided benefits. The problem is particularly acute when a public sector employee exhausts all leave options because of a serious illness. In 1988, Congress passed the Federal Employee Leave Sharing Act. This legislation allows employees to donate a portion of their leave to a colleague who is confronted with a medical emergency. Under such plans the stricken employee does not suffer a loss of income.

Several public employers now offer flexible benefit packages called *cafeteria plans*. Employers like these plans because they are less expensive. Employees like them because benefits are tailored to individual circumstances and needs. Under the cafeteria model the employee chooses a series of benefit menus that suit individual preferences. Normally, there is a core package of benefits that all employees receive—a pension plan and minimum sick leave, for example. Employees then receive benefit credits based upon tenure and salary that can be applied toward the purchase of additional benefits—perhaps extended medical coverage, day care, or dental care. The cafeteria approach provides flexibility for a modern workforce consisting more and more of single parents, dual wage earners, and working women.[15]

It must be noted that these types of reforms are not without their problems. First, AWS may not be applicable in certain agencies. Those employees who are employed in direct service delivery (such as issuers of drivers licenses at state motor vehicle departments) may be required to work the standard eight-hour shift. In addition, AWS is much more easily applied to nonmanagement personnel. Most middle and senior managers in government agencies will attest to the fact that they routinely work sixty hours a week and that AWS is simply not a realistic option. A second problem is that employee benefits such as the direct provision of child care can certainly result in increased costs for the employer. This cost constraint could be particularly burdensome for small local government jurisdictions.

COLLEGE RECRUITMENT EFFORTS

A 1988 study by the U.S. Merit Systems Protection Board revealed that a significant proportion of graduating seniors in such disciplines as engineering and computer sciences did not perceive the government as an employer of choice.[16] The 1989 Volcker Commission Task Force discovered, for example, that only 5 percent of engineering graduates surveyed opted for government employment.[17] As a result, several initiatives have been proposed or implemented to attract talented students. The Presidential Management Internship Program (PMI) is a national competition aimed at attracting the top graduate students in public administration programs across the country. The program is prestigious and very competitive. PMIs are "fast tracked" into the federal system at a GS-9 level. After the first year they are eligible for promotion to GS-11 and, at the end of their two-year internship, they are eligible for *non-competitive* conversion to a permanent position at GS-12.[18] The problem is that PMIs represent only a small fraction of the total supply of personnel that is needed.

A number of public sector agencies utilize a recruitment tool called *on-the-spot-hiring*. Recruiters visit university campuses and offer employment on the spot to graduating students with a grade point average of 3.5 or higher (on a scale of 4.0). This is another means of circumventing the elaborate procedures associated with recruitment.

It is no secret that public sector wages differ markedly from those of the private sector, especially at the senior management level.[19] One alternative reward system that has been applied with some success is *pay banding*. In certain job classifications where the public sector has difficulty competing for the available talent pool (engineering and accounting), the pay scales can be collapsed to create a larger overall salary range. To illustrate, the GS-9 range is $28,900 to $37,600. Pay banding allows recruiters to collapse a series of grades, perhaps GS-9 through GS-11, into one grade. The new range becomes $28,900 to $45,500. This permits flexibility in offering starting salaries and allows for substantial salary growth for the employee within grade. The National Performance Review supported the concept of pay banding by recommending folding "all GS (General Schedule) grades into four, five, or six pay bands within each career path."[20]

CONCLUSION

This chapter examined the nuts and bolts of personnel—position management, classification, and pay. It was noted that effective position management can be used to promote improved organizational productivity, increased motivation of staff, and professional development of agency employees. The quality-oriented position description is the crucible for effective personnel management. It contains all of the pertinent information that is later used to classify positions, assign pay rates, manage performance, and identify training and professional development needs.

Standardized personnel procedures bring a much needed process of uniformity to the world of personnel management. As the National Performance Review documented, they also inhibit attempts at innovation because of their rigidity. A number of reforms in the area of recruitment, retention, and compensation have been implemented in the public sector to maintain equity in the application of personnel policies while at the same time providing some flexibility for agency managers. Cafeteria benefit plans, alternative work scheduling, on-the-spot hiring, and pay banding are only four of a multitude of innovations that federal, state, and local governments have undertaken in an effort to make human resource management procedures more responsive to the needs of both the agency and its employees.

Exercises

4.1 The following is a sample QOPD for the superintendent of an urban forestry program. Utilizing this guide, select a municipal management position (such as planner, city engineer, finance manager), obtain a copy of the current position description, interview the incumbent, and prepare a QOPD for this position.

Position: Superintendent of Forestry
Position Number: 001
Position Category: Existing
Classification: 13
Department: Forestry
Supervisor: Director, Park District
Incumbent:

QOPD: Superintendent of Urban Forestry

A: STATEMENT OF PURPOSE

The position is responsible for the design, maintenance, and coordination of the district's forestry and landscape inventory to ensure quality forestry programs for the city. The position is one of three senior managers who report to the director as part of the district's senior management team.

B: DUTIES/RESPONSIBILITIES/STANDARDS

Critical Element # 1
In conjunction with the two other superintendents, act as a member of the executive management team in advising the director on policy issues affecting the district.
Responsibility   Meet with the director and provide advice on policy issues with respect to resource allocation, personnel matters, and urban forestry.
Standard   Maintain currency with park board policies and with trends and changes in urban forestry standards. Provide written and oral reports in a timely manner.

Critical Element # 2
Develop policies for urban forestry programs.
Responsibility   Develop, implement, and maintain policies and procedures concerning tree care and development for park and berm trees. Pro-

vide direction for the installation and maintenance of landscaping including trees, shrubbery, and floral displays.

Standard All tree care, park development, landscape programs, and other forestry programs will conform to the guidelines established by the National Association of Foresters and the American Society of Landscape Architects.

Critical Element # 3
Prepare forestry department budget estimates.

Responsibility Submit financial estimates and forecasts to the director as required. Provide alternative program funding sources in concert with the overall mission of the park district and policies established by the board.

Standard All documentation will be submitted in an accurate and timely manner. External funding sources such as grants will be maximized. Resource commitments will be managed within the context of the approved budget.

Critical Element # 4
Liaison with municipal, state, and national forestry officials.

Responsibility Ensure that forestry policies and programs reflect changing industry standards.

Standard Represent the park district at meetings with other professionals. Attend professional conferences and make presentations on behalf of the park district.

Critical Element # 5
Liaison with the public.

Responsibility Act as resource person to members of the community in general forestry and tree care matters. Provide professional advice as needed.

Standard Respond to public inquiries and concerns in a timely, appropriate, and professional manner.

Critical Element # 6
Provide design and construction guidelines for new park development and changes to existing developments.

Responsibility Provide professional plans, specifications, and construction guidelines in-house or through the use of professional consultants.

Standard Ensure all developments are carried out in accordance with industry standards and relevant local, state, or national codes and standards.

Critical Element # 7
Supervise forestry department employees.

Responsibility Manage daily activities of subordinates. Provide guidance on district policies and procedures. Prepare and maintain QOPDs. Prepare the performance plan and the achievements review. Provide counsel on training and professional development.

Standard Deal with all employees in a professional manner. Meet at least annually with each employee to develop a performance plan. Ensure that the

QOPDs are updated as circumstances dictate. Meet at least annually with each employee to conduct the achievements review. Make employees aware of training and professional development opportunities. Prepare all documentation in a timely and professional manner. Maintain employee confidentiality. Maintain currency with all district policies and procedures governing human resource management.

Critical Element # 8
Develop neighborhood volunteer programs.

Responsibility   Meet with community groups to establish criteria for tree, shrub, and garden maintenance programs. Specify resources to be committed by the Park District and resources that are the responsibility of the group.

Standard   Maintain contact with the various groups. Ensure that groups are given the credit they deserve for their volunteer efforts.

C: KNOWLEDGE/SKILLS/ABILITIES

1. A four-year undergraduate degree in forestry from an accredited institution.
2. A solid understanding of urban forestry practices, silviculture, and arboculture.
3. A minimum of five years experience in an urban forestry setting.
4. Knowledge of design and maintenance of park developments.
5. Three years experience in the preparation of budget estimates and forecasts.
6. Three years supervisory experience.
7. Eligible for membership in the professional foresters council.
8. Excellent written and oral communication skills.
9. Ability to deal effectively with the public and the media.
10. A general understanding of computer applications in an urban forestry context.

D: SUPERVISORY

Direct supervision of subordinates   This position involves direct supervisory responsibility over the following positions:

1. Forestry Foreman
2. Assistant Forestry Foreman
3. Arborist I
4. Arborist II (3)
5. Horticulturalist

A total of seven positions come under the direct supervision of this position.

Direct supervision of the position   This position bears sole responsibility for all technical aspects of the urban forestry department. The director provides supervisory guidelines in the area of board policy, budget formulation, and human resource management.

E: CONTACTS

This position requires close contact with other forestry professionals, members of the public, members of the park district board, the media, other government and private sector officials, and professional consultants.

F: CONSEQUENCE OF ERRORS

Because of frequency of contact with officials external to the park district, errors in judgment could have serious technical and political ramifications for the park district and the community.

G: WORKING ENVIRONMENT

The position requires extensive field work, particularly during the summer months. The required interaction with the public and the media makes the position politically sensitive.

    4.2 Design what you think would be an appropriate classification system for the QOPD that you developed above. What factors did you include and why? Contact the personnel department and determine what factors they considered in the actual classification of the position. Explain the differences between your model and theirs.

    4.3 Consider some of the personnel management problems, and the possible solutions, that might be raised by flextime, family leave, and compressed work scheduling in government service. Write a memorandum outlining your recommendations.

    4.4 Speculate on the problems that may have prompted the development and eventual adoption of the current models of job and compensation classification systems. Discuss the problems *caused* by these systems and develop plausible solutions. Consider the political and financial costs of your solutions.

Notes

1. Also see Judith A. DeLapa. "Job Descriptions that Work," *Personnel Journal* 68, no. 6 (June 1989).
2. Frederick W. Taylor, *The Principles of Scientific Management* (1911; reprint, New York: W.W. Norton, 1967).
3. W. Edwards Deming, *Out of the Crisis* (Cambridge, Mass.: MIT, Center for Advanced Engineering Study, 1982); Idem, *The Economy for Industry, Government, and Education* (Cambridge, Mass.: MIT, Center for Advanced Engineering Study, 1993).

4. For examples of the human relations approach, see Douglas McGregor, *The Human Side of Enterprise: Twenty-fifth Anniversary Printing* (New York: McGraw-Hill, 1985); Chris Argyris, *Integrating the Individual and the Organization* (New Brunswick, N.J.: Transaction Publishers, 1990).

5. See Brian N. Smith, "The Effects of Job Description Content on Job Evaluation Judgements," *Journal of Applied Psychology* 25, no. 3 (June 1990).

6. A special thanks to Ms. Diane Laub, Assistant Personnel Director, North Dakota Department of Transportation, for providing the information.

7. For a good discussion of application software packages, see Gilbert B. Siegal and James R. Marshall, "The Use of PC Software in Teaching Public Personnel Administration," *Public Personnel Management* 20, no. 1 (spring 1991).

8. This information on the classification process is adapted from the procedures developed by the Central Personnel Division in the preparation of the North Dakota Class Evaluation System, Bismarck, N.Dak.

9. N. Joseph Cayer, *Public Personnel Administration in the United States*, 2d. ed. (New York: St. Martin's, 1986), p. 62.

10. Adapted from the North Dakota Class Evaluation System, Central Personnel Division, Bismarck, N.Dak.

11. Examples of all five can be found in the annual publication entitled *1995 Federal Personnel Guide* (Washington, D.C.: Key Communications Group, 1995).

12. A Report to the President and the Congress of the United States by the U.S. Merit Systems Protection Board, *Federal Personnel Offices: Time For Change?* (August 1993).

13. Al Gore, *From Red Tape to Results: Creating a Government That Works Better and Costs Less: Report of the National Performance Review* (Washington, D.C.: U.S. Government Printing Office, 1993), pp. 20–21.

14. A Report to the President and the Congress of the United States by the U.S. Merit Systems Protection Board, *Balancing Work Responsibilities and Family Needs: The Federal Civil Service Response* (November 1991), p. XI.

15. *Balancing Work Responsibilities*, pp. 59–62.

16. A Report to the President and the Congress of the United States by the U.S. Merit Systems Protections Board, *Attracting Quality Graduates to the Federal Government: A View of College Recruiting* (June 1988), p. vii.

17. The Volcker Commission Report, *Leadership for America: Rebuilding the Public Service* (Lexington, Mass.: Heath & Co., 1989).

18. U.S. Office of Personnel Management, *The Presidential Management Intern Program* (1993).

19. Toni Marzotto, "The Crisis in Pay: Reform or Fragmentation?" in *Public Personnel Management: Current Concerns—Future Challenges*, ed. Carolyn Ban and Norma M. Riccucci (New York: Longman, 1991).

20. Gore, *Report of the National Performance Review*, p. 23.

5

Performance Management

INTRODUCTION

Performance management serves two primary functions. First, it is the daily process of working with employees toward the effective, efficient, and productive operation of the agency. Second, a performance management model also seeks to foster the professional training and development of employees, a term referred to as goal congruence. If employees can fulfill their own personal goals while at the same time accomplishing the goals of the organization, both the organization and the individual benefit. The National Performance Review recognized the need for reform of the current federal performance management systems. Specifically, the report indicates a need for agencies to design and implement their own performance management and reward systems. The report states:

> Performance management programs should have a single goal: to improve the performance of individuals and organizations. Agencies should be allowed to develop programs that meet their needs and reflect their cultures, including incentive programs, gainsharing programs, and awards that link pay and performance.[1]

THE THEORETICAL FRAMEWORK

The theoretical foundation for performance management systems is grounded in the work of a group of scholars collectively known as the organizational humanists. The three primary contributors are Abraham Maslow,

Frederick Herzberg, and Douglas McGregor.[2] Organizational humanism was based upon four core assumptions:

1. Employees have a desire to work and can be motivated to perform quality work.
2. Employees work to satisfy personal and organizational goals.
3. Work is a lifelong pursuit for the employee.
4. The role of management is to promote a positive work environment and to encourage employee creativity.

Maslow, famous for his hierarchy of needs, referred to those workers who used their skills and talents to achieve the highest level of self-fulfillment on the job as "self-actualizers." Once the employee's lower-order needs were fulfilled (physiological and social needs, for example), the employee could self-actualize. Maslow recognized that the ability to self-actualize depended in large part on needs fulfillment both on and off the job, the type of work being undertaken, the relationship with coworkers and, most important, the manner in which the employees were treated by management.

Herzberg surveyed over two hundred accountants and engineers and asked them to describe those aspects of employment that made them feel good as opposed to those that made them feel bad. From the responses, he developed a series of motivators that he called satisfiers. These included employee recognition, delegation of responsibility to employees, progressive responsibility, opportunities for advancement, and so forth. Dissatisfiers, or hygiene factors as Herzberg called them, related to company policies, salary, the technical aspects of employment, and the type of supervision. Herzberg believed that if the dissatisfiers were problematic, the workers would complain. However, even if the working environment was satisfactory, this would not necessarily lead to improved employee motivation and productivity. The only way that management could realize improvements in productivity and employee morale would be to focus on creating an environment that promoted the satisfiers.

Douglas McGregor's studies revealed that most managers had the underlying belief that employees found work distasteful, required constant supervision, were unable to be creative, and responded only to threats of punitive action. He referred to these management perceptions as "Theory X." McGregor presented an alternative view of the typical employee, "Theory Y." The underlying components of Theory Y are that people need to work and actually enjoy working, employees are creative, and that employees will be motivated if the work environment is conducive to motivation.

The applicability to performance management of the principles of organizational humanism outlined above should be obvious. If managers believe that employees are intelligent, capable individuals who derive personal satisfaction from their work and have a vested interest in participating in the success of the organization, performance management should be easy.

Performance appraisal, the actual evaluation of the employee at some point in time, is simply one component of performance management. However, a well-planned performance management approach makes the single appraisal component simple and almost pro forma. In other words, if employees and supervisors work together on a daily basis, there should be no surprises when the formal appraisal takes place.

There are three macro-level problems associated with performance evaluation—problems with the traditional approach, problems with the rater or supervisor, and problems with the appraisal technique. These in turn are discussed below.

PROBLEMS WITH THE TRADITIONAL APPROACH

The comment in the last chapter concerning managers' reluctance to take position analysis seriously is equally applicable when it comes to assessing an employee's performance. Under the traditional approach, the employee and supervisor receive notification from the personnel department that an annual appraisal must be completed by a specific target date. Reluctantly, the supervisor calls the employee into the office, usually the day before the appraisal is due in Personnel, and a scenario such as the following unfolds:

Supervisor: "It's that time of year when Personnel says that I have to do your appraisal. I'm already swamped and really don't have time to meet with you and fill out the forms."

Employee: "I don't really care about the forms. Am I going to get my annual merit increment?"

Supervisor: "The increment is not a problem. Why don't you take the appraisal form and fill it out. I'll sign it and send it to Personnel and then we're done with this hassle for another year."[3]

It should be obvious that this is the antithesis to a performance management system. Unfortunately, in many agencies this scenario is the norm rather than the exception. In these situations it is not that the supervisor is indifferent toward the employee. Rather, most managers are so busy that they find it difficult to schedule one-on-one sessions with each and every subordinate. In many instances, a middle manager has ten or twelve employees reporting directly to him or her. Providing mentoring, monitoring daily performance, assessing training and development needs, and discussing performance plans for the next year can be extremely time-consuming. This is despite the fact that two of the primary responsibilities of supervision include providing guidance and evaluating employees.

In a similar vein, the employee places little importance on the appraisal because the perception is that there is little correlation between performance and the rating received by the employee. This "attitude problem" has prompted some agencies to do away with traditional appraisals altogether.[4]

PROBLEMS WITH THE RATER

Performance evaluation, like grading in college classes, can be a subjective exercise at best.[5] Because the evaluations are conducted by human beings, it is inevitable that problems will occur.[6] *Rater bias* is one such problem. The bias can be unintentional or, in some instances, amount to covert discrimination on the part of a supervisor. The personalities of all of us are such that we form judgments about individuals with whom we work. We might perceive an office mate or subordinate as unmotivated or lazy. These perceptions, whether they are accurate or not, can have an impact on how we evaluate performance. In other words, factors unrelated to the performance of duties can bias the performance rating. When this bias is so pronounced that it takes the form of discrimination on the basis of gender, race, age, or religion, it is illegal but often difficult to prove. Whether or not personal bias of the rater results in illegal discrimination, it is counterproductive for both the employee and the organization.

A second problem associated with how supervisors assign performance ratings is called the *central tendency bias*. This occurs when the manager assigns average ratings to everyone irrespective of any variations in net performance by individual employees; all employees receive a rating of satisfactory. Normally managers do this because they do not want to deal with the "superstar" syndrome whereby employees who are outstanding might become the jealous envy of co-workers, thereby causing behavioral animosity in the workplace. The other problem is that the central tendency bias defeats the purpose of evaluating performance. This bias precludes awarding superior performance ratings for those who deserve them as well as correcting substandard performance on the part of other employees.

The *halo effect* is a third evaluation bias. This occurs when a supervisor's current rating of an employee is influenced by an historic event. For example, suppose a political science major takes three courses from the same professor and deservedly receives an "A" in each course. The student is now taking a fourth course from the same professor. Because of external factors the student cannot devote the time necessary to the course and would be happy with a "B." Yet, she receives an "A." The professor's rating may have been biased by the student's performance in the other courses. This same situation can occur when supervisors evaluate employees in government agencies.

A final problem with supervisory ratings is a function of the fact that performance appraisal is based upon past performance, usually over the past year. This bias is sometimes called *recency error.* Something "good" that the employee did eight or ten months ago is likely to be forgotten. However, something "bad" that happened last week can negatively impact an overall rating that is supposed to be based on the performance over the entire evaluation period.

PROBLEMS WITH THE APPRAISAL TECHNIQUE

There are scores of performance appraisal techniques that are used in the public sector. The instrument selected within a particular public agency depends upon factors such as the agency's mission, legislative direction, regulatory requirements of a central personnel agency, or simply because "it is the way that it has always been done." Each appraisal technique discussed below has strengths and limitations. Remember, what is appropriate for a state transportation department may be inappropriate in a municipal finance division.

The most traditional of the appraisal methods is the *traits approach*.[7] The objective is to identify such presumably key personality characteristics or traits as charisma, intelligence, and assertiveness. Those individuals who possess the desirable traits are rewarded or promoted. Quantifying personality characteristics has its roots in early leadership theory. Good leaders would command high levels of performance in employees, which would lead to improved productivity. Charles Perrow writes:

> The reasoning here is that if one can find out what makes a good leader, and then if one can teach people to be good leaders, or at least find ways to select good leaders, then presumably most of our organizational problems would be solved.[8]

Despite the fact that numerous studies have demonstrated that there is little if any correlation between some personality characteristics and performance, this leadership/traits method is used today. All branches of the U.S. military, for example, use an officer appraisal instrument that at least in part emphasizes leadership characteristics.[9]

The *forced choice*, or forced distribution, technique is a second method used in public sector agencies to evaluate performance. The personnel department provides the supervisor with a series of statements, some of which can be related to personality characteristics. The supervisor's discretion is limited in how the rating is assigned. The supervisor is "forced" to rate the employee on each statement, using a format such as top 5 percent, next 10 percent, next 25 percent, and so forth. Figure 5–1 presents a model that is used extensively in universities in making admission decisions. Students are ranked in such areas as academic performance and oral and written expression. Several municipal agencies also use this format. The problem with this type of instrument is that it is difficult to differentiate between average and outstanding performance.

SUMMARY EVALUATION

Applicant's promise as a graduate student, in comparison with others of similar age and experience.

	Below Average	Average	Above Average	Unusual	Outstanding	Truly Exceptional	Inadequate Opportunity to Observe
	Lowest 40%	Middle 20%	Next 25%	Next 5%	Almost Top 5%	Top 5%	
1. Academic Performance							
2. Knowledge of the Field							
3. Intellectual Ability							
4. Imagination/Creativity							
5. Oral & Written Expression							
6. Professional Accomplishments							
7. Initiative/Resourcefulness							
8. Emotional Maturity							
9. Seriousness about Graduate Study							
10. Promise as a Graduate Student							
11. Promise as a Practicing Professional							
12. Promise as a Scholar							

Please indicate the strength of your overall endorsement by placing an "X" along the scale

|⎯⎯⎯⎯|⎯⎯⎯⎯|⎯⎯⎯⎯|⎯⎯⎯⎯|⎯⎯⎯⎯|⎯⎯⎯⎯|⎯⎯⎯⎯|⎯⎯⎯⎯|⎯⎯⎯⎯|

Not recommended   Recommended with some reservations   Recommended   Highly recommended

Signature _____ Please Print Last Name _____ Date _____

Position _____ With _____

Address _____

FIGURE 5–1

The *Behaviorally Anchored Rating System* is often used as an appraisal tool in the public sector. The assumption here is that a series of desirable and undesirable behaviors can be compiled for each position within a specific task environment—law enforcement, for example. This list of behaviors is then ranked on a Likert scale (from agree to disagree) by a panel of law enforcement experts. The behavioral statements receiving the highest degree of consensus among the experts are then used to develop the appraisal instrument. The instrument is then applied to all police officers within the jurisdiction.

This model tends to be more successful when applied in a highly specialized, mechanized task environment. To continue with the illustration of the law enforcement agency, job-related behaviors expected of police officers are fairly easy to quantify. For example, an officer is required to show competence in the use of a firearm. Attempting to standardize performance behaviors for a city planner or a policy analyst in the U.S. Forest Service may present a more difficult challenge because the duties of these positions may be less technical and therefore more difficult to quantify.

A fourth appraisal instrument is the *narrative essay*. This differs considerably from many of the other techniques because it not only allows but encourages latitude and discretion in evaluating an individual's performance. This narrative format is more conducive to assessing the performance of senior managers, where the emphasis is not so much on how the agency head performed on a specific series of tasks but rather how effective this manager was overall in overseeing the mission of the agency, motivating employees, and recognizing and correcting problems within the agency. This written narrative format is also used in universities to evaluate faculty in the areas of teaching, research, and service.

The *critical element* method is used in the federal system to evaluate middle managers in grades GS-13–15 under the Performance Management and Recognition System. Each primary task or element on which the employee is evaluated is given one of five ratings—Fully Successful, two levels above Fully Successful, and two levels below Fully Successful. The performance rating is then tied to increases in pay.[10]

In recent years several different evaluation mechanisms have been implemented in the public sector. *Team* or group *appraisals* are becoming more common. In this procedure, an "impartial" entity such as an appraisal board reviews the employee's record and assigns a rating. This method attempts to overcome single-rater bias and is used in evaluating members of the federal Senior Executive Service. *Peer reviews* and the use of outside experts are also common, especially in professional fields such as engineering and computer sciences. A peer evaluator participates with the direct supervisor in reviewing the employee's record. This method is incorporated by many universities in granting tenure and promotion to faculty. The peer reviewer assesses the faculty member's record in view of national standards accepted in that particular discipline. The use of *assessment centers* is yet another attempt at removing rater bias from the evaluation process. Assessment can take the form of a written examination, a series of physical exercises that the employee completes, or a mechanical assessment procedure.[11] In using assessment outcomes as the bases to hire, terminate, promote, and fairly compensate employees, the employer is required to demonstrate that the "test" is a valid and reliable indicator of future performance. A second criterion is that *all* individuals within a specific class be treated equally; in other words, a written exam cannot be given to some candidates and not to others. Assessment mechanisms other than written exams include physical endurance tests for fire-fighters, marksmanship tests for police officers, flight simulation tests for pilots, and so on.

Whether an agency selects one of the appraisal instruments described above or whether some other mechanism is used, evaluating employee performance can be one of the least palatable components of employment for both employee and supervisor. Maroney and Buckley note that, despite the fact that most agencies use some model of performance appraisal, few are satisfied with either the process or the outcomes.[12] In a survey of state personnel directors, Hays and Kearney report that the major complaint was the failure of the system to assess employee performance accurately and to reward individuals based upon outstanding performance.[13]

Nonetheless, we believe that the elements of the performance management model that is presented below is workable and, once implemented with the support of senior management, can in fact enhance the operation of the organization and lead to increased employee motivation and productivity.

THE PERFORMANCE MANAGEMENT MODEL

Managing the performance of subordinates involves four components: performance planning, performance managing, achievements review, and feedback.[14]

Performance Planning

Performance planning concerns the establishment of tangible goals and objectives for the next year. The employee and the manager set performance standards together and agree, almost on a contractual basis, to a planning schedule and specific guidelines as to what constitutes satisfactory performance.[15] This must be a collaborative exercise and not something that is imposed from the top down.

The performance plan is the most important component of the performance management model. The following suggestions will assist in working with employees in creating a workable performance blueprint:

1. Set aside an appropriate amount of time to facilitate detailed discussion of the performance plan. Ensure that the time is convenient for both the manager and the employee (i.e., not Friday afternoon). Do not permit any interruptions during the meeting. If necessary, schedule the meeting outside of the workplace.

2. The performance plan should be a written document signed by both the employee and the manager. This does not imply in any way that this is a legal document or that it cannot be amended as circumstances change. Rather, a written plan helps to avoid confusion later on if a question arises as to the plan's content.

3. In developing the performance plan, both the manager and the employee should list specific job tasks of the position. This necessitates that

the manager be familiar with the specifics of the particular position in question. Inevitably some of the tasks on the manager's list will differ from those identified as important by the employee. It is imperative that consensus be reached on the nature of the job.

4. Agree on how the various tasks will be prioritized.

5. Agree on a time line for task completion.

6. Discuss tangible standards for each task. The manager and the employee need to agree on what constitutes satisfactory performance, outstanding performance, and so on. Set realistic but challenging standards.

7. Discuss elements of the performance plan within the context of employee as well as organizational development.

8. Take the employee's comments seriously.

Managing Performance

Performance management is the ongoing monitoring of performance by both the manager and the employee. Periodic meetings are held to discuss areas where performance exceeds targets identified in the performance plan and where performance can be improved. This feedback must always be constructive, whether it is in the form of positive reinforcement or whether it entails discussing and implementing appropriate remedial strategies. Managers should consider the following strategies:

1. Show legitimate interest in the employee and the difficulties that the employee faces within the work environment. Sometimes this involves the manager acting as coach. This helps create an atmosphere of trust and confidence that is often contagious throughout the organization.

2. Immediately identify and address performance deficiencies. Because most of us tend to be conflict-averse, we usually avoid confronting uncomfortable situations until the last minute. However, allowing an employee who is not meeting performance expectations to continue unchecked is unfair to the employee, his or her coworkers, and can ultimately be detrimental to the organization.

3. Attempt to keep accurate documentation of employee performance. This does not have to be an elaborate system, but the documentation is useful in remembering key components of performance several months later. It is also useful in supporting an eventual decision to sanction an employee or in initiating proceedings to terminate employment.

4. Do not hesitate to write a letter of commendation to the file of an employee whose performance goes beyond what is required by the position. This can be an excellent motivator, especially in the public sector, where the allocation of direct rewards and incentives is often difficult or even prohibited.

82 PERFORMANCE MANAGEMENT

5. Recognize external factors that may be negatively affecting an employee's performance—a personal crisis or substance abuse, for example. Refer the employee to a professional for counsel.

Achievements Review

Instead of using *performance appraisal,* a term that connotes top-down evaluation and assessment of a subordinate by a supervisor, we focus on the concept of *achievements review*.[16] An example of an achievements review instrument follows. See the model forms presented in Figure 5–2 (pp. 82–86).

FIGURE 5–2

ACHIEVEMENTS REVIEW SUMMARY
Department:
Employee:
Supervisor:
Date:

Critical Element 1

Rating:
Outstanding:
Satisfactory:
Unsatisfactory:

Assessment Rationale:

Action Required:

Rather than appraisal of performance, achievement review highlights employee accomplishments. The following components of the achievements review differentiate it from traditional appraisal methods:

1. The review should be completed by both employee and supervisor through an interactive, collaborative process.
2. The instrument is used to identify training and development needs of the employee.
3. There is an opportunity for the employee to provide feedback on the organization and the supervisor. This is important because organizational

FIGURE 5–2, *continued*

ACHIEVEMENTS REVIEW SUMMARY
Department:
Employee:
Supervisor:
Date:

Critical Element 2

Rating:
Outstanding:
Satisfactory:
Unsatisfactory:

Assessment Rationale:

Action Required:

barriers unknown to management can often constrain an employee's ability to adequately perform his/her duties.

The performance management model of performance planning, performance management, and achievements review has not gained wide acceptance primarily because it is perceived as too time-consuming. In reality this is an unwarranted criticism. Granted, the initial development of the performance plan requires a modest time commitment. However, once the initial plan is completed, subsequent iterations are simply updated on an annual

FIGURE 5–2, *continued*

ACHIEVEMENTS REVIEW SUMMARY
Department:
Employee:
Supervisor:
Date:

Critical Element 3

Rating:
Outstanding:
Satisfactory:
Unsatisfactory:

Assessment Rationale:

Action Required:

basis as circumstances change. It is not necessary to redo the plan in its entirety every year.

Performance management can be rewarding when employee and supervisor work well together and when the quality of the individual's work and agency productivity are high. Unfortunately, all supervisors at some point are confronted with an employee who does not perform to the standards set out in the performance plan, seems unmotivated or indifferent toward corrective strategies, or seems to be negatively affected by factors outside the organization. Dealing with problem employees is the subject of the next section.

FIGURE 5–2, *continued*

Section B
PERSONAL AND PROFESSIONAL DEVELOPMENT PLAN
This personal and professional development plan is designed by the employee and the supervisor.
Development Area:

Target Date:

Action:

Development Area:

Target Date:

Action:

Section C
Employee Comments of Own Achievements

Section D
Employee Comments on Organizational Effectiveness

86 PERFORMANCE MANAGEMENT

Section E
Signatures
We reviewed and discussed critical elements, job standards, personal and professional development, and the performance plan.

_____   _____
Supervisor   Employee

The employee's signature acknowledges that the review was discussed but does not constitute agreement or disagreement.
Reviewed by: Date:

_____   _____

FIGURE 5–2, continued
Adapted from North Dakota Department of Transportation.

PROBLEMS IN THE WORKPLACE

Employee Discipline

Public managers have the right to discipline employees who are not performing to prescribed standards. The ultimate sanction, dismissal, is also a possibility, although less than 1 percent of the employees in the three-million-strong federal civil service are fired annually. Some argue that the numbers of terminations are low not because there are few poor performers in the federal system, but rather because the termination process is so cumbersome few managers are willing to invest the time to get rid of a problem employee. Recognizing this, the National Performance Review recommended that Congress pass legislation reducing by 50 percent the time required to terminate poor performers.[17]

There are two important points that need to be considered in dealing with problem employees. First, disciplinary action in any form should only be used when all attempts at correcting performance, including counseling, have failed. Second, employee rights outlined in module 4 of the book must be protected. A Government Accounting Office report details a situation in which an employee attacked a supervisor with a baseball bat. The employee was immediately dismissed. The employee won his appeal because it was ruled that the agency did not give sufficient notice. The employee received restitution of back pay and was reinstated.[18] The moral of the story is that the employer must always act in a reasonable manner, have just cause for punitive actions, and afford the employee all of his or her legal and Constitutional rights.

A major problem with disciplining employees is determining what sanction is suitable for the offense. Does the employee simply receive a written reprimand, perhaps a day off without pay, a demotion, or dismissal? Many books on personnel administration recommend dismissal if an employee is involved in theft of government property, is intoxicated or under the influence of drugs while on the job, falsifies an employment record, or accepts a gift from a private citizen. Do we fire an employee who takes a box of computer paper for personal use? What do we do to the employee who accepts an invitation to lunch with a private contractor? Do these kinds of rule violations necessitate dismissal? Is dismissal in these instances reasonable?

Hays and Kearney argue that the "progressive approach," where the severity of the punishment increases as the employee's behavior deteriorates, can exacerbate rather than correct the problem. As an alternative, they suggest a three-stage nonpunitive technique. Once the performance problem is identified, the manager and the employee establish improvement goals and develop an action plan, including identifying training and further supervisory needs. The focus is always positive rather than negative. If this is unsuccessful, the employee can be given a day off with pay to think about the situation. Only as a last resort is the employee dismissed.[19]

Employee Assistance Programs (EAPs)[20]

Sometimes, an employee's performance is adversely affected by factors external to the agency—drug or alcohol problems, AIDS, marital problems, financial problems, or health problems. A telltale sign that something is wrong is when an employee who normally performs at a satisfactory level or higher suddenly begins to act differently; perhaps the supervisor notices unexcused absences, tardiness, excessive use of sick leave, or lethargy.

Most larger public sector agencies provide professional assistance to employees, either in-house through the use of staff specialists or through private EAPs. In the federal government over two million employees are covered by EAPs, most state governments have EAPs, and over two hundred municipalities provide EAPs.[21] The employer normally pays the costs associated with the counseling and treatment. These investments not only help to rehabilitate the employee but reduce direct costs associated with absenteeism and loss of productivity.

A supervisor who suspects that an employee is having personal problems should consider the following:

1. Discuss the situation with the employee. Make the employee aware that professional help is available at no cost to the employee. Explain that the matter will be handled in the strictest confidence.
2. Refer the employee to an EAP professional.
3. Maintain a confidential record.

4. If an employee refuses to acknowledge the problem or refuses to seek professional help, contact a personnel specialist for guidance.
5. The supervisor *should not* try to counsel the employee in substantive terms. These matters are better left to professionals.

Employee Grievances

One vehicle that is made available to employees in most agencies is the opportunity to initiate a grievance against a supervisor or fellow employee when the employee feels wronged in some stipulated way. This process can be particularly elaborate where grievance procedures have been established through collective bargaining agreements with a public sector employees' union.

The agency grievance system should provide explicit guidelines, both substantive and procedural, so that all employees, including supervisors, understand what personnel items are subject to grievance proceedings and the process for handling formal grievances. An employee initiating a grievance normally files a written statement with the immediate supervisor. The supervisor should meet with the employee to discuss the matter. In many instances the problem can be resolved at this first level. If the employee wants someone present during the meeting (a friend or union representative), that individual should be allowed to attend.

If the grievance is denied at the first level, the employee may appeal through the designated management hierarchy. Almost always, the process allows for a final appeal to an independent panel, commission, or board. In the federal system most employees can appeal personnel matters in writing to the Merit System Protection Board, but only after all other avenues have been exhausted.

At the national level, the National Performance Review recommended abolishing existing grievance systems and allowing agencies to modify their grievance procedures or to implement alternative dispute resolution mechanisms. *The Federal Personnel Guide* recommends the following minimum criteria for agency grievance systems:

1. Agency gives prompt attention to each grievance.
2. Agency establishes appropriate due process procedures to afford the employee fair consideration of the matter.
3. Employee has the right to representation.
4. Employee has the right to freedom from coercion or reprisal.
5. Employee has a reasonable amount of time to present the grievance.
6. Agency maintains a grievance file.
7. Agency provides the employee with written notice of the decision.
8. Employee is afforded an avenue for appeal.[22]

CONCLUSION

This chapter emphasized the need in public sector agencies to move from a traditional performance appraisal approach premised upon a periodic performance review, aimed at sanctioning unproductive activity, toward a comprehensive performance management system. The latter involves daily interaction between the employee and the supervisor; the formal appraisal is simply one component of performance management.

Performance management emphasizes employee training and development as well as organizational effectiveness. The performance plan is an integral component of the system in which manager and employee collaborate to identify goals and objectives, establish performance standards, and generally plan the scope of the work for the next year.

In the event that performance is substandard, it was recommended that the manager initiate nonpunitive, corrective action. The employee should be counseled, and the specifics of the improvement plan should be discussed. Managers should always be aware that pressures external to the organization can adversely affect an employee's performance. In the event that the employee is experiencing personal difficulties, he or she should be made aware of the availability of professional help through the employee assistance program. Finally, an employee who feels unfairly treated with respect to a personnel decision has the right to file a formal grievance. The agency must have clearly defined grievance procedures and the employee must be afforded all due process considerations.

Many studies in public sector agencies have shown that performance appraisal does not work. Employees distrust traditional appraisal systems and see little correlation between the appraisal and rewards or reprimands. Most managers hate the thought of conducting annual appraisals, particularly when some element of the performance is substandard. A performance management model is one useful way of rekindling a much-needed focus on improved productivity in the public sector.

Exercises

5.1 In the last chapter you prepared a QOPD and developed a series of factors to classify the position. Now develop a performance management model that is suitable for this type of task environment.

5.2 Write a policy on grievance procedures for this same agency.

5.3 Write a policy on employee assistance programs for your local government.

Notes

1. Al Gore, *From Red Tape to Results: Creating a Government That Works Better and Costs Less: Report of the National Performance Review* (Washington, D.C.: U.S. Government Printing Office, 1993), p. 25.
2. See Abraham H. Maslow, "A Theory of Human Motivation," *Psychological Review* 50 (July 1943); Frederick Herzberg, Bernard Mausner, and Barbara Synderman, *The Motivation to Work* (New York: Wiley, 1959); and Douglas McGregor, "The Human Side of Enterprise," *Management Review* (November 1957).
3. For a more detailed discussion of this, see Douglas McGregor, "An Uneasy Look at Performance Appraisal," *Harvard Business Review* (September/October 1972).
4. McLelland Air Force Base is one such public sector agency that no longer conducts traditional appraisals. An interesting discussion of their model is found in C. Ronald Gilbert, "Human Resource Management Practices to Improve Quality: A Case of Human Resource Management Intervention in Government," *Human Resource Management* 30, no. 2 (summer 1991).
5. See O. Glenn Stahl, *Public Personnel Administration*, 8th ed. (New York: Harper & Row, 1983), chap. 13.
6. The differences between subjective and objective appraisals is discussed in John Nalbandian, "Performance Appraisal: If Only People Were Not Involved," *Public Administration Review* (May/June 1981).
7. An excellent discussion of the methods can be found in Nicholas P. Lovrich Jr., "Performance Appraisal," in *Public Personnel Administration: Problems and Prospects*, eds. Steven W. Hays and Richard C. Kearney, 2d ed. (Englewood Cliffs, N.J.: Prentice-Hall, 1990).
8. Charles Perrow, *Complex Organizations: A Critical Essay*, 2d ed. (New York: Random House, 1979), p. 101.
9. See Don Cozzetto, "The Officer Fitness Report as a Performance Appraisal Tool," *Public Personnel Management* 19, no. 3. (fall 1990).
10. *1992 Federal Personnel Journal* (Washington, D.C.: Key Publications, 1992); Danny L. Balfour, "Impact of Agency Investment in the Implementation of Performance Appraisal," *Public Personnel Management* 21, no. 1 (spring 1992).
11. See Joan Pynes and H. John Bernardin, "Mechanical vs Consensus-Derived Assessment Center Ratings: A Comparison of Job Performance Validities," *Public Personnel Management* 21, no. 1 (spring 1992).
12. Bernard Patrick Maroney and M. Ronald Buckley, "Does Research in Performance Appraisal Influence the Practice of Performance Appraisal? Regretfully Not!" *Public Personnel Management* 21, no. 2 (summer 1992).
13. Steven W. Hays and Richard C. Kearney, "State Personnel Directors and the Dilemmas of Workforce 2000: A Survey," *Public Administration Review* 52, no. 4 (July/August 1992).
14. Kathleen Guinn, "Performance Management: Not Just an Annual Appraisal," *Training* (August 1987).
15. Many agencies use a management by objectives (MBO) approach and this often involves a contractual-type relationship between employer and employee. For a de-

tailed discussion see Charles R. Macdonald, *MBO Can Work!: How to Manage by Contract* (New York: McGraw-Hill, 1982).
16. This is based upon the model implemented by the North Dakota Department of Transportation.
17. Gore, *Report of the National Performance Review,* p. 25.
18. U.S. General Accounting Office, *A Management Concern: How to Deal with the Nonproductive Federal Employee* (Washington, D.C.: U.S. Government Printing Office, 1978).
19. Steven W. Hays and Richard C. Kearney, "Employee Discipline and Removal: Coping With Job Security," in *Public Personnel Administration: Problems and Prospects,* 2d ed. (Englewood Cliffs, N.J.: Prentice-Hall, 1990).
20. There is an emerging body of literature dealing with the structure and effectiveness of EAPs. See, for example, Margaret Coshan, "An EAP Can be Part of the Solution," *Canadian Business Review* 19, no. 2 (summer 1992); Bill McGee, "EAP Evolution: Employee Assistance Programs Provide Stress 'Safety Valve,'" *Denver Business Journal* 44, no. 50 (August 27, 1993); Diane Kirrane, "EAPs: Dawning of a New Age," *Human Resources Magazine* 25, no. 1 (January 1990); Michael J. Major, "Employee Assistance Programs: An Idea Whose Time has Come," *Modern Office Technology* 35, no. 3 (March 1990); Ronald W. Perry and N. Joseph Cayer, "Evaluating Employee Assistance Programs: Concerns and Strategies for Public Employers," *Public Personnel Management* 21, no. 3 (fall 1992).
21. Perry and Cayer, "Evaluating Employee Assistance Programs."
22. *1995 Federal Personnel Guide* (Washington, D.C.: Key Communications, 1995), pp. 152–55.

6

Labor Management Relations

INTRODUCTION

The divergence between private and public sector management is most pronounced in the area of labor-management relations (LMR).[1] This chapter highlights these differences, provides an historical overview of the development of LMR in the public sector, and assesses the role of LMR in the federal system. The collective bargaining process and public sector unions are also discussed.[2]

HISTORICAL EVOLUTION[3]

Although private labor organizations have roots in the United States dating back to the 1640s, their public sector counterparts never really surfaced until the middle of the nineteenth century. One of the first major federal labor disputes occurred in 1839 when workers at naval shipyards in Philadelphia went on strike. The first national labor organization to be established was the National Association of Letter Carriers, founded in 1890. At the local government level, the early years of union activity were focused primarily in the areas of firefighters, police, and school teachers. The International Association of Fire Fighters came into existence in the 1880s.[4] The American Federation of Teachers received its formal union charter from the American Federation of Labor (AFL) in 1915, and the AFL allowed police associations to join as early as 1919.[5] The National Federation of Government Employees was formed in 1917, and the American Federation of State, County, and Municipal Employees was created in 1932.[6]

In 1836 workers in the naval shipyard in Washington, D.C. defied the government and went on strike over a reduced work day. President Jackson capitulated and personally authorized a reduction to a ten-hour work day. Other presidents also became personally involved in dealing with public sector labor organizations. Theodore Roosevelt, growing weary of labor lobbyists descending upon the capitol seeking concessions for public servants, issued an executive order in 1902 prohibiting federal employees from lobbying for personal gain.

By 1912 the postal union, with the assistance of the AFL, succeeded in garnering enough congressional support to ensure passage of the Lloyd-LaFollette Act. This legislation provided guarantees to public sector employees to organize and petition Congress on work-related issues. However, it was not until 1962, with President Kennedy's signing of Executive Order 10988, that federal employees were given the right to bargain collectively.[7]

In the last two decades new tensions have arisen within LMR. At all three levels of government, but particularly at the municipal level, renewed emphasis on outright privatization and contracting-out of government services has been perceived as a serious threat to the very existence of public sector unions. As Naff points out, unions have been turning to the courts in an attempt to overturn legislation mandating contracting-out.[8] These conflicts breed resentment and distrust and do little to help bolster government's low rating in public opinion polls.

The 1978 Civil Service Reform Act provided for the establishment of the Federal Labor Relations Authority (FLRA). It was created in an attempt to centralize all labor relations functions within a single agency and in theory provide a vehicle for the independent assessment and adjudication of all federal labor relations matters. The FLRA has jurisdiction over the determination of bargaining units, the supervision of union elections, and resolving allegations of unfair labor practices.[9]

Hays and Kearney posit that the 1990s present an opportunity for change in the area of labor-management relations.[10] The increasing demands being placed on the public sector in an era of shrinking resources, and calls for greater efficiency and productivity necessitate a move toward what they call a new paradigm—a participative model of LMR where management and labor cooperate to make delivery of government services better. The authors conclude their article with the following challenge:

Increased experimentation in labor-management participation provides a rare and interesting opportunity for the public interest to be served. By fostering a new cooperative spirit between public management and public employees, organizational democracy becomes a natural extension of dominant societal values, and represents a promising new chapter in the American democratic experience.[11]

In 1993, the National Performance Review recommended the establishment of a labor-management partnership at the federal level. The report notes that the current rules and regulations governing LMR are **not** conducive to customer satisfaction and quality improvement. The report states: "We can only transform government if we transform the adversarial relationship that dominates federal union-management interaction into a partnership for reinvention and change."[12] The report advises that the president direct that this partnership be developed and that a National Partnership Council be established to oversee the implementation of the partnership agreement.

The brief historical overview presented above raises an interesting question. Why did it take almost two hundred years (1962) for federal employees to gain labor rights similar to those enjoyed for centuries in the private sector? There are a number of reasons for apparent resistance on the part of politicians and the general public to grant extensive employment rights to public employees. First, opponents of public sector unions argue that government is *sovereign*.[13] In a democratic polity such as the United States, the duly elected representatives of the people exercise a delegated authority. To allow a group such as a public sector union to influence policy and resource allocation decisions without the consent of the people or their representatives is a violation of democracy itself. A Public Service Research Council Report captures the essence of this perspective:

> Currently, collective bargaining excludes major sections of the electorate from decisions affecting budget allocations and policy development. One private interest group, unaccountable to the public, the union, realizes enhanced power over these decisions to the detriment of other legitimate interest groups.[14]

The second major argument in favor of limiting collective bargaining activity relates to what is known as *essentiality*. The public considers many government services to be essential and because government has a monopoly on the provision of these services, the public expects no disruption in their delivery. In the event that collective bargaining fails, labor's withholding essential services through rotating labor stoppages and strikes is considered tantamount to holding the people ransom. Examples of services that are considered essential include police and fire protection, certain military services, and air traffic control operations at the nation's airports.

THE PRIVATE VERSUS PUBLIC CONTROVERSY

The Private Sector Model[15]

There are four major components to LMR in the private sector: equality in collective bargaining; wages and benefits subject to market forces; distributive costs; and the right to strike.

1. When management and labor sit down at the collective bargaining table, both parties are coequal. Statute dictates that management cannot deny labor its rights, and labor cannot expect or demand that management compromise its rights. Both parties must agree on the scope of bargaining before negotiations can begin.

2. Market forces drive the amount of wages and benefits that private sector firms pay their employees. If the firm undercompensates employees, there will be a shortage in the supply of labor and the firm loses its competitive edge. On the other hand, if labor's demands are too high, the firm's profits will erode and again the competitive advantage is lost unless the firm can increase the price of its goods and services without losing market share to its competitors.

3. All private sector firms must ultimately make a profit, or risk bankruptcy. All wages and benefits paid are distributive in nature. In other words, payments to management and labor come out of the same resource pool company profits.

4. If management and labor cannot reach consensus the latter has the legal right to withdraw its services through the use of temporary work stoppages and strikes.

The Public Sector Model

LMR in the public sector (federal) is at the opposite end of the continuum from the private model described above.[16]

1. Parties in this process are not co-equal. Government is certainly not a neutral third party. Furthermore, the government decides what is fit for negotiation. At the federal level, the only components of collective bargaining that are mandated are grievance procedures and occupational safety and health issues. Everything else, including wages, retirement, leave, health care, paid holidays, work assignments, and so forth, is subject to negotiation only at the government's discretion. In other words, government has to agree to include these items in the negotiations. If government does not want to discuss pension plans with its employees, for example, it is not compelled to do so.

2. The market is a remote constraint in the allocation of wages and benefits to public sector employees. In fact, some argue that in many government sectors market indicators cannot be established because of the nature of the work; line activities in defense and the FBI are examples of public sector work activities for which there is alleged to be no significant private sector counterpart. Because most government services are not subject to market competition, unrealistic demands from labor do not have the same effect as they do in the private sector.

3. Most government wage and benefit settlements are hardly distributive. Normally, management and labor post equal gains, something akin to a 4 percent increase across the board. In order to generate the additional resources to pay for the increases, government does not have to worry about profits, so it either raises taxes or increases the deficit.

4. When the negotiations between labor and management break down, labor often does not have the option of going on strike. In many jurisdictions (although not all) strikes are illegal. This was brought to national attention when in 1981 President Reagan ordered striking air traffic controllers back to work and then ordered the dismissal of those who refused to return.

The argument that public sector LMR differs from business sector LMR is certainly not new. In fact, Leonard White's 1949 article, entitled "Strikes in the Public Service," raises some of the same points raised above, although White personally advocated increased employee rights for civil servants.[17] The major difficulty in trying to initiate pro-employee reforms in public sector LMR relates to the political environment to which LMR at all levels of government is inextricably linked. Public servants are placed in an adversarial position with those who pay their salaries, the taxpayers. When management and unions at such private sector firms as IBM or Boeing negotiate and sign a collective bargaining agreement, the terms and conditions of the deal are hardly front-page news or the lead story on the evening news. Yet, if firefighters or elementary school teachers threaten a work stoppage because the bargaining process breaks down or if state civil servants receive a raise in pay, the people rebel. The front page of the newspaper depicts greedy, self-serving, overpaid bureaucrats willing to hold the public, including young schoolchildren, hostage. This is the stuff of which great news is made because the public response is consistent and predictable.

COLLECTIVE BARGAINING

Approximately six million government employees are represented by unions. The Association of Municipal, County, and State Employees is the largest non-federal union, while the postal workers' unions have the largest membership in the federal system.[18] It is important to note, however, that the bulk of collective bargaining takes place at the sub-national level. For example, in certain professions (teachers and firefighters, for example) 70 percent of the employees belong to unions. Forty-four percent of all public sector employees were represented by a union in 1993, a slight decline from 46 percent in 1983.[19] Table 6–1 provides a breakdown of union membership by organization in the federal government.

Most states have passed Public Employee Relations Acts (PERAs) providing the statutory basis for permitting state and local employee groups to bargain collectively.[20] Some states, such as Florida and Massachusetts, allow collective bargaining for all public employees, while such other states as Kentucky and North Dakota limit bargaining to specific classes of employees—firefighters and teachers, respectively.[21] These PERAs normally also identify some state entity to oversee the collective bargaining process, usually some type of labor relations board. These boards typically establish procedures governing selection of bargaining units, the scope of the bargaining, and procedures for impasse resolution.

Despite the fact that union membership in the public sector has remained relatively constant during the last decade, Klingner argues that the situation represents a paradox. On the one hand, public sector unions are perceived by the public to be powerful entities because of the sheer numbers of employees they represent and the amount of resources they command to lobby for improved working conditions and increases in wages and benefits. On the other hand, these same unions see their power bases eroding because of economic, organizational, and political pressures.

The economic impediments to unionization that Klingner refers to come primarily in the area of benefit packages, specifically health and pensions. One of the major appeals of unions in the past has been their ability to negotiate favorable benefit packages. Today, however, as the direct costs of providing these benefits increase, employers respond with reduction-in-force policies and the use of non-benefit employees, sometimes called "kleenex employees." These employees are often part-time (disposable) and thereby reduce significantly the personnel costs within the agency because they receive no benefits. Organizational pressures also sap traditional power bases of public unions. The movement in some sectors away from traditional adversarial collective bargaining tactics to a more participative management approach, such as the one suggested by the National Performance Review part-

TABLE 6–1. Federal Union Representation 1991

American Federation of Government Employees	642,315
National Treasury Employees Union	151,736
National Federation of Federal Employees	146,113
National Association of Government Employees	69,501
Metal Trades Council	63,063
Postal Service Unions	706,265
Other	178,049
Total	1,957,042

nerships, is forcing unions to modify the manner in which they represent their constituents. Moreover, the public sector is increasingly moving toward workforce diversity and diversity training, thereby undermining an important doctrine of the union movement: seniority. Finally, the tremendous growth in white collar jobs in the public sector has refocused the allegiance away from unions and more toward professional organizations (American Society for Public Administration, the American Planning Association, and the International City Manager's Association are examples).[22]

THE PROCESS OF COLLECTIVE BARGAINING

Figure 6-1 shows how the collective bargaining process normally proceeds. In order for a union to act as collective bargaining agent for a group of employees it must be certified. A vote normally takes place, whereby employees indicate a preference for the union that they wish to represent their interests. Once approved, this certification is normally restricted to a fixed time, perhaps one year. After this period has elapsed, rival unions can petition for decertification of the recognized union. Dissatisfaction with the existing union can occur for a number of reasons: employee dissidents demanding a change in representation, lobbying on behalf of rival unions, lobbying on behalf of the employer for a change, union unresponsiveness during contract administration, or the union's inability to secure better wage, benefit, and working concessions from the employer.[23]

Most employers grant *exclusive recognition* for the union selected by the employees. This means that only the designated union will represent all employees within the unit, including nonmembers. Management knows that it has to deal with only a single organization during collective bargaining and when disputes arise during contract administration. In some instances this procedure is fairly straightforward—in the case of police officers or firefighters, for example. On other occasions, several unions attempt to woo or coerce employees in an attempt to secure potential new members. This can lead to controversy and animosity within the agency.

A second problem concerns defining bargaining units for certain classes of employees. The unit "office workers" provides a good illustration because defining the unit as well as the bargaining agent that will represent this unit is not as straightforward a process. Under the category office workers, does one include secretarial staff? What about accounts receivable clerks? Should the office manager, program manager, and finance manager be included in the office workers unit or are these positions excluded entirely from the process because they are designated management (exempt)?

Once the unit is determined and a bargaining agent is certified, the parties to the process must come to agreement on the scope of the bargaining.[24] This is normally discussed within the context of mandatory, permissible, and excluded issues.[25] Mandatory issues are automatically included either by pre-

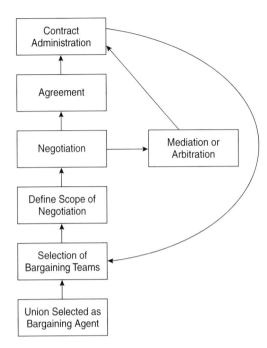

FIGURE 6-1 Collective Bargaining Cycle

vious agreement or by statute. Grievance procedures may be an example of a mandatory issue. Permissible items may include wages, vacation pay, and sick leave. An item excluded from the process entirely might be occupational safety and health.

Assuming that the parties can agree on the scope of negotiation, the actual negotiation then begins. If the process of debate and compromise is successful, both labor and management reach a tentative agreement, subject to ratification by the general membership. If the union members voice their approval for the new agreement, a contract is signed and administered over a specified period of time. This final phase of the process, implementing and administering the provisions of the agreement, is referred to as contract administration.

More often than not, however, the parties come to an impasse as a result of a breakdown in negotiations. If this occurs, there are two primary impasse resolution techniques. The first is mediation. The two parties agree to bring in a neutral outside "expert" to review the proceedings, act as a referee, and recommend a solution. Sometimes this approach is successful, but the problem lies in the fact that neither party is compelled to accept the mediator's recommendations. The second technique is binding arbitration. The process is similar to mediation except that both parties agree in writing to be bound by the recommendations of the arbitrator. An example from professional sports serves to highlight how the process works. Assume that a major league baseball pitcher who in the previous season won twenty games is unsuccessful in negotiating a new contract with his team's management. According to the uniform major league contract, the player and team agree to accept binding arbitration. The arbitrator surveys the market and determines that the pitcher is worth $6 million per year. Even if the parties are unhappy with the decision, they are still legally compelled to abide by it.

STRIKES

The private sector was given the right to strike under the 1935 National Labor Relations Act (Wagner Act). In the public sector, however, employees have historically been prohibited from striking. In the federal system, strikes are still prohibited and government possesses sweeping punitive powers should employees decide to strike. President Reagan's firing of 11,000 air traffic controllers in 1981 is a case in point.

Until 1970, state and local workers were also prohibited from striking. In that year, Pennsylvania became the first state to allow public employees the right to strike (firefighters and police officers were excluded).[26] In most states that allow strikes at all, the right is still tempered by statutory provisions mandating that specific criteria be fulfilled before a strike is permitted. In Montana, for example, health care workers are allowed to strike only after providing written notice thirty days in advance of the strike and only if there is no other health facility planning to strike within a 150-mile radius. Hawaii permits strikes but only after all impasse procedures have been exhausted and ten days written notice of intent to strike has been given.[27] In total, thirteen states permit public employees the right to strike in some form: Alaska, California, Hawaii, Idaho, Illinois, Michigan, Minnesota, Montana, Ohio, Oregon, Pennsylvania, Vermont, and Wisconsin.

By far, the majority of strikes in the public sector occur at the local government level. In the years 1982–1988, there were a total of sixty-three public sector strikes. Over half of these, thirty-five, were in local elementary and secondary education, three occurred in state government, and none occurred in the federal government. During the same time, the private sector experienced 447 strikes.[28] This tends to lend support to the argument that, even in public jurisdictions where strikes are permitted, this right does not appear to be abused when compared to similar activity in the private sector.

Participants in collective bargaining differ across jurisdictions.[29] At the national level, there are over four thousand bargaining units. The procedures are established under the 1978 Civil Service Reform Act and are monitored and enforced by the Federal Labor Relations Authority. The government's negotiation teams are appointed by the heads of the agencies whose employees fall under the unit in question. Management bargainers are usually specialists in the area of labor relations. Each union has its own team of specialists. Congress does not normally involve itself in these matters because they are considered an executive responsibility. However, at the appropriations phase Congress certainly has the power to override any financial compensation packages negotiated by the executive branch.

In some state governments, the management bargaining team is headquartered within the executive branch. The teams might be led by the assistant to the governor, the director of the civil service commission, or the director of the budget office. In other states, collective bargaining offices are established that are staffed with permanent labor relations professionals. As in the case of the federal government, most state legislatures defer to the governor's office during contract negotiations.

It is not surprising that there is little consistency in the establishment and administration of collective bargaining procedures in local government. This is so in part because of the existence of tens of thousands of separate municipal, county, school district, and special purpose jurisdictions. In some instances, the mayor and council actually participate in the negotiations. In other instances, the city manager is the chief negotiator and in still others, the management team comprises senior executive personnel. Some agencies choose to hire outside consultants, and larger cities such as New York City maintain a separate office of labor relations. Finally, some local entities rely on the government attorney to represent management during collective bargaining.

LMR: A SYSTEMS MODEL

All the components of LMR presented above and how they react to external environmental influences can be depicted by the single systems model presented in Figure 6–2. The model of concentric circles places strategic development at the center or the heart of LMR. If the process is successful, collective bargaining is conducted in good faith and an agreement is reached. The inner circle shows the interaction among the actors in the process: labor, management, unions, and the public. The large outside circle is the overarching framework that establishes the parameters governing LMR: statutes, executive orders, regulations, agency rules, court orders, and legal precedent. The constantly changing external environmental factors—political, economic, social, and organizational—highlight the importance for LMR to be able to adapt to changes if the challenges of the twenty-first century are to be met.

FUTURE ISSUES IN LABOR MANAGEMENT RELATIONS

Changing trends in public sector LMR will be a forum for interesting debate in the future.[30] Indeed, some of the discussions surrounding proposed reforms may be among the most controversial components of human resource

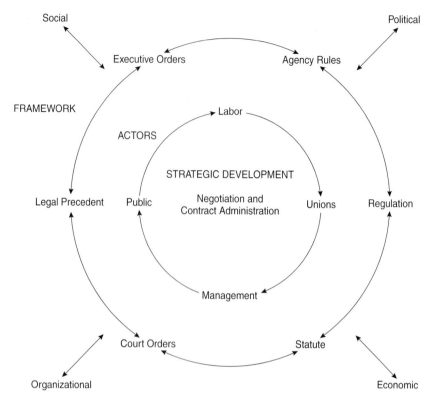

FIGURE 6–2 The LMR Environment

management both for academicians and practitioners. It is clear that several important issues will continue to shape LMR in the foreseeable future.

The first issue involves the potential for erosion in public sector union membership. As government at all levels becomes more technocratic and professionalized, public employees tend to affiliate with professional groups. However, more and more professionals, including two of the authors of this book, have never contemplated joining a labor organization, even though the opportunity exists.

A related aspect is the perception among white- and blue-collar workers that unions have outlived their usefulness. The days of forcing young children to work fourteen-hour shifts in the European coal mines or in American furniture factories are ancient history. Public employees enjoy comprehensive employer-funded benefit packages and favorable working conditions. In fact, many aspects of public employment are now protected by statute and existing contractual agreements. In recent years, some employees have actually gone against the advice of their unions. Workers in certain sectors of the health industry, for example, have opted for four ten-hour workdays per week instead of the traditional eight-hour day. The worker then receives three consecutive days off.

A second issue that will undoubtedly continue to affect LMR concerns the fiscal reality and indeed sometimes fiscal stress affecting most governments. There is no indication that the unwillingness of the public to pay increased taxes or the fear of massive government debt will subside in the near future. It is unlikely, therefore, that public employment will grow; in fact it will probably decline. It is equally unlikely that large wage settlements can be secured during such times of fiscal crisis. The public perception of government inefficiency, coupled with an increased emphasis on privatization of services traditionally delivered by the public sector, will result in a further decline in union membership.

A third major problem concerns underfunded public pension plans, a time bomb waiting to explode. As the ranks of retired former employees swell and as people live longer, resource demands on public retirement systems increase. Employer contributions have not always kept pace with the demand side, and the result is that public employee pension plans at all levels of government are underfunded by hundreds of billions of dollars. Low interest rates and slower growth in financial markets in the early 1990s exacerbate this resource shortfall. This poses a major problem for employers, unions, civil servants, and politicians. What is at stake is the security and well-being of thousands of elderly Americans.

The future role of the courts in the area of personnel in general and LMR in particular is a fourth factor that will have tremendous impact on public employee unions. Court orders mandating the implementation of pay equity and comparable worth policies will increase direct personnel costs in public agencies, leaving a lesser portion of the pie up for grabs during collective bargaining. Court intervention in equal employment opportunity can also erode the union's power base. If the courts decree that for every white male who is promoted, one African American or one woman must also be promoted, this removes from the collective bargaining process, at least in part, the traditional function of unions in negotiating contractual provisions for recruitment and promotion.

Unions will also see a diminished role in grievances. In many public jurisdictions the negotiation of grievance procedures is mandatory. In such personnel areas as employee testing for substance abuse, issues concerning AIDS in the workplace, allegations of discrimination against the disabled, and charges concerning sexual harassment, legislation and court intervention have reduced the need to rely on traditional dispute resolution practices such as the grievance, thereby diminishing the involvement of unions.

The future holds one final challenge for public unions; society's need to *train for technology*. Many services currently provided by government are inefficient because they are technologically obsolete. The U.S. Postal Service is a case in point. The major function of this agency's 750,000 employees is to deliver mail and packages door-to-door throughout the nation. Yet, we currently possess the technology in the form of electronic mail and enhanced cable and fiber optics systems to render a significant proportion of these jobs outmoded. A number of questions come to mind in considering the rapid growth in technology. In an era of reduced resources, how long will unions be able to resist technology-driven change and the reality of massive employment restructuring, including layoffs? How does society retrain technologically obsolete employees so they can continue to be productive? Who pays? The same issues surface when examining the future of other public entities. For example, "smart bomb" technology in the armed forces and advances in aircraft guidance systems installed at the nation's airports make thousands of military and air traffic control jobs obsolete. The inevitable restructuring of the workforce as a result of improved technology will contribute to reduced union membership in all areas of public employment.

One thing is clear about the future nature of LMR in government: it has to change. The adversarial model in which both sides selfishly articulate their respective demands without consideration of the rapidly changing external environment will no longer be acceptable. New cooperative partnerships such as the approach recommended by the National Performance Review appear to be the models of the future. Governments must recognize the need to diversify and retrain the workforce and to reengineer the manner in which work is performed to attain increases in efficiency and productivity.

LMR: A PRACTICAL EXAMPLE

The following events occurred in a municipal special-purpose authority. This past year, several longtime blue-collar employees of the Middletown Park Authority called an after-hours meeting of their colleagues—the topic was unionization.

Middletown is a midwest community with a population of approximately 100,000. The Park Authority has forty-seven full-time employees, forty-three of whom are nonmanagement (the director and three assistant directors comprise management). Salaries and benefits for Authority employees are comparable to those for city and state workers, and there is a high degree of job security. Several of the employees have been with the agency for more than twenty years.

The director believes in a top-down approach to the management of the agency and likes to involve himself in the daily activities of his employees. Personnel matters, however, are not considered a priority, and the director believes that the employees should be thankful for the generous compensation and benefits they receive. In recent months, several personnel problems concerning hours of work, inequities in overtime payments, harassment of female employees, and inequities in the assignment of work have been leaked to the Authority's board of directors.

There is a perception within the agency that morale in general is deteriorating. People not only seem more disgruntled than usual, but their productivity also appears to have declined in recent weeks. The director refuses to discuss employee concerns because he believes that the concerns are not legitimate, and he is annoyed that the board is asking questions related to an "internal" matter.

News of a meeting to consider unionization took the board of directors completely by surprise. The board members wondered what possibly could possess the employees to want to unionize and what long-term effects this would have on the Authority. The board president immediately called a meeting of the employees and the three assistant directors. She knew that inviting the director would be counterproductive and could undermine the employees' willingness to express their views candidly; the board decided to meet with the employees first and then ask the director to join the meeting.

The meeting was very productive. It turned out that the majority of the employees were actually satisfied with the compensation and general work environment. After two hours of discussion it became apparent that the employees were simply asking that their concerns be taken seriously and addressed in a timely manner and that they have some input into the development of personnel policies. Eventually, it was agreed that personnel matters would be handled by a personnel committee comprising three individuals: one elected wage-grade employee, one elected member of the office/secretarial staff, and one of the assistant directors.

The lesson of the story should be clear. Many seemingly insignificant components of LMR in a union or outside a union context can explode into major organizational problems if not addressed in a cooperative and professional manner. The president of the board handled the situation well. She acted responsibly in diffusing the situation, and the formation of the personnel committee was an excellent compromise. The other major piece of the puzzle is what happened to the agency director. Cooperation was too much for him and he ultimately decided to retire.

CONCLUSION

This chapter provided an overview of LMR in government. The private sector has had a much longer, richer history of LMR than has the public sector. Collective bargaining and contract administration is only a few decades old in the latter. The point was made that the processes in the private and public sectors are quite different, primarily because of the political, economic, and organizational factors that are unique to the role of government in modern society.

A typical bargaining cycle was detailed along with impasse procedures aimed at breaking gridlock, including the use of strikes at the state and local level. The chapter concluded with an assessment of the future of LMR in the public sector. Issues such as improvements in technology, changing workforce demographics, the role of the courts, and declining membership send a message to both unions and management that a restructuring in the manner in which LMR is conducted in public agencies is inevitable.

Exercises

6.1 Prepare a memorandum outlining the pros and cons of allowing federal employees the right to strike.

6.2 Find a public agency in your area that permits collective bargaining (e.g., school district, police department). Research the policies and procedures that are currently in place and provide a report including recommendations to improve the process.

6.3 Develop a double timeline of landmark events in the history of private sector and public sector LMR.

6.4 Prepare a memorandum that supports unionization among public sector employees.

6.5 Consider that you are a public sector union organizer and you are confronting a government personnel agency that is resisting the idea of collective bargaining by its employees because it fears strikes. What strategies would you employ that would represent the interests of your prospective members and be acceptable to the government's representative?

Notes

1. This point is made by N. Joseph Cayer, *Public Personnel Administration in the United States,* 2d ed. (New York: St. Martin's, 1986) and in Jay M. Shafritz, Albert C. Hyde, and David H. Rosenbloom, *Personnel Management in Government: Politics and Process* (New York: Marcel Dekker, Inc., 1986).
2. For an excellent series of articles on public sector labor-management relations, see Jack Rabin, Thomas Vocino, W. Bartley Hildreth, and Gerald J. Miller, *Handbook of Public Sector Labor Relations* (New York: Marcel Dekker, Inc., 1994).
3. This section draws heavily upon what is considered the best source on public sector labor relations. For an in-depth treatment of the subject, see Richard C. Kearney, *Labor Relations in the Public Sector,* 2d ed. (New York: Marcel Dekker, Inc., 1992).
4. N. Joseph Cayer, *Managing Human Resources: An Introduction to Public Personnel Administration* (New York: St. Martin's Press, 1980).
5. Charles J. Coleman, *Managing Labor Relations in the Public Sector* (San Francisco: Jossey-Bass Publishers, 1990).
6. Kearney, *Labor Relations in the Public Sector.*
7. A detailed discussion of labor-management relations in the 1960s is in Murray B. Nesbit, *Labor Relations in the Federal Government Service* (Washington, D.C.: The Bureau of National Affairs, Inc., 1976).

8. Katherine C. Naff, "Labor-Management Relations and Privatization: A Federal Perspective," *Public Administration Review* 51, no. 1 (January/February 1991).
9. Kearney, *Labor Relations in the Public Sector.*
10. Richard C. Kearney and Steven W. Hays, "Labor-Management Relations and Participative Decision Making: Toward a New Paradigm," *Public Administration Review* 54, no. 1 (January/February 1994).
11. Ibid., p. 50.
12. Al Gore, *From Red Tape to Results: Creating a Government That Works Better and Costs Less: Report of the National Performance Review* (Washington, D.C.: U.S. Government Printing Office, 1993), p. 88.
13. For a detailed discussion of the sovereignty argument see Sylvestor Petro, *Sovereignty and Compulsory Public-Sector Bargaining,* 10 *Wake Forest L Rev* 25 (March 1974).
14. The Public Service Research Council, *Public Sector Bargaining and Strikes,* 6th ed (Vienna, Va.: The Public Service Research Council, 1982).
15. Shafritz, Hyde, and Rosenbloom, *Personnel Management in Government.*
16. Another excellent discussion of the differences between collective bargaining in the two sectors is Louis V. Imundo, Jr., "Some Comparisons Between Public Sector and Private Sector Collective Bargaining," 24 *Labor Law Journal* 810 (1973).
17. Leonard D. White, "Strikes in the Public Service," *Public Personnel Review* 10, no. 1 (January 1949).
18. Charles J. Coleman, *Managing Labor Relations in the Public Sector.*
19. U.S. Bureau of Labor Statistics.
20. States that prohibit collective bargaining are Alabama, Arkansas, Arizona, Colorado, Louisiana, North Carolina, South Carolina, and Utah.
21. Joan E. Pynes and Joan M. Lafferty, *Local Government Labor Relations: A Guide for Public Administrators* (Westport, Conn.: Quorum Books, 1993).
22. A detailed discussion of the role of professionals in organizations is Mary E. Guy, *Professionals in Organizations: Debunking a Myth* (New York: Praeger, 1985).
23. Kearney, *Labor Relations in the Public Sector.*
24. This relates primarily to state and local government. As noted earlier, in the federal system there is much less latitude in defining scope.
25. John Patrick Piskulich, *Collective Bargaining in State and Local Government* (New York: Praeger, 1992).
26. Coleman, *Managing Labor Relations in the Public Sector.*
27. Pynes and Lafferty, *Local Government Labor Relations.*
28. These data are provided by the Bureau of Labor Statistics. The problem is that the Bureau maintains records only when a strike involves one thousand or more employees.
29. This section is adapted from Kearney, *Labor Relations in the Public Sector,* pp. 125–31.
30. An interesting discussion of some of the future issues is found in Benjamin Aaron, "The Future of Collective Bargaining in the Public Sector," in *Public Sector Bargaining,* eds. Benjamin Aaron, Joyce M. Najita, and James L. Stern, 2d ed. (Washington, D.C.: The Bureau of National Affairs, Inc., 1988).

MODULE III The Human Dimension

7

Human Resource Development

INTRODUCTION

When one thinks of public personnel management, the sub-specialties of compensation and benefits, performance appraisal and management, classification, and labor relations immediately come to mind. This chapter and the following one help shed light on the whole area of human resource utilization. In this chapter we are more specific, in examining the increasingly important human resource development (HRD) dimension. Before defining HRD and exploring it in more depth, we first need to examine the context in which HRD is occurring and will be occurring in the future.

CONTEXT

Change, Change, and More Change

It has almost become trite to talk about the amount of change that organizations are undergoing. Restructuring, reorganizing, redeploying, reengineering, downsizing, rightsizing, mergers and acquisitions, strategic alliances, and a host of other organizational strategies are introducing unprecedented levels of change into business organizations. Government has not remained immune to these developments as it has developed its own strategies for improvement in the form of Total Quality Management, reinvention, and a number of other reform efforts. The point here is not to explore those change movements (see chapter 3), but to point to them as key contextual factors influencing the importance of HRD.

In addition to the reform efforts currently under way, public organizations are learning to live with some other societal trends that have introduced change into the workplace. Three of the more prominent include tight budgets, technological innovation, and workforce composition.

Tight budgets refer to the fact that many government organizations had become accustomed to yearly budget increases and expanding programs throughout the 1960s and 1970s. In the 1980s and 1990s that changed dramatically. Brought into focus by the soaring federal government budget deficit where annual expenditures exceeded revenues, government agencies were suddenly asked to "do more with less." President Carter used a "zero-based budgeting" approach that questioned all spending. Presidents Reagan and Bush were frequently quoted as saying that the problem (the deficit) is not that the taxpayers don't pay enough, but that government spends too much. President Clinton, though a Democrat, also stressed fiscal conservatism in his campaign for the presidency.

Similar trends have taken place at the state and local levels. Republicans were elected recently as mayors in New York City, Los Angeles, and Philadelphia, largely because of their promises to trim government spending. At the state level, Governor Douglas Wilder of Virginia(a Democrat and the first African American governor) will be remembered by many for the budget-cutting over which he presided. Hence, fiscal austerity pervades all levels of government and inserts a huge element of uncertainty into the lives of public employees.

Technological innovation has also been the source of many changes in government. The introduction of the computer, facsimile, voice mail, and overnight delivery systems have fundamentally changed the way work is done. Timesheets and travel vouchers can now be completed on-line and sent electronically to the appropriate office. Legal briefs, contracts, speeches, and other documents can be worked on by professionals in different locations simultaneously.

Similarly, specialized equipment has changed work in government organizations. Local governments are now experimenting with citizen participation on-line rather than in person, over the phone, or by mail. Police are using video recorders to establish a record of encounters with motorists. Land management and military personnel are experimenting with automated global positioning systems to provide them with exact locations rather than relying exclusively on maps and compasses. These few examples are just the tip of the iceberg. Competency in using this technology has become a part of the job. Therefore, as the technology changes so does the work.

Workforce composition has also contributed to change in the workplace.

As was noted earlier in this book, diversity has been replacing homogeneity in the workforce as women and minorities enter the workforce at faster rates than white males. Moreover, restructurings, cutbacks, and the like have brought about changes in the notion that one works in a single profession for the same organization until retirement. As people move in and out of the workplace around changing careers, rearing children, caring for parents, and attending to other personal needs, personnel turnover increases.

In addition, changes in pension plans, such as the replacement of the federal government's old Civil Service Retirement System with the Federal Employee Retirement System (FERS) for all new employees, make workers more mobile. Under FERS, employees' pension plans are more "portable," meaning they can take the benefits with them to a new employer, whereas under CSRS the benefits were not transferable and employees had to work for a long period to receive full benefits. Again, the result is more turnover and change in the workplace. Together, these developments and others make government organizations of today places of great change, signaling a need to successfully assess and manage this change to the benefit of the organization.

Managing Change Through the Learning Organization

Most theorists agree organizations will continue to change at unprecedented rates, precluding a return to "the good old days." Therefore, we face the challenge of managing government organizations in these turbulent times and staffing them with people capable of changing with the times. One of the keys to success will be the ability of individuals and organizations to continue to learn and adapt to the changing environment. Peter Senge's *The Fifth Discipline: The Art and Practice of the Learning Organization*[1] gives us insight into what the future will require of individuals and organizations.

Senge's learning organization calls for some new ways of thinking and acting in order to deal with the change and complexity of today's and tomorrow's worlds. At the core of the learning organization is the notion of systems thinking. Systems thinking calls on individuals to become more aware of the interconnectedness of work issues and to see both the "forest and the trees."[2] By this he means that specialists need to be aware of the larger context in which they work and fully consider the impact of their work. Solving symptoms will not be sufficient; root causes must be addressed. Failure to do so merely guarantees that the problem will continue to haunt the organization.

Consider, for example, how this systems perspective can be applied to the problem of employee absenteeism. One way to fix the problem would be to make sure that the employees are aware of the policy on absenteeism and punish those who violate it. Systems thinking would tell us that the better, long-term approach would be to investigate the cause for the absences and to address the root cause. Such an investigation might show that many employees are also responsible for transporting their children and aging parents to and from appointments. It might also reveal that many of these transportation needs are routine and known in advance (such as taking a child to school). The systems approach solution may be to develop a flexible work schedule so that employees can work hours that accommodate their personal situations, such as caring for family members' needs, and still meet their work obligations.

Systems thinking and building a learning organization will require some new thinking and new behaviors on the parts of employers and employees. Specifically, Senge suggests that central to this shift will be a need for people to become better masters of themselves by expanding their range of skills and capabilities, by employing much more complex mental models that consider the larger system implications, by developing a shared vision of the future with their co-workers, by increasing the ability to learn together as a team, and by exhibiting better personal characteristics such as openness and fully disclosing thoughts and feelings.[3] In the aggregate, these prescribed changes represent a significant developmental challenge for most organizations and their employees. Obviously, HRD is envisioned as a key means of bringing about these desired changes. Yet, before moving into a more detailed description of HRD, we must first look at one more important perspective on the future of our work world.

Rethinking the Kinds of Work We Do

Robert Reich, Secretary of Labor in the Clinton administration, writes convincingly about what the workplace of the future will be in *The Work of Nations*.[4] He states that the labels of today's workers, such as blue- and white-collar and management (upper, middle, and "first line") will become less useful in the future. He offers three categories that better describe the workers of tomorrow:

1. "Routine production services" refers to tedious and repetitive work that accompanies the information era. "The foot soldiers of the information economy are hordes of data processors stationed in 'back offices' at computer terminals linked to worldwide information banks. They routinely enter data into computers or take it out again—records of credit card purchases and payments, credit reports, checks that have cleared, customer accounts, customer correspondence, payroll, hospital billings, patient records, medical claims, court decisions, subscriber lists, personnel library catalogues, and so forth."[5]

They also include low-level supervisors and people performing repetitive checks on people and processes. Government organizations employ many routine production employees in positions ranging from public works employees to Social Security clerks.

2. "In-person servers" also do simple and repetitive tasks but usually do their work with more interactions with customers or clients. "Included in this category are retail sales workers, waiters and waitresses, hotel workers, janitors, cashiers, hospital attendants and orderlies, nursing home aides . . . sellers of residential real estate, flight attendants, physical therapists, and among the fastest growing of all—security guards."[6]

Examples in government organizations would also include cashiers at motor vehicle departments, police officers, receptionists, social workers, and librarians. What is interesting about this category of workers is that it combines some professions not normally considered together because of differences in educational requirements (e.g., social worker and receptionist) and/or compensation (e.g., librarians and cashiers).

3. "Symbolic-analytic" services represent Reich's third type of work. Symbolic analysts work on more complex, less routine matters and often use models, theories, and complex systems to model reality and identify and solve problems. "Included in this category are people who call themselves research scientists, design engineers, software engineers, civil engineers, biotechnology engineers, sound engineers, public relations executives, investment bankers, lawyers, real estate developers, energy consultants, agricultural consultants, armaments consultants, architectural consultants, management informational specialists, organization development specialists, strategic planners, corporate headhunters, and systems analysts."[7]

In addition to many of the professions listed above, government organizations also employ symbolic analysts in personnel services such as policy analysts, program analysts, program evaluation specialists, public affairs specialists, and economic development specialists. Though not always the case, these positions tend to be more highly compensated than many of the positions in production services or in-person services.

Reich's categories of work are helpful in illuminating the types of work that make up the workforce without using the less useful categories of "blue-collar and white-collar," "managers and workers," "exempt and non exempt," "professionals and technicians," and "union and nonunion." They help us to see work as routine and nonroutine tasks, some of which is more "hands on and tangible," such as data entry; some of which is more conceptual (symbolic analysis); and some of which requires personal interaction with clients or other workers while some assignments are more solitary. The categories also clarify the challenges of HRD: helping prepare the workers of today and tomorrow meet their work challenges and the challenges of organizations.

Summary of the Work Context

Extensive and rapid change is a predominant feature in organizations today, including those in government. Tight budgets, technological innovations, and changing workforce composition are specific trends affecting most government agencies and their civil servants. To prosper under such conditions requires new ways of thinking that are more comprehensive and that truly address "root problems." Systems thinking describes one such approach that seems appropriate for contemporary organizations.

Reich's three categories help show one way to conceptualize the work that makes up the modern-day economy and that occurs in government organizations. When one thinks of improvement in routine production services, in person services, and in symbolic analysis, given the trends highlighted above and the need for systems thinking, the challenges for effective human resource utilization are immense. More specifically, the challenge of HRD to prepare workers to perform successfully in this environment is significant. More and more, organizations are realizing that to meet this challenge, investments in HRD and continuous learning are essential toward their becoming "learning organizations."

HRD IN THE EMERGING CONTEXT

Defining Human Resource Development

In the discussion above, we have briefly alluded to HRD as being a part of successful human resource utilization and as a means of preparing for the changes engulfing organizations today. A more precise definition is offered by Nadler and Nadler:

> Human resource development (HRD) is 1. Organized learning experiences provided by employers, 2. Within a specified period of time, 3. To bring about the possibility of performance improvement and/or growth.[8]

This definition needs to be explored in more detail to ensure a common understanding of HRD. "Organized learning experiences provided by employers" signals two main ideas. First, the focus is on organized (e.g., planned, structured, not incidental) learning experiences, such as training classes or temporary work assignments where the objective is for the employee to learn. While it is recognized that employees should be constantly learning from all they encounter in life, HRD is limited to those organized efforts specifically aimed at facilitating learning on the part of the employee within the work environment. Second, the idea is that the training is sponsored by the employer, implying that the learning will be in harmony with the organization's needs. Hence, HRD does not include personal growth efforts not endorsed by the organization, such as training for a new career outside the employee's current organization (e.g., a government personnel clerk taking guitar lessons) or pursuing religious education.

"Within a specified period of time" helps focus the learning experience on a discrete period of time or sequence of events. Hence, an HRD learning experience could be a four-hour training session, a three-day short course at a local university, or a six-month temporary work assignment in a different part of the organization. Having a definite starting and stopping point for the learning experience better enables evaluation of the HRD that has occurred.

"To bring about the possibility of performance improvement and/or personal growth" illuminates the two possible outcomes of HRD: performance improvement and personal growth. Performance improvement refers to the need for all employees to continue to improve their work performance, because in the organizational context of today, continuously working more efficiently and more effectively is expected. Employees often take part in HRD at the start of a new job (as a means of developing new knowledge, skills, or abilities associated with the position) or as a means of improving their performance after a performance appraisal or in response to a development plan indicating developmental needs.

Personal growth, the second HRD outcome, refers less to specific knowledge, skills, and abilities of the job and more to finding and developing aspects of the individual that are unique and undeveloped. According to Nadler and Nadler, ". . . development is sometimes referred to as an activity designed to release human potential. Development provides an opportunity for people to move into uncharted directions. . . . Development can allow individuals to uncover hidden interests and abilities that may, at some time, work to the benefit of the organization, even though that was not the objective."[9] An Outward Bound seven-day trek in the wilderness might be representative of an HRD experience more closely associated with personal growth than increased performance. However, the line between the two is fuzzy as one could find personal growth in an experience designed to increase job performance and vice versa. Most HRD in government organizations is aimed more at improving job performance than at personal growth.

The portion of the definition that says "to bring about the possibility" was carefully worded by the authors. HRD efforts such as training courses cannot guarantee that participants will learn. They can only "bring about the possibility" or create the environment for learning and development to occur. The ultimate responsibility for learning rests with the participants.

A final note about the definition of HRD used here is that it makes explicit the linkage between employer (the organization) and the employee. HRD should represent the intersection of the individual's self-development needs/desires with the organization's perceived needs. HRD efforts that ignore either of these needs are sure to be less than fully successful, as improved performance and/or personal growth will be manifested in the form of changed behaviors in the workplace, where they should be recognized and positively reinforced.

Activity Areas Within HRD

Nadler and Nadler also provide a helpful distinction for areas within HRD where the learning is employee-focused. Though these distinctions are not universally accepted (other authors use different taxonomic schema), they are helpful in thinking through the purpose of an employee participating in an HRD offering. The three areas cited are training, education, and development.[10]

Training refers to those HRD initiatives in which the learning is focused on the current job of the learner. For example, a budget analyst who takes an advanced class in using spreadsheets is doing so for the purpose of doing her current job more effectively. A person who finds her job changing because it will involve more presentations and begins studying and practicing the skills associated with effective communication is focusing on improving performance. Thus, the training, or the learning associated with the training initiative, should ultimately result in both increased job performance and employee satisfaction.

Education in this context refers to those HRD efforts aimed at learning focused on a future job for the participant. For example, the Naval Aviation Administration offers the Senior Executive Management Development Program to upper-middle personnel who have demonstrated potential for executive-level assignments.[11] Though some of the learning can be used immediately, most of the material is offered in preparation for future senior-level assignments. Such is the case for many employees pursuing such degrees as the M.P.A., M.B.A., D.P.A., or Ph.D. on a part-time basis while working full time. Often, their current position doesn't require the degree, but they view the degree as an opportunity for future advancement. These types of education programs are more difficult to evaluate because the learning is focused on positions in the future.

Development differs from training and education in that it is not directly focused toward the job. Often with an objective of encouraging personal growth, these HRD offerings could be about topics as broad as increasing self-esteem or understanding the new emerging world order, or as narrow as exploring a field that is completely new to an individual. In fact, a popular developmental topic is the application of leadership theory to literature classics.[12] Like the education programs discussed above, these HRD programs are also very difficult to evaluate.

From these definitions, it should be clear that it is the perspective of the employee and the organization that determines whether an HRD program is training, education, or development. For example, three people could attend a program on top-level military strategy: a top official at the Pentagon, a junior officer in the Army, and a pharmacist whose hobby is military history. For the first it would be training, for the second it would be education, and for the third, development. Hence, for an HRD offering to be completely training, education, or development, all participants would have to share the same learning objective.

Roles in HRD

For HRD to make a serious contribution to effective human resource utilization in organizations, numerous players must be fulfilling their roles. Given the rapidly changing work environment, HRD is becoming a critical means of helping agencies become learning organizations. In this section we will examine the roles that are crucial to HRD.

Employees are the people who participate in HRD efforts. As discussed earlier, in most government organizations employees receive yearly performance appraisals. Many then establish, with their supervisor's support, an individual development plan (IDP) that spells out training, education, and development needs along with their short- and long-term career goals. HRD offerings such as classes, seminars, conferences, courses, and short-term work assignments are then examined in an effort to find the appropriate mix of learning experiences to best respond to the needs and goals identified in the performance appraisal and IDP. Often in the face of tight budgets and heavy workloads, all of the desired learning experiences do not ultimately get funded.

Supervisors are a key part of HRD because they should work with employees on their performance appraisals and IDPs. Ultimately they often have to allocate the financial resources to pay for the employee to participate in HRD offerings. They also can serve as a valuable link in assessing and reinforcing the learning. For example, in the case of training, supervisors can help give feedback to both the employee and program evaluators about any improvement they have observed in the employee's on-the-job performance since returning from HRD. Their positive reinforcement can serve as added incentive to the employees to use what they learned and to be anxious about improving even more.

Internal HRD professionals are those personnelists who specialize in the process of HRD within their own organizations. Often they work to identify organization needs and to provide HRD offerings that respond to those needs. As in many other professions, the level of specialization of these professionals is often a function of the size of the organization in which they work and the amount of resources the organization spends on HRD. The range is tremendous, from the "one person shop" who handles all aspects of HRD to the highly specialized, such as the person who only designs leadership development programs.

External HRD professionals are those HRD specialists not employed directly by the organization but who provide HRD services to the organization.

This assistance can take many forms including consulting, design and/or delivery of programs and initiatives, evaluation of HRD initiatives, and other services. Unlike some other areas of administration where the organization can make a choice about whether or not it will use external resources to augment its internal force, most organizations' HRD efforts do draw to some extent on outside professionals. This is because it is not usually cost-effective (or, some would argue, possible) to have all the required specialties "in house." Hence, the successful management of an organizational HRD function is often carried out by a team of internal and external HRD professionals working together to meet the needs of the organization and its individual employees.

Organization executives are also key players in HRD for a number of reasons. First, as the positional leaders of the organization, it is their responsibility to scan the environment and develop the organization's strategic direction. That strategic direction should then serve as the starting point for HRD, serving as the indicator of the knowledge, skills, and abilities that will be required of employees. Second, the executive cadre must signal its support of HRD in two ways: (1) by participating in HRD activities themselves—"they will believe what you do, not what you say," and (2) by allocating the necessary financial and human resources to do the job—"talk is cheap." Finally, some executives are playing an even more direct role in HRD by getting actively involved in the delivery of some HRD programs.[13]

Key Issues in HRD

For HRD to play a constructive role in preparing today's organizations and individuals for the challenges of tomorrow, all of the players will have to act in concert. In so doing they will face a number of important issues. Three of those key issues are highlighted below.

Linkage of HRD to other organizational efforts is essential. As was mentioned in the discussion on the organization executives' roles, HRD must be aligned with organizational strategy. HRD should not be preparing employees for a future that is different from the one envisioned by the strategic direction. Likewise, HRD should be complementary to planning efforts to ensure the organization is developing its future executives (called succession planning). HRD is about increasing learning of employees, and the need to guide this learning consistent with the direction of the organization is key. A challenge for the internal HRD professionals is to ensure that their work is linked to other organizational processes.

Funding for HRD is also a key issue, especially in times of tight budgets. Unfortunately, many managers view HRD as a "nice to have" rather than a "must have" item. When compared with paying salaries, funding necessary business travel, and paying fixed costs like rent and utilities, HRD often ends up as the lowest funding priority. The irony of this, of course, is that without employees continuing to learn and develop, the organization will probably be overwhelmed by change. Senge's call for a learning organization as the means of surviving in the future is often lost in the budget battles.

Career development is another key issue in HRD.[14] Because of some of the changes described above in the context section of this chapter, the traditional model of career development is undergoing significant change. The old model of a person pursuing a single professional career at one organization where he/she then retires has become obsolete. People are changing careers and employers at a much more pronounced rate than before. And organizations are changing the work they do as well. This poses significant challenges for HRD in terms of career development.

Two trends in this regard are clear. First, individual employees must begin to assume more responsibility for their own careers and, accordingly, their own career development. No longer can the employer be looked to for HRD from career entry until retirement. Likewise, organizational HRD strategies must begin to emphasize the core skills and competencies the organization will need rather than try to provide each little developmental experience that accompanies each stage in specific professions throughout an entire career.

Emerging HRD Areas

Finally, we turn our attention to five emerging topics that many HRD offerings in government are emphasizing. While different in substance, they are all linked in that they can all be traced to the changing context described earlier in this chapter.

Leadership and executive development programs have become more and more prevalent as the pace of change has affected organizations. The need to read the changing environment, develop a vision for the future, and craft a strategy to attain that vision has become more pronounced as the environment within which organizations exist becomes more and more turbulent. Many organizations developed HRD programs in this area in the late 1980s and early 1990s.[15] Because this is such an important component of effective human resource utilization, the next chapter deals exclusively with this subject.

Diversity is also emerging as a key HRD topic. Driven by an appreciation of the multiculturalism of the United States and its organizations, managers are stressing successful operation in a diverse world. This is a topic that is relevant to all employees, regardless of position or level in the organization. Government organizations, in particular, have led the way in this area, and diversity seems to be a "hot topic" for the foreseeable future.[16]

Technology training, education, and development will continue to be a major topic for HRD. The pace of technology development is not showing signs of slowing down, and all three categories of workers described by Reich will utilize technology to an increasing degree in the future. From the data entry clerk (routine production services) to the police officer (in-person server) to the biotechnology engineer (symbolic analyst), the future holds more technology, not less. HRD should play a key role in making use of technology as easy as possible.

International perspective is another emerging topic area that will continue to be emphasized in HRD. As we move closer to a "world economy," and as transportation and communication systems continue to improve, the international perspective becomes more important. State economic development departments are establishing offices in foreign countries. Federal agencies, such as the Environmental Protection Agency, are realizing that problems such as air and water pollution do not stop at country's borders. And local governments are establishing "sister cities" as a means of facilitating cross-cultural learning. All of this points to a need for public administrators to become "citizens of the world," and HRD will play a part in making this happen.

Government improvement initiatives such as the National Performance Review, Total Quality Management (TQM), and Reengineering, bring with them a language and a process of reforming government that must be learned. (A more complete description of these efforts is included in chapter 3.) HRD has a responsibility to assist this learning by bringing employees into contact with the essential pieces of these reform efforts. For example, TQM places heavy reliance on "customer focus," and many government employees could benefit from rethinking their work in terms of a customer-focus perspective. Likewise, some approaches to TQM utilize statistical control methods that must be learned by certain employees. So once again we see that HRD can play a vital role in something as ambitious as reforming, or "reinventing," government.

CONCLUSION

Human resource development is about blending the needs of the organization with those of its employees. The context surrounding government organizations and employees is turbulent and greatly influences the training, education, and development that is appropriate. HRD efforts should be closely linked to other organizational initiatives and can play a vital role in preparing organizations and individual employees for the future. For this to happen, many players, including employees, supervisors, HRD professionals, and organization executives, must work together.

Exercises

7.1 Identify a relatively large public sector organization. Contact the personnel office and inquire about HRD programs in that agency. Are these programs guided by an overall HRD plan? How are the HRD activities helping prepare the organization and its employees for the future?

7.2 Select a public sector agency and design an HRD plan for that agency that will meet the needs of both the organization and its employees as they face the challenges of the 1990s.

Notes

1. Peter M. Senge, *The Fifth Discipline: The Art and Practice of the Learning Organization* (New York: Doubleday, 1990).
2. Ibid.
3. Ibid.
4. Robert B. Reich, *The Work of Nations* (New York: Vintage, 1991).
5. Ibid., p. 175.
6. Ibid., p. 176.
7. Ibid., pp. 177–78.
8. Leonard Nadler and Zeace Nadler, *Developing Human Resources* (San Francisco: Jossey Bass, 1991). p. 10.
9. Ibid., p. 77.
10. Ibid., p. 4.
11. Terence J. Tipple, *Executive Development Programs: A Framework for Coherence* (Ph.D. diss., Virginia Tech, 1992).
12. Smithsonian Institution, Washington, D.C., "The Smithsonian Campus on the Mall" (fall 1994), p. 28.
13. James F. Bolt, *Executive Development: A Strategy for Corporate Competitiveness* (New York: Harper and Row, 1989).
14. See Richard N. Bolles, *The Three Boxes of Life* (Berkeley, Calif.: Ten Speed Press, 1981).
15. Tipple, *Executive Development*.
16. Ann M. Morrison, *The New Leaders: Guidelines on Leadership Diversity in America* (San Francisco: Jossey Bass, 1992).

8

Executive Development

INTRODUCTION

Almost daily we hear or read about the performance of executives in the public sector. The senior public administrators of today are under close scrutiny to lead and manage their organizations successfully. It seems as though they are constantly being asked to meet increasing expectations, of the publics they serve and of the workforces they manage, with fewer and fewer resources. And they are required to do so in a world becoming ever more complex.

How, then, do public sector executives continue to rise to the challenge of ever-increasing performance demands? Often, the first step is recognizing that the knowledge, skills, and behaviors of yesterday may not be adequate for today, nor those of today for tomorrow. Hence, many successful executives have committed themselves to a professional life of continuous growth and development. This chapter examines the development of executives in the public sector and highlights some specific executive development programs.

WHAT IS EXECUTIVE DEVELOPMENT?

Executive development refers to that portion of human resource development (HRD) targeted at senior members of organizations. Specifically, executive development programs can be defined as "those activities and experiences which are planned and executed in an effort to help top organizational members better lead their organizations."[1]   Opinions on how best to help executives improve their performance and "better lead their organizations" are varied and have led to a plethora of approaches to executive development. In fact, a review of executive development programs will show the professional involvement of many academic disciplines, including public and business administration, education, psychology, economics, counseling, and others.

GROWTH OF EXECUTIVE DEVELOPMENT PROGRAMS

The field of executive development is growing. Both government and nongovernment organizations are encouraging executives to participate in structured developmental programs. Organizations are trying, through the use of executive development, to remain well-positioned and competitive within their respective environments. Executive development has become a strategic tool of the organization.[2]

Similarly, many individual executives have adopted a mode of "lifetime learning" in which they recognize that the pace of change today demands that they stay current on emerging developments.[3] Graduation from degree programs, such as the master of public or business administration, no longer signifies the end of formal learning as more and more executives are enrolling in seminars, short courses, workshops, and programs on a wide variety of topics. In fact, recent years saw the emergence and growth of executive M.P.A. and M.B.A. programs specifically tailored to working managers.

Organizational and individual pursuit of continuous development has helped make executive development a large component of the overall HRD effort. Stephan and others estimate that 12.2 percent of training and development expenditures, or $7.32 billion, goes toward business executive development in the United States.[4]   When government and not-for-profit organizations are added, the total spent on executive development is even larger. Hence, when public administrators decide to pursue some developmental effort in order to improve their performance, they have a great deal of company.

Academic institutions have participated in the growth of executive development, as have specialized staff units within organizations, which facilitate managerial and executive growth. In 1988, Green and Lazarus reported on the rapid growth of both corporate and university programs. Clark and Freeman[5] describe over 100 university and not-for-profit leadership programs that have "open enrollment" policies, meaning executives from any organization can participate. Executive development programs now serve as an important link between universities and organizations, where theory and practice come together.

EXECUTIVE DEVELOPMENT PROGRAMS EMPHASIZE LEADERSHIP

Though executives participate in numerous developmental sessions on everything from computers to personal fitness, many of the programs aimed at generally improving their performance as executives focus on leadership. Either implicitly or explicitly, leadership is an underpinning for many executive development programs. This strong interest in leadership grew significantly in the 1980s.

Prior to the 1980s, much of the literature referred to the work of executives in terms of discrete roles or managerial functions. For example, a public sector executive's work might be seen as consisting of budgeting, personnel, policy formulation and execution, and legislative affairs. Often popular in public administration circles was the longstanding acronym PODSCORB, which helped many graduate students recall the functions of planning, organizing, directing, scheduling, coordinating, and budgeting.[6] A business executive might be described as working in the areas of finance, marketing, business strategy, and information systems.

In the 1980s and 1990s, much attention shifted to the whole of the executive's responsibilities rather than the component parts. Writings on leadership from earlier decades by Chester Barnard[7] and Phillip Selznick[8] were built upon and popularized. What emerged was a picture of a more fluid existence in which the divisions between planning and organizing, and between finance and strategy, were more conceptual than real.[9] Kotter's work, in particular, was highly influential in constructing the image of the modern executive, not as someone who had mastered the knowledge of one or several functional areas but as a person with a broad-based background within a particular industry who succeeded by effectively utilizing people and resources throughout a network that spanned formal and informal channels.[10] Interestingly, nearly forty-five years earlier, Barnard had written about the importance of three executive functions—maintenance of organizational communication (through formal and informal channels), securing essential services from individuals, and formulating purpose and objectives.[11] Hence, though the importance of leadership has been highlighted lately, management theorists have been aware of its importance for many years.

The writings on leadership of the past fifteen years have helped fuel a growth of interest in leadership and a growth in executive development programs that focus on leadership. No single description or definition is accepted as the universal explanation of leadership. Rather, what has emerged are a number of perspectives on leadership, all of which emphasize certain aspects of successful executive behavior. Some of the more common areas of emphasis follow:

1. *Self-awareness.* Executives must be aware of their own strengths and weaknesses, attitudes, behaviors, and the effects they have on others (subor-

dinates, peers, supervisors) if they are to lead successfully. Often, this information is gathered through specially designed questionnaires, or diagnostic instruments, which are completed by the executives and by others with whom they interact. Examples of such instruments that are used in executive development programs to increase participants' self-awareness are the Heresy/Blanchard Situational Leadership Instrument, the Myers Briggs Type Indicator, and the Center for Creative Leadership's Leadership Survey Instrument and Benchmarks. Typically, the results of these instruments are shared with the executive in a process called "giving feedback." Executive participants then use this feedback to prepare individual development plans that will guide their development into the future.

A portion of the benchmarks instrument is reproduced in Figure 8–1. The questions shown are answered by the executive, the executive's supervisor, some of the executive's peers, and by direct reports. All of these responses are aggregated and shared with the executive during a feedback session.

2. *Clear understanding of the operating context.* For both public and business executives, understanding the environment in which their organiza-

FIGURE 8–1 Excerpt from Benchmarks

1 = Strongly disagree
2 = Tend to disagree
3 = Hard to decide
4 = Tend to agree
5 = Strongly agree

This person:
15. does not pay enough attention to detail.
16. does not handle pressure well.
17. isolates him/herself from others.
18. relies too much on natural talent.
19. disagrees with higher management about how the business should be run.
20. is emotionally volatile and unpredictable.
21. has chosen to stay with the same boss too long.
22. makes direct reports or peers feel stupid or unintelligent.
23. might burn out, run out of steam.
24. has left a trail of little problems.
25. might lose a powerful advocate within the organization.
26. has left a trail of bruised people.

A "5" response is always negative.

tion operates is seen as a critical component to successful leadership. For public administrators this is particularly true as the actions of so many players (e.g., elected officials, citizen groups, unions) can affect the success of their organizations. Hence, many leadership development programs aimed at public executives focus on increasing their levels of understanding of the complex world of public policy and administration. Examples include many of the sessions sponsored by think tanks and universities, where a topic such as the impact of falling interest rates on local government financing is discussed in detail. In these sessions participants get a clear understanding of the operating environment and how it might change.

In many sessions that provide a clearer understanding of the operating context, executives often learn as much from discussions with each other as they do from listening to lectures from university professors or other "experts." Accordingly, professional organizations such as the National Academy of Public Administration, American Society for Public Administration, and the International City Management Association play a key role in providing opportunities for executives to work with and learn from each other. Often, some of the problems they encounter are new developments for which no theory or recommended approach yet exists. For example, when AIDS first entered the public consciousness, questions were raised about the proper approach for an organization to take in working with an employee (and that employee's coworkers) diagnosed as HIV-positive. In many instances, practicing executives can work together to develop innovative and collaborative solutions to emerging problems.

Such experiences can contribute greatly to providing the public executive with timely information on how best to manage difficult situations: often the ones that will influence their perceived success or failure as executives.

3. *Vision for the organization.* Many leadership theorists[12] and executive development programs emphasize the need for leaders to have a strategic vision for their organization. It is felt that it is an executive leadership responsibility to articulate a vision or central purpose for the organization that is clear and compelling to all members of the organization (e.g., employees) and all external stakeholders. Without a clear vision, it is argued, organizations can get lost in the day-to-day challenges and lose sight of the overall organizational mission. Hence, leaders are charged with providing a clearly defined state toward which organization can work. One of the most popular examples of a vision in the public sector is NASA's original charge "to put a man on the moon before the end of the decade."

Few organizational visions are as dramatic (or brief) as the one that accompanied this country's venture into space exploration. But all should share a common characteristic of focusing the organization's efforts toward major areas of emphasis and away from lower-priority work. This establishment and articulation of an organizational vision is very much considered an executive function.

Providing a vision for an organization in the public sector is particularly challenging because so much for which the organization is responsible is spelled out in law, charter, or some form of legislative mandate. For example, the executives at the U.S. Environmental Protection Agency (EPA) must direct their agency to enforce statutes such as the Clean Air Act and the Clean Water Act, as they are a specific part of the EPA's legislative mandate. At the same time, there is still room for executive discretion and interpretation such that an EPA administrator could decide to emphasize, for example, nonprofit sources of water pollution. The point is that, within the legal and administrative mandates, public administrators still retain discretion over how their own organizations operate. Many leadership theorists encourage administrators to channel their discretionary efforts toward a vision for their organizations.

From 1985–1993, Chief F. Dale Robertson led the U.S. Forest Service, in part, based on a vision for that organization. In addition to having a vision for what the agency's focus was, Robertson felt a need to articulate a vision for what the Forest Service should be. That vision is reproduced in Figure 8–2. Note that though the vision is describing a future state, it is written in the present tense to help employees and key stakeholders better relate to the vision.

Vision for the U.S. Forest Service
F. Dale Robertson, Chief (1993)

We are recognized nationally and internationally as a leader in caring for the land and serving people.

We are a multicultural and diverse organization. Employees work in a caring and nurturing environment where leadership is shared. All employees are respected, accepted, and appreciated for their unique and important contribution to the mission. The work is interesting, challenging, rewarding, and fun—more than just a job!

We are an efficient and productive organization that excels in achieving its mission. Responsibility and accountability for excellence are shared by employees and partners. The American people can count on the Forest Service to perform.

FIGURE 8–2

4. *Understanding and managing change.* A fourth leadership area involves the executive's special responsibility to anticipate and manage the changes he or she and the organization will encounter in pursuit of the vision. Successfully managing change requires recognition that change occurs at many levels—individual, team (group, project, department), intergroup, organization, and society.[13]

A change for an individual might mean an employee will soon finish an executive M.P.A. program and look for a position with more responsibility. Change at the organizational level might be a city government department facing a 10 percent reduction in staffing as a result of a budget cut imposed by city council.

The public sector executive is constantly being bombarded by change at all levels and is expected to help the organization successfully navigate the rapids of change. What are the truly significant changes? How should the organization respond? When should the organization try to bring about changes in the operating environment? These and other similar questions are addressed by public executives regularly.

One key way that executives lead organizations through change is by monitoring and managing the organization's culture. "Corporate culture is the system of norms, beliefs, and assumptions, and values that determine how people in the organization act—even when that action may be at odds with the written policies and formal reporting relationships."[14] Hence, the leader is challenged with influencing employees' norms, beliefs, and assumptions and, as Snyder says, being fully aware that written policies and formal reporting relationships are not always followed. Executives then must use formal and informal mechanisms to align the culture of the organization with their vision and the significant changes taking place in the operating environment.

Public executives face a special challenge in managing organization culture as two factors come together. The first is the perception on the part of many that government employees are incompetent and lazy. The second is that the resources available to the public manager seem to be constantly decreasing with budget cuts and personnel freezes. And public expectations seem to be continually increasing. Amidst these factors, how can a public executive manage change and the organizational culture so that the public interest is served and the organization remains healthy?

Bardwick[15] suggests that the executives and their organizations must focus on creating cultures where high performance is the central characteristic. She argues that performance is maximized when the organization culture is characterized neither by entitlement (where employees feel entitled to their positions and benefits and have no anxiety about job loss) nor by high levels of fear (where employees are extremely anxious about job loss and have no feeling of control). Rather, the healthy organization culture is characterized by a sense of "earning" where employees have moderate amounts of job anxiety, yet they know that if they produce at high levels they will have some control over their own destiny. This relationship is shown graphically in Figure 8–3. As the figure shows, the challenge for any executive is to create an earning culture where productivity is the highest.

The sucessful public sector executive attempts to manage the organizational climate in such a way that employees experience neither of the anxiety extremes shown in the figure. A very low anxiety level, called "entitlement," would be associated with an office that changes little from day to day, year to year, and where employees could be thought to have "an attitude"—namely, they are confident they are in no danger of losing their jobs regardless of their level of performance. A very high anxiety level (characterized by fear) refers to an organization where employees are paralyzed by change and believe their jobs are constantly at risk regardless of their performance. Executives need to pay attention to the anxiety level and attempt to influence it in the direction of higher productivity.

Some city managers and public works directors have helped bring about an earning culture by allowing private contractors to compete against government crews for work, such as trash collection. The work is awarded to the lowest bidder. Hence, the city crews must earn the work and productivity must be high. Likewise, some training and development departments are forced to recover all of their operating funds from the other departments whose employees they train via tuition and fees. Efforts such as these to manage change and organization culture are going a long way toward changing the "entitlement" stereotype of government, and they are a key part of the public sector executive's leadership responsibility.

5. *Developing skills and competencies.* The fifth and final area of emphasis regarding leadership we have broadly called skills and competencies.

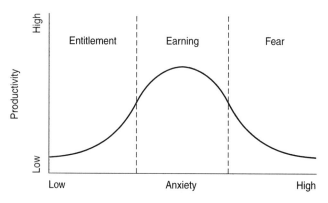

FIGURE 8–3 Different Organizational Cultures as Characterized by Productivity and Anxiety Levels

Source: Bardwick, Judith M., *Danger in the Comfort Zone* (New York: American Management Association, 1991).

Much of the leadership literature will point to a skill or area of competency thought to be critical to the success of an executive. Many executive development programs will feature one or a few skills and allow the participants to develop proficiency and demonstrate competency. Some of the more common ones include systems thinking, resolving conflict, negotiating, and giving feedback. Often, the proficiency is developed through role-playing in which participants act out a role designed to give them practice in the skill area. For example, a participant may be asked to develop an agreement with a peer for sharing a computer system (negotiating) or to help settle a dispute between two department heads (resolving conflict).

Since many of the skills included in this area are behavioral, they can be practiced (via role plays and other methods) and demonstrated. Many executive developmental programs use video tape to record performance and allow participants to see their behaviors. Often, the instructors will work individually with the participants to review their recorded performance and suggest ways to improve. As the saying goes, the camera doesn't lie. Managers for executive development programs at the World Bank and Center for Creative Leadership find skill development and the use of the video recorder very helpful in developing leadership among executives.[16]

SAMPLE EXECUTIVE DEVELOPMENT PROGRAMS

This section profiles three well-known and highly respected executive development programs. It provides an insight into real attempts to develop the leadership capabilities of executives, most of whom work in the public sector. This should be useful for readers who are pursuing a profession in human resources management as well as for those who adopt a personal course of continuous learning as an executive. The descriptions are written to highlight different approaches to executive and leadership development, to show some of the ways programs focus on leadership areas of emphasis (such as self-awareness), and to help the reader understand the experience of being a participant in an executive development program.

Senior Managers in Government (SMG)

The Senior Managers in Government (SMG) program is for government executives and is held for three weeks each summer at Harvard University's Kennedy School of Government. Senior executives from the federal government's executive and legislative branches join with a lesser number of executives from foreign governments and private corporations for a three-week period. Executives from state and local governments are not included as the Kennedy School has other programs for them.

Sleeping in dormitories, attending classes in university classrooms, and eating some meals in the cafeteria gives the program a true feeling of being a university experience. The participants spend concentrated periods of time together and often develop long-lasting professional networks. Faculty and program support staff reinforce the message that the participants are truly public policy and administration elites. Faculty members generally are from the Kennedy School or the Harvard Law School.

The bulk of program time is spent studying and discussing cases about major public policy and administration issues. The cases are written descriptions, approximately ten to thirty pages, describing an actual situation that occurred in the public policy arena. For example, one case describes the challenges faced by Alice Rivlin (now Clinton administration Director of the U.S. Office of Management and Budget) as the first director of the Congressional Budget Office (CBO). Participants are given the case in advance and asked to come to class prepared to discuss it. Their preparation is guided by study questions such as: "The case describes a number of the decisions Alice Rivlin must make regarding organizational design, staffing, and process. What do you recommend she decide on these points, given her goals and strategy for the C.B.O.? Be prepared to make recommendations and defend them."[17]

The discussions of the cases typically take about eighty minutes, during which the faculty person will facilitate a dialogue among the participants. The participants are, in essence, asked to put themselves in the place of the main figures in the cases and describe what they might have done similarly or differently. Again, this has the effect of treating the participants as true policy elites (like Rivlin and other figures in the cases) by asking them to assume hypothetical leadership positions at the very highest levels of government.

Another major component of the SMG program is the time spent in lectures and seminars with public administration and policy elites. For example, the class of 1990 heard from a number of speakers, including Robert Reich (Clinton administration Secretary of Labor), Peggy Noonan (former President Reagan's speechwriter), and former Massachusetts governor and presidential candidate Michael Dukakis. All of them shared "insider accounts" of their view of the public administration and policy process.

From the above description of SMG it should be evident that the program's effort to develop effective leadership capabilities among executives involved in federal policy and administration is grounded heavily in the second leadership emphasis area, developing a clear understanding of the operating context. The case studies and the lectures and seminars with prominent people all help participants better understand the nuances of the context surrounding public administration and policy in Washington. Participants are given a chance to read and hear insider accounts, share ideas with fellow executives and faculty, and to map out their own hypothetical leadership strategies. Finally, participants are asked to relate the program content back to their position in government to which they will return at the end of the three weeks.

Leadership Development Program (LPD)

The Leadership Development Program (LPD), sponsored by the Center for Creative Leadership, lasts five and one-half days and is open to executives from all organizations—business, government, and not-for-profit. Programs such as this are called "open enrollment" because their participant mix is not limited to one organization or even one sector, but represents a true cross-section of organizations. Because of this mix from different operating contexts, the emphasis of this program is not on the second leadership emphasis area. Further, this program embodies a belief that leadership is not organization-specific.

LPD is representative of a large number of executive development programs that focus on the first leadership emphasis area: self-awareness. And because the focus is on self-awareness, the lessons about leadership transcend organizational boundaries, allowing the same materials to be used regardless of the executive participant composition. By focusing on self-awareness, the program is adopting a point of view that says leadership is generic; that is, leading as an executive for a state government human services organization is similar to the leadership challenges faced by an executive at a major corporation. The key for LDP is to get participants to examine their own individual strengths, weaknesses, and leadership operating styles. This is done largely through participant self-examination and through information provided by others who work with that participant on a regular basis.

The program begins with a series of diagnostic instruments that give the participants feedback about themselves. Specifically, participants receive the results of the Myers Briggs Type Indicator, the Kirton Adaptor Inventory, and the Leadership Survey Instrument—all of which they complete before arriving at the program site. The results give them a profile of their personality preferences, their tendencies toward innovation (coming up with completely new approaches) or adaptation (modifying existing approaches to meet new challenges), and some insights about their leadership style (e.g., directive versus facilitative). Additionally, on the first day of the program, participants also complete some assignments and activities that give them further insights into other characteristics, such as their intelligence level.

Armed with this array of data about themselves, the majority of the program is then aimed at helping the participants understand the data and develop a personal development plan that will guide them in their quest to be a more complete executive. For example, an executive participant may learn that she is highly intelligent, prefers to work alone, and is a strong adapter. LDP faculty would work to help her see that her profile may not serve her well in cases requiring involvement of many other people and consideration of innovative solutions. She then may develop a personal plan that might attempt to broaden her approaches to leadership by prescribing her to work on teams addressing highly complex problems. Executives are encouraged to develop a broad range of leadership styles and approaches.

The Center for Creative Leadership's LDP is offered around the world to executives from all kinds of organizations. Participants are offered an opportunity to be introspective about some of the factors that contribute to making them unique executives. Then they are asked to consider their strengths and weaknesses in various generic leadership assignments, such as decision making. Finally, participants develop personal plans for expanding their strengths and preferred operating styles identified by the diagnostic instruments and program faculty.

Leadership for a Democratic Society (LDS)

Leadership For a Democratic Society (LDS) is the premier executive development program offered by the U.S. Office of Personnel Management for senior federal government executives. This four-week program has been offered for over twenty years and now is held at the Federal Executive Institute (FEI) located in Charlottesville, Virginia, near the home of Thomas Jefferson (Monticello) and the University of Virginia. The FEI is a self-contained campus with classrooms, leisure facilities, and sleeping and eating accommodations. The current LDS design includes program segments that touch on all of the leadership emphasis areas. Participants experience a variety of content topics—ranging from constitutional history to personal fitness—and process approaches—ranging from elective classes to large blocks of unstructured free time.

In many ways, the LDS is a hybrid of the SMG and LDP described above. As in the SMG program, the participants are from the federal public administration and policy arena and work to improve their understanding of the operating context; they do so in small group discussions and lectures by top government officials. As in the LPD, participants work on improving their self-awareness through the use of diagnostic instruments such as the Myers Briggs Type Indicator. Yet, overall the intent of the LDS is to provide a much broader leadership experience than either the SMG or the LDP.

The broad perspective of the LDS touches on all the leadership emphasis areas. In addition to building self-awareness and a better understanding of the operating context, the program also encourages participants to develop personal and organizational vision by having them develop an executive case about their organization. It also addresses the topic of change by offering a number of relevant elective courses such as "The Organizational Impacts of Information Technology." Finally, it presents multiple opportunities for skill/competency development on topics such as media relations, computer usage, and negotiations.[18]

The LDS program is also characterized by its explicit attention to the "personal side" of the public executive's life; those aspects normally considered "off the job." For example, LDS addresses subjects such as nutrition, physical fitness, and personal financial planning. The argument for doing so is that a person is a complete being who is only artificially separated into the "work life" and the "personal life." In reality, this perspective says, the personal life greatly affects the work life, and vice versa. Hence, the only appropriate way to improve overall executive performance is to address the complete life of the leader, not just the work life.

LDS serves as a key developmental experience for many federal managers who are in, or aspire to be in, the Senior Executive Service—the elite core of executives who are the top leaders in federal departments and agencies. In addition to building professional networks and learning from each other, participants in the LDS program are exposed to a very broad-based approach to executive leadership development.

Summary of Executive Development Programs

Structured executive development programs such as the three profiled above play an active part in trying to enhance the leadership capabilities of today's and tomorrow's public sector executives. Theories about leadership and how best to develop it lie at the heart of all three. Yet the programs differ in their focus on the various leadership areas of emphasis. Prospective participants and human resource development professionals should be aware of these differences as they work to increase the leadership capabilities of public sector executives.

OTHER FORMS OF DEVELOPMENT

Although much of this chapter has focused on one important aspect of executive development, executive development programs, other efforts aimed at enhancing the capabilities of executives are also important. Some of those efforts are described briefly in the following sections.

Career Planning

It is often said that events of today are often the results of yesterday's planning. So it is with the career of an executive. Many public sector executives attribute some of their success to gaining substantive knowledge and experience in critical areas (such as budgeting, procurement, human resource management) while in positions earlier in their careers. Others emphasize having diversifed their work experiences to include both line and staff assignments. Increasingly, career development and planning are becoming more formalized, and human resource professionals are being asked to play a significant role in career planning for employees of their organizations.

Rotational Assignments

Many organizations encourage employees to participate in short-term "rotational assignments" outside their normal work unit to help expand their knowledge and skills. For example, an employee working in a public works department of a municipality as an operations manager may go to work in the budget office for three months to help prepare the municipality annual budget. In doing so, he helps the budget office manage an intense work period while gaining personal knowledge and skills in budgeting that will serve him and the public works department well. Likewise, it may offer a developmental opportunity for someone to assume some of his operations responsibilities back in the public works department. Over the course of a career, carefully planned and executed rotational assignments can contribute greatly to building executive capabilities.

Within the federal government rotational assignments are used extensively as a development tool. The Presidential Management Intern (PMI) program, the premier professional entry program, encourages participating agencies to use rotational assignments as means of developing PMIs. Similarly, many agency-sponsored Senior Executive Service candidate development programs include rotational assignments. Often, participants will work in another agency or even in a not-for-profit or business organization in an effort to gain a particular knowledge or skill that will be valuable as public sector administrators. Finally, some professional associates sponsor rotational assignments for executive-branch employees. An example is the American Political Science Association's Legislative Fellowship program, which enables agency pre-executives to work in the legislative branch on Capitol Hill for one year to gain valuable perspective on the legislative branch and its interface with the executive branch.

Continuing Education

As was noted earlier, the entire field of executive development has been growing. Not an insignificant part consists of those professionals who go back to school to pursue degrees that will enhance their executive capabilities. "Executive programs," those designed to meet the schedule needs of practitioners, often offer all of their classes at night and on the weekends. Many practitioners are pursuing general administration programs such as the M.P.A., M.B.A., and D.P.A. At the same time, others are going back to school to specialize further (in areas such as information technology or social work) or to change professions. The organizations that employ these part-time students often become involved in these educational pursuits through their sponsorship of tuition reimbursement programs and through career development and planning initiatives. The human resource management professionals who work in this area can play a pivotal role in helping employees select a program of study that meets their career development needs as well as further the organization's interests in a well-developed workforce.

AVOIDING DERAILMENT

The above sections have described many of the efforts that are made toward assisting individuals in their pursuit of success in top-level executive positions. Yet, the reality is that many of those who seek such a goal status never achieve it. Some are selected for a position and fail while others receive their last promotion long before they reach the executive suite. McCall and Lombardo[19] and Lombardo and Eichinger[20] have studied this process, which they call derailment. They have identified many of the causes of it and have suggested approaches to help avoid it. Certainly, any executive development strategy should implicitly embrace an attempt to avoid derailment.

Interestingly, but not surprisingly, many of the major fatal flaws (reasons for derailment) identified are aspects of leadership addressed by many executive development programs. A few of the top fatal flaws are shown below to highlight the importance of the content frequently addressed in executive development initiatives:[21]

- Being insensitive to others; having an abrasive, intimidating, bullying style;
- Being cold, aloof, arrogant;
- Overmanaging; failing to delegate or build a team; or
- Being unable to think strategically.

Hence, whether framed in the positive perspective of helping executives succeed or in the more negative approach of avoiding derailment, the challenges of executive development are the same. Executive development is about preparing individual employees to successfully assume the challenges of managing and leading organizations from the top-level positions. Both individual employees and their organizations share responsibility for ensuring that executives are prepared (developed) to do so.

CONCLUSION

A critical HRD challenge is that of executive development. Central to being a successful public sector administrator is the willingness to be a life-long learner and to work continually at improving one's leadership capabilities. Leadership is described in a variety of ways and is at the core of many executive development programs. Programs vary in their focus on five leadership areas of emphasis: self-awareness, the operating context, vision for the organization, understanding and managing change, and skills and competencies.

Career planning, rotational assignments, and continuing education all can play significant roles in helping executives avoid derailment and achieve success in leading and managing our public organizations.

Exercise

8.1 Utilizing the same agency from exercises 7.1 and 7.2, design an executive development plan for senior management.

Notes

1. Terence J. Tipple, *Executive Development Programs: A Framework for Coherence* (Ph.D. diss., Virginia Tech, 1992), p. 9.
2. James F. Bolt, *Executive Development: A Strategy for Corporate Competitiveness* (New York: Harper & How, 1989).
3. Robert E. Kaplan, Wilfred H. Drath, and Joan R. Kofodinos, "High Hurdles: The Challenge of Executive Self Development," *The Academy of Management Executive* 1, no. 3 (1987): 195–205; Ronnie Lassem, *Development Management: Principles of Holistic Business* (Colchester: Basil Blackwell, 1990).
4. Eric Stephan, Gordon E. Mills, R. Wayne Pace, and Lenny Ralphs, "HRD in the Fortune 500: A Survey," *Training & Development Journal* 42 (January 1988): 26–32.
5. Miriam B. Clark and Frank H. Freeman, *Leadership Education 1990; A Source Book* (West Orange, N.J.: Leadership Library of America, Inc., 1990).
6. Luther Gulick and Lyndall Urwick, eds., *Papers on the Science of Administration* (New York: Institute of Public Administration, 1937).
7. Chester I. Barnard, *The Functions of the Executive*. (Cambridge, Mass.: Harvard University Press, 1938).
8. Phillip Selznick, *Leadership in Administration* (New York: Harper & Row, 1957).
9. Henry Mintzberg, *The Nature of Managerial Work* (New York: Harper & Row, 1973); John P. Kotter, *The General Managers* (New York: Free Press, 1982).
10. Kotter, *The General Managers.*
11. Barnard, *The Functions of the Executive,* pp. 215–34.
12. Stephen R. Covey, *Principle Centered Leadership* (New York: Simon & Schuster, 1990); Craig R. Hickman and Michael A. Silva, *Creating Excellence: Managing Corporate Culture, Strategy and Change in the New Age* (New York: Penguin Books, 1984); Noel M. Tichy and Mary A. Devanna, *The Transformational Leader* (New York: Wiley Press, 1986).
13. Warren G. Bennis, Kenneth D. Benne, and Robert Chin, *The Planning of Change,* 4th ed. (New York: Holt, Rinehart & Winston, 1985), p. 49.
14. Richard C. Snyder, "To Improve Innovation, Manage Corporate Culture," in *The Planning of Change,* pp. 164–76.
15. Judith M. Bardwick, *Danger in the Comfort Zone* (New York: American Management Association, 1991).

16. Tipple, *Executive Development Programs.*
17. Ibid., p. 107.
18. Ibid.
19. Morgan W. McCall and Michael M. Lombardo, "Off the Track: Why and How Successful Executives Get Derailed," *Technical Report #21* (Greensboro, N.C.: Center for Creative Leadership, 1993).
20. Michael M. Lombardo and Robert W. Eichinger, "Preventing Derailment: What to Do Before It's Too Late," *Application Report* (Greensboro, N.C.: Center for Creative Leadership, 1989).
21. McCall and Lombardo, "Off the Track," p. 6.

MODULE IV The Legal Dimension

9

The Constitutional Dimensions of Employment Law

Public personnel administration has in recent decades been increasingly faced with litigational issues involving rights of public employees. The growing salience of constitutional issues in public employment can been seen in a statistical review of the U.S. Supreme Court's docket. In 1970, the Supreme Court received only 33 petitions involving an issue of public employment. In 1994, the number of petitions for certiorari involving public employment issues and employee rights totaled 180, a six-fold increase.

It is evident that employee rights have become a paramount concern for personnel administrators. Administrators must be sensitive to issues of employment discrimination, employee harassment, invasions of employee privacy, restrictions or infringements on fundamental rights, health and safety concerns, and fair dealing in any matter involving employment status, compensation, terms, and conditions of employment. If adverse actions are taken, the employer must provide adequate due process.

Several factors have contributed to increasing friction between public employers and their employees resulting in litigation and a commensurate development of law on public employment issues. Beginning in the 1950s and accelerating in the 1970s, the courts extended a due process umbrella over many of the decisional processes embracing personnel matters. Concurrently, Congress addressed a number of personnel issues with legislative enactments. Beginning with the Equal Pay Act of 1963 and the Civil Rights

Act of 1964 (Title VII) and proceeding to the Civil Rights Act of 1991, the Americans with Disabilities Act of 1990, and the Freedom of Religion Act of 1993, public employees came under a widening umbrella of protection. State statutes also addressed perceived loopholes in the federal statutes.

The 1990s confront any public personnel administrator with a complex maze of federal and state laws and mandates and a myriad of regulations coming out of federal and state agencies and municipalities. Internal agency rules and policy manuals expand a contractual system of rights governing public employer/employee relations. Add to this a persistent rain of new court decisions at all levels and personnel administrators often feel they have need of a law degree or an in-house counsel. The rising number of public employment legal claims has also been a reflection of social and cultural trends. An increasingly litigious society stimulates public employment litigation as well. Empowerment of different groups that have experienced some measure of employment deprivation or discrimination has led to suits for redress. Courts have also removed many of the threshold barriers to filing such suits, broadened court jurisdiction, eased standing requirements, allowed class action suits, and lowered threshold standards for injury.

Among employees there has also developed a heightened perception of unfair treatment in the workplace. Many grievances demonstrate linkage with discrimination or harassment issues that may operate overtly or covertly in the employment environment. Tensions and disagreements between administrators and employees more frequently easily escalate into formal grievances. The inevitability of grievances has directed public agencies and offices to formally address the problem through the development of juridical frameworks that include personnel policy manuals, institutionalized grievance procedures, appeals procedures, arbitration panels, and sensitivity training.

These trends reflect employees' perceived high stakes in their jobs. Jobs are very important in defining an employee's sense of self-worth and personal security. The loss of a position or a disruption in working conditions creates stress equal in intensity to that of a divorce or death in the family. Employees feel that they must challenge any threats to job status or privileges and conditions of employment.[1]

The growing body of employment law provides a means to protect job interests and to provide remedies where employees perceive themselves ill-treated. These trends operate in a dual manner. On one hand, they reflect a heightening of tensions between employer and employee. On the other hand, they have led to juridical channeling of disagreements into settings where fair procedures and fairness to all parties are stressed. However uncomfortable these matters are for those concerned, at least the mechanisms exist for civil resolution of employee grievances and for the improvement of employer/employee relations. An increasingly legalized work environment is certainly preferable to the phenomenon of employees expressing their frustrations in directed or random acts of violence, another unfortunate trend.[2] The relationships between public employer and employee have also become more strained as public bureaucracies themselves have come under stress. Budget cuts, an uncertain economy, and downsizing and restructuring of public institutions increase the risk of career disruption for public employees at all levels. If such institutional changes are accomplished under authoritarian leadership, workers may particularly feel victimized and express that victimization in disabling depression, alcohol or drug abuse, or confrontation with the employer.[3] Such trends also engender anger and prejudice that are directed against new groups of individuals recruited into public agencies. This backlash mitigates against efforts to diversify the public workforce and open opportunities to candidates of all backgrounds; it also leads to more grievances and litigation.[4] In the midst of these changes the challenge for public administrators is to maintain and maximize the expectations of fairness for all in the public workplace.

PROCEDURAL DUE PROCESS

Only a few decades ago, public employees had few rights to employment. Employment was regarded as a privilege that the public employer could condition as that employer saw fit. The very right to hold a position was rejected by the courts. Justice Oliver Wendell Holmes in *McAuliffe v Mayor of Bedford*[5] in 1882 upheld the termination of a policeman for engaging in First Amendment activity.

> There is nothing in the Constitution . . . to prevent the city from attaching obedience to this rule as a condition to the office of policeman and making it a part of the good conduct required. The petitioner may have a constitutional right to talk politics but he has no constitutional right to be a policeman. There are few employments for hire in which the servant does not agree to suspend his constitutional rights of free speech, as well as idleness by the implied terms of his contract. The servant cannot complain as he takes the employment on the terms offered him.

In 1947 the Supreme Court introduced the doctrine of unconstitutional conditions in *United Public Workers v Mitchell*.[6] This doctrine indicated that government could not bar employment to one or require an employee to relinquish employment for engaging in a constitutionally protected activity. But the issue remained as to whether a public employee was to be given due process protections, notice, and fair hearing where government did act to deprive a person of employment. At first, in *Bailey v Richardson* (1951)[7] a federal district court rejected the claims of a government employee that he was entitled to a hearing of a quasi-judicial type upon dismissal on grounds of alleged "disloyal connections" made by anonymous accusers. The court noted that

> never in history had a government administrative employee been entitled to a hearing of the quasi-judicial type upon his dismissal from government service.

That record of a hundred and sixty years of government administration is the sort of history that speaks with great force . . . to hold office at the will of a superior and to be removable therefore only by constitutional due process of law are opposite and inherently conflicting ideas. Due process is not applicable unless one is deprived of something to which he has a right.[8]

That was the rub. Public employment was not a right, and a job contained neither a property interest nor liberty interest to invoke the due process clause. However, on the same day that the Supreme Court affirmed *Bailey* it also decided *Joint Anti-Fascist Refugee Committee v McGrath* (1951)[9] in which Justice Jackson in a concurrence noted that individuals may have the right to be heard before being condemned to suffer grievous loss of any kind even though it may not involve the stigma and hardship of a criminal conviction.

The Supreme Court moved to recognize in *Greene v McElroy* in 1959[10] that a public employee might have a right to a hearing when the adverse action involved a security clearance that was an essential element in continuing employment. Other courts also recognized that liberty interests could not be adversely affected without adequate hearing. An adverse decision affecting reputation could be taken only after procedures were followed that would determine if legitimate grounds existed to justify a dismissal.[11]

It was becoming clear that the concept that public employment as a privilege that could be withdrawn at will was under challenge. A retreat from this doctrine was sounded by Professor William Van Alstyne when he called for the extension of due process to public employment decisions.[12] Van Alstyne discounted the premise that government could deny employment to or withdraw it from an individual simply because it was publicly funded. He found it difficult to legitimate government prerogatives of exercising arbitrary power or demonstrating unfairness in its conduct in any public undertaking.[13] Van Alstyne also felt that a constitutional right to procedural due process should operate over the full range of adverse actions that might be directed against employees.

> The character of the hearing to which a person may be constitutionally entitled may depend on the importance of what he stands to lose, of course but his constitutional right to procedural due process entitles him to a quality of hearing at least minimally proportioned to the gravity of what he otherwise stands to lose through administrative fiat.[14]

In a pair of cases decided in 1972, *Board of Regents v Roth*[15] and *Perry v Sinderman*,[16] the Supreme Court dealt with two college professors who were denied re-employment. One claimed that he had been terminated without the hearings that due process demands; the other claimed that, in addition, he had been let go for exercise of First Amendment rights. The decision in each case turned on whether each professor had a property interest imbedded in his employment status. In *Roth*, the Court noted that the professor had only a temporary contract that contained no expectations for renewal. The fact that he was not given a hearing was irrelevant. In *Sinderman,* the Court found that Sinderman was summarily dismissed in a system where policies and practices gave employees an expectation of continued employment with four years of service. A property interest was recognized that triggered the due process clause to at least obligate college officials to grant a hearing that would review the claim that the college had refused to renew the teaching contract on an impermissible basis (the exercise of free speech rights).

When the courts moved to a recognition of public employment, property interests, and associated liberty interests, they also focused on the precise nature of "those proceedings that are fairly due one" when one is subject to an adverse employment decision. In 1975 the Supreme Court adopted the concept of proportional due process that had been suggested by Van Alstyne. In *Goss v Lopez*[17] the Court dealt with the issue of what proceedings should be accorded a public school student who was suspended for ten days for alleged misconduct. The Court found that the misconduct charge triggered the due process clause since liberties involving reputation and good name were at stake. As to what process was due, the Court noted that even with the minor sanctions directed against the student, notice and some kind of hearing were indicated. The decision has impact on employment law where employees may be subject to a wide range of sanctions ranging from simple reprimands to termination. Limited due process can thus attach to any disciplinary or demoting action.

Finally, in *Cleveland Board of Education v Loudermill* (1985)[18] the Supreme Court outlined a laundry list of procedures for persons facing employment termination. Utilizing a balancing approach between the employee's interests in defending his continued employment and the interests of a public employer in maintaining institutional functions and in avoiding administrative burdens and intolerable delays, the Court indicated that pre-termination protections were essential.[19] These would include oral or written notice, some form of pre-termination hearing, opportunity for the employee to present his side of the case, and explanation of adverse evidence. A full post-termination hearing at a reasonable time would round out the requirements. These pre-termination hearings, though necessary, need not be formal or elaborate. Procedures could vary depending on the nature of the interests involved and in light of available post-termination procedures.[20] There is still a legal uncertainty as to what procedural elements must be provided or what issues resolved prior to termination and what elements can be carried over to a post-termination hearing. Employees have laid claim to an immediate hearing when stigmatizing information was placed in their personnel files and made a point in an internal affairs report. The Eleventh Circuit, in *Buxton v City of Plant City, Florida* (1989),[21] indicated in cases where liberty interests arising from reputational damages are implicated, a name-clearing hearing need not take place prior to an employee's termination or prior to that information being published or becoming part of a public record.

CONSTITUTIONAL CONDITIONS: FREE SPEECH IN THE WORKPLACE

One of the more common conflicts involving a constitutional protection concerns free speech claims. Free speech claims come up hard against administrative interests. The ventilation by public employees before the public or to the media of grievances, policy disputes, administrative failings, or personality clashes within a public agency can negatively affect the functioning of an agency. In a 1968 case, *Pickering v Board of Education*,[22] the Supreme Court identified the interests that a public agency or office might advance to justify an adverse decision against an employee who had made public intra-agency conflicts. These included:

1. the effect of the speech on conduct and discipline of employees by superiors;

2. the effect on harmony among the employee's coworkers;

3. the breach of relationships, which require personnel loyalty and confidence;

4. the effect of speech on job performance;

5. disruptive impact on the functions of the agency. Disruption can be broadly interpreted to extend to effects beyond the immediate workplace such as an undermining of public confidence in the agency.

The Court in *Pickering* found that a teacher's criticism of a school board and its policies through letters written to the editor of a local newspaper was protected from retaliation. The Court noted that similar cases would require a balancing between the interest of the employee as a citizen in contributing to debate of a matter of public concern and the interests of the public agency as an employer in performing its publicly legitimated functions and ensuring that those functions are not disrupted.

The *Pickering* balancing test has formed the cornerstone of doctrine on free speech issues involving public employees.[23] The problem is that public concern may wear many faces. Public concern is easily implicated in cases where actual wrongdoing or breach of the public trust on the part of public officials is publicized as a consequence of employee speech. The rights of employees on such overriding matters of public concern are reinforced through at least twenty-eight different federal statutes whose provisions protect whistle-blowing employees.[24] The difficult cases are those that do not take on significance outside the workplace or that deal primarily with a personal grievance of an employee who widens the circumference of the audience and who elevates the personal conflict to a generalized policy issue (such as discrimination). The effect of this is to turn a personnel matter into a mixed motive case, that is, a case in which an adverse decision against an employee involves both justifiable grounds and impermissible grounds. A series of cases showed the application of the *Pickering* test to mixed motive cases. In *Mount Healthy City Board of Education v Doyle* (1977),[25] the courts dealt with a situation in which a schoolteacher had, within the scope of his duties, engaged in a series of unrestrained and inappropriate behaviors. The board moved to terminate his employment, but Doyle claimed that he had been fired for exercising his right to freedom of expression. The Supreme Court noted that the initial burden lay on the employee to demonstrate that his questionable conduct was constitutionally protected and that it was a substantial or motivating factor in his dismissal. The Supreme Court found that Doyle met this burden, but the school board was able by a preponderance of the evidence to show that it would have reached the same decision as to his reemployment discounting the protected conduct. In *Givhan v Western Consolidated School District* (1979),[26] the Supreme Court affirmed the "but for the protected conduct" rule noting that, while the primary reason for firing Givhan was her criticism of her employer, there was still a sufficient cause to justify not rehiring her on other grounds.

A true borderline case, *Connick v Myers* (1983),[27] represented an increasingly common issue, that of aggressive subordinates who seek to become a catalyst for reform in their agencies. Following disputes with her superiors and a plan by them to transfer her, Shiela Myers circulated a questionnaire among her coworkers soliciting their views on transfer policies, grievance procedures, and confidence in their superiors. In applying the balancing test articulated in *Pickering,* the Supreme Court established a threshold inquiry to determine to what extent the employee's expressive activity was a matter of public concern. Examining the questionnaire item by item, the Court found only one item focusing on pressure to work for political campaigns a matter of public concern. The Court said that "The First Amendment does not require a public office to be run as a roundtable for employee complaints over internal office affairs,"[28] and placed administrative gadflies on notice that causes devoted to purely internal agency matters can be hazardous to continued employment.

However, the division between purely internal matters and matters of public concern cannot be easily drawn. In *Jurgensen v Fairfax County Virginia* (1984),[29] a public employee of the Fairfax County Police Department was demoted for releasing an internal report of the review of an Emergency Operations Center to a reporter of the *Washington Post*. The newspaper ran a story on some of the administrative problems of the office. The story was inoffensive because it revealed no corruption, misconduct, or mismanagement. The release of the story appeared to cause no disruption in the office. But Jurgensen's superiors moved to demote him for going out of channels. Jurgensen then contested his demotion, claiming that the action was taken in retaliation for his free speech activities. The Fourth Circuit concluded that the agency was justified in demoting an employee for clear violation of department regulations. As to retaliation for free speech activity, the court noted that Jurgensen had voiced his complaints to coworkers, superiors, and before meetings of the Civil Service Commission without experiencing any censorship or disciplinary action. Jurgensen had crossed a threshold that took him into the area of civil disobedience. The court also took into account the nature of the employee's position, recognizing that the expectations of restraint of speech may vary with the job. In this case the weight to be given a particular position was to be arrayed on a spectrum from university professors at one end (least restraint) to policemen (most restraint).[30]

Following *Connick,* the Supreme Court decided *Rankin v McPhereson* (1987),[31] which arose out of a discharge of a clerical worker in a law enforcement office who, upon hearing that President Reagan had been shot by an assassin, said, "If they go for him again, I hope they get him." Rankin's employer felt that such comments revealed a disrespect for law incompatible with her service in a law enforcement agency. The Supreme Court saw the statements as addressing a matter of public concern and applying the *Pickering* balancing test saw little occasion for such remarks to disrupt the functions of the agency. The Supreme Court also broadened the definition of speech of public concern to embrace matters of public interest and controversial and provocative speech.[32]

In June 1994, the Supreme Court decided *Waters v Churchill,*[33] addressing the issue of workplace speech that draws sanctions because it is disruptive and insubordinate. A plurality of the court upheld the prerogative of a supervisor in a hospital facility who fired an employee on the basis of third-party reports that the employee was "knocking the department" and criticizing her superior before trainees. The employee argued that her speech involved matters of public concern and were protected under the *Connick* test. The Supreme Court focused on the procedural foundations of the decision. While the supervisor may not have appreciated the fact that statements made by the employee were constitutionally protected, the supervisor did conduct a reasonable investigation and could reasonably conclude from that investigation that the statements were disruptive and not an expression of concern over policy. The plurality also found that a person's disruptive statements are not immunized because they are surrounded by protective speech. In dicta, Justice O'Connor also appeared to carve out an exemption of First Amendment protection for certain speech in the public workplace.

> We have always assumed that . . . government as an employer has far broader powers than does government as sovereign. The assumption is simply borne out by considering the practical realities of government employment and the many situations in which . . . most observers would agree that government must be able to restrict its employees' speech.[34]

Certain internal matters within agencies demand public exposure. These include issues of fiscal mismanagement, nepotism, discrimination, harassment, improprieties with clients, misuse of staff, and failures of agencies to address mandated responsibilities. Whistle-blowing speech finds protection only insofar as it involves publicity. Investigatory activities by themselves on the part of employees seeking to expose irregularities in their agency are insufficient to gain free speech protection. This was indicated in the case *Maciarello v Sumner* (1992),[35] a case involving the demotions of two police officers who had suspected that a superior officer had tampered with evidence in a case. Not trusting their superiors, they commenced their independent investigations and even went with their suspicions to a local judge (who informed them that they should talk to the city attorney). Their investigatory activities surfaced, and the chief decided to demote them for failing to report their suspicions or going through proper channels. The officers then filed a suit claiming that they had been demoted for pursuing and voicing matters of public concern. However, the court of appeals easily concluded that the investigatory activities were not speech. "Though they claim that they intended to speak out eventually, their intention expresses nothing. A hen may intend to lay an egg someday, but the omelet must await it."[36]

Protection of the free speech of whistle-blowers is more firmly established for federal workers than for state and local employees, who rely upon the judicial standards discussed to this point. In 1989 Congress amended the Civil Service Reform Act (CSRA) to expand protections for federal employees who reveal illegal or improper conduct.[37] The law now protects an employee from retaliatory personnel actions where an employee has a good faith, reasonable belief that an illegal act, gross mismanagement, waste of federal funds, abuse of authority, or tolerance of danger to public health or safety has occurred in the agency. The protections of the act are triggered only when the employee is discharged or sanctioned. A federal employee can prevail by demonstrating that the disclosure was a contributing (motivating) factor in the adverse action. The employer can escape corrective action only if it can prove by "clear and convincing evidence" that the adverse action would have been taken independent of any disclosure. The Special Counsel of the Merit System Protection Board has the responsibility for enforcement of the CSRA and conduct of investigations on complaint. The Special Counsel has the authority to prosecute retaliation claims against agencies within specified timeframes.[38]

The free speech rights of employees may also embrace speech and associational behavior that is not carried on in the workplace. This activity is usually governed by the disruption test. An example would be an off-duty police officer who participates in an antiabortion rally, disturbing coworkers whose duties might include keeping peace at such demonstrations. Employees can also press the outer limits of associational rights by participating in movements whose activities or positions might be irritating. A nexus test would likely be applied by the courts, as in the case of *Curle v Ward* (1979),[39] where a New York Court of Appeals directed reinstatement of a correctional officer who possessed a membership in the Ku Klux Klan. If the membership was discreet and there was no detrimental effect on the performance of duties, the expressive activity is to be tolerated.

Symbolic expression may also invade employment situations. This may arise when public employees exhibit messages on their clothes and person. Here the *Pickering* and *Connick* balancing tests can also be applied. Superiors in the Immigration and Naturalization Service (INS) ordered their uniformed employees to cease and desist from wearing small union insignia and penholders with union insignia and mottos. The employees then filed an unfair labor practices charge against the INS. The Federal Labor Relations Authority found the displays small and unobtrusive. In *I.N.S. v F.L.R.A. and A.F.G.E., A.F.L.-C.I.O.* (1988),[40] a federal court of appeals however, found that a public interest was at stake, and the Civil Service Reform Act of 1978 affirmed the rights of public managers to "run their shop" in a manner consistent with an effective and efficient administration. The existence of the management rights provision in 5 U.S.C. sec. 7106 precluded the application of balancing tests such as provided in *Connick*. Whether the deference shown to disciplinary regulations could extend beyond agencies of a nonparamilitary or law enforcement function is unresolved. Could an agency bar the wearing of a pin of the National Rifle Association, a religious symbol, or even a Phi Beta Kappa Key? A recent private sector decision would indicate that a display that was disruptive could be prohibited.[41]

The exercise of free speech rights in the workplace can also implicate libel law.[42] Libel actions take place outside the universe of normal personnel decisions. Comments directed to superiors or to coworkers that are libelous in character may in fact lead to adverse personnel actions where those comments disrupt the functions and harmony of a workplace. An employee's statements will not be protected if they are slanderous or knowingly or recklessly false.[43] Libel actions initiated by superiors are exceedingly difficult to pursue under the *Sullivan* rules,[44] which allow an official or person in a position of public responsibility to recover for injuries of defamation only when it can be demonstrated that the libel was committed with actual malice, malice being defined in terms of a reckless disregard of the truth or intentional assertion of provably false statements of factual connotation.[45]

Defamation suits still survive where employees claim injury to their reputations through statements spread or made public by their agency superiors. But courts have been drawn to extend protection against suit because the statements were categorized as "opinion" or because the statements were regarded as so outrageous as to strain credulity. A case illustrating the difficulty of prevailing in a defamation suit involving employees and their superiors is *Bross v Smith*, a 1992 Ohio case.[46] Two police officers sued their assistant chief and chief of police for defamation and intentional infliction of emotional distress. The particular police department was experiencing a bitter feud dividing the department into two hostile factions. Bross and others belonging to one faction were the object of letters and postings on bulletin boards that accused them of being rats, "dopers," and "pill heads," of engaging in sexual misconduct (swapping mates), of stealing ammunition, and falsely accusing the chief. The individuals victimized by these statements brought suit against their superiors when they came on evidence that the superiors had drafted a missive containing vulgarity and use of terms used in the rat letters. The Ohio Court, relying upon Supreme Court decisions on libel, in particular *Hustler Magazine v Falwell* (1988)[47] and *Milkovich v Lorain Journal Co.* (1990),[48] held that the police officers could not maintain actions against heads of their section based on defamation or on emotional distress. The court did not dispute the jury's conclusions that the letters were outrageous and the product of sick, paranoid minds. The court found the general tenor of the communications so exaggerated and subjective in tone that reasonable persons could only conclude that the author was stating opinion. The decision raises questions because many of the assertions in the rat letters are arguably provable as true or false.

RELIGIOUS FREE EXERCISE AND EMPLOYMENT

Of the substantive rights protected under the First Amendment, none creates more sensitive issues than that of religious free exercise. Generally, religion cases in employment involve one of the following four issues:

1. a conflict between the demands of the workplace and an employee's religious beliefs and behavioral imperatives;
2. discrimination against an employee based on a public employer's failure to recruit, hire, promote, or provide equal terms of employment because of that employee's religious identity or profession;
3. creation, maintenance, or tolerance of a workplace environment that is perceived to reflect hostility toward an employee because of that employee's religion;
4. violation of the Establishment Clause by someone bringing religious activity or symbols into the workplace.

The first issue generally involves the refusal or reticence of an employee to work on Sabbath or holy days. Beginning with *Sherbert v Verner* (1963),[49] the Supreme Court noted that employees should not be put into the predicament of choosing between employment and conformity with their religious beliefs. Congress then passed the Civil Rights Act of 1964 that explicitly prohibited discrimination in employment on religious grounds in regard to the terms, conditions, or privileges of employment. It was not long before the question arose as to whether it was a discriminatory action to refuse to hire an employee or to discharge the employee upon refusal to work during normal work days because of religious reasons.[50] The Equal Employment Opportunity Commission (EEOC) set out a regulatory requirement that placed an obligation on the employer to make reasonable accommodation to the religious needs of an employee when such accommodation could be made without undue hardship.[51]

The courts affirmed the regulation,[52] and Congress responded by amending the religious provision of Title VII of the Civil Rights Act in 1972 to provide for reasonable accommodation to all aspects of religious observance, practice, or belief unless the employer demonstrates an inability to do so without undue hardship on the conduct of the employer's business.[53] The accommodation requirement has given rise to a number of recurrent issues:

1. What constitutes a prima facie case of discrimination?
2. What is a reasonable accommodation?
3. What constitutes an undue hardship?
4. What constitutes improper retaliation for religious actions?

To establish the fact that employees have experienced religious discrimination, the employees must show:

1. that they have a bona fide belief that compliance with a work requirement is contrary to their religious beliefs;
2. that they have informed the employer about the conflict;
3. that they have been disciplined or discharged for refusing to comply with the employer's work requirement.[54]

In effect the employee must lay the foundation for accommodation to take place. Public employers can protect themselves against prima facie claims by establishing policies that allow for the resolution of such conflicts in advance through work release taken through annual or personal leave, or through arrangements that the worker can make with coworkers.

The key to resolving these conflicts are reasonable accommodations. But what constitutes a reasonable accommodation? This also requires a reasonable demand on the part of the employee (such as need to observe a holy day, a period of mourning, or a devotional imperative).[55] The courts have indicated that the accommodation may constitute what may be minimally necessary for an employee to serve his or her religious conscience as long as the employment status of the employee does not change. This was indicated in *Ansonia Board of Education v Philbrook* (1986).[56] The *Ansonia* decision involved Philbrook, a teacher working under a collective bargaining agreement that allowed three paid days off for religious observances and use of three accumulated days' leave for personal reasons. Philbrook, a fundamentalist Christian, sought leave for at least six days of religious observances. He even offered to pay for a substitute to cover his duties during the days he was absent. The Second Circuit found that Philbrook had proposed a reasonable accommodation that did not cause any undue hardship for the district.[57] However, the

Supreme Court, with Chief Justice Rehnquist speaking for the majority, rejected this ruling, holding that the district was not under an obligation to accept an employee's proposal for accommodation unless it caused undue hardship. That would provide an incentive for an employee to hold out for the most beneficial accommodation to him. Rehnquist found that the district's provision of unpaid leave was a reasonable accommodation. It allowed the individual to fully observe his religious holy days and give up compensation only for the days he did not work. That would be a temporary (and voluntary) loss of income for the period not at work, with no effect on employment status. *Ansonia* weighed the scales in favor of employers on developing accommodations. The decision also overruled EEOC guidelines[58] mandating an employer to choose the alternatives that least disadvantaged the employee in regard to employment opportunities.[59]

The legislative provisions on accommodation also relieve the employer of an obligation to accommodate if that would create an undue hardship for the employer. What constitutes an undue hardship? That was addressed by the Supreme Court, even prior to Ansonia, in *Trans-World Airlines v Hardison*[60] in 1977. Hardison, a member of the Worldwide Church of God, observed the Sabbath by refraining from work from sunset Friday to sunset Saturday. When Hardison informed his employer of the conflict between his work schedule and religious scruples, the employer made various arrangements that satisfied Hardison, but a transfer again placed Hardison in conflict. He did not have the seniority to obtain shift preferences and coworkers did not cooperate in voluntary accommodation. The Supreme Court ruled that TWA was not obligated to meet Hardison's needs by shifting people or paying employees overtime. Neither was the company to be pressed to deviate from collective bargaining agreements containing seniority rules. In an important dicta the Court noted that an accommodation causes an employer undue hardship whenever the accommodation results in more than a *de minimis* cost to the employer.[61] The upshot of the *Hardison* and *Ansonia* decisions is that while employers do have an obligation to offer an accommodation, the reasonableness of that accommodation can be defined in terms of the realities of the workplace. If the accommodation causes inconveniences, delays, disruption of personnel practices, diminution of production or services, or conflict with contracts and bargaining agreements, it also causes an undue burden.[62]

Issues of retaliatory action against an employee on religious grounds are handled as discrimination cases under Section 704, Title VII of the Civil Rights Act. Here the complaining party must establish a prima facie case of discrimination on a factual demonstration that:

1. his or her job performance was satisfactory;
2. direct or indirect evidence supports a reasonable inference that discharge was predicated on religious grounds;
3. he or she was thereafter replaced by a person outside the protected group.[63]

Retaliation cases predictably are heavily fact-centered. An example is the case *Lawrence v Mars Inc.* (1992),[64] a case involving a Jewish employee who took a day off to observe the holy day of Rosh Hashanah under a company policy that permitted employees to take off days for religious observance but counted them against their vacation days or as floating holidays. Lawrence took the days off during the company's executive conference period, an event carrying an expectation of mandatory attendance. An executive colleague told Lawrence, "There is no excuse for missing McClean Weeks. The only excuse is if you're dead and that is not a good excuse." Two weeks later during a business trip to Europe, Lawrence got into a verbal altercation with another executive. On his return he was informed that his employment was terminated. Lawrence later filed charges of religious discrimination with a county human rights commission and with the EEOC (both of which rejected his claims). Ultimately Lawrence filed an appeal with the Fourth Circuit Court of Appeals. The court assessed the facts of the case and concluded that Lawrence's performance at the time of the discharge was not satisfactory. As to the remarks indicating displeasure with his giving priority to his religious intentions over the demands of his job, the court noted that such remarks came from persons having no supervisory authority over him. The court interpreted the adverse employment decision as properly motivated.

Free exercise issues also attach to the practice of wearing of religious garb by employees performing public duties, especially schoolteachers.[65] Relying on the Establishment Clause, courts have affirmed the power of the state to prohibit religious garb, noting that allowing such garb would be incompatible with the commitment of the state toward maintaining an atmosphere of neutrality in religion. To allow public employees to wear such garb might also be perceived as a state endorsement of religion or a message of symbolic union between church and state. This position was reaffirmed in *Cooper v Eugene School District* (1986).[66] The Oregon Supreme Court affirmed the revocation of a tenured teacher's certification for violating a state anti-religious garb statute. The teacher had attempted to wear traditional Sikh garments in the classroom. A federal case, *Goldman v Weinberger* (1986),[67] saw the Supreme Court affirm an Air Force regulation that prohibited a Jewish Air Force chaplain from wearing a religious skull cap in conjunction with his uniform. Goldman had argued that his practice of wearing religious headgear was an expression of a silent devotion that had no impact upon his duties. In this case the Court found that free exercise interests were overridden by interests of the military in promoting discipline and uniformity in the armed forces. Congress then passed curative legislation that now permits armed forces personnel to wear items of religious apparel if they are "neat and conservative" and do not interfere with the performance of a member's military duties.[68] Setting aside the possible problems of vagueness of defining what is conservative, the congressional action can be interpreted as the expression of a developing norm that allows the toleration of religious identification under something akin to an undue burden test. Clearly if the display has a *de minimis* impact, the employer should have no interest in restricting such displays.

Employees may also raise issues of religious offense or harassment. Certain elements of the workplace or a work routine may be offensive to certain employees' religious sensitivities. Such claims are to be assessed in terms of the impact of an employee's own beliefs. Certainly, a public employee who observed religious dietary taboos could not be forced to handle foodstuffs that violated those precepts. On the other hand certain incidents of offense may reflect a personal issue of conscience for the employee.[69] A Jewish federal clerical employee, Fagele benMiriam, protested the use of the abbreviation A.D. on a government form because it forced her to subscribe to a Christian dating system, thus violating her free exercise rights.[70] The court utilized the three-prong test of impact on religious exercise enunciated in *E.E.O.C. v Pacific Press Publishing Assn.* (1982).[71] Courts must weigh three factors:

1. the magnitude of the exercise of the religious belief;
2. the existence of a compelling state interest justifying the burden on exercise of religious belief;
3. the extent to which an exemption would impede valid state objectives.

The court found that the impact on benMiriam's beliefs was minimal or nonexistent. The case illustrates the difficulties which spring from personally defined interpretations of "free exercise" as they embrace beliefs, practices, and personal identity, dignity, and hostility issues. The difficulties are increased with efforts to achieve neutrality and remove religion from the workplace, raising the issue that the employer is hostile to religion.[72]

Special accommodations have been legislated to accept certain claims of free exercise. For instance, Congress exempted employees of certain religions that conscientiously objected to the payment of union dues from having to join or contribute to unions. This accommodation required a reciprocal accommodation on the part of the employee to contribute sums equivalent to the dues to religious charities.[73]

Religious harassment suits have been rare. These can be brought as Title VII discrimination cases or as 1983 suits. A federal district court in *Weiss v U.S.* (1984)[74] applied the standards for racial or sexual harassment to religious harassment. The court outlined two varieties of harassment, a "condition of work" harassment, where an employee may be repeatedly subjected to demeaning and offensive religious slurs by coworkers or supervisors, and "quid pro quo" harassment, where a supervisor demands that an employee alter or renounce some religious belief or practice in exchange for job benefits. Weiss, who was Jewish, was an employee of the Defense Logistics Agency. He was subjected to repeated and vulgar religious slurs. When he complained to his superiors, they took a course of retaliatory actions, giving him difficult and unreasonable work assignments, rating his work performance substantially lower than they had prior to the complaints, and frequently berating and demeaning his performance in front of others. He was then rated as having an unsatisfactory work performance and terminated. His employers saw the case as a mixed motive one in which Weiss would have been let go in any case for poor performance and difficulty in dealing with his superiors. The court ruled that the employer could not point to lowered performance as a legitimate basis for removal when the employer through discriminatory and retaliatory actions caused the subpar performance.

A recent 1994 case raised the issue of sanctioning a county employee for bringing religious activity into the workplace. In *Brown v Polk County, Iowa*,[75] a county employee was terminated from his position after refusing to stop using county resources to support religious activity. He had held before-hours prayer meetings and had used his office for religious counseling. He was also ordered to remove religious objects, including a Bible, from his office. The court balanced the free exercise rights of the employee against the state's duties to avoid Establishment Clause violations and to protect the religious beliefs of other employees. The court ruled against the employee, noting that the employer had a strong interest in preventing disruption in public functions. Judge Arnold in dissent would have, however, narrowly restricted a prohibition to the aim of preventing religious harassment directed against fellow employees.

From 1989 to 1993 the EEOC received 123 complaints of religious harassment. The EEOC unveiled proposed guidelines in October 1993 that would have protected workers from religious offense and harassment. However, the proposals unleashed a firestorm of protest in Congress and drew fire from religious groups in the notice and comment period. Religious groups interpreted the new guidelines as permitting the sanctioning of employees for expressing their beliefs in the workplace, although the EEOC said they were aimed at protecting employees who might be harassed because of their religious beliefs.[76] Congress then directed the EEOC to withdraw the regulations and to draft new guidelines to make it clear that display of symbols or expression of religious belief in the workplace is consistent with the First Amendment and the Religious Freedom Restoration Act of 1993.[77]

Free exercise activity has in rare instances constituted an impediment to employment where the religious activity is illegal. An example is the case of *Potter v Murray City* (1985)[78] that dealt with the issue of a police officer terminated for his practice of plural marriage. He contended as a member of a polygamous sect that his termination violated his rights of free exercise. The courts dismissed his claim, holding that the decision in *Reynolds v U.S.* (1878)[79] was still controlling in that states may subject activities, even when religiously based, to the regulation of the states to promote health, safety, and welfare objectives. Some practices are not of such certain illegality, as illustrated in the conflicts that have arisen over Native American Church member usage of peyote.[80] In *Warner v Graham* (1985)[81] a human services drug counselor (who was not non–Native American) was suspended and then terminated after admitting to the use of peyote in association with religious practices of the Native American Church. The district court ruled that while the state could assert a compelling interest in removing her from a counselor position (the notoriety of the case negated her effectiveness), it could not terminate her employment as long as a less onerous and less restrictive means of implementing its compelling interests was available, such as a transfer to a less sensitive position.

Accommodation was also the approach for a Native American who engaged in ceremonial peyote use and applied for a position with a trucking company.[82] The company first refused to hire him because it felt that usage would create safety hazards and put the company at risk of violating U.S. Department of Transportation regulations preventing drivers under the influence of controlled substances from driving. The candidate filed a religious discrimination suit with the New Mexico Human Rights Commission. The company then offered to hire him under an accommodation that would require him to take vacation days after incidents of religious use of peyote. The candidate refused the accommodation, but the court found that the company's offer cured the original act of discrimination and that the offer was a reasonable one. A conflict between religious exercise and business necessity must often be resolved through bilateral cooperation and an applicant's decision to spurn such an offer vitiates the discrimination claim.

The Supreme Court addressed the issue of religious practices disqualifying persons from employment in *Employment Division v Smith* in 1990.[83] Smith and another Native American who were hired as drug counselors were terminated for "misconduct" when they were found to have used peyote during religious ceremonies. The Court found that the misconduct rooted in the violation of an Oregon statute did not merit any exemption because it was grounded in legitimate religious practices. The Oregon law could be sustained because it was a substance abuse law of general application that was not directed against a specific religious practice. The fact that a prohibited practice was accompanied by religious convictions did not immunize persons from sanctions for the practice.

The *Smith* case was widely condemned in academic and religious circles. Of the first sixteen law review articles and notes written on the case, all but one condemned the decision.[84] In December 1993 Congress passed the Religion Freedom Bill,[85] which has the effect of returning the law to the pre-*Smith* period. States would need to have a compelling interest to enforce any laws, regulations, or policies that place a substantial burden on religious practices.

CONCLUSION

The development of the law of public employment has shown the need for a greater awareness of constitutional and rights concepts by public personnel administrators. This chapter, which is an overview of the rapidly growing and changing field of public personnel law, is an introduction to a glossary of legal concepts, standards, and variables. These can serve as a foundation for a checklist that administrators can consult for employment situations that require their response. This checklist can help administrators comply with the growing body of law and in developing internal policies, allowing for harmonious, fair, and efficient administration of public sector agencies.

PUBLIC ADMINISTRATOR CHECKLIST: APPLICABLE PERSONNEL LAW QUESTIONS

1. Are the employment interests involved privileges, contractual rights, or vested rights?
2. What property interests (monetary or job security) can be identified in an employment situation?
3. What liberty interests can be identified in an employment situation? Is a name-clearing issue involved?
4. Does adverse employment action impact on employment opportunities?
5. What is the measure of due process to which an employee is entitled in deprivational action?
6. How are the procedures tailored to the severity of the adverse action involved? (*Goss* principle)
7. What procedures must be adhered to prior to termination? Which can be postponed to a post-termination hearing?
8. What unconstitutional conditions may be implicated in a personnel case?
9. What interests can be balanced in a free speech case? (*Pickering* and *Connick* principles)
10. Are there multiple (mixed) motives for making an adverse personnel action? May some of the motives be impermissible?
11. Can the motivating or substantial factors be identified in an adverse employment action?
12. What evidence indicates that the adverse action would have been taken irrespective of free speech activity ("but for rule")?
13. Can one identify and distinguish between issues of public interest, public concern, and purely internal matters?
14. Have policies and channels for bringing issues of public concern to superiors been established?
15. Is the action statutorily protected "whistle-blowing?"
16. What is the impact of employee political activity on the workplace?
17. Is speech (employee or employer) disruptive? Harassing? Con-

tributory to lowered performance? Reckless in terms of defamatory falsehoods?

18. Can adverse employment actions be perceived as retaliatory? Once an employee raises issues of discrimination, harassment, or chilling of rights, employer can take steps to resolve issues but not in any way to punish or remove employee.

19. Does employee have sincere religious obligation creating conflict with employment?

20. Has employee properly notified superiors of conflicts and concerns?

21. Have accommodations for religious needs of employees been extended? Is accommodation a reasonable one? For employee? Employer?

22. Can costs to accommodation be measured as more than *de minimis*? What compelling state interests burden the employee?

23. Do work terms or conditions impact religious beliefs? What is the magnitude of that impact?

24. What alternatives of accommodation can be advanced? What are the least onerous or burdensome of the alternatives?

EXAMPLE OF EMPLOYER FREE SPEECH POLICY

One personnel issue affecting both public and private employers is the bounds for employee speech both in and outside the workplace, especially the speech focusing on the activities of the employing institution and matters of internal administration. Court decisions and an increasing number of federal and state statutes have extended an umbrella of protection to employees who publicize matters that expose malfeasance, misfeasance, and nonfeasance within the employee's insitution. These whistle-blower statutues set the parameters for protecting speech where a public interest overrides the interest of the agency in efficient or harmonious or unimpeded administration. However, carving out zones of protected expression does not give rise to a general protection of all that an employee might choose to ventilate publicly of institutional matters or activities. Court decisions indicate that a balance must be drawn between the legitimate interests of an institution or organization and the public interests and concerns in the activities of that institution. Firm rules are hard to draw because the interests of the public institution and the public concerns vary according to circumstance. Thus we are left to decide on a case-by-case basis whether particular communications by employees are permissible or impermissible, whether they can be tolerated, or whether they jeopardize the functioning of an agency. This does not mean that certain standards may not be employed in drawing up a policy to guide administrators.

DISCLOSURE OF INFORMATION BY EMPLOYEES

1. Prohibited action: A public employer shall not discharge, discipline, threaten, or otherwise discriminate against or penalize an employee regarding the employee's compensation, terms, condition, location, or privileges because the employee or person acting on behalf of an employee in good faith reports the following:
   a. violation of state or federal law or regulations;
   b. theft, embezzlement, fraud, or personal enrichment;
   c. bribery or corruption;
   d. obstruction of justice, falsification of information;
   e. abuse of governmental authority;
   f. safety or health violations or complaints;
   g. unfair treatment of clients, persons served by agency;
   h. failure of the agency to fulfil statutory or legal mandates.

2. Information on above issues is entitled to unrestricted public disclosure as being inherently a matter of over-riding public concern.

3. This policy does not permit an employee to make statements or disclosures knowing that they are in reckless disregard of the truth.

4. This policy does not permit disclosure that would violate federal or state privacy laws or would diminish or impair the rights of any person to the continued protection of confidentiality of records or communications as provided by common law.

5. Not all reports and communications rise to the level of overriding concerns indicated above. When an employee publicly speaks out on institutional or agency matters, disputes, or internal issues that may be matters of public concern but also may negatively impact on an agency's functions and public service responsibilities, any disclosure must be judged in terms of a balancing of the agency's interests and the public concerns that may be implicated. Such interests are to be balanced on a case-by-case basis and an analysis must weigh:
   a. any impedence the disclosure may have on the employee's ability to perform duties;
   b. the need to maintain confidentiality of the information disclosed;
   c. the need to maintain discipline and harmony among coworkers;
   d. the importance of encouraging and maintaining close working relationships between superiors and coworkers;
   e. the time, place, and manner in which a speech is delivered;
   f. the context in which the underlying dispute arose giving rise to the disclosure.

6. To provide for a balancing of these factors at the earliest stages, an employee has the prime responsibility of making such reports through chan-

nels. Complaints should be directed to the employee's supervisors or to an appropriate official or supervisor in a bypass procedure in which the disclosure may implicate the supervisor.

7. The employer should respond to the report or complaint within a reasonable time (such as 72 hours). In the response the employer shall utilize the opportunity to:

  a. address the matter, dispute, or concern;
  b. inform the complainant of information that carries the protection of confidentiality;
  c. inform the complainant of any false or inaccurate information in the report or contemplated disclosure;
  d. inform the complainant of the consequence of any comments or public disclosure in disrupting the efficient operation of the agency or the harmony of the workplace;
  e. inform the complainant that the complainant's comments are protected only on matters of public concern that are not outweighed by the state's interest of effective and efficient administration. Complainant given notice that complainant may be subject to discipline or sanction if state interests are found to prevail.

8. Protection of employee's comments applies only where report relates to matters of public concern. While a matter of public concern may be raised in the midst of a personal dispute, a personnel matter that is personal in nature and limited to employee's own situation is not a matter of public concern unless it reflects a pattern of behavior, an explicit or implicit policy, or a systemwide problem. Such individual concerns or complaints merit response, particularly if they involve incidents of harassment or discrimination. However, the employee is directed to pursue redress within the agency first and to utilize any and all available grievance procedures before engaging in public disclosure.

9. A report or comment may not address a matter of public concern while issues are being processed and considered under internal procedures. The agency has an interest in restricting indiscriminate, premature, or insubordinate release of material. Employees cannot assert a constitutional "right to leak." This can apply to such matters as internal audits, personnel evaluations, policy reviews, agency self-studies, preliminary rulemaking, grievance procedures in progress, or other operations that have not run their course. While such issues may ultimately address matters of public concern, premature disclosure preempts the agency in making its own public release of information and may be considered serious misconduct, probably fatal to already difficult employment relationships. Prohibition of such disclosure by employees should be interpreted as a short-term prior restraint.

10. Public safety organizations such as police, law enforcement, or fire departments have a more significant interest than typical government employers in regulating speech activities of its employees in order to promote efficiency, foster loyalty, keep up morale, maintain discipline, and instill public confidence within the organization. Such organizations may not be able to accept the amount of disruption tolerated in a typical public agency. Particularly serious are comments that are attempts to undermine authority. Employees are directed to ventilate concerns or issues through direct channels or bypass channels within the organization.

Exercises

9.1 One issue in free speech cases is the separation of communication that is of public concern from that which relates to internal matters only. Using a law library find and read the case *Mekss v Wyoming Girls' School*, 813 P2d 185 (Wy 1991). Critique the case and indicate the factors that support the plaintiff and those which support the institution. What guidance is given by the free speech policy in the chapter? Would the recent Supreme Court decision in *Waters v Churchill* alter the law brought to bear in the case?

9.2 One of the issues raised in this chapter relates to due process considerations in employment practices. Personnel Grievance 2 in Appendix A involves in part the issue of due process. Prepare a memorandum stating whether or not the complainant is justified in raising questions of due process and provide specific substantiation for your position.

9.3 An agency of several hundred employees includes many different faiths: Jewish, Islamic, fundamentalist Christian, and Catholic. Devise a workplace policy that strikes a balance between free exercise of religion and avoidance of offense and harassment.

9.4 Personnel Grievances 6 and 9 involve allegations concerning the free exercise of religion. Discuss each of these cases and determine how a grievance board would address them.

Notes

1. See Ross P. Laguzza, *Assessing Attitudes and Beliefs: Employment Cases Stir Jurors' Emotions*, National Law Journal, 28 June 1993, pp. 27–28.
2. Postmaster General Marvin Runyon in an address at a national forum (Washington, D.C., December 16, 1993) on workplace violence noted that in 1993 over 750 people were murdered in workplace incidents in the United States. The U.S. Post Office recorded over 34 such deaths in ten incidents over the period of a decade. Also see National Institute for Occupational Safety and Health, Washington, D.C., "Fatal Injuries to Workers in the United States, 1980–1989" (Dec. 2, 1993), which notes that workplace homicides claimed 7,603 lives of 63,589 workplace fatalities for the decade.
3. Dennis Johnson, President of Behavior Analysts and Consultants, speaking at the National Forum on Workplace Violence, Washington, D.C., Dec. 16, 1993.

4. See investigative report by Jeff Thomas, "White Male Backlash," *Colorado Springs Gazette Telegraph*, 2 January 1994, p. 1.
5. 155 Mass 216, 220 (1882).
6. 330 US 75 (1947). The doctrine is set in dicta at p. 100.
7. 182 F2d 46 (DC Cir 1950), aff'd by an equally divided Court, 341 US 918 (1951).
8. 182 F2d at 59.
9. 341 US 123 (1951).
10. 360 US 474 (1959).
11. *Birnbaum v Trussell*, 371 F2d 672 (2d Cir 1966).
12. *Demise of the Right-Privilege Distinction in Constitutional Law*, 81 Harvard L Rev 1439 (1968).
13. Ibid. at 1461.
14. Ibid. at 1452.
15. 408 US 564 (1972).
16. 408 US 593 (1972).
17. 419 US 565 (1975).
18. 470 US 532 (1985).
19. The Court also saw that the public employer also had substantial interests in providing a full range of procedural protections. The public employer has an interest in avoiding erroneous decisions, unnecessary litigation, and the cost of training replacement employees. A government employer also has the interest in keeping citizens usefully employed instead of forcing them on the welfare rolls. Ibid. at 542–43.
20. Ibid. at 545.
21. 871 F2d 1037 (11th Cir 1989).
22. 391 US 563 (1968).
23. See D. Gordon Smith, *Beyond "Public Concern": New Free Speech Standards for Public Employees*, 57 U of Chicago L Rev 249 (1990); Craig D. Singer, *Conduct and Belief: Public Employees' First Amendment Rights to Free Expression and Political Affiliation*, 59 U of Chicago L Rev 897 (1992); and George T. Roumell Jr., *The Impact of Free Speech on Arbitrable Review of Discipline in the Public Sector*, 3 Detroit College of L Rev 807 (1992).
24. This includes such major legislation as the National Labor Relations Act, the Civil Rights Act of 1964, and the Civil Service Reform Act.
25. 429 US 274 (1977).
26. 439 US 410 (1979).
27. 461 US 138 (1983).
28. Ibid. at 149.
29. 745 F2d 868 (4th Cir 1984).
30. Ibid. at 880.
31. 483 US 378 (1987).
32. Before *Rankin*, a number of circuits had attempted to make a distinction between speech of public interest and speech of public concern, the latter restricted to bona fide attempts to alert the public to actual or potential wrongdoing or

breaches of the public trust. See *Gomez v Texas Dept. of Mental Health,* 794 F2d 1018 (5th Cir 1986) and *Egger v Phillips,* 710 F2d 292, 316–17 (7th Cir 1983).
33. 62 Law Week 4397 (31 May 1994).
34. Ibid. at 4400.
35. 973 F2d 295 (4th Cir 1992), cert denied, *Maciarello and Rowell v City of Lancaster,* 122 L.Ed.2d 356 (19 January 1993).
36. 973 F2d at 299.
37. 5 U.S.C. sec. 2302 (b)(8)(A).
38. For a discussion of the whistle-blower issue, see Martin W. Aron, *Whistleblowers, Insubordination, and Employees' Rights of Free Speech,* 43 Labor L J 211 (April 1992).
39. 389 N.E.2d 1070 (NY 1979).
40. *Immigration & Naturalization Service v Federal Labor Relations Authority and American Federation of Government Employees, AFL-CIO,* 855 F2d 1454 (9th Cir 1988).
41. See *Wilson v U.S. West Communications,* 860 F.Supp. 665 (D. Neb. 1994) in which a court upheld the termination of an employee who had refused to stop displaying a graphic antiabortion pin and who had refused some accommodations to wear the pin but cover it.
42. See Robbin T. Sarrazin, *Defamation in the Employment Setting,* 29 Tennessee Bar J 18 (6) (May-June 1993).
43. The Supreme Court in *Pickering* held that absent proof of false statements knowingly or recklessly made, a teacher's right to speak out on matters of public importance would not furnish the basis for dismissal from public employment. 391 US at 564.
44. *New York Times v Sullivan,* 376 US 254 (1964).
45. Malice has a technical meaning equivalent to statement of bald-faced lies. Simple expression of ill will or animus will not suffice to demonstrate malice. It is also necessary for challenged statements to carry a factual connotation and not the expression of speculation, guess, hunch, or hyperbole.
46. 608 N.E.2d 1175 (Ohio App. 12 Dist., 1992), cert. denied by U.S. Supreme Court, 124 L.Ed.2d 251 (17 May 1993).
47. 485 US 46 (1988).
48. 497 US 1 (1990).
49. 374 US 398 (1963).
50. The demands of different religious groups vary widely. Orthodox Jews eschew both employment and travel on the Sabbath and seek time off on Yom Kippur, Rosh Hashanah, and Succoth; Seventh-Day Adventists abstain from work on Saturday; Islamic workers seek accommodations during Ramadan and on Fridays; Ethiopians on the Feast of Maksal; and Native Americans may seek excuse from work during powwow religious ceremonies.
51. 29 C.F.R. sec. 1605.1 (EEOC, 1967).
52. *Kettell v Johnson & Johnson,* 337 F.Supp. 892 (D. Ark 1971).
53. 42 U.S.C. sec. 2000e et seq., sec. 701(j).
54. See *Equal Employment Opportunity Commission Compliance Manual,* sec. 628: 0015, 0016, 0019 (1984).
55. A reasonable demand on the part of an employee would also include a commit-

ment of the employee to cooperate with the employer and also share the burden of accommodation, making such adjustments in his or her own working life to resolve a conflict. See *Brener v Diagnostic Center Hospital,* 671 F2d 141 (5th Cir 1982).

56. 479 US 60 (1986).
57. *Philbrook v Ansonia School Board,* 757 F2d 476 (2d Cir 1986).
58. 29 C.F.R. sec. 1605.2(c).
59. 479 US at 69, n.6.
60. 432 US 63 (1977).
61. Ibid. at 84.
62. For a comprehensive case review of the accommodation issue, see Robert M. Preer, *Reasonable Accommodation of Religious Practice: The Conflict Between the Courts and EEOC,* 15 Employee Relations L J 67 no. 1 (summer 1989).
63. See *Anderson v Bessemer City, North Carolina,* 470 US 564, 572 (1985).
64. 955 F2d 902 (4th Cir 1992).
65. "Wearing of Religious Garb by Public School Teachers," 60 ALR2d 300 (1958).
66. 723 P.2d 298 (Oreg. 1986), cert. denied, 480 US 942 (1986).
67. 475 US 503 (1986).
68. PL 100–180, 101 Stat. 1086–87, sec. 508 (1987).
69. A religious adherent's beliefs may be entirely sincere but protection of the freedom of religion "does not afford an individual's rights to dictate the conduct of the government's internal procedures." Chief Justice Burger in *Bowen v Roy,* 476 US 711–12 (1986).
70. *benMiriam v Office of Personnel Management,* 647 F.Supp. 84 (M.D. N.C. 1986).
71. 676 F2d 1272, 1279 (9th Cir 1982).
72. For a discussion see Laura S. Underfuffler, *Discrimination on the Basis of Religion: An Examination of Attempted Value Neutrality in Employment,* 30 William and Mary L Rev 581 (1989).
73. See 29 U.S.C. sec. 169 (as amended 1980). For a test of this accommodation by a person claiming a "personal" religious abhorrence to supporting labor unions, see *Stern v Teamsters "General" Local Union No. 200,* 626 F.Supp. 1043 (E.D. Wis. 1986). This exemption involved a reciprocal accommodation that requires the employee to contribute a sum equal to the dues to a charitable cause.
74. 595 F.Supp. 1050 (E.D. Va. 1984).
75. 37 F3d 404 (8th Cir 1994).
76. See W. John Moore, "Possibly One 'Thou Shalt Not' Too Many," *National Journal,* 21 May 1994, p. 1191.
77. 3 *Employment Discrimination Reporter* 99, 27 July 1994; 3 *EDR* 228, 24 Aug. 1994 (BNA, Washington, D.C.).
78. 585 F.Supp. 1126 (D. Utah 1984), aff'd. 760 F2d 1065 (10th Cir 1985), cert. denied, 474 US 849 (1985).
79. 98 US (8 Otto) 145 (1878).
80. Religious use of peyote is not federally illegal. The Bureau of Narcotics and Dangerous Drugs has added a religious-use exemption to its Schedule I: "The listing of peyote as a controlled substance in Schedule I does not apply to the non-drug

use of peyote in bona fide religious ceremonies of the Native American Church." 21 C.F.R. sec. 1307.31 (1983).
81. 675 F.Supp. 1171 (D. N.Dak. 1985).
82. *Toledo v Nobel Sysco*, 651 F.Supp. 483 (D. N.Mex. 1986).
83. 494 US 872 (1990).
84. See James E. Ryan, *Smith and the Religious Freedom Restoration Act: An Iconoclastic Assessment*, 78 Virginia L Rev 1407 (Sept. 1992), n.6 at 1409.
85. H.R. 1308.

10

Public Employment and Privacy

A constitutional umbrella was not extended over privacy concerns in general until 1965 and the case *Griswold v Connecticut*.[1] The U.S. Supreme Court began an incremental process of extending privacy protections into those areas and spheres of activity where individuals professed and the public supported "expectations of privacy."[2] This chapter will review the role of public institutions and personnel managers in recognizing such expectations while pursuing valid governmental objectives that happen to touch on individual privacy. The balancing of administrative interests against privacy matters will be discussed with respect to:

1. gathering and using personal information in recruitment of persons into public employment;
2. issues of personal appearance and behaviors as they relate to job performance and agency functioning;
3. issues of personal off-duty behaviors;
4. issues of personal space in the workplace;
5. issues of workplace monitoring and surveillance.

RECRUITMENT

Intrusions into a prospective employee's private life can begin with the recruitment process. Before hiring anyone, employers pursue background checks that look to educational levels, skill levels, work history, and criminal records. Pre-employment inquiries and application forms can focus on such relevant job factors as education, experience, particular skills, work-related attitudes, or ability to respond to unusual work schedules or assignments. They can also attempt to extract information on matters irrelevant to job performance or administrative necessity. Antidiscrimination policies have ruled out self-identifications by race or national origin. To reinforce the color-blind nature of the recruitment process, photos are not included as an application requirement. Inquiries as to marital status, children, or companionship relations have increasingly been put out of bounds. California and Minnesota make marital inquiry illegal. There is even a suggestion that the initial screening process for new employees should be gender-blind as well as color-blind, the applicants revealing their identities only through initials. Beyond the formal application, the unstructured interview provides potential for intrusions into matters that are within a private domain. Interviews serve to provide indications of compatibility between employer and employee and also allow the employer to probe the commitment of an applicant to institutional goals. Once, it was common for an an employer to ask about an applicant's family, child-rearing demands, or any other "dependent" obligations, but this has been viewed as providing a basis for discrimination against women with children. The employer may ask about the applicant's hobbies, use of free time, or his or her experiences (to see whether they were broadening). The interview cannot include a question such as "How's your love life?" Such questions are totally improper. Yet they are very difficult to eradicate from a process that has as a goal the development of complete knowledge on a prospective employee. A public employer should be guided by the same principles that were enunciated for proper testing and consideration of applicants in *Griggs v Duke Power Co.* (1971)[3]—that any test or qualification for a job must be *job-related* and that any test or qualification should measure the person for the job and not the person in the abstract.

Job-related questions and inquiries may still focus on very personal matters. A Department of Defense questionnaire asks those holding "secret" security clearances to divulge their entire life histories; their criminal arrests, their travels, their credit ratings, their mental health problems, and any instances of drug or alcohol abuse. Federal employees filed a suit challenging the use of the questionnaire as an invasion of privacy and a violation of the Fifth Amendment provision against self-incrimination. The Court rejected their contention, ruling that the self-incrimination provision would apply only if the government pursued a criminal prosecution. The only element of compulsion lay in the notice that "failure to answer the questions might result in our being unable to complete our investigation and result in your not being considered for clearance." The information requested was highly relevant to the responsibilities and behavioral expectations of a person holding a security clearance.[4]

These inquiries are often accompanied by physical examinations. Again, the issue is one of a job-related inquiry. An employer can inquire about those physical or mental conditions that affect the performance of the job in question. To go beyond that would be to intrude into private matters. Questions as to pregnancies, abortions, or health procedures dealing with the reproductive system would appear to show little job-relatedness. A question as to whether a person has a condition such as diabetes or asthma may have no relevance to ability to perform the job, particularly with the availability of treatments that control any expression of the disease. Can the employer ask the general question whether the applicant has any condition of which knowledge might be useful to both employer and employee in event of a medical emergency? The passage of the Americans With Disabilities Act in 1990[5] would appear to rule even this out. Preemployment medical examinations and inquiries (questionnaires or oral inquiries) are generally prohibited under Title I of the Act. For a discussion of this topic, see chapter 13.

Physical examinations may be augmented by psychological tests and inventories and attitudinal instruments to screen applicants. These instruments can also be used to monitor current employees and identify personnel problems. The key case supporting the legitimacy of such testing was a 1978 case, *McKenna v Fargo*.[6] The Jersey City Fire Department used psychological tests to screen applicants. The objective was to recruit applicants who could make decisions under stress, maintain discipline and emotional control, and be able to handle job experiences without post-traumatic stress. The testing procedure involved a two-step process, beginning with the administration of the Minnesota Multi-Phasic Personality Inventory (MMPI). Those with "flags" on the MMPI would be administered a full battery of affirmation tests. The MMPI has a vast array of items that have been utilized to construct specific subscales focusing on such psychological attributes as manifest anxiety, ego strength, or religiosity.[7] Three plaintiffs who were eligible for employment resisted the test requirements. They were intimidated by the religiosity questions and the follow-up interviews that focused on family upbringing, alcoholism, and family mental histories. One was disturbed by the Thematic Apperception Test and questions on dating. The court addressed the issues of the intrusiveness of tests, violation of freedom of belief, and the necessity of this particular testing process as a reasonable hiring procedure. The court upheld the use of the tests, noting that there was no attempt overtly to test for social or political beliefs or to ensure that applicants who were chosen exhibited attitudes and beliefs in conformity with Jersey City residents. The court did note that the questions did touch on privacy interests and liberty interests of honor and reputation. But this intrusion was justified in terms of the compelling state interests of recruiting employees able to meet the rigorous psychological qualification of a firefighter. The tests were useful in identifying those applicants who would be high-risk candidates for the jobs.

The *McKenna* rationale served as guiding law, at least for testing applicants for positions serving a compelling state interest. The courts are now taking a more protective position of privacy interests of employees. A case contrasted with *McKenna* is *Soroka v Dayton-Hudson* (1992).[8] This case involved a challenge of the use of a psychological screening battery by a department-store chain in hiring store security officers for its stores. The battery used such true or false questions as:

T. or F.	I feel there is only one true religion
T. or F.	I am strongly attracted by members of my own sex
T. or F.	I have trouble starting or holding a bowel movement
T. or F.	A person is foolish to vote for an increase in their taxes

The California Court of Appeals ruled that the chain's preemployment requirement of psychological screening violated California's constitutional and statutory provisions protecting privacy interests. The tests improperly inquired into the religious, social, and personal beliefs of applicants, and the tests were not essential to business necessity.[9]

While such blatant attempts to screen the inner opinions and predispositions of job applicants appear destined to be regarded as unnecessary invasions of privacy, such may not be the case with integrity tests—tests aimed at testing potential trustworthiness of employees. They are seen as predictors of all sorts of negative work behaviors, including wayward impulse behavior, employee deviance, organizational delinquency, or drug risk.[10] While the stated objectives of the tests appear to reflect compelling administrative interests, questions remain whether these tests are valid or reliable. Employees can readily spot the contentious questions and provide evasive or false responses, thereby skewing the results. Validation is also problematic because of the difficulty of identifying all the employees actually guilty of theft or abuse of institutional resources. Correlations between test profiles and employees who actually demonstrate the undesired behaviors are often lacking.

One preemployment screening device that has been put under restriction is the polygraph examination. In 1988, Congress passed the Employee Polygraph Protection Act, which prohibits employers involved in or affecting interstate commerce from utilizing polygraph tests to deny employment opportunities.[11] The act proscribes the use of mechanical or electrical methods to arrive at diagnostic findings regarding the honesty or dishonesty of employees. Prospective employers are also deterred from suggesting or leading applicants to take a "voluntary" test. These protections, however, have no application in public employment because Section Seven of the act exempts all public employees of federal, state, and local governments and any contractors or consultants of the federal government. There still remains the question of whether a public employee or applicant might raise due process claims for improper use of polygraphs by a public employer, such as the use of non–job-related information obtained through such examinations to make an adverse decision against the employee.

LIFESTYLE ISSUES IN EMPLOYMENT[12]

Prior to the 1970s public employers could attach almost any conditions to employment, and off-duty behaviors could jeopardize employment. High standards of personal behavior were seen as legitimate expectations in light of the public trust placed with public employees. Public agencies as well as private institutions also were quite concerned about institutional reputation. Certain public roles, especially those connected with law enforcement, were particularly held to expectations of morally correct behavior. In *Briggs v North Muskegon Police Dept.* (1983)[13] and in *Thorne v City of El Segundo* (1983),[14] courts ruled that private off-duty sexual activities having no impact on job performance could not be used to adversely affect the job status of employees. In each case an employee having an affair with married persons not their spouse was dismissed or rejected for employment. The courts ruled that the adverse actions violated associational and privacy rights of the employee. However, the judge who wrote the opinion in the *Briggs* case ruled in a related case that a policeman could be dismissed for entering into a relationship with a woman who had asked for police assistance.[15] The distinction was that the policeman became involved while investigating the woman's citizen complaint and thus the conduct was related to and was connected to his performance. Improper relationships, such as those of police officers with prostitutes, also cannot be condoned because such activities create conflicts of interest, compromise their performance as officers, threaten the morale of the department, and jeopardize the departments' reputation in the community.[16]

An issue that is more commonly encountered is that of the involvement of two employees within an agency. A typical case was *Kukla and Kukla v Village of Antioch* (1986).[17] A male police sergeant and a female police dispatcher were discharged for cohabitation, in violation of a regulation prohibiting socialization between employees of a different rank. The couple, who married as their case progressed through channels and into the courts, maintained that their relationship had constitutional protections of both privacy and association. They maintained that there was no evidence that their job performance was diminished because of their relationship.

In reviewing a wide range of cases of this genre, the court in *Kukla* did not line up neatly behind the position of either the employees or the employer. The court said that these cases are heavily fact-dependent and they turn on the extent to which the employees' private choices relate to the governmental necessities involved. In effect, the court adopted a balancing test analogous to the *Pickering* balancing test in expression cases.[18] The court looked at such unique factors in this case as the existence of a department regulation prohibiting fraternization, the effect on morale in a small department, and the effect that the relationship had on public perception of the department in a small community. The discharges were upheld.

In a similar case, *Shawgo v Spradlin* (1983),[19] a circuit court upheld the termination of police officers for violating regulations prohibiting cohabitation. In this case the circuit court saw the special demands of discipline in a quasimilitary organization as overriding the privacy interests of employees, who are expected to forgo some of the rights and privileges assumed by ordinary citizens. Applying the fact-dependent analysis advanced in *Kukla,* one might reason that the turning fact was not so much the off-duty behaviors of these employees as the fact that sexual behaviors might corrupt superior/subordinate relationships.

The key to any institutional interest in the private lives of employees must be a nexus between behavior and job performance. Legislatively, the trend is emerging to protect employees from adverse employment decisions because of what employees do in their off-duty hours as long as those activities are legal. New York in 1992 amended its labor law to prohibit "discrimination against engaging in legal activities during non-working hours."[20] The law protects employees in their political activities, recreational activities, and in the legal use of consumable products.[21] Employers would not be in violation of the statute where actions were taken pursuant to established substance or alcohol abuse programs or where individual actions were illegal, or if behavior constituted habitually poor performance, incompetency, or misconduct.

The New York law is undergoing legal challenge. A major retailer terminated two employees who were dating. The retailer had implemented an "Improper Workplace Conduct Policy" stating that "workplace conduct arising from a romantic relationship between two or more associates in the same work location is improper when it adversely impacts safe, orderly, and efficient operations." The two employees who were discharged took extended work breaks, engaged in open displays of affection, disrupted work routines, and offended coworkers. The employer asserted that this ceased to be a privacy issue when the employees brought their relationship into the workplace. Employers also see such situations as ripe for sexual harassment suits if the relationships sour.[22] The first appellate decisions on the termination, alleging violation of the new law, have, however, ruled that dating is not a recreational activity, and persons terminated for romantic activities cannot rely on the statute for relief.[23]

Reviewing these issues of personal behaviors that may affect job performance, workplace atmosphere, or the reputation of the institution reveals a tangled skein of legal, moral, ethical, and management issues. As public administrators can attest, relationships between individuals are hardest to manage. Management can approach these matters along two tracks. One approach is to draw up a set of rules or expectations, set standards of behavioral excellence, and monitor the workforce. This may create a work environment that pits administrators against employees. Employees may simply become surreptitious in their behaviors, gossip will permeate the work environment, and employees may turn in other employees. Another approach is to attempt to integrate behavioral expectations into the *esprit de corps* of the organization. The idea is to communicate to employees the point that a responsible personal lifestyle is institutionally appreciated and rewarded. Sensitivity should prevail in counseling those who may be acting irresponsibly in their personal lives. Some might argue that this approach is still, however, coercive toward conformity and conducive to an organization that is rigid in values, behavior, and appearance. However, this need not be the case for an organization that prides itself on its responsible members and its diversity. Thus, the agency becomes a community of members who are quite different in their personal externalities but dedicated to each other and the institution.

If an agency or organization accumulates sensitive personal information about its employees, it may also be liable to suit at common law.[24] There are three tort actions available to employees in the case where an employer misuses personal information. These torts include intrusion upon seclusion, publicity given to one's private life, and publicity placing a person in a false light.[25] In intrusion upon seclusion, an employer's surveillance of a person's off-duty activity could lay the basis for such a tort claim. A borderline situation is indicated where an employer might refer an employee to a counselor or psychologist and reports and communications between the employer and the counselor would disclose revelations the employee would consider privileged.[26] As to tort actions in which the employee claims the employer gave publicity to the employee's private life, a fine line exists between disclosure of information to those supervisors or employees who need to know and those who do not. Disclosure of information to the public at large, to the media, or to so many people that the matter would certainly become one of common knowledge would support such a tort action. If, however, the employee goes public or makes information known to co-workers, that employee waives privacy rights.[27] The issue of publicity placing a person in a false light is likely to emerge in cases where employers and employees are involved in grievances and the parties make public details within the controversy or breach the confidentiality provisions of any settlements that might be reached. Employers may be under intense pressure to provide information (especially to the press), but preservation of confidentiality serves the interests of both employer and employee.

Sexual Orientation[28]

Another privacy issue involves sexual orientation. This issue involves both incidents of individual discrimination and patterns of discrimination directed against male and female homosexuals. This matter is covered in this chapter on privacy and lifestyle because the federal courts so far have not designated these people as classes protected under the equal protections clause or Title VII of the Civil Rights Act, but this remains a possibility. In *Frontiero v Richardson* (1973),[29] in an opinion by Justice Brennan, a plurality set down the following criteria for strict scrutiny of laws impacting a protected class:

1. The class is identified by an immutable characteristic which is an accident of birth;
2. The class has experienced a long history of pervasive and even invidious discrimination.
3. The identifying characteristics of the class bear no relation to the ability to perform or contribute to society.
4. The class lacks political power or influence to redress its grievances.[30]

While this multiprong test has not been applied to classes of sexual orientation by the Supreme Court, it has gained some acceptance in lower federal courts.[31]

Gay men and lesbians face discrimination and adverse employment actions in three areas of public employment: in the military, in sensitive positions that carry security clearances, and in the ranks of the civil service. The military has maintained an uncompromising position excluding and expelling persons of homosexual orientation from its ranks. It has also maintained an uncompromising discharge policy for homosexual conduct and for disclosure of homosexual conduct. These policies are grounded in the Universal Code of Military Justice and its antisodomy provisions as well as in what has been regarded as the special requirements of command, discipline, unit cohesion, and privacy interests of nonhomosexuals. That policy changed somewhat in July 1993 with an executive order signed by President Clinton that allows for homosexuals to serve as members as long as they are totally discreet in regard to their orientation and do not engage in homosexual conduct. It remains to be seen whether this is protective of homosexuals who choose to serve in the military under those requirements.

In sensitive and security areas, the federal government has generally barred employment of homosexuals and the courts have supported this position, as in *Padula v Webster*[32] where the court upheld the FBI's refusal to hire a lesbian job applicant on grounds that FBI activities often involve classified matters that cannot be entrusted to employees who may be subject to blackmail.[33] In *High Tech Gays v Defense Indus.*[34] a federal district court applied a strict scrutiny standard to the government's policy of denying clearances to those persons who had participated in homosexual activity within the past fifteen years. An appeals court overturned the decision, ruling that strict scrutiny need not be applied and that the policy in question was rationally related to a legitimate interest in protecting national security.[35]

The federal civil service has, on the other hand, exhibited a more tolerant and accepting stance toward the employment of gay men and lesbians. Before 1969 the guiding law was articulated in *Dew v Halaby* (1963),[36] which held that an employee might be discharged for any reason that could have justified not hiring him in the first place. That changed in 1969 when the D.C. Circuit in *Norton v Macy*[37] applied the due process clause to actions where federal employers either fired or refused to hire a homosexual. To justify such a termination or exclusion, the acting agency had to establish a rational relationship between the person's sexual orientation and the efficiency of the agency's operations. Norton's behavior was private, off-duty, discreet, and posed no threat to the efficiency of government operations. Following *Norton,* the Civil Service Commission issued guidelines for evaluating the suitability of individuals for federal employment.[38] Under the guidelines, one of the factors to be considered as the basis for disqualification is criminal, dishonest, infamous, or notoriously disgraceful conduct. The key was notoriety. Even though conduct might be regarded as offensive to some, if it was not generally known or the object of public scandal, adverse findings would not be appropriate. A concluding note indicated that commissions and agencies have been enjoined not to find a person unavailable for federal employment "solely" because a person is a homosexual or has engaged in homosexual acts.[39] The basis for adverse action still remains activity involving public notoriety. In *Singer v U.S. Civil Service Comm.*[40] the court upheld the dismissal of a federal employee who made a public issue of his sexual orientation, "openly and publicly flaunting his homosexual way of life while identifying himself as a member of a federal agency."

Presently, federal regulations protect employees under guidelines that condition protection on keeping activities private and discreet with no occasion for public notoriety. The policy exhibits parallels with the recently declared military policy, which can be capsulized, "Don't ask, don't tell, don't flaunt." Borderline situations are bound to arise, particularly if they involve political expression. Such situations would implicate a free speech issue. However, only one state court has ruled that self-affirming statements of homosexual identity are protected as political expression (and that was under the state's labor code and not the U.S. Constitution).[41] Would a federal employee participating in an ACT-UP[42] demonstration jeopardize his employment? Would appearance on a talk show, particularly one of the tabloid variety, present a sufficient case to affect an agency's missions or functions? The court rulings stress the need to establish a nexus between private behavior and job performance.

The increasing attention given to sexual harassment in the workplace has raised the question of sexual harassment of gays, or by gays.[43] Courts have already begun to entertain suits under Title VII alleging that employees who happen to be homosexuals were subjected to sexual harassment and forced to work in a hostile and abusive work environment. Federal district court decisions, however, have rejected the claims, ruling that the harassments suffered by the plaintiffs were because of their sexual orientation rather than because of their gender. The harassing actions did not come under Title VII because it was not the type of conduct that Congress intended to sanction when it passed Title VII.[44] A number of employees have attempted to make the case that sexual harassment may be encountered within the same gender group. Courts have, however, made a distinction between inter-sex harassment, which involves exploitation of a power position to impose demands or pressures on an unwilling but less powerful person, and situations where a person of a particular gender was selected for sexual attention. Employees may have been harassed, but the courts have not acknowledged that is was part of an antimale workplace environment.[45] It is possible that new cases may be decided with a closer attention to the Equal Employment Opportunity Commission (EEOC) guidelines that define a hostile work environment in terms of "unwelcome sexual advances," "requests for sexual favors," and "verbal or physical conduct of a sexual nature."[46] These guidelines stress not the gender target of harassment but the sexual nature of the harassment involved. They also judge the harassment in terms of results, that being interference with an employee's job performance. It would also appear that Title VII quid pro quo suits could also embrace homosexual harassment. If a male supervisor is heterosexual, he may exploit female employees. If he is homosexual, male employees may be the target of his demands. Present semantic hairsplitting over the protective ambit of Title VII appears to ignore common sense. What is developing is that many agencies, particularly those at the state and local level, have put in place rules and standards that judge harassment not in terms of the male/female dichotomy but in terms of the sexual nature of the harassment involved. It appears that the workplace may be ahead of the federal judiciary on this issue.

If federal jurisdictions have been inertially resistant to extending the coverage of Title VII to issues of sexual discrimination against homosexuals, twelve states as of 1992 have independently extended protection to this class of workers and have limited employers' discretion in the areas of sexual preference.[47] In addition, sixty-five municipalities and counties have enacted antidiscrimination legislation on the basis of sexual preference. That includes most of the major cities in the country.[48] In fact, some cities have taken the lead where the states have failed to do so.[49] Ironically, this has reduced the pressure on the EEOC and the federal courts to deal with the issue of discrimination because victims of discrimination have more likelihood of success in pursuing their case through state or local courts utilizing independent state grounds.

Dress, Grooming, Personal Habits

Diversity in lifestyle is often reflected in terms of dress and grooming practices. The key case is *Kelley v Johnson*, decided by the Supreme Court in 1976.[50] A police benevolent association challenged a county police department's rules applicable to male employees governing hair length and facial hair, contending that the regulations were violative of free expression, guarantees of due process, and equal protection. A court of appeals found that the choice of personal appearance is an ingredient of an individual's personal liberty and that the police department failed to show a relationship between the regulation and a legitimate department interest. The Supreme Court, however, found that the state need not establish a genuine public need. It remained for the employees to prove that the regulations were so irrational as to be branded as arbitrary. The regulations were sustainable in terms of rather vague objectives as deference to the organizational structure of the police force and the county's possible desire to make officers more readily recognizable to the public. This is close to a *de minimis* justification. Such considerations would hold true for law enforcement and quasimilitary organizations, but could they be applied to all public employees? The Ninth Circuit evidently thought so when it upheld suspensions and ultimate terminations of employees of the Maricopa Assessors Office for not complying with rules that male employees wear hair cut above the collar.[51]

Grooming regulations focusing on hair styles and facial hair also run against antidiscrimination provisions especially if the grooming practice is linked to race, sex, or religion. Employees have frequently challenged grooming violations, claiming that they violate Section 703(a) of the Civil Rights Act.[52] In addition to relying on Title VII, an employee might seek relief on constitutional grounds as in the case of claims that an Afro hairstyle worn by an African American employee was so exclusively a cultural symbol of African American identity that its suppression was per se an automatic case of racial prejudice. A number of cases have ruled that a no-beard policy has a disparate impact upon African Americans, who disproportionately suffer from folliculitis and must refrain from shaving for health reasons. However, the general grooming requirements could be sustained if they provided for medical exceptions.

As to dress regulations, where there is no prescribed uniform, employers, including public employers, may draft a dress or grooming code, but any dress code must not involve a burden on one sex but not the other. Thus, an airline company was cited for violating Title VII because it forbade women cabin attendants to wear eyeglasses but allowed their male counterparts to do so. Similarly a more defined or specifically directed dress code for one sex but not the other may be discriminatory. Inordinate preoccupation with the appearance of female employees can be a violation of Title VII.[53] On the other hand, a requirement that male employees comply with hair length requirements or be required to wear ties was upheld even though collateral requirements were not placed on the female employees.[54] Pressing the dress code requirements beyond general requirements of neatness or professional acceptance would appear to raise more problems than any improvement in agency image would warrant. A make-up requirement raises issues of sexist stereotypes, health issues (allergic employees), unwarranted and disparate financial burdens on employees, and possible religious objections. This is an area for common sense to prevail, not fine legal distinctions.

Another recent workplace issue involving personal lifestyle choice is that of smoking. After the passage of the Rehabilitation Act of 1973, employees who suffered health problems as a result of passive (second-hand) smoke began to sue their employers, asking that their employers make a reasonable accommodation to their medical reactions to environments allowing the smoking of tobacco. Suits were filed as common-law actions (right to a safe workplace), under OSHA statutes, and as constitutional due process and privacy actions. Few of these suits were successful.[55] However, the Federal Labor Relations Authority did allow bargaining between employers and organized workers over such issues as designation of offices or work areas as smoking areas or non-smoking areas, separation of smokers and nonsmokers, partitions between smokers and nonsmokers, and requirements that smokers refrain from smoking if requested to do so. Many issues were also resolved through the arbitration process in which an employee files a grievance against an employer. Grievances were brought by nonsmokers seeking accommodation or a totally smoke-free workplace as a remedy to their discomfiture in a smoky environment and also by smokers who were disciplined for violating non-smoking rules or who felt that unilaterally imposed smoking restrictions were unfair. A trend began to emerge that saw the affirmation of the imposition of no-smoking rules that had a direct relationship with a business objective.[56] Employers were also seen as acting on their authority to change workplace rules or impose new ones and in most cases to do so without having to negotiate smoking restrictions with a union. A federal appeals court in 1987 also upheld department rules that forbade probationary firefighters from smoking on or off the job. Such rules had a rational relationship to the state's interest in promoting health and safety. It also upheld the firing of a probationary firefighter for taking three puffs on a cigarette during an unpaid lunch break.[57]

In the 1980s, restrictions on smoking in the workplace became a general norm for both private and public employers. Reports on the health hazards of passive smoke on those not smoking were issued by the Surgeon General of the United States, the Environmental Protection Agency, and the Centers for Disease Control and Prevention. This information was very influential in leading employers to establish voluntary smoke-free work policies in thousands of workplaces, especially in offices. It has also led to a trend whereby employers adopt policies allowing them to refuse to hire or discipline employees who smoke off the job. By 1993, some 6 percent of employers had adopted hiring bans or firing threats against smokers.[58] These particular policies were attacked by the Tobacco Institute, ad hoc smokers' groups, and by the American Civil Liberties Union as violating rights of privacy and the right to engage in lawful activity off the job. Smoking interests reframed the debate from one focusing on health issues to one of privacy and civil rights.

In response to this trend, smoker rights interests were able to mobilize efforts at the state level to pass smoker protection legislation. In 1989 and 1990, seven states passed such legislation. By August 1992 the number had risen to twenty-five. The statutes vary in terms of scope of protection. In most states it is tobacco use or smoking that is made an illegal hiring consideration. In states like Colorado and North Dakota, the anti-discriminatory factor is the employee's engaging in "any lawful activity." In the states of Illinois, Minnesota, Nevada, New York, and Wisconsin protection extends to employees using or consuming "any lawful product." In sixteen of the states, the laws prevent an employer from discriminating against a smoking employee on the basis of compensation or benefits. This prevents public agencies from imposing high health insurance payments or premiums on smoking employees. Some of the statutes permit exceptions allowing an employer to refuse to hire a smoker because of a bona fide occupational qualification, or if the hiring of a smoker would create a conflict of interest. This deluge of legislation does not point to what state sovereignty proponents call a tranquil diversity. Half the states have no laws protecting the employment rights of smokers, and many states of the other half have laws that protect such rights to the detriment of employers. While the laws protect smokers in their off-duty activity, they go so far as to restrict employers in dealing with employees who are unable to perform their jobs when health problems due to smoking finally do arise. That situation also raises new questions of accommodation under the Americans with Disabilities Act (see chapter 13).

WORKPLACE SEARCHES

In recent years, privacy concerns have also been raised in terms of employee expectations of privacy within the workplace itself. Three areas where conflicts have arisen between an employer's prerogative of conducting searches and employee privacy interests include (1) the search of private spaces and properties within the workplace; (2) requirements of drug or substance abuse testing for employees; and (3) the electronic monitoring of work activities and the surveillance of employees' work performance.

While the Supreme Court had developed an extensive body of law in regard to searches and seizures, it was not until *O'Connor v Ortega* (1987)[59] that the Court explored the dimensions of searches in the workplace. The decision addressed a number of privacy-in-employment concerns: societal expectations of privacy in the workplace, privacy interests created in the context of personal needs, and sanctity of areas exclusively utilized by individual employees. Against these privacy interests, there are employer interests in supervising and monitoring employee activity, deterring illegal conduct, protecting employer property, and efficiently administrating business.

The Supreme Court recognized that searches and seizures by government employers of the private property of employees is subject to Fourth Amendment restraints rooted in both societal and worker expectations of privacy. These expectations can vary widely with the operational realities of different workplaces; a reasonableness assessment must be attached to each circumstance. Privacy expectations must also be balanced against the government's needs. A public employer's need to have access to or to retrieve work-related material or data as well as the need to investigate violations of workplace rules can override the ordinary rule that office files and drawers have a reasonable expectation of privacy. The need to conduct work-related investigations also makes a probable cause requirement impractical. The Supreme Court found that the search of Dr. Ortega's desk was thus a "reasonable search" even in the absence of a hospital policy on searches or advance notice of possible searches.

Ortega provided employers with a range of policy alternatives that would legitimate their policies of pursuing searches and seizures in the workplace. *Ortega* allowed employers to escape restrictions on their search and seizure policies by:

1. reducing the opportunity for privacy in the workplace;
2. arranging workplaces, filing areas, and property stores to eliminate expectations of privacy;
3. giving notice to employees of search policies;
4. making employee areas repositories of information to which the employer must have access;
5. requiring employees to conform to certain work standards (like keeping their desks clean).[60]

The triggers of Fourth Amendment protections are entirely within the employer's control. Unless the reasonable expectation of privacy threshold is crossed, no search has occurred. And even where employer and employee interests must be balanced, government interests may be strengthened by advancing multiple work-related purposes for conducting a search.[61]

The balancing test leaves open the question of a distinction between professional and nonprofessional work environments. Professional employees (teachers, researchers, scientists) often integrate their personal and research libraries and data into their office libraries. They may possess files and correspondence relating to their professional and associational activity within files provided by their employer. While professionalism and collegiality would indicate a high respect for a colleague's professional resources, the rare occasions when a person's research is called into question and issues of scientific integrity could demand the opening of those files. In such instances subpoenas may be the proper approach to get at mixed properties. The Fourth Amendment protects a person's papers and effects and only the necessity to produce those papers in a court of law could compel their discovery.

DRUG TESTING

As the problems of drug use spread through society, public agencies find that these problems can also exist in their workplaces. President Reagan initiated a response to these problems with the promulgation of Executive Order

12564 on September 15, 1986.[62] Recognizing that employees using drugs on and off duty impeded the efficiency of government agencies, Reagan directed all agency heads to develop plans for achieving a drug-free workplace, to set up programs to test for the use of illegal drugs by employees in sensitive positions, to set up programs for voluntary drug testing, and to provide for treatment and rehabilitation of employees found to be using drugs.

Agencies responded with programs tailored to their own functional requirements, and individual programs soon came under constitutional challenge. The Supreme Court reviewed the constitutional dimensions in 1989 in *Skinner v Railway Labor Executives Assoc.*[63] and *National Treasury Employees Union v Von Raab.*[64] In the *Skinner* case, the challenged regulations of the Federal Railroad Administration permitted drug testing of any employee when supervisors had a reasonable suspicion that the employee was using drugs or had violated certain rules. Mandatory drug tests were to be performed on employees involved in any major train accident, especially if they involved fatalities. In the *Skinner* case, the Court found that the normal requirements to obtain warrants need not be followed. Evidence of drugs or alcohol would be lost if the government were delayed in making tests by obtaining a warrant. Publication of the policy gave employees notice, a purpose served by warrants, and the need for a neutral magistrate to assess justifying facts seemed superfluous in the face of such obvious facts as a train wreck. Noting that the policy allowed for reasonable, warrantless searches, the Supreme Court balanced the interests of employees against those of the government. The Court recognized that urinalysis tests were particular invasions of personal privacy[65] but also recognized that train workers should have a diminished expectation of privacy given the importance and public responsibility of their duties and the overriding concerns of public safety.

In the *Von Raab* case, there were not the overriding safety considerations or the pressing interests of the need to get to the bottom of a transportation accident. Here, the United States Customs Service required mandatory drug tests of all employees involved in on-the-border enforcement of drug and customs laws. This policy applied to all persons who were authorized to carry firearms. The Court found that government had a vital interest in inquiring into the trustworthiness and readiness of officers and employees who were to come in contact with criminal elements. Employees who take on such duties should reasonably expect inquiry into their fitness and probity.[66] In addition, different members of the Court found other vital governmental interests that were served by the testing policies: deterrence against corruption of employees, protection of sensitive information, preventing bribery, and bypassing the difficulty of discovering drug use by the more normal means of observing employee behavior on the job. These two cases laid out an ad hoc program-by-program balancing approach to drug testing, one that addresses a wide variety of specific procedures and objections to such procedures as well as allowing for flexibility in dealing with issues that lack established standards. It also leaves the door open to what Justice Thurgood Marshall in *Skinner* termed a "manipulable balanced inquiry." This is where the courts can see diminished expectations, diminished intrusions on one hand, and greater probability of harm, or greater breach of public trust, on the other.[67]

Justice Marshall's concerns have materialized in the cases that followed *Skinner* and *Von Raab*. The various agencies of the federal government set up drug programs that introduced different protocols of drug testing. These protocols included preemployment testing, post-accident testing, periodic random testing of employees, testing on reasonable suspicion of drug usage, and testing upon an employee's return to duty following drug or alcohol rehabilitation.

Preemployment drug testing has been consistently upheld by the courts. Even before *Skinner* and *Von Raab*, a court had upheld preemployment chemical testing for prospective employees who would work in special areas of nuclear power plants.[68] The privacy rights of applicants are distinguished from those of employees. Applicants can avoid costs to privacy by not applying for that particular position. The denial of possible employment is not seen as intrusive or deprivational as is the loss of a job. Preemployment testing carries with it advance notice of the tests themselves. Finally, the very process of being considered for a position carries with it a lesser expectation of privacy as prospective employers scrutinize the applicant's full employment history and all job-related background variables. A preemployment drug test is a one-time intrusion, is integrated into physical examinations that are part of the recruitment process, and does not allow for exercise of employer discretion that is necessarily present in post-accident, for-cause, or random testing.[69]

The *Skinner* decision made clear the overriding interests of the government in the imposition of drug tests in accident investigations. However, testing procedures and criteria must meet a two-prong reasonableness standard. First, testing must be applied only to those employees who caused or contributed to the accident. Second, testing of employees can be initiated after crossing a reasonably defined threshold of injury or property damage. Courts have affirmed testing programs where an accident has resulted in a fatality, significant injury, or property damage of at least $2,000.[70] However, courts have rejected a protocol that required drug tests of any employees of the Office of Personnel Management who were involved in any accident involving death or personal injury and damages greater than $1,000. A court found that isolated auto accidents did not evidence issue of a risk to the safety of the public.[71] The court also rejected the protocols of the Navy that allowed local officials discretion in setting the thresholds of personal injury and monetary damage.[72]

More challenges have been raised against systematic random testing than any other testing protocol. The reasonableness of such testing programs has hinged both on the nature of the governmental interest and the duties of the employees covered. Random drug testing protocols must be justified under compelling governmental interests, or special needs. These involve issues of public safety, protection of truly sensitive information, and maintenance of employee and agency integrity. The *Von Raab* decision justified on a public safety rationale the random testing of those law enforcement personnel who carry firearms. Dicta also extended the possibility of random testing of persons in those occupations where the discharge of duties is at all times "fraught with such risks to others that even a momentary lapse of attention can have disastrous consequences."[73] This consideration was extended to employees of private industries presenting hazards to the public and operating under close governmental regulation, such as the natural gas and liquid pipeline industries[74] and truck drivers using the nation's roads.[75] The overriding interest in securing safe airline traffic for the public made all commercial airline employees, including flight attendants, subject to random testing.[76] Within the federal government, safety considerations have been differentially applied. After the Navy and other branches of the armed services drafted a policy of random drug testing of service personnel, the Navy, in the interest of creating a totally drug-free workplace, drafted a policy for its civilian employees requiring random testing for forty-five different job classifications. The court found that a requirement of random testing for those involved in "equipment maintenance" or those who were employed in public health was overly broad. Such broad classifications brought the electric bulb changer and the dental hygienist under the policy. The defense agencies were to establish a clear nexus between the drug impairment for a particular job and a grave risk to public safety. Thus, random tests would be justified for those operating public carriers or nuclear vessels but not for an employee in a clerical position.[77] Courts have affirmed the application of random tests to federal employees who regularly drive motor vehicles, including bus drivers and chauffeurs.[78] The court suggested that in determining which employees were subject to tests, a line might be drawn between testing individuals whom government pays to transport passengers and testing individuals who drive on their own time. A gray line appears to exist between circumstances where risks of drug use affect the public safety and those where the danger is limited mainly to the individual to be tested.[79]

Random drug testing has also been approved for employees who handle sensitive information. Courts have indicated that random drug testing may be required of those employees with access to "secret" or "top secret" information. Government employees with such access have diminished expectations of privacy because of the sensitive nature of the information they handle and the processing they undergo for security clearance.[80] Beyond that such tests must be applied discriminatingly. A testing program that extended to all prosecutorial personnel in the U.S. Department of Justice was held to be overly broad. Internal agency security needs were not sufficient to justify systematic random tests.[81]

Random tests have also been justified in terms of maintaining employee integrity. *Von Raab* acknowledged that front-line drug interdiction personnel must exhibit unimpeachable integrity in performing their functions. Similarly, personnel who would be in contact with Department of Defense drug rehabilitation patients would come under the umbrella of random testing.

Another drug testing protocol involves subjecting an employee to a drug test on reasonable suspicion that the employee is engaging in abuse of a controlled substance. This suspicion must be based on specific objective facts and reasonable inferences drawn from these facts. Five criteria establish a reasonable suspicion:

1. direct observation of drug use or possession;
2. a pattern of abnormal conduct or aberrant behavior;
3. arrest or conviction for a drug-related offense or becoming the focus of a criminal investigation involving drug crimes;
4. information provided by reliable, credible sources with corroboration;
5. newly discovered evidence that employee has tampered, adulterated, or substituted a drug test.

The reasonable suspicion issue raises the question of moving forward with tests on the basis of off-duty behaviors and observation of off-duty impairment. Courts have, however, upheld such moves to the extent that such behaviors increase the risk of on-duty drug impairment or otherwise detract from job performance.[82]

TECHNOLOGICAL SURVEILLANCE

New technological advances have made available to employers a wide array of devices for monitoring the activities of employees. These include the accounting and monitoring of phone calls, oversight of the efficiency and accuracy of computer operations, computerized surveillance of vehicle usage, tracking of employee location, auditing of employees' computer files, tapping of E-mail transfers, and observation of the workplace areas by video cameras.[83]

These surveillance efforts are prompted by legitimate concerns. In the public as well as the private sector, theft of goods by employees may be a substantial problem. Surveillance may operate both as an enforcement mechanism and a deterrence against unauthorized or illegal activity. It may be used to determine if employees are following agency policies and if they are using their work time properly. Increased surveillance may be prompted by a heightened sense of liability to suit. The monitoring of the safety of operations may be important not only in preventing accidents but preventing lawsuits. But the best of motives may be open to abuse. For instance, the surveillance efforts may be focused on union-organization efforts, or concentrate on protected classes of employees to allow employers to prevail in mixed-motive personnel actions, or be used to identify whistle-blowers and troublemakers. Such abuse may be rare, but even with proper motives the techniques employed per se involve intrusions on the privacy expectations of individuals, expectations that must be balanced against the needs of the employer. Expectations of privacy may vary, with diminished expectations in the monitoring of performance and productivity to heightened expectations in the monitoring of behaviors (both on and off duty) to highest expectations in the monitoring of personal states (e.g. personal health, financial affairs, family relations, love life, political and social attitudes, personal stresses) where employees expect to be "left alone."

For instance, the monitoring of conversations in lounges during work breaks would be regarded as a monitoring of behaviors outside the employer's sphere of interest. The heightened expectation of privacy attached to oral conversations is recognized in legislation like the Federal Wiretap Act,[84] which prohibits both private and public employers from intercepting and recording the "wire communications" of employees. It is the conversations that are protected. For instance, employers may utilize cameras to observe employees and to provide security. But providing those cameras with audio capability could violate the Federal Wiretap Act. This is consistent with employees who may tolerate surveillance of bursar windows or mailrooms for security reasons but draw the line on any attempt to record their conversations.

The Federal Wiretap Act contains some critical exceptions that permit surveillance, exceptions that threaten to negate the protective benefits of the act. First, surveillance may proceed if employees give their consent to be monitored. Such consent may be implicit with an acceptance of employment. The second exception is known as the "business extension" exception, which excludes an expectation of privacy on the phones or other electronic devices provided for and used in the business.[85] Internal institutional policies can also be drafted to give notice to all employees that they restrict their use of phones or computers to agency business. Employers may intercept calls to determine if employees are making calls that are not authorized. However, an employer may not intercept a call to determine its contents or use the discovery of interspousal or private contents against an employee.[86] A California court has also indicated in dictum that employer eavesdropping would need to be limited to a particular place, time, and purpose to come under the business exception.[87] The growing utilization of E-mail in both private and public business has raised the issue of employer interception and review of E-mail files.[88] Interception and review of E-mail files is itself a reaction to possible abuses by employees who can utilize bulletin boards not only to discuss agency matters and exchange valid information but also to criticize administrators, libel employees, and generally disrupt efficient administration. By blocking the source of messages or using their own passwords, users can attempt to preserve the anonymity of their communications.[89] A recent case involving these issues has been decided in favor of employers. An employer had intercepted and reviewed personal E-mail messages, some including sexual messages. Terminated employees sued, claiming invasion of privacy. Employees claimed they had expectations of privacy since they were given their own passwords. The court, however, found that employees had no reasonable expectations of privacy in light of common knowledge that E-mail files were read by persons other than intended recipients.[90] In a more recent decision, a court in California ruled that company supervisors did not invade the privacy of an employee in monitoring and reading hundreds of messages the employee had sent through E-mail.[91]

The workplaces of the future can present an intimidating threat to the privacy interests of employees, particularly if the trend to develop full background information on employees and the trend to put close surveillance on their work activities merge. This scenario was developed in an article, "The Case of the Omniscient Organization," by Gary T. Marx, published in the *Harvard Business Review*.[92] A hypothetical industry called Dominion-Swann Industries subjected its employees to exhaustive medical and psychological testing at entry level and compiled a comprehensive employee database including full educational, credit, driving, military, and court histories. Periodic medical tests were employed to monitor long-term health. Workplace activity was electronically monitored and analyzed by computers. Periodic peer reviews were documented. The company collected a hard drive of information on every employee. Supposedly this allowed the company to achieve goal congruence whereby the organization and its employees would both fit into a specific organizational culture. It also helped the company make appropriate assignments, predict employee productivity and potential for advancement, and reduce employee turnover, sick leave, workplace accidents, theft, and disruptions of workplace harmony.

But the accomplishment of these goals comes at considerable cost. Intrusion becomes an organizational prime function that draws off considerable resources. In public agencies, the organization may be distracted from its public missions. The model of a "representative bureaucracy" that mirrors the pluralist views of society at large would be lost in the pursuit of internal goals that stress conformity. Public agencies expected to demonstrate respect for the civil rights and privacy expectations of citizens would betray that public trust.

CONCLUSION

This chapter examined the important factors related to privacy and employment. At issue is how public employers balance management's rights against employee privacy rights in the areas of recruitment, sexual orientation, grooming habits, workplace searches, drug testing, and technological surveillance. The complex web of statutes coupled with a voluminous amount of judicial opinion concerning privacy make the job of public management increasingly difficult. Managers must ensure that any intrusion in the area of privacy must be job-related. The checklist that follows is intended to assist with the development of agency policies in this very important personnel area. The sample substance abuse policy provides a concrete example of how agencies need to develop definitive policies with respect to privacy issues.

CHECKLIST FOR PUBLIC ADMINISTRATORS: PERSONNEL LAW QUESTIONS

1. Are recruitment applications and interviews purged of questions or inquiries that probe into areas where persons have a reasonable expectation of privacy?

2. Is information gathered in the recruitment or promotion process relevant to job performance or work potential?

3. Can all questions and inquiries in the recruitment or promotion process be validated in terms of skill measurement or prediction of job performance?

4. Do off-duty activities demonstrate a nexus to job performance or job and agency integrity?

5. Does the agency or office have a policy to react to possible charges of harassment of individuals because of their lifestyles? Is there an agency or office policy expressing a policy against discrimination of individuals for lifestyle?

6. Does the agency or office have a publicized policy giving notice to employees as to what behaviors may bring notoriety and discredit to the agency? Does the policy provide a rationale for such guidelines?

7. Is a drug-testing policy necessary for certain employees in terms of public safety considerations? Trust and integrity considerations?

8. Does the agency or office have a rehabilitation policy for employees with drug or alcohol problems?

9. Does a non-smoking policy for the workplace include commitments to assist employees in complying with the policy and becoming nonsmokers?

10. Is there a policy allowing for expectations of privacy in the workplace, for private space for employees in the workplace?

11. Are employees given notice of an agency policy that may allow entry of private spaces or work files?

12. Is there a clear policy as to the authorized uses of vehicles, office equipment, and communications?

13. Is any accounting of phone use, computer communications, and FAX use limited to time and destinations and not content?

14. What policy measures ensure the confidentiality of any employee's files?

15. Does the agency permit employee access of their own personnel files?

EXAMPLE OF SUBSTANCE ABUSE POLICY FOR FACULTY AND STAFF

Purpose

The University recognizes that the use of illegal drugs and abuse of alcohol and prescription drugs is a serious problem within our society. In response to this concern, the University is committed to the following goals:

1. To establish and enforce clear campus policies regarding the use of alcohol and illegal drugs.
2. To educate members of the campus community for the purpose of preventing alcohol abuse and illegal drug use.
3. To create a campus environment that promotes the individual's responsibility to him/herself and to the campus community.
4. To provide resources through counseling and referral services for students, faculty, and staff who experience alcohol- and other drug-abuse problems.

Policy

University policy prohibits the abuse of alcohol and use of illegal drugs as well as reporting for work or engaging in work or other University-related activities under the influence of alcohol or illegal drugs. Behaviors that suggest alcohol/drug abuse include (but are not limited to) the following:

1. Repeated accidents (on or off campus).
2. Repeated illness absences.
3. Chronic lateness or early departures.
4. Significantly diminished task performance (with no other explanation).
5. Odor of alcohol, slurred speech, unsteady gait, disorientation, paranoia, hallucinations, and other physical signs of impaired function not caused by a known medical condition.

A faculty or staff member who suspects that a colleague or co-worker is under the influence of alcohol or illegal drugs should contact his/her department chair or supervisor immediately. A faculty or staff member who suspects a supervisor or department head is under the influence of alcohol or other illegal drugs should contact the next level of supervision or administration.

If a department chair, supervisor, or administrator has been contacted or suspects that an individual is under the influence of drugs or alcohol, he/she should contact the Director of the Employee Assistance Program (Director of

Student Health), Personnel Services, or the next level of administration for assistance. The individual will be given an opportunity to discuss the situation. A person suspected or found to be under the influence of alcohol or other drugs and/or who may be incapable of performing his/her job will be sent home in a taxi. Anyone who insists on driving while suspected of being under the influence of alcohol or other drugs will be reported to authorities.

If a person admits to being under the influence of alcohol or illegal drugs, drug or alcohol testing of the individual may not be necessary. In these cases, a mandatory referral will be made for evaluation by a licensed addiction counselor on or off campus.

If it is determined that testing is necessary because of a critical incident in the workplace or because of safety concerns for the individual, colleagues, or coworkers, blood and/or urine testing procedures will be used. The University will pay the cost of all required drug or alcohol testings. Drug or alcohol testing may be conducted at the Student Health Service or other appropriate health agency, with test samples sent to a certified laboratory for analysis. Random drug or alcohol testing is not explicit or implicit in this policy.

An individual suspected or found to be under the influence of alcohol and/or illegal drugs will be referred for evaluation to a licensed addiction counselor and, if indicated, will be expected to participate in an appropriate treatment program for rehabilitation. If an individual refuses evaluation, refuses to participate in the appropriate treatment program, if it is indicated, or does not successfully complete the program, he/she will be subject to disciplinary actions up to and including dismissal.

If the individual is able to continue working while involved in the treatment program, his/her supervisor, department head, or department chair will determine if the individual is capable of performing regular job duties. If it is decided that the person should not work at his/her regular job, a temporary alternate job may be offered if one is available for which the person is qualified, or he/she will be placed on leave of absence with or without pay based on the appropriate leave of absence policy.

Conviction of Criminal Drug Statute Violation

Any faculty or staff member convicted of violating a criminal drug statute in this workplace must inform his/her department chair or the supervisor of such conviction (including pleas of guilty and nolo contendere) within five working days of the conviction occurring. Failure to so inform will subject the individual to disciplinary action up to and including dismissal for the first offense. Under the Drug-Free Workplace Act of 1988, the University will notify the federal contracting officer within ten days of receiving such notice from a faculty or staff member on a federal grant or contract or otherwise receiving notice of such a conviction.

The University reserves the right to offer individuals convicted of violating a criminal drug statute in the workplace participation in an approved rehabilitation or drug assistance program as an alternative to discipline. If such a program is offered and accepted by the faculty or staff member, he/she must satisfactorily participate in the program as a condition of continued employment.

Aftercare

Upon completion of the initial alcohol/drug treatment program, the individual may be monitored for up to two years by the supervisor/department head as determined by the treatment program.

As a part of the aftercare program, monthly reports from the licensed drug/alcohol treatment program will be submitted to the supervisor or department chair on the individual's progress while he/she is in the program. Reports of relapses and/or missed aftercare meetings also will be reported to the supervisor or department chair by the licensed alcohol/drug treatment program.

Noncompliance in the above-stated elements of the aftercare program will result in disciplinary actions up to and including dismissal.

Prescription Drugs

Although prescription drugs and over-the-counter drugs are legal, their use may be unsafe under certain circumstances. A person who is using a drug that impairs mental or physical functioning should inform his/her supervisor or department chair. The supervisor will be responsible for evaluating the individual's ability to work. If necessary, the faculty or staff member may be requested to obtain a statement from the prescribing physician authorizing the individual to work. If it is determined that it would be unsafe for an individual to work in the regular work setting, an alternative, temporary job may be offered if one is available for which the person qualifies. If no suitable job is available, the impaired person will be sent home.

Sale, Transfer, Possession of Illegal Drugs

Possession of illegal drugs (except possession of current prescription drugs) is prohibited and anyone in violation shall be subject to discipline. Any person who sells, manufactures, or distributes any illegal drugs on University property will be reported to the authorities and will be subject to dismissal.

Exercises

10.1 Personnel grievance 2 in appendix A concerns a privacy issue. Evaluate the facts and provide a memorandum assessing the merits of the case raised by the complainant.

10.2 Personnel grievance 5 challenges workplace regulations concerning smoking. Assess the merits of the employee's allegations.

10.3 Personnel management training has in recent years included sensitivity and training sessions that have as their objective the opening and improvement of channels of communication between employees and management. The sessions also incorporate activities that promote cultural diversity and greater interemployee tolerance. As part of these training sessions employees may be encouraged to reveal their concerns and problems in working with different groups or personalities. These training sessions often include role-playing and role reversals in which trainees act out unwelcome behaviors or problem relationships; group sessions in which participants reveal life histories, past experiences, or personal incidents of abuse, discrimination, or harassment; or stress scenarios in which participants are subjected to provocative or physically and mentally intimidating situations.

Discuss how these sessions might go so far as to violate the privacy of the participants or coerce participants to provide personal information that is not essential to job performance. Note the fact that the participants may believe that advancement depends on successful completion of the training program and compliant involvement. How might the personal information be misused?

10.4 An office manager has set up an electronic "suggestion box." Employees can register suggestions or complaints into an intra-office bulletin board that is read only by the director. The program blocks the source. When the suggestion box included some abusive and obscene comments and some unfounded and libelous allegations about another employee (who belonged to a protected class), the director utilized a tracer program to pinpoint the terminals from which the messages originated. The employee was disciplined, but he claimed that someone put out the message from his terminal and that the utilization of a tracer program was a violation of an entitlement to anonymity in putting messages into the suggestion box. The director claims he will respect the anonymity of sources but only as long as those communications are not libelous, threatening, or obscene. Discuss this issue.

Notes

1. 381 US 479 (1965).
2. See, for example, *Katz v U.S.*, 389 US 347 (1967), which extended the right to expectations of privacy in communications, and *U.S. v Orito*, 413 US 139 (1973), which extended expectations of privacy to those matters involving marriage, procreation, motherhood, childhood, and education. However, the Court more recently has tempered the "expectations" doctrine by holding that certain behaviors are not protected if they carry an assumption of risk of public exposure. *Smith v Maryland*, 442 US 735 (1979).
3. 401 US 424 (1971).

PUBLIC EMPLOYMENT AND PRIVACY 189

4. *National Federation of Federal Employees v Greenberg,* 789 F.Supp. 430 (D.C. Cir 1992), vac 983 F2d 286 (D.C. Cir 1993).
5. 42 U.S.C. sec. 12101–12213 (1991).
6. 451 F.Supp. 1355 (D. N.J. 1978).
7. See W. Grant Dahlstrom and Leona Dahlstrom, *Basic Readings on the M.M.P.I.: A New Selection on Personality Measurement* (Minneapolis: University of Minnesota Press, 1978).
8. 1 Cal. 2d 77 (1992).
9. This issue did not get a review before California's Supreme Court, which had granted review in the case. Before the court heard the case, the parties settled the suit, with the four plaintiffs splitting a $60,000 settlement. *National Law Journal,* 26 July 1993, p. 15.
10. Paul R. Sackett, Laura Burris, Christine Callahan, "Integrity Testing for Personnel Selection: An Update," *Personnel Psychology* 42 (1989), p. 491.
11. PL 100–347, 102 Stat. 646, et seq., 29 U.S.C. 2001.
12. For a comprehensive treatment of this subject, see Marvin Hill Jr. and Emily Delacenserie, *Procrustean Beds and Draconian Choices: Lifestyle Regulations and Officious Intermeddlers—Bosses, Workers, Courts, and Labor Arbitrators,* 57 Missouri L Rev 51 (1992).
13. 563 F.Supp. 585 (W.D. Mich. 1983).
14. 726 F2d 459 (9th Cir 1983), cert. denied, 469 US 979 (1984).
15. *Jackson v Howell,* 577 F.Supp. 47 (W.D. Mich. 1983).
16. *Fugate v Phoenix Civil Service Bd.,* 791 F2d 736 (9th Cir 1986).
17. 647 F.Supp. 799 (N.D. Ill. 1986).
18. *Pickering v Bd. of Education,* 391 US 563 (1968).
19. 701 F2d 470 (5th Cir 1983), cert. denied, 464 US 965 (1983). In a rare set of dissents to a denial of certiorari, Justices Brennan, Marshall, and Blackmun expressed outrage at the terminations. They felt that the employees were terminated without due process that afforded them notice of prohibited activity. There was no hint in the city's rules forbidding off-duty, legal, consensual sexual relations.
20. New York Laws 1992, chap. 776 (1992), codified in *N.Y. Labor Laws* (McKinney 1994), sec. 201d.
21. This would prohibit employment bars for off-duty smoking or drinking. An employer thus could not bar the employment of persons for having a smoking habit (such as is the policy of Cable News Network).
22. See Randall Samborn, "Love Becomes a Labor Law Issue," *National Law Journal,* 14 Feb. 1994, pp. 1, 33.
23. *New York v Wal-Mart Stores,* NY Sup. Ct., App. Div. 70609 (Jan. 1, 1994).
24. David S. Hames and Nickie Dierson, *The Common Law Right to Privacy: Another Incursion into Employers' Rights to Manage Their Employees?* 42 Labor L J 757 (Nov. 1991).
25. American Law Institute, "Restatement of the Law," *Torts,* 2d. ed. (1981), pp. 376–403.
26. See *Leggett v First Interstate Bank of Oregon,* 739 F2d 1083 (9th Cir 1987).

27. See *Cummings v Walsh Construction Co.* 561 F.Supp. 972 (D. Ga. 1983).
28. See *Note: Developments in the Law—Sexual Orientation and the Law*, 102 Harvard L Rev 1509 (May 1989), and Rhonda R. Rivera, *Queer* Law: Sexual Orientation Law in the Mid-Eighties*, 10 Dayton L Rev 481 (1985).
29. 411 US 677 (1973).
30. *Note: Constitutional Status of Sexual Orientation: Homosexuality as a Suspect Classification*, 98 Harvard L Rev 1285 (1985).
31. See *High Tech Gays v Defense Indus. Sec. Clear. Off.*, 668 F.Supp. 1361 (1987); *Watkins v U.S. Army*, 847 F2d 1329 (9th Cir 1988), 875 F2d 699 (9th Cir 1989).
32. 822 F2d 97 (D.C. Cir 1987).
33. The FBI also does not hire admitted homosexuals on grounds that agents must be free to be transferred to assignments in any of the states of the union, several of which still maintain sodomy laws. An agency will not accept the risk of an agent breaking local laws.
34. 668 F.Supp. 1361 (C. D. Calif. 1987).
35. *High Tech Gays v Defense Indus. Sec. Clear. Off.*, 895 F2d. 563 (9th Cir 1990).
36. 317 F2d 582 (D.C. Cir 1963). The case involved an air traffic controller fired after the employee admitted homosexual conduct. He was discharged even though he was married and had a son and a psychiatrist testified that the conduct represented an isolated incident of adolescent experimentation.
37. 417 F2d 1161 (D.C. Cir 1969).
38. U.S. Civil Service Commission, Orders 731-3, 41 Law Week 2032 (July 3, 1975).
39. *Ibid.*
40. 530 F2d 247 (9th Cir 1976).
41. *Gay Law Students Ass'n v Pacific Tel. and Tel. Co.*, 595 P2d 610–11 (Calif. 1979).
42. ACT-UP is an acronym for AIDS Coalition to Unleash Power. It has a tendency to put on demonstrations or displays that can be interpreted as outrageous or offensive and certainly as confrontational.
43. See Samuel A. Marcosson, *Harassment on the Basis of Sexual Orientation: A Claim of Sex Discrimination Under Title VII*, 81 Georgetown L J 1 (1992).
44. 54 Fair Empl. Prac. Cas. 81 (C. Kans. 1990).
45. See *Goluszek v Smith*, 697 F.Supp. 1452 (N. Ill. 1988); *Garcia v Elf Atochem North America*, 28 F3d 446 (5th Cir 1994); and *Hopkins v Baltimore Gas & Electric Co.*, (C. Md.), No. H-934167 (Dec. 28, 1994). These decisions have focused on hostile environments or lack thereof instead of the issue of quid pro quo advances whereby employment may have been on the line.
46. 29 C.F.R. sec. 1604.11(a).
47. See Hill and Delacenserie, *Procrustean Beds and Draconian Choices,* Note 114. The states are Alaska, Connecticut, Delaware, Hawaii, Maine, Massachusetts, Montana, Nebraska, North Dakota, Oregon, Virginia, and Washington.
48. *Ibid.* at Note 178, p. 89.
49. An example is California where Governor Pete Wilson vetoed a bill to protect homosexuals against job discrimination. But some thirteen cities have enacted antidiscrimination ordinances.
50. 425 US 139 (1976).

51. *Jacobs v Kuenes,* 541 F2d 222 (9th Cir 1976).
52. "Annotation: Employer's Enforcement of Dress or Grooming Policy As Unlawful Employment Practice Under Sec. 703(a) of Civil Rights Act of 1964 (42 U.S.C. sec. 2000e-2(a)) 27 ALRFed 274 (1976)."
53. *Drinkwater v Union Carbide Corp.,* 56 Fair Empl. Prac. Cas. 483 (1990). However, this is not to be regarded as a hostile environment bordering on sex harassment.
54. See *Knott v Missouri Pacific R.R.,* 527 F2d 1249 (8th Cir 1975); and *Fountain v Safeway Stores* 555 F2d 753 (9th Cir 1977).
55. For a survey of those cases, see Mollie H. Bowers, *What Labor and Management Need to Know About Workplace Smoking Cases,* 1992 Labor L J 40 (Jan. 1992).
56. These would include such concerns as health of patients under care of employees, handling of flammable materials, possible food contamination, or increase of health risks (as in the case of firefighters).
57. *Grussendorf v City of Oklahoma City,* 816 F2d 539 (10th Cir 1987).
58. Donald W. Garner, *Protecting Job Opportunities of Smokers: Fair Treatment for the New Minority,* 23 Seton Hall L Rev 417 (1993).
59. 480 US 709 (1987).
60. See *U.S. v Takela,* 923 F2d 665 (9th Cir 1991).
61. Heather L. Hanson, *The Fourth Amendment in the Workplace: Are We Really Being Reasonable,* 79 Virginia L Rev 243, at 258 (1993).
62. See Fed. Reg., vol. 51, no. 180 (Sept. 17, 1986). For a record of presidential remarks on the occasion, see *Weekly Compilation of Presidential Documents,* vol. 22, no. 38.
63. 489 US 602 (1989).
64. 489 US 656 (1989).
65. In addition to the loss of dignity involved in a urinalysis test, those tests could reveal a whole host of private medical facts about the employee.
66. *Von Raab,* 489 U.S. at 672.
67. For a discussion of the balancing issue, See Laura A. Lundquist, *Weighing the Factors of Drug Testing for Fourth Amendment Balancing,* 60 The George Washington L Rev 1151 (1992).
68. *Alverado v Wash. Public Power Supply System,* 759 P2d 427 (Wash. 1988). This case, decided in state court, affirmed the preemptive character of federal regulation in the area of nuclear power.
69. See Jonathon Hotzman, *Applicant Testing for Drug Use. A Policy and Legal Inquiry,* 33 Wm & Mary L Rev 47 (1991).
70. See *American Federation of Government Employees, Council 33 v Barr,* 794 F.Supp. 1466, 1477 (N. Cal. 1992), setting damage threshold at $2,000; *Int'l. Brotherhood of Teamsters v Dept. of Transportation,* 932 F2d 1292 (9th Cir 1991), setting damage threshold at $4,000; and *National Treasury Employees Union v Yeutter,* 733 F.Supp. 403, 416–17 (D.C. Cir 1990), which affirmed a threshold of $10,000 in property damages.
71. *Connelly v Newman,* 753 F.Supp. 293 (N.D. Calif. 1990).
72. *AFGE Local 1533 v Cheney,* 754 F.Supp. 1409, 1423–24 (N.D. Calif. 1990).
73. *Von Raab,* 489 US at 670.

74. *International Brotherhood of Electrical Workers, Local 1245 v Skinner,* 913 F2d 1454 (9th Cir 1990).
75. *International Brotherhood of Teamsters, Chauffeurs, Western Conference of Teamsters v Dept. of Transp.,* 932 F2d 1292 (9th Cir 1991).
76. 53 Fed. Reg. 47024 (Nov. 21, 1988), affirmed in *Bluestein v Skinner,* 908 F2d 451 (9th Cir 1990); and *Independent Union of Flight Attendants v FAA,* 908 F2d 451 (9th Cir 1990).
77. *American Federation of Government Employees, Local 1533 v Cheney* 754 F.Supp. 1409 (N.D. Calif. 1990).
78. See *AFGE v Skinner,* 885 F.2d 884 (D.C. Cir 1989), cert. denied, 495 US 923 (1990); and *National Treasury Employees Union v Yeutter,* 918 F2d 968 (D.C. Cir 1990).
79. See Lawrence A. Michaels and Adam Levin, "Courts are Divided on Drug Tests," *National Law Journal,* 24 Oct. 1994, p. B8.
80. *Harmon v Thornburgh,* 878 F2d 484 (D.C. Cir 1989); and *Hartness v Bush,* 919 F2d 170 (D.C. Cir 1990), cert. denied, 111 S. Ct. 2890 (1991).
81. *AFGE v Barr,* 794 F.Supp. 1466 (N.D. Calif, 1992).
82. See *Accord, AFGE v Cavazos,* 721 F.Supp. 1361, 1376–77 (D.C. Cir 1989); and *AFGE v Cheney,* 754 F.Supp. 1409 (N.D. Calif. 1990).
83. For a comprehensive discussion of the issues, see Robert G. Boehmer, *Artificial Monitoring and Surveillance of Employees: The Fine Line Dividing the Prudently Managed Enterprise From the Modern Sweatshop,* 41 DePaul L Rev 739 (1992).
84. 18 U.S.C. secs. 2510-2521 (1988) as amended by *Electronic Communications Privacy Act of 1986,* PL 99-508.
85. See 18 U.S.C. sec. 2510(5)(a). It excludes from the definition of electronic device "any device furnished to the subscriber or user by a provider of wire or electronic communication service . . . that is used by the subscriber or user or by the provider of the service in the ordinary course of its business."
86. *Watkins v L. M. Berry & Co.,* 704 F2d 583 (11th Cir 1983).
87. *People v Otto,* 9 Cal. Rptr. 2d 596 (1992).
88. Michael Traynor, "Computer E-Mail Privacy Issues Unresolved," *National Law Journal,* 31 Jan. 1994, p.S2f.
89. See Jonathon Gilbert, *Computer Bulletin Board Operator Liability for User Misuse,* 54 Fordham L Rev 439 (Dec. 1985); and Terri A. Cutrera, *Computer Networks, Libel, and the First Amendment,* 12 Computer L J 555 (No. 4, Dec. 1992).
90. *Bourke v Nissan Motor Corp. in U.S.A.,* B068705 (Cal. App., 2d Dist., Div. 4 (July 26, 1993)).
91. *Shoars v Epson America,* SWC 112749 (Ct. of Appeals for 2nd Dist. Calif.–L.A. (June 1994)), unpublished decision.
92. Gary T. Marx, "The Case of the Omniscient Organization," *Harvard Business Review* (Mar./Apr.) 1990, p. 12.

11

Racial Discrimination in Employment

Legal protections against racial and other forms of discrimination in employment date back to the days of the post-Civil War era. Congress passed the Civil Rights Act of 1866, which extended to all persons in all states and territories the same rights as white persons to make and enforce contracts, sue, be parties in action, and have full and equal benefit of all laws and proceedings for security of persons and property. Congress followed this with the passage of amendments in 1871 that allowed parties to use the federal courts to seek relief to remedy actions whereby persons acting under color of state or territorial law deprived those citizens of any constitutional right or privilege.[1] The reach of these statutes was not extended to the property interests and contractual dimensions of public employment, and suits to redeem employment rights were almost nonexistent until 1961.[2] Public employers were also insulated from suit by the doctrine of sovereign immunity.[3] At present, suits under Sections 1981, 1983, and 1985 of Chapter 42 of the U.S. Code (which have their source in the 1866 and 1871 Civil Rights Acts) cover many of the same claims that constitute intentional discrimination under Title VII of the 1964 Civil Rights Act.[4]

At the federal level, the first legal protections against employment discrimination came in 1940 when Congress mandated employment on the basis of merit in the federal government without regard to race, creed, or color.[5] As a result, African Americans moved into the federal government employment in large numbers, especially into postal positions. Yet even there they remained crowded into the lower ranks.[6]

From 1941 to 1960, Presidents Roosevelt, Truman, Eisenhower, and Kennedy took executive actions to ensure nondiscrimination in federal employment. President Franklin Roosevelt established a Fair Employment Practices Committee in 1941 to bar discrimination in defense industry employment.[7] President Eisenhower indicated it was public policy to promote equal employment opportunity for all qualified persons employed on government contracts. President Kennedy reinforced that position with the executive order of March 6, 1961.[8] In the implementation of that order, the President's Committee on Equal Employment Opportunity drew up a ten-point plan that outlined the first affirmative action steps directing public employers and state employment offices to reanalyze all available jobs to ensure consideration of minority group members; to seek out, recruit, refer, and encourage the application of minority group members; to establish training programs that would bring such applicants to qualified status; and to monitor all efforts to bring minorities into the federal workforce.

It was not, however, until the passage of Title VII of the Civil Rights Act of 1964 that a broad-based anti-discrimination statute was put in place able to address discrimination in employment in plenary fashion. The act prohibited discrimination in the hiring and discharge of any individual or in respect to compensation, terms, conditions, or privileges of employment because of an individual's race, color, religion, national origin, or sex. Title VII applied to private employers, labor unions, and employment agencies. Amendments in 1966 broadened the definition of employer to include state and political subdivisions insofar as they employed persons working in hospitals, institutions, or schools.[9] In 1972 Congress extended coverage of the act to state and local governments, citing principles of the Constitution of the United States, especially the due process clauses and the enabling clauses of the Thirteenth and Fourteenth Amendments.[10]

TITLE VII: CIVIL RIGHTS ACT OF 1964 APPLICATIONS

Title VII on its face is applicable to employment decisions that are discriminatory, whereby employers or supervisors reject, demote, or terminate an employee on the basis of an employee's race, religion, national origin, or sex, or whereby they subject that protected employee to working conditions different from those imposed on the workforce generally. The Equal Employment Opportunity Commission (EEOC) is charged with implementation of the statutes, and all charges of Title VII violations must first be brought before the EEOC or a state referral agency. The statute did not define discrimination as such and left to the courts the identification of discrimination in different employment circumstances. Courts would recognize two ways in which an employer could violate the statute. One was disparate treatment of an employee, the less favorable treatment of an employee vis-à-vis the other employees because of race or one of the other impermissible reasons. Disparate treatment is challenged in individual cases, and a plaintiff must demonstrate that the employer had intentionally discriminated against the employee or had an unlawful motive. The processing of claims of disparate treatment begins with the initiation of a complaint with the EEOC. The EEOC will investigate the claim and, if the agency finds "reasonable cause" to believe that discrimination was directed at an employee the EEOC will notify the employee that he or she has a cause and a right to sue in federal court. Reasonable cause to sue is easy to establish where there is direct evidence of discriminatory conduct (e.g., a sign on the hiring door, "Blacks need not apply"). The Supreme Court also recognized that a complainant may have a prima facie case (one where it is more likely than not that the defendant has discriminated) where certain circumstances provide an inference of discrimination. In *McDonnell-Douglas Corporation v Green* (1973)[11] and *Texas Dept. of Community Affairs v Burdine* (1981),[12] the Supreme Court identified threshold conditions that would establish a prima facie case of individual and intentional discrimination.[13]

1. The aggrieved employee demonstrates that he or she is a member of a class protected under Title VII.
2. The applicant applied for a vacant position and had the qualifications to perform the job.
3. Although the applicant was qualified, the applicant was rejected.
4. After rejection, the position remained open and the employer continued to seek applications for persons equally qualified.

All this provides an adverse inference that an applicant was rejected because of his or her minority status. This creates a factual foundation that stands until rebutted by the employer. An employer can rebut a prima facie case by proffering a legitimate and nondiscriminatory reason to account for the rejection or adverse action.[14] In *McDonnell-Douglas,* the employer was able to justify the refusal to hire an employee by bringing up incidents of prior misconduct. The employee had taken part in an unlawful, disruptive stall-in as a protest to the employer's policies. The rebuttal did not end the matter. The Court ordered that the employee be afforded a fair opportunity to show that the stated reason for the employee's rejection was only a pretext for rejecting him on racial grounds. Such a hearing would clarify the hanging question as to whether McDonnell-Douglas had rehired or retained white employees who had also participated in the disruptive activities attributed to the black employee. In this process the burden of persuasion shifts back and forth. The employee alleges discrimination; the employer raises a different and legitimate motive; the employee claims the motive is pretextual. Within this process, the plaintiff always has the burden of proof and the ultimate task of persuading fact finders and a court.[15]

This was affirmed in a 1993 decision of the U.S. Supreme Court in *St. Mary's Honor Center v Melvin Hicks*.[16] A correctional officer became the subject of repeated and increasingly severe disciplinary actions. He was suspended, reprimanded, demoted, and finally discharged. The officer then brought an action under 42 U.S.C. 1983, alleging that he had been discharged because of his race. The district court concluded that Hicks had proven the existence of a crusade to harass and intimidate him on the job, but he had not proven the existence of a crusade that was racially motivated.[17] The court of appeals discredited the employer's proffered reasons and thus the prima facie case stood unrebutted. The issue remained whether as a matter of law the plaintiff would prevail.

The Supreme Court sided with the district court. The Supreme Court devised a two-prong test to determine whether a proffered reason was a pretext for discrimination. One had to demonstrate both that the reason given for the adverse action was false and also that racial animus was the real reason. It was not enough to disbelieve the employer. Evidence of intentional racial discrimination must exist and be persuasive with the trier of fact.

While some commentators have labeled the *Hicks* decision as one that is unfair to those bringing discrimination claims,[18] a realistic application of the decision to the real world of personnel administration provides instructive lessons to both claimants and employers. The court decision emphasizes the importance of the development of a complete record of what gave rise to the suit. Employees need to construct a file of those incidents that give both direct and inferential evidence of discriminatory conduct or predisposition. Employers need not only to profer a nondiscriminatory reason to rebut a prima facie case, they should also be prepared to back any reason with a documented record of what might have led to the adverse action (incidents of misconduct, incompetence, or violations of rules and policies). Both parties should be prepared to back up anecdotal information and to respond to discovery motions. Fact finders will thus have sufficient articulated evidence in which to ground their decision.

The Supreme Court has also recognized a second means of establishing violations under Title VII, that of demonstrating that employer practices had a collective adverse and discriminatory impact on a class of employees. These practices or rules may be nondiscriminatory on their face but they may create differentials between whites and minority groups in hiring or advancement rates or may carry a vestige of past discrimination. In *Griggs v Duke Power Company* (1971),[19] the Supreme Court laid out the finding that employment policies or decisions that had the effect of collectively disfavoring a protected class or eliminating or diminishing employment opportunities for a protected class could be interpreted as illegal discrimination. Disparate impact of an employment practice or policy on a protected class can be grounds for a charge of discrimination. In the *Griggs* case, the issue was a power company's reliance on high school diplomas and a general intelligence test as occupational qualifications for field workers. Under these testing procedures,

Blacks were disparately affected because statistically fewer Blacks than whites qualified for the positions.

Griggs provided a two-step analysis for determining whether selection criteria violated Title VII as a disparate impact case.

1. The determination of whether selection and promotion criteria have an adverse impact on members of any race or ethnic group. Without a finding of disparate impact the court is precluded from further inquiry.

2. Once it is shown that a given requirement or selection criterion selects applicants in a racial pattern different from the pool of applicants, the employer bears the burden of showing that the requirement has a clear relationship to a qualification for employment. The employer must prove that the tests are validated for job-relatedness. The touchstone of a legitimate requirement or test would be business necessity and relation of the selection procedure to job performance. *Griggs* also removed the necessary condition of intention to commit discriminatory acts. It proscribed not only overt acts of discrimination but also those "built in headwinds to minorities" that are fair in form but discriminatory in result by either conscious or unconscious design.

The Supreme Court further developed the standards that allow for a determination of disparate impact. In determining whether the recruitment process tended to screen out minorities, the fact finder was to consider the qualifications of the position and then relate the recruitment levels for minorities to the proportion of minority members in the available community who were qualified for those positions.[20] Disparate impact cases thus involve complex statistical and demographic analysis to determine whether it is more likely than not that the employer has engaged in discriminatory practices.[21] The employer, in rebuttal to charges of employing a discriminatory selection or promotion system, can defend the system in terms of a business necessity. For instance, the employer may argue that his selection criteria promotes greater safety in the workplace. The Supreme Court relaxed the business necessity justification in the decision *Wards Cove Packing Co. v Antonio* in 1989.[22] The Court indicated that a challenged practice affecting personnel selection did not have to be so necessary to the functioning of the business that it was indispensible. It only had to serve a legitimate employment goal. The decision may be compared with *Washington et al. v Davis* (1976),[23] where the Supreme Court upheld the District of Columbia Police Department's use of a standard personnel test focusing on verbal competencies even though it had the effect of disproportionately disqualifying African Americans. A legitimate public sector goal thus might involve a collateral asset to a bona fide occupational qualification. This might involve the upgrading of the workforce communication skills or the recruitment of persons with a higher level of awareness of public issues. Such an interpretation was, in fact, the object of a legislative compromise in the 1991 Civil Rights Act in which employment rights proponents won a codification of the disparate impact theory and employer interests obtained a recognition that the employer's defense of business necessity would prevail if the challenged practices were job-related.[24]

The public workplace is also not immune from a form of discrimination that has been termed "systematic intentional discrimination."[25] In such instances a substantial proportion of a protected class in the workplace is subjected to disparate treatment and individualized discrimination. Work rules, policies, disciplinary actions, and advancements are enforced to favor one class of employees over another. Class-action suits under Title VII may be instituted to establish a prima facie case under both the disparate treatment and disparate impact theories. Anecdotal and statistical evidence on disparities can build such a case. High-level federal agencies such as the Drug Enforcement Agency (DEA) and the Federal Bureau of Investigation (FBI) have been the target of such suits.[26] African-American agents in the DEA and Hispanic agents in the FBI sued their agencies because of alleged discrimination in allocation of assignments, supervisory evaluation, discipline, and promotion. The courts in both cases recognized many of the claims of the plaintiffs and ordered the agencies to devise and implement procedures that would prevent a dual standard of personnel administration.

RACIAL HARASSMENT IN THE WORKPLACE

Under the differential treatment standard, Title VII extends protections against racial harassments in the workplace. Judge Goldberg in *Rogers v E.E.O.C.* (1971) expressed the view

> that employees' psychological as well as economic fringes are entitled to protection from employer abuse and that the phrase "terms, conditions or privileges of employment" in Section 703 is an expansive concept that sweeps within its protective ambit the practice of creating a working environment heavily charged with ethnic or racial discrimination . . . One can readily envision working environments so heavily polluted with discrimination as to destroy completely the emotional and psychological stability of minority group workers and I think section 703 of Title VII was aimed at the eradication of such noxious practices.[27]

Like discriminatory action claims, hostile environment charges of this sort are filed with the EEOC. The employer is notified of the charges and the EEOC typically investigates, then attempts to arrange a conciliation between the parties. The role of the agency is to educate and to encourage cooperation and voluntary compliance as a preferred means of settling these disputes.

Courts have ruled that a working environment dominated by racial slurs constitutes a violation of Title VII. However, to rise to the level of a statutory violation, the derogatory behavior must be ongoing, frequent, and part of a pattern. Racial comments or jokes that are part of a casual conversation, that are accidental or sporadic do not trigger Title VII sanctions.[28]

Hostile environment harassment charges have shown a tendency to become entwined with disciplinary actions and terminations. An employee may be fired for a "legitimate" reason; the employee then raises the issue of a pattern of racial insensitivity that suggests that racial animus played a part in the employer's decision. As the case *Bibbs v Block* (1985)[29] illustrates, the issue then becomes one of determining whether race was a discernible factor in the decision. A finding that it was a discernible factor establishes intentional discrimination and liability under Title VII. With the employer proffering nondiscriminatory reasons for an adverse action, it becomes the role of the court to determine if the racial factor was a substantial, motivating, and determining factor in the adverse decision.[30] "But for the racial element," the employee would have been promoted. In *E.E.O.C. v Alton Packaging* (1990)[31] evidence of stray racial slurs by the employer was found to constitute direct evidence of discrimination, but the employer demonstrated through a preponderance of evidence that the African-American employee would not have been promoted in any case. When the employer brought forward a record of nine reprimands for unexcused absences, tardiness, production errors, and falsification of records, he was able to show that the complainant was simply not qualified to be a supervisor. Claims of racial harassment also bring up questions of constructive discharge. The employer may not terminate the employee but the atmosphere may be perceived as so intolerable that an employee is forced to resign and the employer is held liable for the termination.

Employees facing adverse action may also file complaints of harassment or a racially hostile environment in anticipation of adverse action. If the employer then terminates the employee, the employee may raise the issue of retaliatory discharge for filing a complaint against the employer.[32] While there may be cases where marginal employees may attempt to utilize hostile environment charges as a distraction from performance or misconduct issues, discrimination victims appearing before congressional committees have testified that many workers simply want the harassment to stop and would raise the issue but are afraid to speak out for fear of losing their jobs.[33] The outcome of these cases is very much influenced by the factual circumstances. Any resolution must involve a disentanglement of the facts and conflicting claims. Documentation becomes critical in providing the EEOC or the court of the correct picture of the working environment.

It should be noted that a retaliation constitutes an independent violation under Section 704 of Title VII of the Civil Rights Act, a charge that can be raised by an employee for bringing any claim of discrimination. A retaliation can involve a wide range of actions in which the employer alters the grievant employee's job status or conditions of employment. It can include subjecting the employee to additional harassment, selective enforcement of work rules against the employee, taking away an employee's resources or job functions, keeping exclusively adverse records about an employee, or transferring the employee laterally to a different position even without any reduction in salary or benefits.[34]

REVERSE DISCRIMINATION

It is well established that white persons may bring suits under Title VII or Sections 1981 or 1983. The title makes any race a class protected against race discrimination. That was indicated in *McDonald v Santa Fe Trail Transportation Co.* (1976),[35] when two white employees who were discharged for theft made the case that their discharge was discriminatory because a black employee who was also involved was not sanctioned. White employees can even bring reverse discrimination suits under 42 U.S.C. 1981, which gives the same contractual rights to black and white employees. Of course, the *McDonnell-Douglas* requirement of belonging to a racial minority does not apply in establishing a prima facie case of discrimination against whites. In place of this requirement, those attempting to develop the inference that the employer's minority preference policy discriminates against whites support their claims with a bill of particulars of background circumstances.[36] What these background circumstances may be can vary both as to incidental evidence and weight of that evidence. It can include such things as evidence of political pressure, monopoly of personnel and selection decisions by minority members, irregular acts of favoritism, and inconsistency in applying selection criteria.[37] One defense that employers may raise to counter claims of reverse discrimination is that actions were taken in accordance with a bona fide affirmative action plan.

AFFIRMATIVE ACTION

Title VII forbids discrimination in employment. But the exposure and sanction of discriminatory acts and practices is only an initial step in achieving and assuring conditions of equal opportunity within the affected workplace. The key to achieving a condition of equal opportunity is not only to eliminate the illegal practice but also to make things whole. In the case of discrimination that has effected a harm on an individual employee, a series of different remedies may be directed, such as re-evaluation, reinstatement, promotion, backpay, or damages. In the matter of disparate impact cases, the question becomes "What can be done to remedy practices that have deprived employment opportunities to unknown numbers of minority employees or applicants?" Affirmative actions are taken to make things whole but even after thirty years of experience with Title VII, a great deal of controversy still exists over the range of allowable actions that may be taken to affirmatively address a discrimination problem.

Affirmative action may be remedial, prophylactic, or preferential.[38] The following is a rank order of actions to affirmatively address employment opportunity issues along a continuum from remedies that simply eliminate discriminatory rules and procedures to those that require a restructuring of the employment environment, that change employer/employee relationships, and that diversify the workplace and create a representative bureaucracy.[39]

Affirmative Action Ladder

1. Rules, practices, norms, or qualifications that have an effect of discriminating against an employee are invalidated and prohibited.
2. Employer implements alternate selection tests or measures that exhibit a more valid relationship to job performance (which may be put forward by litigants in the suit to show that other tests or selection devices without an undesirable racial effect would still serve employer's legitimate interests).
3. Employer undertakes affirmative recruitment of minorities and protected classes by advertising for open positions in the minority labor pool. Employer makes effort to contact potential minority applicants, to encourage minority applicants to seek positions and promotions. This is known as targeting.
4. Employer assists applicants in meeting employment qualifications by providing preemployment training and remedial education, a practice known as bootstrapping.
5. Employer makes minority or protected status (e.g., race, gender, or disability) a consideration in selection or promotion.
6. Employer may adjust qualifications to allow minorities or protected class to meet requirements at standards different than normally relied upon. This is often termed adjustment of threshold scores or within-groupnorming.
7. Employer takes steps to redress imbalance of minority or protected workers in the workforce. This may be done by establishment of goals and timetable to meet those goals or by utilization of quotas in selection and promotion processes.

Within this scale four affirmative action policies have been particularly controversial. These are quotas, threshold measures to gauge violations, race-norming, and voluntary affirmative action.

Quotas

Quotas as an affirmative action mechanism have always been suspect. During the debate on the civil rights bill in 1963 and 1964, even liberal sponsors like Rep. Immanuel Cellar and Sen. Hubert Humphrey expressed the concern that nondiscrimination rules would mandate employers to create a racially balanced workforce. Amendments to the Civil Rights Act of 1972 clearly indicated that no employer would be required to grant preferential treatment to any individual or group on account of an imbalance that may exist with respect to total number or percentage of persons of any race, color, sex, or national origin.[40] While this provision prohibited agencies from requiring employers to give preferential treatment to groups that were underrepresented in an employment classification, it did not take away the power of the courts to utilize quotas as *remedial* instruments to redress injuries incurred through past discrimination.

Following the *McDonnell-Douglas* case, courts not only enjoined use of tests that produced disparate impacts but they also imposed selection procedures that employed set-asides and quotas. A pool of qualified applicants would be established and a public employer was to make appointments and promotions from such a pool according to ratios determined by the court.[41]

The Supreme Court has been inclined to favor quotas only where it is necessary to address and redress the lingering effects of past discrimination. In the case *U.S. v Paradise* decided in 1987, the court by a narrow margin affirmed a judicial order imposing on the Alabama Department of Public Safety an order to hire and promote African Americans on a one-to-one basis with white officers. The quotas were justified in light of a four-decade record of the Department's exclusion of African Americans and a record of delay and frustration in implementing orders dating back to 1972. A one-to-one requirement was necessary to eliminate the effects of long-term open and pervasive discrimination.[42]

The position of the Court in upholding quotas as remedial mechanisms hangs by a slender thread. In the *Paradise* case Justices White, O'Connor, Rehnquist, and Scalia found quotas an impermissible approach to remedy past discrimination. This bloc has consistently rejected the use of strict racial quotas or any mechanisms that had the effect of displacing innocent nonminority workers. They have rejected the view that affirmative action policies can be utilized to remedy societal discrimination, and they would also limit the remedies to those applicants or workers who were actually the object of discriminatory acts.[43]

Thresholds for Violations

In response to the *Griggs* case and its attention to the consequences of using selection procedures that produce a disparate impact on candidates for employment, the EEOC issued guidelines for employers covered by Title VII that would assist them in complying with it.[44] These guidelines were not administrative regulations issued under the rule-making procedures set in the Administrative Procedures Act but were published as interpretive rules of Title VII.[45] The guidelines emphasized requirements that the tests utilized in job selection be job-related and professionally validated for job-relatedness. The guidelines also defined discrimination as the use of any selection procedure that had an adverse impact on a protected group. A mathematical measure for disparate impact was provided in terms of a four-fifths rule that would regard as evidence of adverse impact a selection rate for any race, ethnic group, or protected group as 80 percent less than the selection rate for the highest group.[46] To ensure that companies and agencies meet these standards, employers are required to maintain and have available records showing the number of persons hired, promoted, and terminated for each job by race, sex, and national origin. Records are to be maintained for each race and national origin group constituting more than 2 percent of the labor force in the relevant labor area. These guidelines were challenged but the Supreme Court upheld them in *Albemarle Paper Company v Moody* in 1975[47] and *Connecticut v Teal* in 1982.[48] The Court indicated that one of the primary purposes of Title VII was the prophylactic one of achieving equality of employment opportunities and removing barriers to such equality. The EEOC guidelines have a strong impact on the playout of discrimination charges against employers. EEOC investigations into the pattern or practice of discrimination focus on employment statistics to determine if there are disparities in hiring or recruiting that could not be expected on the basis of chance.

While the EEOC guidelines are prophylactically intended to prevent employers from falling into discriminatory practices, the specific approaches indicated, such as the four-fifths rule, the mapping out of relevant labor markets, and the comparative analysis to determine which applicants on file are hired as vacancies occur, are all race-conscious employment practices that in effect encourage implicit quotas. Employers who fail to keep adequate race data records are particularly vulnerable to complaints and suits charging discrimination. Employers who take the view that they will be color-blind and hold that race or ethnic origin is totally irrelevant in employment decisions may be open to charges of rejecting an indistinguishable Native American or Honduran or Mormon or any member of a protected group constituting more than 2 percent of the employers' labor market. Employers could protect themselves by asking about minority status, but employers are not allowed to ask.[49] The guidelines, while intended to assist employers public and private, also have the effect of making them walk a tightrope in which they render themselves vulnerable to charges of reverse discrimination while attempting in good faith to avoid possible disparate impact charges.

Race-Norming

The practice of adjusting scores to facilitate the hiring of qualified minority applicants was affirmed as a remedial practice in *Connecticut v Teal*, in which an adjustment of the passing score was made to lessen the disparate impact of the test involved.[50] Race-norming was a practice of choosing applicants not strictly on the basis of the highest scores of the entire applicant population but on the basis of the highest *qualifying* scores within each group of applicants classed by race or ethnic origin. The Department of Labor in 1981 encouraged state employment agencies to use score adjustment strategies in administering the General Aptitude Test Battery.[51]

Court decisions also affirmed adjustment of scores where steps had to be taken to compensate for a history of racial discrimination. In *Guardians Association of N.Y. City Police Dept. v Civil Service Commission of City of New York* (1981),[52] the Second Circuit ruled as discriminatory the administration of a test that had a passing rate for whites of 49 percent, 20.5 percent for Hispanics, and 17 percent for African Americans. While not explicitly affirming race-norming, the court did press the commission to focus on using content-valid tests that identified all those who would be qualified for the open positions, minority or nonminority. The commission could then identify the qualified minority applicants who had to be recruited to compensate for prior discrimination. The courts would also affirm the race-norming practice as long as it did not render an exclusionary effect on nonminority candidates.[53] Race-norming was an approach to prevent those who score better on employment tests generally, irrespective of the predictive value of those tests on job performance, from dominating in the selection procedure and disproportionately getting most of the jobs.[54]

However, Congress in 1991 placed an express provision in the Civil Rights Act of 1991 that made it an unfair labor practice for employers to adjust scores, use different cutoff scores, or otherwise alter employment-related tests because of race, color, religion, sex, or national origin.[55] Congressional proscription of race-norming appears to have been a sacrifice to political accommodation to allow for passage of the 1991 Civil Rights Act.

Following passage of the Act, a remedial practice known as "banding" was challenged as violating a provision of the Act that indicates that an unlawful employment practice is established when the complaining party demonstrates that race, color, religion, sex, or national origin was a motivating factor for any employment practice even though other factors motivated the decision.[56] Banding replaces strict rank-order selection with selection of candidates from a band of scores embraced by the statistical-measure standard deviation. Differences between scores within a band are considered to be statistically insignificant and are treated as identical. Minority candidates within a band or distribution of most qualified individuals would be selected first. When no minorities remained, the highest scorers would be selected until the band "slid" down to encompass additional minority candidates. Race would thus be the paramount consideration in selection of candidates within a band. San Francisco utilized a banding selection system in evaluating and promoting its police officers; police officers' associations challenged the practice as violating Sections 107(a) and 106, which made it unlawful to "adjust the scores of or use different cutoff scores for or otherwise alter the result of employment related tests on the basis of race, color, religion, sex or national origin." The Ninth Circuit upheld the selection procedures.[57] It noted that the procedure was a necessary remedy to supplant examinations that had been ruled to have produced adverse impacts on minorities. To meet the requirements of a consent decree the public employer proposed to band the scores, a procedure that would mitigate adverse impact of the examinations. The court noted that the procedure was itself approved by the U.S. Supreme Court as a mitigation of test scores as an imprecise measure of future job performance.[58] It also saw that the practice was consistent with *The Uniform Guidelines on Employee Selection Procedures*,[59] which were not displaced by the 1991 Civil Rights Act. The Court did not address the question extended by the police associations that any plan or remedy that even utilized race as a "plus" would be an impermissible approach to correct racial imbalance.

Voluntary Affirmative Action

The first case in which the Supreme Court dealt with an affirmative action program at a public institution was the landmark case *Regents of University of California v Bakke*,[60] decided in 1978. The Supreme Court had the opportunity to review the use of a special program that admitted a finite number of minority applicants into a California medical school. Justice Powell was able to obtain sufficient support on the Court to declare the program unconstitutional. The program provided for a quota-based selection process that was closed to whites. The compelling reason that justified remedial quotas was absent in this case because there was no indication of a previous history of racial discrimination in the medical school's short history. Justice Powell in dicta did not rule out consideration of race in selection systems. Because selection of a diverse student body was an important objective for the medical school, the school could, in a competitive process between individual applicants, attach a plus to an applicant's race. But race would be only one factor among many merit factors and could not by itself be determinative of selection.

Then the Supreme Court reviewed a private sector voluntary affirmative action plan in *United Steelworkers of America v Weber* (1979).[61] While the case involved a bargaining agreement between a major corporation and a union, the Court's approval of the affirmative action plan involved did provide a three-prong test that was applied to public sector affirmative action plans.

1. The plan is designed to break down entrenched and existing patterns of racial segregation (or exclusion) and hierarchy. It is structured to "open" opportunities for those to which employment was closed.
2. The plan does not necessarily trammel the interests of white employees.
3. The plan is a temporary measure. It is not intended to maintain a racial balance but to eliminate a "manifest" racial imbalance.

The federal government has been pursuing the goal of introducing affirmative action plans into federal agencies since 1969 when President Nixon issued Executive Order 11478,[62] which mandated that all agencies establish affirmative action programs that would provide maximum feasible opportunities for minorities and women to enter and enhance their skills in the federal workforce. These early programs for the most part adhered to steps 1 through 4 of the affirmative action ladder (see below). Following *Weber* and *Bakke*, the EEOC in January 1979 published its final affirmative action guidelines.[63] The guidelines provided that employers or labor organizations could voluntarily develop affirmative action plans in the absence of a requirement to develop such a plan by court order or direction of a federal agency or a state employment rights agency. These voluntary plans would be classed as "unapproved plans." In order to protect an employer against reverse discrimination claims, such voluntary plans had to meet the following criteria:

1. An affirmative action plan must be designed to achieve the objectives of Title VII, to break down old patterns of segregation and hierarchy, and to overcome effects of past discrimination.

2. An affirmative action plan must be designed to solve a problem disclosed by self-analysis. An employer need not admit to past or present discrimination to adopt a plan, but the analysis should determine whether discrimination existed in the past or still exists and whether steps taken have done enough to remedy that discrimination.

3. Self-analysis is the process by which an employer determines whether its employment practices limit, exclude, or restrict employment opportunities for minorities or women. A self-analysis should look for the existence of adverse impact, disparate impact, or policies and practices that leave uncorrected the effects of past discrimination. It should include a review of compliance with all federal, state, and local laws prohibiting employment discrimination. It should include a review of procedures used for hiring, promotion, merit increases, demotions, discharge, and layoffs to determine if any produce an adverse impact on employment opportunities for minorities and women. Finally, it should include a determination of possible underutilization of minorities and women by means of a demographic analysis (this may vary from a locality survey to a Standard Metropolitan Statistical Area survey to a national survey of employment patterns).

4. An affirmative action program must be a comprehensive, reasoned program rather than a reaction to one or more isolated corrective actions.

5. An affirmative action program must be temporary, in effect only as long as necessary to achieve the plan's objective.

6. An affirmative action plan must avoid unnecessary restriction on the opportunities of the workforce as a whole.

7. An affirmative action plan must contain specific objectives, numerical or otherwise, for a workforce operating under conditions of equal opportunity. Goals and timetables may be included. The exact steps to achieve goals need not be specified but intentions must be stated.

8. An affirmative action plan should include monitoring procedures, an internal audit, and a reporting system to measure the effectiveness of the program.

Public agencies tended to stretch the envelope in terms of the parameters of these guidelines, and the issue of voluntary action plans of public agencies came to the dockets of the courts.[64] In *Johnson v Transportation Agency of Santa Clara County* (1987),[65] the Supreme Court addressed the issue of a local government affirmative action plan that established a goal of redressing an underrepresentation of protected groups (ethnic minorities, women, and disabled) in the county's workforce at all job positions. The affirmative action plan was invoked in the selection of a woman for "road dispatcher." After considering the top candidates, the selection board considered the sex of the applicant as a factor in meeting its affirmative action goals only after an affirmative action director had intervened. A male with a marginally higher score challenged the selection and the plan. When the Supreme Court received the case it had before it two prime issues, whether a plan that was directed at responding to a "manifest imbalance" in job hires of protected classes was constitutionally permissible, and whether consideration of gender (or another protected classification) in a closely competitive selection was justified in terms of legitimate objectives or whether it was determinative of the choice and thus impermissible. The Court by a narrow 5-4 margin found that an affirmative action plan could address a manifest imbalance in the workforce, especially in a case where a class was egregiously underrepresented (or represented by an inexorable zero as noted by Justice O'Connor).[66] The consideration of the applicant's gender to meet affirmative action goals was legitimate in that this did not insulate the applicant from being compared with all other applicants in regard to all qualifying factors. Also, the challengers did not have an entitlement to the position. Seven of the applicants were qualified and the director could choose any one of them.

Following *Johnson*, courts have demonstrated a spotty record in approving voluntary affirmative action plans. Federal courts have not given a general green light on voluntary affirmative action plans. In the District of Columbia, courts muddled through several cases involving public agencies.[67] In *Hammons v Barry*[68] in 1987, the Court of Appeals for the D.C. Circuit struck down a plan to provide that 60 percent of the new hires in the fire department be black. Judge Kenneth Starr found this to be "a hard-core, cold-in-the-dock quota." He rejected the notion that affirmative action could be pressed on grounds of a manifest imbalance in the workforce in the absence of a definitive ruling as to what constituted a manifest imbalance.

Voluntary affirmative action plans instituted by municipalities have also been subjected to scrutiny. The city of Providence, Rhode Island, drafted an affirmative action plan for recruiting minorities into its fire department by setting up a two-track recruitment system, in concept, not unlike the special task force program that was struck down in *Bakke*.[69] In *Bertoncini v City of Providence*

(1991),[70] a district court struck down the plan. The plan purportedly caused irreparable damage to white applicants who would lose seniority even if selected in an upcoming round, and it utilized preferential mechanisms to redress societal discrimination. While the city had argued that this was to address a "manifest" imbalance in the firefighting positions, the court found that the balance should be measured in terms of the qualified pool of applicants in the population, especially if the public employer was seeking applicants with some expertise. The tests per se established the pool of "qualifieds."

Other requirements emerge in regard to the drafting of affirmative action plans. One is that there must be a strong showing of past discrimination in an institution's employment history in order to justify race-conscious policies, especially those with numerical goals. Claims of discrimination must be tied to actual injuries, not just to assertions that not enough had been done to attract or promote minorities.[71]

Can an employer implement an affirmative action plan to forestall formal findings of discriminatory policies and court-ordered plans? A recent Chicago case suggests that a litigational history pointing to a prima facie case of racial discrimination would be enough to sustain an affirmative action plan that was drafted through a collective bargaining agreement with unions pursuing discrimination claims.[72] Questions also remain as to the nature of a manifest imbalance that can justify an affirmative action plan. How does a court reviewing an affirmative action plan determine that positions being filled are ones from a restricted qualified pool of applicants in which minority representation is the fewest in number? How does a court decide if a position requires special training or expertise and cannot be filled from a general labor pool? And once a labor pool is established, what is the geographic extent of that pool?[73] These questions have particular relevance for public administrators because a significant portion of public sector employment must meet specific educational, administrative, or technical requirements. A public administrator would appear to withstand reverse discrimination charges as long as each hiring or promotion is tied to individualized competitive assessments, with protected status given "a plus" in order to increase diversity.

What precisely can be pursued by agencies in their efforts to maximize employment opportunities for members of all groups? Consideration of race has become a common feature of recruitment practices in many public agencies and institutions. Advertisements for positions frequently announce that the public employer is an "equal opportunity employer" or "an affirmative action employer." Advertisements not only may encourage minorities or women and the disabled to apply but also may say that these applicants are preferred or that the employer seeks diversity.[74] Public employers tread a delicate line between the pursuit of diversity in their workforce and the possibility of excluding qualified applicants who may have cause to initiate a reverse discrimination action. An agency cannot overtly solicit an applicant for a position on the basis of race. As an example, the decision of a county board to hire an African American for the position of executive secretary of the county's human relations commission was violative of the rights of a qualified white applicant, even though the county's preference for an African American was made in good faith and subjectively reasonable.[75] Recruitment of personnel not on the basis of their race but on the basis of their race-related functions may be more defensible. Thus the search may be directed not to find a person of a specific race or national origin but to find human relations directors able to work with minority residents or students, or to find persons qualified to teach "Black Studies," or to recruit a person who has a task of representing minority interests.

The nature of public agencies with their professionalized staffs and cadres of supervisors and administrators call for specific affirmative actions to expand the professional opportunities available in the agency. Minority members or women brought into positions of responsibility should be given the same opportunities as other professionals, including challenging work assignments, participation in conferences, professional skills training, client contact, and meaningful social interaction with higher-echelon administrators. Attention should also be paid to fair resource allocation in terms of staffing, space, office services, travel funds, and research materials. At the same time the agency may also need to be sensitive to cultural differences and extend accommodation in terms of religious or cultural holidays, dietary restrictions, and dress requirements.[76]

Affirmative action demands implementation at every stage of the competitive selection process, from the minimum qualifications rating stage to the screening panel stage to the interview stage. Once members of protected classes are recruited into a workforce, the efforts to achieve "equal employment opportunity" shifts to promotion issues. Performance appraisals and evaluations are the preferred mechanisms for determining who will be advanced or promoted within the professional and administrative ranks of the agency. This process should be susceptible to external audit in the same manner as is selection or discharge. Recommendations by superiors should be grounded on identifiable criteria of job performance. In evaluating leadership potential and initiative, it is important that evaluators avoid subjective assessments or those that focus on personality or image traits.[77] Too often the advancement of persons was tied to the exhibition of traits associated with previous role occupants. Not only did this involve stereotypical expectations associated with white males but white males who fit a certain image involving an authoritarian style, professional family origins, orthodox dress, and physical fitness. At one time, administrators were expected to look and act like typical bankers, corporation heads, or graduates of military academies. This had the effect of discriminating against a high proportion of white males as well as women and minorities. These leadership expectations became part of a supervisory culture and are perpetuated in "good old boy" networks. It is an ongoing task to eradicate both the roots and fruits of these modes of recruitment and assessment.

Affirmative action programs, especially unapproved programs, can encounter resistance. Private firms moving toward more diverse workforces have had to deal with feelings of displacement and hostility as old-line employees see the changes brought about by affirmative action programs as threats to their interests and status.[78] An existing agency culture is often responsible for the creation and maintenance of these attitudes. It has thus become necessary to provide diversity training to the officers and employees of an agency. Diversity training has grown into a cottage industry of its own in the 1990's as small teams of consultants assist both private and public institutions in meeting the integrational problems of the workforce. Diversity training begins with a survey of the prevailing attitudes of officials as well as rank-and-file employees and their receptivity to functioning as a diverse workforce. The training generally involves one- to three-day workshops that involve development of an open atmosphere, removal of authority barriers, ventilation of concerns, and discussion of diversity issues. Using simulations, games, and role-playing, the trainers prepare the workforce to function in an atmosphere of mutual respect and collegial reinforcement. This involves the first steps in changing an agency's organizational culture and reversing the conditions that necessitated affirmative action in the first place.[79] Diversity training programs must be carefully crafted. Diversity programs may generate backlash if they are used to promote the political views of the trainers, promote change only for one group, or are insensitive to different styles of participation.[80] Diversity training highlights the importance of managing diversity once the minorities and historically deprived classes have been recruited into the workforce. Only then can a truly representative bureaucracy be achieved as an administrative result.

The Future of Affirmative Action

The preceding narrative, which marks the twists and turns of affirmative action doctrine, is not complete. In fact, affirmative action programs are at a political crossroads. With the Supreme Court's mixed and divided view on affirmative action programs, interests have moved to put affirmative action on the political agenda. While repeal of affirmative action policies was not part of the Republican Contract of 1994, it is no secret that many Republican politicians are making it a cutting-edge issue for the 1996 elections. Many of the party's presidential aspirants have indicated they would reverse or alter government's role in promoting affirmative action, one candidate going so far as to pledge that his first act as president would be an executive order repealing all previous executive orders mandating affirmative action in the federal government. In California a group has embarked on a petition drive to put a proposed California Civil Rights Initiative on the ballot to amend the state constitution to prohibit state and local governments from giving preference to women and minorities in jobs, promotions, contracts, and college admissions. Even the Democratic opposition is devising an affirmative action strategy, one option being a counter ballot initiative that would allow remedies to discrimination to be based on socioeconomic considerations rather than those of race, ethnicity, and gender. Not waiting for legislative action, Governor Pete Wilson in June 1995 signed an executive order rescinding all state regulations and programs implementing affirmative action for state entities. It is clear that the present state of the law will change but to what extent is uncertain.

CONCLUSION

This chapter highlighted important case law and statutes governing racial discrimination in the workplace. Public managers are directed to identify and eliminate those work rules or policies that have the effect of discriminating against any employee or potential employee on the basis of race. Moreover, any indications of racial harassment in the work environment must be immediately addressed. The most contentious issue with respect to affirmative action is the use of policies to ensure employment opportunities for members of all segments of the population that have suffered from historic discriminatory employment practices. While there may be some uncertainty in the utilizations of quotas, timetables, and goals, public managers should develop plans with confidence that maximizing opportunities for all, assisting workers in all classes to realize their highest potential, and striving to maintain a working environment of mutual respect serves productivity, efficiency, and agency success.

PUBLIC ADMINISTRATOR CHECKLIST

1. Does the agency have a history that reflects racial mono-representation in the ranks of employees? Have supervisory and administrative positions reflected mono-representation or something close to that?
2. What positive steps are taken to recruit employees of diverse backgrounds? Has the agency access to a market analysis of the labor market in terms of minorities available for recruitment?
3. Have recruitment efforts been extended to a market encompassing minority populations? What is the relevant market (in terms of reasonable commuting distances) for a recruitment effort?
4. Has an effort been made to determine the population of qualified candidates for a position and the pool of qualified candidates in minority populations?
5. To what extent are recruitment and selection criteria and preemployment tests job-related? To what extent do they predict job performance? Have these tests been validated?
6. Is any group of employees subject to differential treatment or different work rules?

7. Does a personnel practice or policy make a disparate impact as indicated in statistical measures on one class of workers as contrasted with another class? Is it an adverse effect?

8. Are minority applicants and candidates as successful as white applicants and candidates in the screening process? Do minority classes meet the four-fifths rule? Can parity be achieved in the screening ratio for all classes being recruited (noting that the four-fifths rule is still a barely passing standard for employers)?

9. To what extent are recruitment or promotional processes infused with subjective criteria? Are the subjective criteria capable of objective evaluation? What do interviews seek to show?

10. Are any recruitment or promotional criteria a product of stereotypical perceptions? To what extent are higher-level positions based on stereotypical expectations?

11. Once minority members have been recruited into the agency workforce, what efforts are made to ensure that procedures involving promotions, merit raises, and advancements are not only open to minority candidates but also allow minority candidates to be evaluated on performance standards alone?

12. Once minority personnel have been recruited into supervisory or higher-level positions, what efforts does the agency take to ensure that these people are treated the same as others in being given challenging assignments, travel opportunities, offices, research resources, and support?

13. After a removal or transfer action taken against an employee, did the employer replace the removed employee with a member of the same protected class?

14. In the instance of an adverse action against a member of a protected class, to what extent are permissible reasons for the adverse action documented?

15. Does a survey of the agency reflect particular administrative cultures that mitigate against introduction or cultivation of a diverse administration?

16. To what extent are recruits to administrative positions given the widest possible latitude to do their jobs effectively?

17. To what extent are minority candidates included in the informal networks that operate in the institutional setting?

18. How can affirmative action steps be introduced without displacement, with improvement of communication between new and old employees, and with the achieved result of improved productivity and morale?

19. Does the implementation of an affirmative action program raise any problems in terms of perceptions of favoritism or displacement on the part of current workforce members?

20. How can the implementation of an affirmative action program involve the participation and cooperation of members of the current workforce? In education programs, through mentoring programs?

EQUAL OPPORTUNITY/AFFIRMATIVE ACTION POLICY STATEMENT

A. Equal Employment

The University practices a policy of non-discrimination in recruiting, hiring, and promoting all of its employees—faculty, staff, and students. It is committed to administering all personnel actions—demotion, transfer, use of facilities, treatment during employment, rates of pay or other forms of compensation, selection for training, layoffs, or termination—without regard to race, color, national origin, religion, sexual orientation, sex, age, creed, marital status, veteran's status, political belief or affiliation, or physical, mental, or medical disability unrelated to the ability to engage in activities involved with the job. The University actively supports an affirmative action program in order to provide equal employment and educational opportunity in all areas: academic, support, and construction.

B. Educational Programs and Activities

It is the policy of the University that no person shall be discriminated against because of race, religion, age, creed, color, sex, disability, sexual orientation, national origin, marital status, veteran's status, or political belief or affiliation, and that equal opportunity and access to facilities shall be available to all. This policy is particularly applicable in the admission of students in all colleges and in their academic pursuits. It is also applicable in University-owned or University-approved housing, food services, extracurricular activities, and all other student services. It is the guiding policy in the employment of students either by the University or by outsiders through the University and in the employment of faculty and staff.

Exercises

11.1 Using a legal library, find and read the following case that went through several appeals: *Aikens v United States Postal Service Bd. of Governors*, 642 F2d 514 (D.C. Cir 1980) and *Postal Service Bd. of Governors v Aikens*, 665 F2d 1057 (D.C. Cir 1981), 460 US 711 (1983). The case deals with discrimination in selection of high-level managers in the public sector and with agency discretion to make such selections. What was the agency's basis for rejecting Aikens? Is there evidence for a prima facie case that the agency's actions were discriminatory? Did Aikens demonstrate the requisite qualifications to get the position? Critique the decision.

11.2 Personnel Grievance 1 concerns allegations by an American Indian of racial discrimination affecting the terms and conditions of employment. Develop a strategy to deal with this case.

11.3 In Personnel Grievance 10, Mr. Greenbusch alleges that the forestry department's affirmative action policies constitute reverse discrimination. Assess his claim.

Using the table below, determine if the hypothetical agency is meeting affirmative action thresholds under the four-fifths rule. Do the calculations change when dealing with only those who qualify for positions?

TABLE 11-1. Hiring Record of a Natural Resource Agency

	APPLICANTS	# MINORITY (# REJECTED)	# NON-MINORITY (# REJECTED)
Clericals	30	6 (3)	24 (12)
Field Workers	120	30 (20)	90 (50)
Foresters	20	3 (2)	17 (10)
Administrators*	60	4 (2)	56 (52)

* National search.

$$\text{Rate of selection} = 100 - \text{rate of rejection}$$

$$\frac{\text{Selection rate for minorities}}{\text{Selection rate for non-minorities}} = >.80 \text{ or } .80<$$

How would calculations change if the public employer indicated that of the field workers only 12 minority members were qualified and only 70 non-minority members were qualified?

Notes

1. These provisions are included in current federal law as 42 U.S.C. 1983.
2. The Supreme Court would breathe new life into Section 1983 in *Monroe v Pape*, 365 US 167 (1961), holding that individuals could use federal courts to sue state officers acting under state authority or under pretense of authority for damages in cases involving deprivation of their constitutional rights by those officers.
3. See Mayer G. Freed, "Suits to Remedy Discrimination in Government Employment—The Immunity Problem," *Columbia Human Rights Review* 383 (1973).
4. While suits filed under 42 U.S.C. 1981, 1983, and 1985 represent parallel avenues of seeking relief, the charges of racial discrimination brought under these suits are governed not by Title VII standards but by constitutional equal protections

standards embracing such concepts as strict scrutiny, compelling interests, and invidious discrimination. See for example *Wade v Mississippi Cooperative Extension Service*, 528 F2d 508 (5th Cir 1976), on remand, 424 F.Supp. 1242, 1255 (5th Cir 1976).

5. An Extension of the Civil Rights Act, sec. 3(e), also known as the Ramspeck Bill, 54 Stat. 1214 (1940).
6. See Daniel H. Pollitt, *Racial Discrimination in Employment: Proposals for Corrective Action*, 13 Buffalo Law Rev 59 (1963).
7. Executive Order 8802, 6 Fed. Reg. 3109 (1941). The Committee passed out of existence in 1946 when Congress directed its liquidation.
8. Executive Order 10925, 26 Fed. Reg. 1977 (1961).
9. PL 89-601, 80 Stat. 830 (Sept. 23, 1966). The law put these public institutional workers under the Fair Labors Standards Act, whose workers were covered by Title VII.
10. H.R. Rep. 238, 92d. Cong., 1st. sess. 19, 1971. Legislative history presented in *1972 Cong. and Admin. News*, 92d Cong., 2d. sess., 2152.
11. 411 US 792 (1973).
12. 450 US 248 (1981).
13. This threshold is not the only one that establishes a prima facie case. Plaintiffs may offer their own circumstantial or direct evidence to indicate that employment discrimination has occurred.
14. Employers have only to proffer a reasonable nondiscriminatory justification for their action. They do not have to prove it.
15. See *Texas Department of Community Affairs v Burdine*, 450 U.S. 248 (1981).
16. 125 L.Ed.2d 407, 113 Sup.Ct. 2742 (1993).
17. *Hicks v St. Mary's Honor Center*, 756 F.Supp. 1244 (C.D. Mo. 1991). The district judge recognized the animosity between the two parties but was unable to conclude that it was racial rather than a conflict of personalities.
18. See the comprehensive treatment of the issue in Melissa A. Essary, *The Dismantling of McDonnell-Douglas v. Green: The High Court Muddies the Evidentiary Waters in Circumstantial Discrimination Cases*, 21 Pepperdine L. Rev 385 (1994).
19. 401 US 424 (1971).
20. See *Hazelwood School District v U.S.*, 433 US 299, n.13 (1977). Also see *Mayor v Educational Quality League*, 415 US 605 (1974).
21. Plaintiffs attempt to show that the representation of a minority in the workforce is lower than the numbers that would be expected were employers to make employment decisions on a random basis without regard to race or sex. If the disparty shows a difference greater than two standard deviations from the mean, it is regarded as statistically significant.
22. 490 US 642 (1989).
23. 426 US 229 (1976).
24. Civil Rights Act of 1991, PL 102-166, 105 Stat. 1071.
25. It has also been termed "pattern of intentional discrimination" and "institutionally intentional" discrimination.

26. *Segar, et al. v Civiletti*, 508 F.Supp. 690 (D.C. Cir 1981); and *Perez v F.B.I.*, 714 F.Supp. 1414 (D. W. Tex. 1989).
27. 454 F2d 234, 238 (5th Cir 1971).
28. See *Johnson v Bunny Bread Company*, 646 F2d 1250 (8th Cir 1981).
29. 778 F2d 1318 (8th Cir 1985).
30. This standard has been codified in the 1991 Amendments to the Civil Rights Act. See sec. 703(m).
31. 981 F2d 920 (11th Cir 1990).
32. An example is provided in the case *Valdez v Mercy Hospital*, 961 F2d 1401 (8th Cir 1992), where a hospital worker with a record of negative evaluations facing termination for unsatisfactory performance filed a complaint attributing to his superior such discriminatory and injurious acts as passing around under the table publications like the "Polish Sex Manual" and the "Mexican Sex Manual."
33. H. Rept. 102-40(I) on Civil Rights Act of 1991, p. 71.
34. For an extensive inventory of actions that may be regarded as retaliatory, see secs. 247, 248 of "Job Discrimination," in 45A Am Jur 2d (1993).
35. 427 US 273 (1976).
36. See *Parker v Baltimore & O. R. Co.* 652 F2d 1012 (D.C. Cir 1981).
37. For references on raising an inference of reverse discrimination through background circumstances, see sec. 131 of "Job Discrimination," in 45A Am Jur 2d 189 (1993).
38. This three-tier model represents the author's expansion of a two-tier model defined by John A. Gray, *Preferential Affirmative Action in Employment*, 1992 Labor L J 23 (Jan. 1992).
39. The term "representative bureaucracy" originated with J. Donald Kingsley, *Representative Bureaucracy* (Yellow Springs, Ohio: Antioch Press, 1944) and was applied to the American system by Samuel Krislov, *Representative Bureaucracy* (Englewood Cliffs, N.J.: Prentice-Hall, 1972). The concept elucidates a goal of both providing some proportional equity in the distribution of goods or privileges and an affirmation of the principle that all groups have a right, an access to position and influence in the making and administration of public policy impacting their interests.
40. Title VII of Civil Rights Act of 1964 as amended by sec. 703(j). 78 Stat. 257 (1972).
41. *E. N. Bridgeport Guard Inc. v. Members of Bridgeport Civil Service Comm.* 482 F2d 1333 (2d Cir 1973). The Supreme Court denied certiorari, 421 US 991 (1975).
42. 480 US 149 (1987).
43. For expression of these positions, see Rehnquist in *Weber*, 443 US 193, 220–54; Powell in *Bakke*, 438 US 265, 309; O'Conner in *Wygant v Jackson Bd. of Educ.* 476 US 267, 499 (1986); Scalia in *Wygant*, at 521–27; White and Rehnquist in *Local 93, Int. Assoc. of Firefighters A.F.L.-C.I.O. v. E.E.O.C.*, 478 US 501, 532–45 (1986); O'Connor, White, and Rehnquist in *Local 28 of Sheet Metal Workers v E.E.O.C.*, 478 US 412, 489–500 (1986); O'Connor in *City of Richmond v Crosen*, 488 US 469, 499 (1989); Scalia in *Crosen* at 521–27.
44. C.F.R. sec. 1607.1–1607.14, 43 Fed. Reg. 38295, 383112, Aug. 25, 1975.
45. Interpretive rules do not carry the force of law but are generally given great weight by the court when decisions made under them are challenged.

46. The standard has its origin in *Connecticut v Teal,* 457 US 440 (1982). An example of the four-fifths rule: If an agency hired 72 out of 120 qualified white applicants (60 percent), then it would be expected that the agency would find a way to hire at least 24 out of 50 qualified black applicants.
47. 422 US 405 (1975).
48. 457 US 440 (1982).
49. For a discussion read Tama Starr, "So Sue Me Already: In the Age of Hyperfairness, a Business Owner Swims through Litigious Waters," *Washington Post National Weekly Edition,* 19–25 April 1993.
50. 457 US 440 (1982).
51. For a discussion of race-norming see Richard A. Epstein, *Forbidden Grounds: The Case Against Race Discrimination Laws* (Cambridge, Mass.: Harvard University Press, 1992), pp. 238–41.
52. 630 F2d 79 (2d Cir 1980), cert. denied, 452 US 940 (1981).
53. *Bushey v New York State Civil Service Comm.,* 733 F2d 220 (2d Cir 1984).
54. For a thorough discussion on this issue see Mitchell F. Rice and Brad Baptiste, "Race Norming, Validity Generalization, and Employment Testing," in *Handbook of Public Personnel Administration,* ed. Jack Rabin et al. (New York: Marcel Dekker, 1995), pp. 451–65.
55. PL 102-166, sec. 106. See discussion *Congressional and Administrative News,* 102d Cong., 1st sess. (1991), H.Rept. 102-40(II), pp. 749–50.
56. 107(a), 105 Stat. at 1075 (codified as amended at 42 U.S.C. sec. 2000e-2(m)).
57. *Officers for Justice v Civil Service Commission of the City and County of San Francisco,* 979 F2d 721 (9th Cir 1992).
58. *Castaneda v Partida,* 430 US 482, 496–97, n.17 (1977).
59. 29 C.F.R. sec. 1607 (1990).
60. 438 US 265 (1978).
61. 443 US 193 (1979).
62. 34 Fed. Reg. 12985, Aug. 12, 1969; see C.F.R., Title III, Chap. 2.
63. *Equal Employment Opportunity Commission Compliance Manual,* sec. 607: 0003-0033 (BNA: Washington D.C., 1992).
64. In the early tests, courts tended to support the constitutionality of the plans. See *Bushey v N.Y. St. Civ. Serv. Com'n.,* 733 F2d 220 (2nd Cir 1994); *Bratton v City of Detroit,* 704 F2d 878 (6th Cir 1983), cert. denied, 464 1040 (1984); and *La Riviere v E.E.O.C.,* 682 F2d 1275 US (9th Cir 1982).
65. 480 US 616 (1987).
66. In the county none (the inexorable zero) of the 238 skilled craft positions was held by a woman.
67. See *Ledoux v District of Columbia,* 820 F2d 1293 (D.C. Cir 1987), reh. granted, 833 F2d 368 (D.C. Cir 1987), vacated, 841 F2d 400 (D.C. Cir, 1988); and *Hammon v Barry* 606 F.Supp 1082 (D.C. Cir 1987), rev'd, 813 F2d 412 (D.C. Cir 1987), reh. denied, 826 F2d 73 (D.C. Cir 1987), cert. denied, *Barry v U.S.,* 486 US 1035 (1988), vacated, 841 F2d 426 (D.C. Cir 1988).
68. 826 F2d 73 (D.C. Cir 1987)

69. Of the 60 highest ranked applicants, 58 were white and two were African American. The plan chose the 48 highest-scoring whites and 12 selections made in rank order from among the minority and female applicants.
70. 767 F.Supp. 1194 (D. R.I. 1991)
71. *City of Richmond v Crosen*, 488 US 469 (1989).
72. *Chicago Firefighters v Washington*, 736 F.Supp. 923 (N.D. Ill. 1990).
73. *Finding a "Manifest Imbalance": The Case for a Unified Statistical Model for Voluntary Affirmative Action Under Title VII*, 87 Mich L Rev 1987 (1989).
74. This raises a semantic issue. Does the recruiter mean that applicants of the protected classes will be accorded a plus in consideration, or does it mean that the protected classes will be hired if they demonstrate the requisite qualifications?
75. *Butta v Anne Arundel County*, 473 F. Supp. 83 (D. Md. 1979).
76. These suggestions are drawn from guidelines for affirmative action in law firms that are analogous to public agencies in terms of their talent profiles. See Valerie A. Fontaine, "Cultivating a Diverse Work Force: Firms' Profiles Need to Reflect Reality," *National Law Journal*, 10 Jan. 1994, pp. 25–27.
77. Courts have looked on disfavor at evaluation criteria that are subjective and that resist objective evaluation. See *Crawford v Western Electric*, 614 F2d 1300, 1313–17 (5th Cir 1980). But compare with *Hill v Seaboard Coast Line R. Co.*, 885 F2d 804 (11th Cir 1989), which recognizes that bona fide subjective criteria may exist. Also see Donald R. Stacey, *Subjective Criteria in Employment Decisions Under Title VII*, 10 Georgia L Rev 737 (1976).
78. See Jeff Thomas, "White Male Backlash in the Workplace," *Colorado Springs Gazette Telegraph*, 2 Jan. 1994, p. 1.
79. Ann Perkins Delatte, "Eight Guidelines for Successful Diversity Training," *Training* 30 (Jan. 1993), 55.
80. Michael Mobley and Tamara Payne, "Backlash: The Challenge to Diversity Training," *Training and Development* 46 (Dec. 1992), 45; Kara Swisher, "Diversity Training: Learning from Past Mistakes," *Washington Post, National Weekly Edition*, 13–19 Feb. 1995, p. 20.

12

Gender Discrimination in Employment[1]

Protection of employment rights for women employees begins with the passage of the Equal Pay Act of 1963.[2] Employers covered by the commerce clause were not to discriminate between employees on the basis of sex by paying wages to employees at a rate less than that paid the opposite sex for equal work, the performance of which required equal skills, effort, and responsibility and which were performed under similar working conditions. It also contained a number of statutory exceptions. Equal pay was not mandated when differential payments were made pursuant to a seniority system, a merit system, any system measuring earnings by quantity or quality of production, or a differential based on any other factor other than sex.

It remained for the passage of the Civil Rights Act of 1964 to provide women with protection against discrimination in employment. "Sex" was added as one of the protected classes through an amendment offered by Rep. Howard Smith of Virginia, who thought that such an extension would jeopardize passage of the bill. The House accepted that amendment on a 168-133 vote.[3]

The 1964 Act brought gender under the same broad general prohibition against employment discrimination that applied to race, religion, and national origin. There was such concern that this would allow the intrusion of women into positions that were appropriately to be performed by men that in 1972 Congress inserted the following amendment into the Civil Rights Act:

> Notwithstanding any other provisions of this title it shall not be an unlawful employment practice . . . to admit or employ any individual in any such program on the basis of his religion, sex, or national origin where religion, sex, or national origin is a bona fide qualification reasonably necessary to the normal operation of that business or enterprise.[4]

The bona fide occupational qualification (BFOQ) represented a loophole that employers attempted to utilize to avoid integration of a workforce by gender. Employers utilized every possible gender stereotype to be permitted to deal with women differently in the workforce. In 1977 the Supreme Court addressed the issue of BFOQs as bars to employment of women in prison-guard positions in *Dothard v Rawlinson*.[5] Women employees challenged necessary height and weight requirements, which had the effect of disproportionately excluding women from serving as corrections officers. In addition to this disparate impact claim, the women also claimed disparate treatment in their exclusion from service that would put them in contact with inmates in maximum security facilities. The Court found that women were disparately impacted by these physical requirements and that, on their face, these requirements did not show a relationship to job performance. However, the Court noted that the males-only requirement for contact guards in the "jungle" of a maximum security prison was a bona fide gender consideration necessary to the "business" of administering a penal institution. The Court had difficulty in accepting a role for women guards in dealing with predatory prisoners or with prison riots.

The issue of the validity of BFOQs arose mainly in private employment cases such as *Diaz v Pan American World Airways* (1971),[6] and *Wilson v Southwest Airlines* (1981).[7] The *Wilson* case established a two-part test applicable to private and public cases to determine if there is a BFOQ based on gender. The employer must demonstrate that a member of the opposite sex cannot do the job; if that is so, then the employer must demonstrate that the conduct of business would be undermined if members of the wrong sex were hired. The conduct of business applies in the broad sense to the business of governance and administration, such as the business of running a penal institution.

In 1982 the Equal Employment Opportunity Commission (EEOC) came out with interpretive guidelines for the BFOQ provisions. The guidelines held that hiring on the basis of unfounded assumptions would violate the statute (e.g., assumptions that turnover rate among women is higher than among men, that pregnancies will cause instability of assignments in the workforce, that women are less aggressive salespersons, or that a woman in a position would generate hostility among coworkers, clients, or customers).

BFOQ issues have waned as the work culture has changed and as it becomes almost impossible to define employment positions or functions that are to be limited to one sex. Except for exclusively biological functions, such as sperm donor or surrogate mother, one might remove the BFOQ on sex from the agenda. However, it can still rear its head on occasion as in the case *Torres v Wisc. Dept. of Health and Social Services* (1988)[8] in which a court of appeals found it was permissible for a state to employ only women guards at a women's maximum security prison if the state could prove that it was necessary. The state asserted interests in protecting inmate privacy and promoting rehabilitation that the court accepted without need of validation. The case demonstrated that a BFOQ based on sex-linked, sex-supported attributes might still be raised as in the case of an employer who seeks employees of a particular sex to serve as role models or, as in this case, trust figures. Cases in gender discrimination can focus on differential treatment in which an employer singles out an employee for different and less favorable treatment. Disparate treatment cases involve claims of intentional discrimination. The employer uses a different set of rules for each gender, administers a neutral rule differently for each gender, or exempts a person from a rule on the basis of gender. In an allegation of intentional discrimination, the complainant can utilize the three-stage process that was outlined for racial discrimination cases in *McDonnell-Douglas Corp. v. Green* (1973)[9] and *Texas Department of Community Affairs v Burdine* (1981).[10] In the first stage, the complainant presents a prima facie case that demonstrates that the employee is a member of a protected class, that she applied for a job or promotion and was rejected, and that the employer hired a male of equal qualifications or continued to seek to fill the position with persons of those qualifications. The second stage allows the employer to rebut the claim by articulating some legitimate nondiscriminatory reason for not hiring, not promoting, or firing the individual. The third stage provides an opportunity for the complainant to persuade the court that the reasons proffered for the employer's decision are not credible or pretextual.

Gender discrimination suits also involve adverse actions that may be governed by mixed motives. In *Price-Waterhouse v Hopkins* (1989),[11] a woman employed as a senior manager in a professional accounting firm was considered for a partnership. The evaluations of the woman solicited from all partners (all men) split. Positive evaluations highlighted her conscientious work habits, knowledgeability, independence, self-reliance, strong character, and integrity. She was credited with having secured major contacts for the firm. On the other hand, she was seen as impatient, abrasive, harsh, pushy, and lacking in interpersonal skills. One evaluation said she was "too masculine" and should walk, talk, and dress more femininely. She was denied the promotion. She then filed a suit alleging discrimination based on sex. The federal district court acknowledged that sexual stereotyping was involved in the evaluations but that the firm should simply have not given any credence or effect to partners' comments reflecting such stereotyping. The appeals court viewed it as a mixed motive case, saying the firm could avoid not only equitable relief but liability if it could prove it would have made the same decision had discrimination not played a role. For the Supreme Court the key issue was the effect to be given to evidence that the employer may have also relied on non-discriminatory motives to deny an employee a privilege of employment. A plurality opinion by Justice Brennan affirmed the principle that an adverse employment decision based on sex would constitute discrimination. A review of the circumstances surrounding the denial of her admission to partnership indicated that gender was taken into account at all stages in the process. Her employers objected to women who showed aggressive management traits, yet they required such traits in the position. That placed women in an intolerable and impermissible Catch-22. They were out of a job if they behaved aggressively and out of a job if they didn't.[12] The Supreme Court, however, noted that even where an employee proves her gender was a motivating factor in the decision, the employer can avoid a finding of liability by a preponderance of evidence that it would have made an adverse decision independent of any gender consideration. Justice White reinforced this position by stating that the unlawful motive had to be the substantial factor if the employee was to prevail. The case was remanded to district court to determine if Price-Waterhouse would have arrived at the same decision regardless of the considerations of sex. The district court concluded that Price-Waterhouse "does not want her and would not admit her" and ruled that the firm failed to prove that non-discriminatory reasons prevailed in the case.[13]

The Supreme Court's remand of *Price-Waterhouse* providing that an employer would prevail if the employer could demonstrate that it would have made the same decision on nondiscriminatory grounds was regarded as a setback for women confronting sex discrimination in the workplace. If a lawful factor was implicated in the case, the complainant lost the case.

Overturning of aspects of *Price-Waterhouse* became a key objective of the proponents of the 1991 Civil Rights Act. Section 203 of that act with the addition of 703(1) to Title VII now requires that the complaining party must demonstrate that discrimination was a contributing factor in an employment decision. Once it is established that gender was a factor influencing the decision, the violation is established. The employer may still make the point that an adverse decision would have been taken against the employee in any case, but the employer would not be able to avoid all liability. Under subsection 706(g) of Title VII the employer would not be required to hire, reinstate, promote, or provide back pay to the complainant if the employee is not qualified to receive those privileges. Under the new amendments the employer may be liable for injunctive relief, monetary damages, and attorney's fees to redress the personal injury resulting from the invidious acts directed at the employee. The new changes in the law have the effect of restoring the rule applied in many federal circuits before the *Price-Waterhouse* decision that employers were liable for any discrimination playing a part in employer-employee relations.

A high proportion of Title VII disparate treatment cases contains to some degree a mélange of motives. As noted above, employers prevail against a claim of gender discrimination if they can advance a nondiscriminatory reason behind an adverse decision and show by a preponderance of evidence that the decision would have been made but for the sexist considerations. A review of case law has illustrated the magnitude of the conflict.[14] Employers base adverse decisions on such grounds as alleged lack of leadership skills, alleged lack of experience, alleged lack of improvement, alleged lack of interpersonal skills, or alleged lack of interest or enthusiasm in the job. Whether the proffered reasons are accepted as genuine or held to be pretextual depends on the evidentiary analysis. Courts explore the full personnel file to review the standards to which employees were held (and to determine if there were different standards for members of one sex). They review performance evaluations of the complainant and co-workers (with an eye to comparison of the evaluation process and any disparate results between men and women). If an employer demonstrates a pattern of promoting candidates of the other gender who demonstrate similar or inferior job performance, that supports a challenge that the reasons are pretextual.[15] An employer's reliance upon subjective assessments (such as an alleged lack of leadership skills) are given heightened scrutiny by the courts especially if the evaluators are not members of the protected class. Adverse testimony that is "unfocused" or "undocumented" will not pass such scrutiny.[16] A personnel record that contradicts allegations of inadequate performance can undermine the nondiscriminatory reason for adverse action. Any proffered reasons that focus on interpersonal difficulties (with superiors, coworkers) must be corroborated by testimony independent of the evaluators. A clear and complete record is necessary to raise a credible defense against a gender discrimination claim.

Sex discrimination in employment can also be demonstrated through findings that employment policies or practices work a disparate impact on employees of one gender. In this form of discrimination, discriminatory actions are not directed at specific individuals but the personnel practices employed have the effect over time of disfavoring or placing at a disadvantage members of one gender. These practices may not be overtly discriminatory and may be regarded as neutral. They may involve tests, physical requirements, evaluation systems or criteria, or job expectations that independently of valid performance measures tend to screen out or act as a barrier to members of one gender.

An ongoing case involving female foreign service officers in the Department of State illustrates the creation of a disparate impact case.[17] Female foreign service officers sued the department in 1985, alleging that department policies and practices governing advancement of officers within the system were disadvantageous to female officers and resulted in widely disparate advancement rates to the highest grades of the service for male and female officers. The female officers pointed to seven different employment practices that put more males into the coveted political branches, that disproportionately assigned more males into the more preferred "stretch" assignments, that disproportionately favored males in the evaluations for potential, and that disproportionately allocated superior honor awards to males. Evidence was introduced that produced the anomaly that female officers with high performance ratings were still scored much lower than males in the critical "evaluation for potential." Lower courts indicated that the promotion process itself was not conducted in a manner to discriminate against candidates by gender. However, the Appeals Court for the D.C. Circuit noted that many of the practices demonstrated an overwhelming statistical gender disparity in how the State Department assigned and rewarded its officers. The State Department failed to rebut the prima facie findings with articulate nondiscriminatory explanations. The court noted that while the final promotion board evaluated candidates on an equal footing, those promotions were made on the basis of what was in an officer's personnel file. Assignments, awards, and the evaluation for potential were critical in a competitive promotion process. Thus the promotion materials were discriminatorily tainted and infected the final process.

The State Department cases illustrated the importance of identifying the subtle and subjective factors that may influence the conduct of what ostensibly appears to be a neutral evaluation and promotion process. Subjective practices are implicit in the creation of what has been termed "the glass ceiling," that undefinable barrier that seems to block the advancement of women into the higher levels of organizational structures.[18] The impediments to advancement are often imbedded in attitudes that color and corrupt personnel practices. These attitudes may range from a general tendency to underestimate women's potential to an attitude that women are less committed to their careers than men. They may involve the view that women are less mobile than men or that women will be distracted by family responsibilities. Existent attitudes may also downgrade the measures of performance by women. For instance, women may be held to higher standards of achievement than men and be held more accountable for any mistakes or deficiencies.[19] A barrier may also be raised in a tendency for promoters to restrict advancement to those of long-term acquaintanceship, a tendency that tends to deny advancement to any new class coming into the administrative workplace.

These barriers are often the product of gender stereotyping.[20] Stereotyping may emerge in the hiring process. Questions directed to applicants that ask about childbearing plans or whether a spouse would object to her working with men raise subtle reservations about hiring a woman.[21] Inquiries of this type are irrelevant and discriminatory. Stereotyping continues in the assignment and evaluation processes for employees where assumptions portray the woman employee as less than totally committed to her job. Surveys have revealed that many of these stereotypes are contradicted by the facts. For instance, surveys show that 95 percent of women say they are very committed to their jobs (compared with 93 percent for men); that 89 percent of women are always enthusiastic about their job (compared with 88 percent for men); and that 78 percent of women indicate that they are willing to devote whatever time is necessary to advance their careers (compared with 74 percent for men).[22] Surveys taken within an agency may provide the basis for an education campaign to demonstrate that the women employees have loyalty, commitment, and professional values that square with those of their male counterparts. The Merit System Protection Board also notes that mentoring practices are useful in providing aspiring candidates who are members of protected groups with a counterbalance against the barriers that exist within an institutional culture. It also found that inclusion of such candidates in the informal networks that operate within institutional settings is also necessary to break down the covert barriers.[23]

AFFIRMATIVE ACTION

The *Weber*[24] and *Bakke*[25] cases indicated that there was a basis for the voluntary implementation of affirmative action plans by employers seeking to expand employment opportunities to classes that had experienced employment deprivations. However, *Weber* and *Bakke* diverged on a key point. *Weber* indicated that an affirmative action plan might be implemented to break down traditional patterns of segregation and hierarchy (societal discrimination), while *Bakke* was clear in stating that an affirmative action plan must be a response to past discrimination. These nuances were addressed in a case involving an affirmative action plan to open employment opportunities for women, *Johnson v Transportation Agency of Santa Clara County* (1987).[26] This case, already discussed in chapter 11, involved a challenge of a promotion of a woman in a voluntary affirmative action program intended to increase employment opportunities for women as well as minorities. The county saw an underrepresentation of women employees in many job categories. The plan was intended to achieve a statistically measurable yearly improvement in the hiring, training, and promotion of minorities and women throughout the agency in all major job classifications. In a competition for the position of road dispatcher, Diane Joyce and Paul Johnson both qualified and the agency chose Joyce for the job. Johnson filed a suit under Title VII, alleging that as a qualified candidate who had a better score,[27] he had been discriminated against since Joyce obtained the position because the employer considered her gender and utilized that as the determinative factor. For Joyce the issue was also cut-and-dried. "She took a test. She qualified. They could choose anyone on the list. They chose her."[28] When the case reached the Supreme Court, the Court, with Justice Brennan speaking for the majority, found that the plan was permissible. It addressed an egregious underrepresentation of women in many job categories. The court continued to maintain that affirmative action plans should be predicated on redressing past discrimination. In this case a firm basis existed for the agency's believing that past sex discrimination existed in the fact that not one woman (an "inexorable zero") had been hired into the skill craft positions. As to the "plus" of gender that was added into the hiring officer's final evaluation, that was simply a factor through which the hiring officer could advance forward-looking legitimate employment policies that stood apart from a need to remedy any sin of past discrimination. He was free to do that with the final pool of applicants, all of whom were qualified for the position. The dissenters led by Justice Scalia thought that the district court's finding that Joyce's gender was the *determining* factor in her selection rendered the selection a violation of Title VII, which states that race or gender shall not be the basis for employment decisions.

The dissenters argued that Joyce would not have obtained her position "but for her gender." Gender was considered a factor for employment, but was it considered too much—was it the motivating factor for her selection? It is true that Johnson had a marginally higher score than Joyce but this score included an interview component that contained subjective evaluations that might express unarticulated criteria (appearance, ability to fit in, etc.). Women applying for positions traditionally held by men are at a particular disadvantage vis-à-vis men in such evaluations. Thus the consideration of sex as a factor may not be so much a plus for the applicant as a balancing factor to even the playing field.[29]

Affirmative action to remedy old patterns of segregation, hierarchy, and presumptive classification need not await litigation and compliance with orders issued from courts or equal employment agencies. Agencies can initiate voluntary affirmative action plans that allow for a more accessible, welcome, and representative workplace for female employees. Voluntary affirmative action plans to alleviate gender issues are different from voluntary affirmative action efforts designed to open work-places to racial minorities.[30] The most obvious difference relates to the scope of integrational efforts. Affirmative action plans seek to restructure workforces in conformity with the proportion of qualified workers of a class or group within the accessible labor market. Women comprising half of the workforce population and moving into almost all job categories will impact an institutional workforce more than any minority.

Society's response to racism and sexism is also different. Any belief that racial differences reflect differences in intellect or competence is generally regarded as an illegitimate racist viewpoint.[31] On the other hand, many people are of the opinion that gender distinctions in work roles actually exist (note perceptions underlying the "glass ceiling"). Even Supreme Court decisions have rejected the notion of gender parity in all societal circumstances, preferring to hold that distinctions may be entertained in laws and regulations if it can be demonstrated that men and women are "not similarly situated."[32] As a consequence, gender enjoys only a heightened judicial scrutiny, not a suspect status in equal protections doctrine. However, it should be noted that the implementation of affirmative action programs for women generates a higher level of acceptance than programs for racial minorities. Surveys have indicated that affirmative action programs for women are less threatening to existing employees than those for racial minorities.[33] The great number of bilaterally employed husband-wife pairs also enlists many male employees into support of programs that advance the opportunities for what they perceive as a working partnership. A particular problem is that there is a linkage between race discrimination and sex discrimination. The consequence is that women and persons of color then are placed in competition for the benefits of affirmative action. Voluntary affirmative action plans should address such issues comprehensively and provide for the monitoring of the progress of each group separately to ensure that one is not benefiting at the expense of the other.[34]

As indicated in chapter 11, affirmative action policies are undergoing review and challenge. This may have profound effect upon recruitment and promotion of women into the public workforce, especially in promotion of women into upper-level administrative positions. Women comprise the one group that has benefited the most from affirmative action in the public sector, for the most part from voluntary programs. A review of the changing profile of the federal workforce reveals that at the upper levels, women increased their percentage at the GS-12/13 levels from 11 percent in 1982 to 27.8 percent in 1992. At the GS-14/15 levels, they increased their percentage from 5.7 to 17.8 and at senior executive levels they increased their percentage from 4.9 to 13 for the decade.[35] However, one may note that these dramatic increases may not be due solely to the existence of affirmative action programs but to the fact that the federal government has not only recruited women but has attracted exceptionally well-qualfied women entrants. This has been noted for the influx of women attorneys into the federal service. Still encountering problems in finding appropriate opportunities (except for token hires) with private sector law firms, highly qualified women found a more inviting employer in the federal service.[36] If public service can attract women as the better-qualified hires, then alterations in affirmative action rules may not diminish equal opportunity for the class.

SEXUAL HARASSMENT

Title VII of the Civil Rights Act did not have a provision specifically directed at sexual harassment. Even after *Rogers v E.E.O.C* (1971)[37] recognized a cause for action based on a discriminatory work environment, courts rejected sexual harassment claims under Title VII with decisions holding that a rebuff of a sexual proposition to an employee of the opposite sex followed by adverse employment actions against the employee did not constitute sex discrimination but only improprieties not covered by Title VII.[38] The courts also ruled that an individual action of sexual bribery did not constitute a systemic pattern of harassing women as a class of employees.[39] A supervisor's sexual demands on an employee simply constituted abuse of authority for personal purposes.[40] Finally in 1976 in *Williams v Saxbe*,[41] a federal district court found in favor of a female employee who had rejected her supervisor's advances and was fired shortly thereafter. The court rejected the notion that sexual demands could be made on either or both sexes. The actions of the supervisor "created an artificial barrier to employment which was placed before one gender and not the other."

In 1980 the EEOC issued guidelines to define sexual harassment.[42] Sexual harassment was to embrace unwelcome sexual advances, requests for sexual favors, or other verbal or physical conduct of a sexual nature. A nexus was also established between conduct and employment status and conditions of employment. The above conduct would violate Title VII if:

1. submission to such conduct was made explicitly or implicitly a term or condition of employment;
2. submission to or rejection of such conduct was used as a basis for employment decisions affecting the individual;
3. the conduct had the purpose or effect of unreasonably interfering with the individual's work performance or creating an intimidating, hostile, or offensive work environment.

It became clear to the courts that harassment violated Title VII if the harassment was tied to tangible losses of an economic character. In *Henson v City of Dundee* (1982)[43] the courts established the prerequisites for what is known as quid pro quo harassment. To establish a case, an employee must prove:

1. the employee belongs to a protected class (both men and women qualify);
2. the employee was subjected to unwelcome sexual advances;
3. the harassment complained of was based on sex (but for her (or his) sex there would have been no harassment);
4. the employer's reaction to the harassment complained of affected tangible aspects of an employee's compensation, terms, conditions, or privileges of employment.

The *Henson* decision set standards to deal with the common pattern that includes acts of retaliation for resisting sexual harassment: sexual advances are made by superiors against employees; employees rebuff advances; employer retaliates utilizing nondiscriminatory performance measures (victim is charged with poor performance, absenteeism, disruptive behavior, or insubordination). Retaliation may arise only after the grievant raises a harassment issue.

Henson-type cases were based on a nexus between harassment and the terms of employment but the question arose, "What if there is no adverse economic or job status decision?" Courts also recognized a second form of sexual harassment to violate Title VII, the creation and maintenance or allowance of a hostile work environment. This hostile environment need not require any sexual advances, propositions, or economic considerations. It need only involve harassing behaviors directed at an employee "as a woman."[44]

The EEOC amended its guidelines in 1981 to reflect a working conditions theory that made the employer liable for coworker harassment if the activity interfered with work performance or created an intimidating atmosphere.[45] That same year the case *Bundy v Jackson*[46] indicated that a sexually hostile environment standing alone could constitute a violation of Title VII. This hostile environment would be created by verbal abuse, offensive behaviors, or offensive atmosphere. The *Bundy* court noted that the law to that point had not permitted a woman's claim of harassment to prevail unless the employer had taken tangible actions resulting in economic disadvantage against her.

> And this in turn means that so long as the sexual situation is constructed with enough coerciveness, subtlety, suddenness or one-sidedness to negate the effectiveness of a woman's refusal, or so long as her refusals are simply ignored while her job is formally undisturbed, she is not considered to be sexually harassed. . . . The employer can thus implicitly make the employee's endurance of sexual intimidation a "condition" of employment. The woman then faces a cruel "trillemma." She can attempt to oppose it, with little hope of success, either legal or practical, but with every prospect of making the job even less tolerable for her. Or she can leave her job with little hope of legal relief and the likely prospect of another job where she will face harassment anew.[47]

Judge Wright's dicta in *Bundy* emphasized the disparate power relationships in workplace environments that engender incidents of sexual harassment. Supervisory personnel possess a wide range of power resources besides physical dominance and male assertiveness that put subordinates at distinct disadvantages. They control access, opportunities, and conditions of employment. They can invoke seniority privileges and administer both tangible and intangible sanctions like social exclusion, criticisms, extra work demands, or demotion within implicit pecking orders. Probably the most insidious power resource is to manipulate the situation to provide a rationale to sanction or deprive the employee of a job benefit on independent grounds.

The Supreme Court finally addressed both the quid pro quo and hostile environment issues in *Meritor Savings Bank v Vinson* in 1986.[48] The *Meritor* case involved a woman employee of the bank who claimed that a supervisor had pressured her over a three-year period to initiate and continue an affair with him under what she described as conditions of duress. During this period she was afraid to report the harassment. When she took excessive sick leave, ostensibly to deal with attendant stress, she was fired. A district court decision found that if the supervisor and employee had a sexual relationship it was merely voluntary. A circuit court found this interpretation did not fit the EEOC guidelines, which defined as sexual harassment any conduct which was "unwelcome." The court also found that the district court had not allowed in evidence that which might have shown that there was a pattern of sexual harassment involving other employees. The circuit court also ruled that the bank itself could not be held liable under EEOC guidelines regardless of whether the acts complained of were authorized or forbidden by the employer and regardless of whether the employer knew or should have known of their occurrence. When Meritor appealed to the Supreme Court, the government was put in the position of defending its EEOC guidelines. EEOC Chairman Clarence Thomas urged the administration to take a stand against poisoned environments, "Forcing a woman to work in a hostile environment is like forcing a Jewish employee to work in an office covered with Nazi memorabilia."[49] The Solicitor General's brief on behalf of the EEOC, however, attempted to narrow the standard of a hostile environment and to keep the EEOC out of personal relationships that might develop in the workplace.[50]

The Supreme Court's decision in *Meritor*, with Justice Rehnquist writing the opinion, affirmed the concept of "hostile environment" harassment. The Court also upheld the appeals court finding of sexual harassment and affirmed Vinson's claim. The gravamen was not whether the behavior was voluntary but whether it was "unwelcome." On the issue of whether the bank itself was liable for this set of events, the Supreme Court was ambivalent. It rejected the appeals court decision that employers are automatically liable for misconduct of their agents. Yet neither the employer's lack of knowledge of the incidents nor the fact that a grievance procedure was in place insulate the employer from suit. Liability would be determined on a case-by-case analysis of circumstances.

In quid pro quo cases, the employer is generally liable for the acts of supervisory employees who allocate the rewards and benefits of employment. Where the harasser was a coworker or supervisory employee, courts attached a constructive responsibility to the accountable employer.[51] In 1980 the EEOC issued interpretive guidelines applying what is known as the *Wood*[52] standard to sexual harassment cases, the principle that officials are not immune from damage suits if they knew or reasonably should have known that actions taken violated the constitutional rights of persons. To assess liability on the employer, one must determine:

1. whether the employer knew or should have known of sexual harassment in the workplace;
2. whether on being notified, employee took prompt and effective remedial action to address it.[53] The guidelines also imposed an affirmative obligation on employers to prevent and deter possible harassment by taking such steps as raising the subject, expressing strong disapproval, informing employees of their right to raise issues of harassment and developing appropriate sanctions.[54] Courts have also held that when an employer receives a complaint, that employer has an affirmative duty to investigate the complaint and take appropriate action. Failure to do so is evidence of acquiescence.[55]

The *Meritor* decision still left many issues unresolved. Harassment is indicated in terms of behaviors that are unwelcome or offensive. These are very subjective standards. The area between what is merely inappropriate and what is offensively impermissible is an ambivalent gray. A supervisor surprises a female employee with a statement about her perfume, "I don't know what you're wearing but it's a sensual experience." Is that an innocent compliment, double entendre, or a veiled advance? Would giving a female secretary a "Sweetheart of the Office" card be a quaint but embarrassing gesture or a labeling that compartmentalizes the female workers into a differently and less-valued component of the workforce? Is it harassment if a boss insists that an employee go out to dinner with him?[56] The debate on these issues is drawn between those who would define as harassment only those actions that are hostile or exploitative in intent and those who view as harassment all those symbolic acts, conscious or unconscious, that affirm the operation of a patriarchal hierarchy within the workforce. Because of the fact that men and women may have been socialized or culturally directed to have different perceptions of these interpersonal behaviors, there may be a gender gap in terms of evaluating the offensiveness or unwelcomeness of different behaviors. Socialization into certain male cultures may also promote attitudes, expectations, and stereotypes that engender dominating and predatory actions against women.[57]

The first suggestion of a "reasonable woman" standard to judge claims of sexual harassment was put forth by Judge Keith in dissent in *Rabidue v Osceola Refining Co.* (1986).[58] In ruling on a discrimination suit alleging insulting and demeaning verbal abuse directed against a female employee, the court ruled that "sexual jokes, sexual conversations, and girlie magazines may abound, and Title VII was not meant to change this. . . or the social mores of American workers." Keith argued that asessing the behavior of the supervisor by the reasonable person standard failed to account for the wide divergence between men and women as to what behavior or speech or display is inappropriate in the workplace. Judge Keith argued that courts not be allowed to utilize notions of reasonable behavior fashioned by the offenders, namely men.

In *Andrews v City of Philadelphia* (1990),[59] the Third Circuit developed a comprehensive four-part test for an employee to establish a sexual harassment claim:

1. She must demonstrate she was discriminated against on the basis of sex.
2. She must show discriminating conduct was pervasive, not isolated.
3. She must show that discrimination injured her.
4. She must demonstrate that discrimination would affect a reasonable person of same sex in that position.

The court would make a woman's perspective a critical factor in adjudicating a claim. At the same time its reference to a "reasonable" woman would protect the employer from an employee who manifests a hypersensitive or idiosyncratic viewpoint.

The Ninth Circuit was the first to adopt a reasonable woman standard in the case *Ellison v Brady* in 1991.[60] A female IRS employee filed a sexual harassment claim in response to actions of a male employee who constantly pestered her and bombarded her with bizarre love letters. Ellison saw this behavior as threatening. The district court found the behavior immature but trivial. The circuit court overruled the district court and found a prima facie case of sexual harassment under a reasonable woman standard. The court felt a reasonable person standard tended to be male-biased and inherently ignored the experiences of women. The court also found that the agency was liable for the hostile environment even though a female supervisor arranged a temporary transfer (cooling-off period). The agency failed to reprimand the offending employee, put him on probation, or even warn him that his repeated harassment could result in suspension or termination.

The reasonable woman standard has gained acceptance in a growing number of circuits.[61] The reasonable woman standard has also been applied in dealing with the issue of what is meant by actions that are unwelcome or offensive. In the case of *Burns v McGregor Electronic Industries*,[62] a female employee brought a Title VII harassment suit against her employer, alleging harassment by coworkers and by a supervisor who verbally demeaned her, calling her every name in the book and forcing her resignation. A district court utilizing a reasonable man standard found that much of this harassment might be unwelcome but it should not have been considered offensive given the fact that the employee had the notoriety of having appeared in nude photographs in a motorcycle magazine. The circuit court reversed, holding that while the language used by fellow employees may have been unobjectionable to some groups of men, the incidents must be viewed from the victim's perspective, and in this case the victim was a woman. The court also emphasized the necessity of judging these cases solely in terms of the workplace and work-related conduct. Burns did not engage in provocative behavior in the workplace. An employee's private life, her past conduct, her off-duty reputation is irrelevant to an employee's treatment in the workplace. The goal of Title VII is to rid the workplace of any kind of unwelcome harassment.

An important issue in a finding of sexual harassment is the determination of psychological injury. In *Meritor* the Supreme Court stated that the proper standard for a sexual harassment claim was that the improper behavior be sufficiently severe or pervasive to alter the conditions of the victim's employment and create an abusive working environment.[63] Three federal circuits had determined that improper conduct must not only be offensive but also seriously affect the psychological well-being of the victimized employee.[64] On November 9, 1993, the Supreme Court decided *Harris v Forklift Systems*[65] in which both the district and circuit levels had insisted on a requirement of psychological harm to demonstrate hostile work environment sexual harassment. Teresa Harris noted a persistent pattern of insult and sexual innuendo on the part of her employer, which affected her personal calm and normal personality. She became upset, cried frequently, took to drinking, and experienced instability in her familial relationships. While the lower federal courts found the employer's behavior very offensive it was not so severe as to affect the employee's psychological well-being. The employer argued that to establish that the conduct created an environment affecting conditions of employment, there should be a measureable impact of harm, either in performance or through a professional or medical diagnosis. Harris, on the other hand, argued that a plaintiff should be able to prevail without proof of negative impact on work performance or psychological harm. The proof of offensive conduct should be sufficient to sustain a harassment claim.

The Supreme Court rejected both of these propositions. It said that "merely offensive" conduct by itself was not actionable. But the Court also said that it was not necessary to establish tangible psychological injury or impact on performance to proceed with a harassment claim. As Justice O'Connor noted, Title VII comes into play before the complainant has suffered a nervous breakdown. The defining issue is whether the behaviors were so pervasive and severe as to create an "abusive working environment." To determine if a claim is warranted, the Court set up a totality of circumstances test. Whether an environment is hostile or abusive will be determined by looking at the frequency of the discriminatory conduct, the severity of the behavior, whether it is threatening or humiliating, whether it is an isolated incident, and whether it unreasonably interferes with an employee's work performance. Justice Ginsberg in a concurrence elaborated on the last point, holding that a case was presented if working conditions were so altered as to make it more difficult for the employee to do her job. The Supreme Court did not address the "reasonable person" standard directly except to state that the harassing behavior be severe enough to alter the "victim's" condition of employment. The decision also did not articulate a set of objective indicators to identify what was hostile or abusive. Juries are thus left without guidance in determining whether sex-related behaviors are egregious enough to warrant damage awards. Courts are still operating within a limbo of standards as indicated in the first post-*Forklift* harassment case, decided in the Seventh Circuit. The court ruled that an employee had failed to establish a case because an objective test of whether a reasonable person would find the work environment hostile or abusive was not satisfied. The behavior, while viewed as inappropriate and unprofessional, did not appear to the court to change the workplace environment.[66]

An additional development in 1991 also enhanced the protective umbrella of Title VII in sex harassment cases. Under the Civil Rights Act of 1991, victims of sex discrimination can seek compensatory and punitive damages up to certain limits on the size of the employer's workforce (from a maximum award of $50,000 for a business with 15 to 100 employees to a maximum of

$300,000 for a business with over 500 employees). This leaves some questions as to the size of a unit a public employee may fit under (the local field office or the entire agency?). Under previous law, a victim of sexual harassment could only get back pay (in quid pro quo suits), and in hostile environment cases they could only obtain equitable relief.[67]

The debate concerning permissible or impermissible behaviors distracts from the broader question of the scope of the sexual harassment problem and the response to it. Sexual harassment suits have increased progressively. In 1975 only seventy-five complaints were filed with the EEOC. By 1984 they had increased to over five thousand, and by 1988 they had increased to over seven thousand. In a two-month period in 1992 (October to December), over sixteen hundred cases were filed, four hundred more than had been filed for that period in 1991.[68] Polling data show that sexual harassment is widespread and pervasive. A Harris Survey taken in the spring of 1994 found almost 31 percent of women and 7 percent of men said they had been sexually harassed at work. Forty-three percent of the women reporting harassment said it was a supervisor who was the harasser, and 27 percent said it was a senior employee.[69]

With the greater number of sexual harassment claims, employers are urged to be more reactive to complaints.[70] Employers are under a legal obligation to make an immediate investigation. The outcome of the investigation is to be documented and recorded in the employer's files. The documentation should include whatever disciplinary or remedial measures were taken. If the investigation is inconclusive, the results should be communicated to the complainant and the accused employee. However, disciplinary steps taken against an employee are to be kept confidential. The object of the harassment is only informed that disciplinary action was taken along with such steps as are necessary to prevent further harassment.[71]

In many instances, victims demand that parties guilty of sexual harassment be terminated, transferred, or at least suspended. In *Barrett v Omaha Nat'l. Bank* (1984),[72] the court determined that it is only necessary that a sanction be immediate and appropriate. In *Barrett* the party was reprimanded, placed on probation, and warned that repetition would lead to discharge. Victims may press for more severe sanctions or question the reasonableness of the employer's response. EEOC standards indicate that an employer's action is appropriate where it "fully remedies the conduct without adversely affecting terms and conditions of employment for the charging party"(e.g., as in asking the victimized employee to work at a less desirable location).[73] This still leaves open the issue of whether nonpunitive responses are adequate. A Ninth Circuit decision supported a sexual harassment victim in requiring the employer to impose more severe disciplinary measures to end the harassment after separation and counseling proved ineffective.[74] Judge Keep's concurrence in that case suggests the need for a standard to guide employer responses, a standard that would require steps most likely to put a stop to the unlawful behavior and that might require immediate termination in the most egregious cases.[75]

This is a more widespread problem than one might think. When a complaint is adjudicated in court, a judge can find an agency guilty and issue sanctions against it. However, any disciplinary action against the harasser is left to the agency and agencies cannot be compelled to discipline those employees. An EEOC study of its recommendations to federal agencies concerning its 1989 caseload revealed that the agencies rejected the EEOC findings in 58 percent of the cases. In fact, in many instances the parties accused of harassment are not disciplined, especially if they are management officials. The irony is that if the harassment is tied to a work-related personnel matter within the scope of the supervisor's duties, the agency becomes the defendant and agency attorneys will defend the actions of the official.[76] Sexual harassment is said to be part of the social and work culture. The investigative reports demonstrating harassment on the part of high officials, including those with a special responsibility for civil rights (EEOC officers), show that the problem penetrates into the management culture.

Even when agencies have sexual harassment policies and procedures to deal with complaints, employees and victims may not obtain satisfaction. A recent study of an institution of higher learning's experience with its policy discovered a disjunction between form and practice.[77] While the sex harassment policy engendered positive responses, dissatisfaction with the implementation of the policies was substantial. Complainants noted that accusers were treated as guilty parties, that the policy was biased in favor of the accused, and accusers' confidentiality interests were breached. Highest levels of dissatisfaction were registered with responses of the institution. Some 32 percent reported that little to nothing was done about the accusations. Where sanctions were applied they were viewed as too lenient by the accusers. The most surprising finding was that those experiencing harassment preferred dealing with the harassment through informal approaches rather than the formal investigations and hearings that marked the policy. Grievances of this nature take on the form of adversary proceedings, which become very uncomfortable for the parties involved. Surveys relating to implementation of antiharassment policies would indicate that prevention programs rather than reaction would serve employer and employee interests best.

SEX-LINKED DISCRIMINATION

Certainly one issue that profoundly affects women and their employment rights and privileges is pregnancy. Pregnancy involves not only physical changes that affect expectations of performance but also the issue of inevitable interruptions in the work history of the employee. As a result pregnant employees were often the object of discrimination and immediate expulsion from the workforce. Typically, a female employee would inform her employer that she had just discovered she was pregnant. The employer would then regard her announcement as the fifteen-days' notice for termination of employment. The courts were not initially responsive to pregnant workers. In a 1948 case, a judge expressed the opinion that a woman who took time off for pregnancy was not unlike "one who deliberately maims himself to unfit himself for work."[78]

The first cases to reach the Supreme Court involving pregnancy issues dealt with forced-leave policies, a common practice, especially applicable to women in the teaching profession. The Cleveland Board of Education required women to initiate a leave from employment at least five months before the child was due and to continue that leave until three months after birth. In *Cleveland Board of Education v LaFleur* (1974),[79] the Supreme Court addressed possible constitutional violations in the policy. It bypassed the equal protections issues and found the policy violated due process standards by unduly burdening a woman's fundamental right to bear a child. While restrictions may be placed on such liberties under the due process clause, the board of education policy represented an irrebuttable presumption that women were per se unfit to perform occupational duties within the bracketed period of eight months.

The passage of the 1964 Civil Rights Act, which indicated that there shall be no discrimination on account of sex, did not answer the question as to whether discrimination against pregnant women might violate the act. In *Geduldig v Aiello* (1974)[80] the Supreme Court found that a medical disability plan for state employees did not violate the equal protections clause of the Constitution by excluding from its coverage women who lost time from work for pregnancy-connected medical problems. The state plan did not exclude women from obtaining benefits; it only excluded those persons who manifested certain medical conditions.

The Supreme Court then decided a pregnancy discrimination case brought under Title VII, *General Electric Co. v Gilbert* (1976).[81] Here the Court found that the General Electric Company had not violated Title VII with an unlawful employment practice by excluding from its disability coverage women who lost time from work for pregnancy-connected medical problems.[82] Again the Supreme Court, with Justice Rehnquist providing the rationale, ruled that this did not involve discrimination in terms of the standard male/female dichotomy. Rehnquist conceded that only women get pregnant, but he said it was a unique condition that was desired and voluntarily entered into.[83] Even more remarkably, the decision rejected EEOC guidelines that stated that pregnancy, childbirth, miscarriage, or abortion should be treated as any other health or temporary disability condition.[84] Rehnquist brushed off the guidelines, saying they were only interpretive rules that flatly contradicted rules the EEOC had in place earlier. Justice Stevens in dissent thought the Court erred in drawing distinctions between pregnant persons and non-pregnant persons (that would include women). It should have made the distinction between those who were at risk for pregnancy (all women) and those who were not.[85] The Court also ignored the invidious double standard in the policy that covered male reproductive conditions but not female reproductive conditions.

The *Geduldig* and *Gilbert* decisions generated such outrage that Congress passed the Pregnancy Discrimination Act of 1978(PDA). It amended Title VII to include section 701(k), which stated:

> the terms because of sex and on the basis of sex include but are not limited to, because of or on the basis of pregnancy, childbirth, or related conditions; and women affected by pregnancy, childbirth or related medical conditions shall be treated the same for all employment related purposes including receipt of benefits under fringe benefit programs, as other persons not so affected but similar in their ability or inability to work.

What the PDA proscribed was refusal to hire a woman because she is pregnant, any inquiry as to whether an employee is pregnant or intends pregnancy,[86] forcing a pregnant woman to leave work if she remains willing and able to perform her job functions, and abrogating or terminating any privileges or benefits of employment such as accrued seniority.

The language of the PDA would appear to clearly proscribe termination of employees on the grounds of pregnant status. However, the PDA did not eliminate the mixed motive action. In 1992 the Second Circuit decided *Zaken v Boerer*.[87] Rona Zaken was hired as a sales representative for a company owned and headed by a female CEO, Bonnie Boerer. After Boerer learned of Zaken's pregnancy she became cold and hostile to the employee and put Zaken under evaluation. The evaluation found fault with Zaken's record-keeping skills and the employee was terminated. The employee then filed a suit under Title VII and New York antidiscrimination laws alleging discrimination based on pregnancy. To make such a claim she introduced evidence, largely hearsay, that indicated that the employer had terminated previous employees because of pregnancy. Immediate supervisors "hinted" that pregnancy was a factor in the decision ("Your pregnancy doesn't help your case"). The case became a typical mixed motives case with the employer proffering reasons other than pregnancy for termination. The case was remanded by the appeals court to the district court to allow the employee to demonstrate by a preponderance of evidence that pregnancy was a motivating factor in her termination.

The PDA created multiple complications on leave issues. One issue became the extension of leave privileges to pregnant women, which other workers considered preferential. Some states such as California also enacted th' own legislation allowing women to take up to four months of unpaid p' nancy disability leave and guaranteeing their reinstatement.[88] By the end o1 1992 sixteen states and the District of Columbia had enacted statutes providing for maternity leave.[89] With such a diversity of policies, there always remained the issue whether the PDA would preempt state laws or whether state laws were so preferential or discriminatory to classes similarly situated that they would fall of their own constitutional infirmities.[90]

The passage of the Family and Medical Leave Act of 1993(FMLA)[91] went a long way to addressing the lack of uniformity in state policies and providing an omnibus solution to it. Under the FMLA, employers both private and public with more than fifty employees[92] are to allow unpaid leave for a variety of reasons: serious illness, childbirth, adoption, or serious illness of children, spouse, or parents. They may take up to twelve weeks of leave at one time or intermittently, and status and benefits of employment (including health insurance premiums) are not to be effected by the leaves. What the act does is to remove the issue of differential treatment of pregnant and non-pregnant employees, of pregnant employees and those otherwise temporarily disabled, of female and male caregivers, of birth and adoption of a child, and of short-term and long-term plans. Title IV of the act also addresses the diversity issue, noting that the FMLA does not affect any state laws that provide greater leave benefits. However, the FMLA will supersede state laws that are less protective of employees and less stringent on employers. It also serves to reinforce federal legislation, not to alter it, noting that nothing in the act should be construed to modify or affect in any way federal laws prohibiting discrimination, including the basic provisions of the Civil Rights Act of 1964 and its 1978 amendments (the PDA).

CONCLUSION

Gender discrimination in the workplace and personnel issues impacting women represent some of the more contentious areas in public personnel management. The most prominent issue of late is sexual harassment. Increasing numbers of women are bringing allegations of sexual harassment against public employers. Public agencies must implement policies that make explicit that sexual harassment will not be tolerated. Employees engaged in harassing behavior must be dealt with swiftly. The checklist and sample policy on sexual harassment that follow provide guidance in establishing agency policies and procedures that safeguard against gender discrimination.

PUBLIC ADMINISTRATOR CHECKLIST

1. Are all agency positions open to persons of either gender?

2. Do qualifications reflect valid predictors of job performance? Do any qualifications unfavorably impact one gender or another? Are physical qualifications fair to recruitment of both genders?

3. To what extent can objective screening criteria replace subjective screening criteria?

4. What subjective screening or evaluation criteria may overtly or subtly reflect stereotyped gender-linked expectations? In the interview process how may gender neutrality be maintained?

5. In the agency, how do the advancement patterns of men and women employees compare? Is there evidence of a "glass ceiling"?

6. To what extent are there incentives or encouragements to female employees to compete for advancements?

7. To what extent are resources, assignments, and contacts equitably distributed between men and women employees?

8. Has the agency developed an environment that preserves dignity and respects feelings of all employees? Does the environment express disapproval of sexual harassment?

9. Has the agency informed employees of their rights in raising sexual harassment charges? Does it have a policy in place to deal with sexual harassment complaints? Does it provide a channel for complaint that can allow parties to bypass their immediate superiors? Do the policies allow for confidential investigations and hearings? Is there a publicized code of sanctions for improper behaviors?

10. Does the agency provide sensitizing education programs on sexual harassment and proper workplace etiquette?

11. To what extent are women employees included in an agency's social networks?

EXAMPLE OF SEXUAL HARASSMENT POLICY

Agency: Metropolitan Park District
Policy: Sexual Harassment

The Metropolitan Park District guarantees to all employees the right to work in an environment free of sexual harassment. Sexual harassment is offensive both physically and emotionally, undermines employee morale, and affects the productivity of the victim and his/her coworkers.

Sexual harassment is defined as *unwelcomed* verbal comments or physical contacts of a sexual nature. Specifically, sexual harassment occurs when these unwelcomed actions:

1. are made a condition of employment;
2. are used as a condition for an employment decision (e.g., promotion, salary adjustment, training program, and so forth);
3. affect the performance of the employee's duties;
4. create an offensive, hostile, or intimidating work environment.

Any employee who is aware of a potential sexual harassment situation should immediately contact his/her supervisor or the director. Upon receipt of any complaint alleging sexual harassment in the workplace, the Park District will investigate the complaint and take immediate corrective action. All employees should be aware that the Park District will not condone or tolerate sexual harassment in any form. Any employee found to have engaged in *any* act of sexual harassment is subject to disciplinary action, including dismissal.

TEN TOP QUESTIONS TO ASK WHEN INVESTIGATING SEXUAL HARASSMENT COMPLAINTS*

1. Who harassed you? (The higher-ranking the harasser, the more likely a formal complaint or suit.)
2. What did they do? (Specifics are vital.)
3. When did they do it? (Were there repeat offenses?)
4. Where did it happen? (Whether it was on agency property is immaterial.)
5. Were there any witnesses? (Look for corroboration.)
6. Who did you tell? (Were other persons informed?)
7. Who else has been harassed? (Is this a broader problem?)
8. What did you do in response?
9. What do you want done? (Employer should document what employee thinks is appropriate as protection should employee later claim different action was requested.)
10. Do you feel that you need counseling or some assistance (therapy) to help you deal with this? (If employee indicates such a need agency should refer employee to appropriate caregiver and underwrite such assistance. If answer is no, document that in case of later claims of emotional distress resulting from alleged harassment.)

Exercises

12.1 Personnel Grievance 3 in the appendix concerns an allegation of sexual harrassment in the workplace. How would you have handled this situation? Draft an agency policy on sexual harrassment.

12.2 Personnel Grievance 8 partly involves discrimination based upon gender. Examine the facts and advise management on how to proceed.

12.3 Personnel Grievance 9 filed against the director of the Sunshine Center also involves an allegation of discrimination based upon gender. Assess the merits of this case.

12.4 Personnel Grievance 12 is filed against a policy analyst and involves an allegation of sexual harassment and retaliation for bring a harassment complaint. Assess the merits of this case.

*Derived from 14 *BNA Communicator* No. 3 (Fall 1994), p. 9. © Bureau of National Affairs, Washington, D.C. All rights reserved.

Notes

1. For an excellent review of gender discrimination issues, including those in employment, see Susan Gluck Mezey, *In Pursuit of Equality: Women, Public Policy, and the Federal Courts* (New York: St. Martins Press, 1992).
2. 29 U.S.C. 206(d).
3. The amendment was not offered as a serious proposal but as a sarcastic and cynical attempt to introduce a controversial element into the legislation that would jeopardize its passage. See Charles Whalen and Barbara Whalen, *The Longest Debate: A Legislative History of the Civil Rights Act* (New York: Mentor Books, 1985), p. 117.
4. Civil Rights Act of 1964 Amended (1972). Sec. 703(e)(1).
5. 433 US 321 (1977).
6. 442 F2d 385 (5th Cir 1971).
7. 517 F.Supp. 292 (N.D. Tex. 1981).
8. 859 F2d 1523 (7th Cir 1988).
9. 411 US 792 (1973).
10. 450 US 248 (1981).
11. 490 US 228 (1989); 737 F.Supp. 1202 (D.C. Cir 1990).
12. Ibid. at 251.
13. 737 F.Supp. 1202 (D.C. Cir 1990). Judge Gessell particularly faulted Price-Waterhouse for failing to separate out the tainted sexist comments from those free of sexism in evaluating Hopkins.
14. Martha Cleary, *Sufficiency of Defendant's Nondiscriminatory Reason to Rebut Inference of Sex Discrimination in Promotion or Demotion of Employee as Violation of Title VII of Civil Rights Act of 1964*, 111 ALR Fed 1 (1993).
15. See for example *Ezold v Wolf, Block, Schorr, and Solis-Cohen*, 751 F.Supp. 1175 (E.D. Pa. 1990).
16. See *Bruhwiler v University of Tennessee*, 859 F2d 419 (6th Cir 1988); and *Jones v Rivers*, 722 F.Supp. 771 (D.C. Cir, 1989).
17. See *Palmer v Schultz*, 616 F.Supp. 1540 (D.C. Cir 1985), 815 F2d 84 (D.C. Cir 1987); and *Palmer v Baker*, 905 F2d 1544 (D.C. Cir 1990).
18. See Ann M. Morrison, Randall P. White, and Ellen Van Velsor, *Breaking the Glass Ceiling: Can Women Reach the Top of America's Largest Corporations?* (Reading, Mass.: Addison Wesley, 1982); and Mary M. Hale and Rita Mae Kelly, *Gender, Bureaucracy, and Democracy* (New York: Greenwood Press, 1989).
19. A Report to the President and the Congress of the United States by the U.S. Merit Systems Protection Board, "A Question of Equity: Women and the Glass Ceiling in the Federal Government" (Oct. 1992).
20. See Tracy L. Bach, *Gender Stereotyping in Employment Discrimination: Finding a Balance of Evidence and Causation Under Title VII*, 77 Minn L Rev 1251 (1993).
21. See *Barbano v Madison County*, 922 F2d 139 (2d Cir 1990).
22. "A Question of Equity," p.18.
23. Ibid., pp.24–25.

24. *United Steelworkers of America v Weber,* 443 US 193 (1979).
25. *University California Bd. of Regents v Bakke,* 438 US 265 (1978).
26. 480 US 616 (1987). A full-length case study is presented in Melvin I. Urofsky, *A Conflict of Rights: The Supreme Court and Affirmative Action* (New York: Chas. Scribners, 1991).
27. The scores of the qualifying applicants ranged from 70 to 80. Johnson was tied for second with a score of 75, Joyce was third with a score of 73.
28. Urofsky, p. 56. The statement was made by Michael Baratz, public employees union representative.
29. An observation advanced by Ruth Bader Ginsberg during her confirmation hearings for Supreme Court Justice in respect to her experiences with employment interviews.
30. See Susan D. Clayton, "Remedies for Discrimination: Race, Sex and Affirmative Action," *Behavioral Science and the Law* 10 (1992), p. 245.
31. See P.T. Reid, "Racism and Sexism: Comparison and Conflicts," in *Eliminating Racism: Profiles in Controversy,* ed. P.A. Katz and D.A. Taylor (New York: Plenum, 1988), pp. 203–21.
32. See Rehnquist opinion in *Michael M. v Sonoma County,* 480 US 616 (1981).
33. A. Szymanski, "Racism and Sexism as Functional Substitutes in the Labor Market," *Sociological Quarterly* 17 (1976), p. 65.
34. Clayton, "Remedies," p. 252.
35. OPM, *Demographic Profile of the Federal Workforce,* PSO-OWI-5 (Washington, D.C.: 1992), appendix II, pp. 79, 103.
36. See Cynthia Fuchs Epstein, *Women in Law* (Urbana, Ill: University of Illinois Press, 1993). See chap. 7, "Government Practice."
37. 454 F2d 234 (5th Cir 1971).
38. 13 Fair Empl. Prac. Cas. 123 (D.C., 1974). This decision was finally overruled in *Barnes v Costle,* 561 F2d 983 (D.C. Cir 1977).
39. *Miller v Bank of America,* 418 F.Supp. 233 (N.D. Calif. 1976).
40. *Tomkins v Public Service Electric and Gas Co.,* 422 F2d 553 (D. N.J., 1976). Following *Saxbe, Tomkins* was overruled at the circuit court level, 568 F2d 1044 (3d Cir 1977).
41. 413 F.Supp. 654 (D.C. Cir 1976).
42. 29 C.F.R. sec. 1604.ll (1980).
43. 682 F2d 897 (11th Cir 1982).
44. See *Kyriazi v Western Electric Company,* 461 F.Supp. 894 (D. N.J. 1978). A district court found that coworkers who conducted a constant campaign of insults, ridicule, and sexual aspersions against a disliked female employee had altered her conditions of employment.
45. 29 C.F.R. sec. 1604.11(a) (1981). For a discussion of the implementation of a working conditions theory of harassment see Joseph G. Allegretti, *Sexual Harassment of Female Employees by Co-workers: A Theory of Liability,* 15 Creighton L Rev 437 (1981–82).
46. 641 F2d 934 (D.C. Cir 1981).
47. Ibid. at 945–46.
48. 477 US 57 (1986).

49. David C. Savage, "Thomas Urged Reagan Administration to Toughen Stand Against Harassment," *Minneapolis Star Tribune*, 10 Oct.1991, p. 6A.
50. The government brief tried to make the case that what the guidelines proscribed was a "hostile environment" affecting the workplace, other workers, clients, or customers, not a social and personal relationship originating in sexual attraction. The government brief also tried to discredit Vinson's case totally, noting that for three years she had made no complaint, had received all expected perquisites of employment, and was not observed by coworkers to have exhibited any stress that would indicate harassment. So much for the EEOC's brief on behalf of a protected employee under Title VII. Brief for the United States and the Equal Employment Opportunity Commission as amicus curiae in the matter of *Meritor Savings Bank v Vinson*, DKT. N. 84–1979, 15–18.
51. See *Tomkins v Public Service Electric and Gas Co.*, 568 F2d 1044 (3d Cir 1977).
52. See *Wood v Strickland*, 420 US 308 (1975).
53. 29 C.F.R. sec. 1604.11(d),(e).
54. Ibid. at (f). See Michele Hoyman and Ronda Robinson, "Interpreting the New Sexual Harassment Guidelines," *Personnel Journal* (Dec. 1980), pp. 996–1000.
55. See *Mumford v James T. Barnes and Co.*, 441 F.Supp. 459 (E.D. Mich. 1977).
56. For a discussion of changing attitudes, see Richard Morin, "Think Twice Before You Say Another Word: A Poll Shows the Definition of Sexual Harassment is Changing," *Washington Post Weekly Edition*, 28 Dec. 1992–3 Jan. 1993, p. 37.
57. For a discussion of this issue, see *The Reasonable Woman Standard: Preventing Sexual Harassment in the Work-place*, 18 William Mitchell L Rev 795 (1992).
58. 805 F2d 611 (6th Cir 1986), Keith dissent at 626.
59. 895 F2d 1469 (3rd Cir 1990).
60. 924 F2d 872 (9th Cir 1991).
61. Eric J. Wallach and Alyse L. Jacobson, "'Reasonable Woman' Test Catches On," *National Law Journal*, 6 July 1992, pp. 21–25. Federal courts in Pennsylvania, Hawaii, Michigan, Minnesota, and New Jersey applied or at least partially relied on the reasonable woman standard.
62. 955 F2d 559 (8th Cir 1992), on remand, 807 F.Supp 506 (N.D. Ia. 1992), revs'd, 989 F2d 959 (8th Cir 1993).
63. 477 US at 67.
64. *Rabidue v Osceola Refining Co.* 805 F2d 611 (6th Cir 1986); *Scott v Sears Roebuck*, 798 F2d 210 (7th Cir 1986); and *Brooms v Regal Tube*, 830 F2d 1554 (11th Cir 1987).
65. 126 L.Ed.2d. 295 (1993), 114 S.Ct. 367 (1993).
66. *Saxton v American Telephone & Telegraph*, 10 F3d 526 (7th Cir 1993). See *National Law Journal*, 20 Dec. 1993, p.6.
67. Cora S. Koch, "Rights Act Reshapes Remedies," *National Law Journal*, 30 Mar. 1992, pp. 23–25.
68. *EEOC Compliance Manual*, no. 173 (Mar. 31, 1993).
69. 14 *BNA Communicator*, no. 3 (fall 1994), p. 15.
70. See Hoyman and Robinson, "Interpreting the New Sexual Harassment Guidelines."
71. See *Swentek v USAir*, 830 F2d 552 (4th Cir 1987).

244   GENDER DISCRIMINATION IN EMPLOYMENT

72. 726 F2d 424 (8th Cir 1984).
73. See *EEOC Compliance Manual,* sec. 615.4(a)(9)(iii) at 3213(1988).
74. *Interlekofer v Turnage* 973 F2d 773 (9th Cir 1992).
75. Ibid. at 783.
76. See Dana Priest, "When the Enforcer Commits the Sexual Harassment: Federal Agencies Often Don't Discipline Their Wrongdoers," *Washington Post Weekly Edition,* 9–15 Dec. 1991, p.32; and Bill McAllister, "Atlanta's VA Hospital: A Top-Level Conspiracy of Silence: Blatant Sexual Harassment Persisted for Years," *Washington Post Weekly Edition,* 15–21 March 1993, pp. 31–32. Also see Bettina B. Plevan, "Harassment Gets Taken Seriously," *National Law Journal,* 30 Mar. 1992, pp. 23–25, and Janice Goodman, "Sexual Harassment Laws Face Lax Enforcement," *National Law Journal,* 11 Jan. 1993, p. 17.
77. Laura A. Reese and Karen E. Lindenberg, "Staff Perceptions of Sexual Harassment Policy: Content and Recommendations" (paper delivered at the 1993 Annual Meeting of the American Political Science Association, Sept. 2–5, 1993).
78. *Moulton v Iowa Employment Security Commission,* 34 N.W.2d. 21 (1948).
79. 414 US 632 (1974).
80. 417 US 484 (1974).
81. 429 US 125 (1976).
82. The General Electric plan prohibited any disability payments for medical leave taken for pregnancy, miscarriage, or childbirth. Medical conditions arising during pregnancy were not covered either. Males could, however, obtain disability payments for medical conditions involving their reproductive systems.
83. The Court was stating sub rosa that rational decisions to have children involved voluntary absences that should not be rewarded by an employer.
84. 29 C.F.R. sec. 1604.10(b) (1975).
85. 429 US 125, Stevens dissent at 162.
86. See *King v Trans World Airlines,* 738 F2d 255 (8th Cir 1984). Employer asked employee eligible for rehire questions as to her pregnancy, marital status, number of children she had, legitimacy of those children, child care arrangements, future childbearing plans. Court of Appeals for 8th Circuit ruled that under sec. 701, questions about pregnancy and childbearing are unlawful in absence of bona fide qualifications. Employer also cannot have two-interview policies for job applicants, one for men and a more scrutinizing one for women.
87. 964 F2d 1319 (2d Cir 1992).
88. The California Maternity Leave Act was declared constitutional by the U.S. Supreme Court in *California Federal Savings and Loan v Guerra,* 479 US 272 (1987). While California's provisions were different from the PDA, Justice Marshall said it was the intent of Congress that the PDA contain a floor beneath which pregnancy disability benefits would not drop, not a ceiling above which they might not rise.
89. See Patricia J. Bejarano, *Labor Pains: The Rights of Pregnant Employees,* 43 Labor L J 780 (Dec. 1992), p. 782; and Tim Barnett, Winston N. McVea Jr., and Patricia A. Lanier, *An Overview of the Family and Medical Leave Act of 1993,* 44 Labor L J 429 (July 1993), p. 432.
90. There even remained the question, whether some of these laws, even if compatible with the PDA, contained provisions that violated the Equal Protections clause.

91. PL 103-3 (H.R. pt. 1), Feb. 5, 1993.
92. The term employer in the act includes "any public agency" as defined in sec. 3 of the Fair Labor Standards Act of 1938. Sec. 108 of the act has special provisions concerning employees of local educational agencies, and Title II extends leave for civil service employees of the federal government.

13

Discrimination Based on Age and Disability: Accommodation and Adjustment

This chapter extends the discussion of discrimination into the additional areas of age and disability. It will conclude with a discussion of the issue of personal and family leave. While most of the focus in discrimination in employment has concerned racial or sex discrimination suits, age discrimination cases are becoming more salient. In 1992, age discrimination suits filed by the Equal Employment Opportunity Commission (EEOC) constituted 28 percent of its caseload, outnumbering racial cases (25 percent) and exceeded only by gender discrimination suits (36 percent). These cases show a high correlation with suits challenging discriminatory discharge. Moreover, age discrimination cases involve higher financial stakes than the usual case. In fiscal year 1992, the EEOC recovered $71.1 million for victims of employment discrimination. Over $56 million of that was for suits filed under the Age Discrimination in Employment Act (ADEA).[1]

It was once a given that employers could release employees whose age, physical, or mental disabilities caused them to perform below employer expectations. There was also a long-held and irrebuttable presumption that employees could be expected to perform duties until the age of sixty-five. This threshold was regarded as a practical one that would accommodate both the need of business or agencies to create job opportunities for younger persons with potential for development and the expectations of the older workers looking forward to retirement. This "compulsory" retirement at sixty-five was a workplace norm until the passage of the ADEA in 1967.[2] This act originally applied only to employers in the private sector covered by the Commerce Clause of the U.S. Constitution, but 1974 amendments extended the coverage of the act to federal, state, and local governments.[3] The ADEA prevents employers from subjecting an older qualified worker to compulsory retirement, demotion, or discharge in order to make room for a younger worker. The act protects workers over forty years old and protects them from compulsory retirement and adverse actions in which age is the reason for the action.[4] One important exemption is for executives or administrators who occupy policy positions for at least two years prior to a retirement date. The exemption applies solely to those involved in making executive decisions, not to senior employees such as counsel or scientists who happen to earn as much as policymakers.

Age discrimination questions that particularly affect public administrators fall into the following contexts:

1. failure to hire older persons or rejection of those persons for reasons that are age-linked;
2. failure to promote older persons, or promotion of younger persons over older or more experienced candidates;
3. reductions-in-force (RIFs) that terminate or force retirement on older workers, either exclusively or disparately in numbers, or that adversely affect older workers;
4. termination of older workers for reasons of lowered performance or medical problems associated with age.

The protection of older workers begins with the hiring stage. Older applicants must not be excluded or discouraged from seeking employment. Employment notices and advertisements that call for applicants below forty years of age or that are specifically directed to younger applicants violate the act unless the employer can demonstrate the age restriction is job-related. Even borderline issues such as notices that are targeted to "recent graduates" have been interpreted as violating the spirit of the act.[5]

Often older workers, particularly those who have been displaced, may find that their experience and talents are a liability. They have been rejected as "overqualified." Two court cases, *Taggart* I and *Taggart* II, were the first to deal with the potential age discrimination involved in rejecting applicants because they were "overqualified."[6] When Taggart was passed over for a less-qualified individual because the position was a "junior position," he sued. The district court found no problem in dismissing the claim.[7] Under an employment discrimination case, a person who challenges a rejection must meet the requisite condition of being "qualified" for the position. The court determined that this was one instance in which the applicant was "not appropriately qualified." The court of appeals reversed, noting that it was a fallacy to conclude that an overqualified person is an *unqualified* one (emphasis added).[8] The court noted that "overqualified" may also serve as a euphemism for being too old, in which case the challenger has grounds to raise the issue of discrimination with pretext. The question of whether the "sole reason of overqualification" was equivalent to "age being the sole reason" was left to a jury to decide.

When older workers are denied promotions, the issue comes down to whether the person is qualified for advancement and whether the older person's qualifications are competitively superior to other candidates irrespective of consideration of age. What some older employees may not realize is that they can prevail against an adverse action only if they can establish by a preponderance of the evidence that they were not promoted "because of age." Private employers covered under the ADEA would be free to deny a promotion to or even dismiss an older worker for any reason or no reason, provided only that the reason is not age. As the court noted in *Partington v Broyhill Furniture*,[9] "Nothing in the age discrimination law provides tenure to competent older workers. . . . The market like the jungle to which it is compared is pitiless." For instance, in a competition for a promotion, less-experienced or less-qualified persons might be chosen. If a candidate were chosen on the basis of nepotism, that might appear odious but would not be regarded as a violation of the ADEA.[10] Public employees would receive some additional protection under the due process clauses of the Fifth and Fourteenth Amendments in that those clauses prohibit adverse actions for purely arbitrary reasons. Denial would have to be based on a rational nondiscriminatory reason. The public employer would need to establish nondiscriminatory grounds for the employment decision, but that is easily accomplished. The reasons advanced might be:

1. some special qualification of the person chosen;
2. other applicants did better in their interviews;
3. the older employee had some negative references or evaluation in his or her file;
4. the older applicant was not denied or rejected but ranked equally with others and put on short list whereby the employer had discretion to choose any of the top candidates;
5. the older applicant expressed differences with superiors on matters of policy.

Even federal employers have been able to circumvent the age reason with some impunity. In *Odum v Frank*,[11] a recent case involving denial of promotion to a fifty-four-year-old black male in the postal inspectors branch, the court decided in favor of the Postal Service. The older candidate "was simply not the top ranked candidate." While the court acknowledged that the promotion seemed to be predicated on the perpetuation of an old boys' network, with decision-makers going through the motions to ensure that the top administrator would get the person he wanted to fill the new position, the court also noted;

> But even if that impression is correct, it does not amount to racial or age based discrimination. . . . Even though the Service's process might not pass the smell test and might well raise some eyebrows, Odum failed to adduce sufficient evidence to demonstrate that discriminatory intent motivated the acts and omissions.[12]

Adverse employment such as denials of promotions are made ostensibly on the basis of valid nondiscriminatory reasons. While such reasons may be challenged by an older employee covered by the ADEA as pretextual and a mask for a discriminatory motive, it has become difficult to rebut the proffered nondiscriminatory reasons especially since the adverse decision may involve mixed motives. Under the 1991 Civil Rights Act amendments, an employee must persuade the court that age was the motivating factor in the dismissal. What one must provide is a "smoking gun" demonstrating overt expression of prejudice against an older worker. Statements of employers and supervisors that aim at "getting rid of the good ole joes" or the "old buzzards" or the "Alzheimer brigade" may be probative that age was the controlling factor in the adverse decision against the employee. Remarks and cryptic allusions that workers were "out of date," "not sufficiently trendy," "over the hill," or "burnt out" may be dispositive in a close case, courts ruling that they were not simply stray words but probative of intention to discriminate.[13]

The 1991 Civil Rights Act amendments provide for disposition of age discrimination claims in jury trials. A resultant jury verdict may be subject to review and reversal if it failed to take into consideration the weight of nondiscriminatory factors. In *Walker v A.T.&T. Technologies,*[14] a female applicant for a promotion was able to convince a jury that a less-qualified candidate was chosen. She reinforced her position with evidence that most of her coworkers were upset over what was termed a patently wrong choice. However, the court of appeals noted that there is no principle of law that a business decision be popular with employees. It overturned the verdict, noting that the instructions to the jury failed to firmly impress the point that an employer has the right to assign work to an employee, to change employee duties, to refuse to assign or even to discharge an employee for good reason, bad reason, or no reason at all absent intentional age discrimination.[15]

Adverse actions against older workers are often associated with RIFs, an increasing phenomenon of the late 1980s and 1990s in public organizations as agencies deal with budgetary cutbacks.[16] RIFs are often coupled with restructuring objectives that seek to inject new ideas, new spirit, and new energy into a department while getting rid of exhausted, stagnant, or functionally obsolescent personnel. RIFs are conventionally perceived as targeting older employees. The decision of an organization to implement a RIF is not a violation of the ADEA. Such actions may be a business or administrative necessity. It becomes a violation only when the RIF has an exclusive or strongly disparate impact on those over forty years old. If the RIF is targeted at positions and not at occupants in those positions of a particular age range, the RIF is likely legitimate.[17] If an agency intends to cut back its management positions, the effect is more likely to impact older workers (who may be concentrated in management positions). While such an action may disparately impact the older portion of the workforce, the focus on positions may demonstrate that the organization exhibited no intent to discriminate against older workers.[18] Current law is unsettled in allowing employers some discrimination between older and younger workers in a protected class (keeping workers in their forties and releasing those over fifty).[19] RIFs must be evaluated in terms of the final mix of positions and employees at different age brackets.

The ADEA stresses the continued employment of qualified workers over forty. It focuses on promoting the employment of workers based on ability rather than age. For some employees, age will mark the onset of declining health and disabling conditions that progressively affect job performance. Before the passage of the Americans with Disabilities Act (ADA) in 1990, older employees were in the same position as other workers adversely affected by decisions based on reasonable factors other than age, including physical or mental inability to carry out the functions of a position. Now, under the ADA, a substantially limiting age-linked impairment could be considered a disability. Employees able to demonstrate that they have a disability under the broad definitions of the ADA would be able to require the employer to make reasonable accommodations that would realistically enable the employee to carry out the job functions and thus maintain the position.[20] Specific disability questions are discussed in the following section.

EMPLOYMENT DISCRIMINATION: DISABILITIES AND HANDICAPS[21]

The workplace, both private and public, has always incorporated a sampling of employees who were able to responsibly fulfil the requirements of their jobs in spite of the fact that they had obvious disabilities and handicaps. But the reality was that disabled and handicapped individuals were more often than not the victims of discrimination based on apparent disability without regard to ability to perform. The recognition of employment rights for the disabled began with the passage of the 1948 amendments to the Civil Service Act, which prohibited employment discrimination based on physical handicap in the U.S. Civil Service.[22] In 1968 Congress passed the Architectural Barriers Act, which required that new and remodeled buildings be made accessible to persons with physical impairments. Then Congress enacted the Rehabilitation Act of 1973, which prohibited employment discrimination against otherwise qualified handicapped employees in any executive agency or the U.S. Postal Service.[23] Collateral sections also mandated affirmative action programs for hiring of the handicapped in government agencies and by government contractors.[24] The EEOC and the Office of Federal Contract Compliance drafted regulations to implement these provisions.[25] The Rehabilitation Act and its implementation reflected a congressional intention that the federal government be a model employer of the handicapped.[26]

After 17 years of experience with the Rehabilitation Act of 1973, Congress passed the Americans with Disabilities Act (ADA) of 1990. The act broadened the protection of persons with disabilities in employment to public employees in state and local governments and to the entire private sector. An umbrella of protection was extended to an estimated 43 million Americans who exhibited some type of disability.[27] The act has the potential for protecting employment and other rights of every American. The class of persons protected under the act is the only one of which persons may become a member at any time. As someone waggishly put it, those persons without disabilities can be classed as "the temporarily able bodied."[28] The scope of the act addressed issues of employment discrimination, public accommodations, public services, public housing, education, transportation, communication, and even voting. The employment provisions of the ADA basically follow the patterns of the Rehabilitation Act of 1973 and includes concepts expressed in administrative regulations issued by the EEOC under Section 504 of the Rehabilitation Act.[29] It also incorporates by reference the procedural requirements and remedies of Title VII of the Civil Rights Act of 1964.[30] Except for some special positions within the federal workforce that require preentry examinations, the requirements of the two acts can be discussed concurrently.

The Rehabilitation Act of 1973 addressed both the issue of the accommodation of the workplace itself for handicapped individuals and the issue of the qualifications of the handicapped to hold employment. The issue of physical barriers is perhaps the least controversial. Handicapped individuals must have a reasonable access to and from their place of work, and their workstations must involve physical arrangements that allow them most efficiently to carry out their duties.[31] One problem is the substantial capital investments that must be made to make workplaces fully accessible. Progress continues on the accessibility objectives of the Rehabilitation Act and the more recent Americans with Disabilities Act. A 1992 study by the General Accounting Office noted that 67 percent of 231 buildings surveyed were in compliance with federal accessibility guidelines. Accessibility is relative to the structures involved. The most accessible building had 92 percent compliance and the least accessible building met the standards for 40 percent of its features.[32]

The more critical issue is the opening up of the workforce to persons whose handicaps raise the issue of qualifications. Public employers can be naturally expected to search out and hire the most qualified individuals, hire those individuals who require no adjustments or material modifications of the work environment, and hire applicants who give promise of long, uninterrupted employment. Prior to the Rehabilitation Act, agencies like the Postal Service attached the requirement that its employees be in "good physical condition" in order that they be able to perform a variety of arduous tasks. This contemplated the use of physical examinations to screen out applicants for employment. However, the Rehabilitation Act and the ADA have established guidelines for preemployment medical examinations and inquiries. Originally, a person with a medical condition such as epilepsy, diabetes, or cancer in remission would apply for a position. A candidate would be asked to fill out a medical questionnaire and take a medical examination. The candidate would then proceed through the process of interviews and providing references and would then be denied the job. There would be no way for the applicant to know that the disability factor was crucial to denial. In 1977 regulations issued by the Department of Health, Education and Welfare (HEW) restricted an employer from having a candidate submit to any medical examination or to provide a medical history. The employer could ask questions only as to limitations a candidate might have in regard to specific job functions. Once an employer had determined that the candidate had the qualifications to perform the job and had offered the job, the employer could require the applicant to undergo medical exams or respond to medical inquiries (only if such examinations were given to all new personnel). The results of the medical examination could not be used to withdraw the offer of employment unless results indicated that the candidate would not be able to perform the duties under the job description. Also, if the exam uncovered a medical condition of concern (such as deafness in one ear, a heart problem, HIV infection), the employer could not use those results to discriminate against the person if the person was still qualified for the job.[33]

The federal government treads a fine line between avoiding inquiries that would screen out individuals unfairly and making inquiries that would be in the interest of the employee's safety. The regulations state that an agency may not conduct a preemployment medical examination or make an inquiry whether a candidate has a handicap or how severe that handicap is. This can involve a test of abilities for safe and efficient performance of duties. An agency may also make inquiry whether an applicant has particular medical needs to which the individual might need access with the government serving as a guarantor of that access. The Department of Defense, for instance, inquired whether persons posted to distant foreign-duty stations (e.g., Saudi Arabia) have any chronic or recurring physical or mental impairment or allergy that requires availability of medical care, services of specialists, maintenance of prostheses, medication, hospitalization, or special food.[34] Similarly, the Department of State requires considerable medical information on employees posted overseas.[35]

On medical inquiries under the ADA, certain questions are appropriate; others are not.[36]

Appropriate Questions

1. Are you able to perform certain tasks?
2. How would you perform those tasks and with what accommodations?
3. Are you able to meet the job's work, hour, and schedule requirements?

Inappropriate Questions

1. Have you ever been treated for the following conditions or diseases?
2. Please list any conditions or diseases for which you have been treated in the past three years.
3. Have you ever been hospitalized? For what?
4. Have you ever been treated for a mental condition? Have you been treated by a psychiatrist? Psychologist?
5. What prescription drugs are you taking?
6. Have you ever been treated for drug addiction or alcoholism?
7. Is there any health reason that might prevent you from doing the type of work you will be doing?

A primary question in employing persons with physical or mental conditions is to ascertain who is an otherwise qualified person with a disability. Under the Rehabilitation Act[37] and the ADA, an individual with a disability is a person who has a physical or mental impairment that substantially limits one or more life activities, a person with a history or record of such impairment, or a person regarded by others as having such an impairment. Physical impairments include any physiological disorder, deficit, or condition that affects body systems or processes. They do not include temporary medical traumas or conditions (bodily injuries, episodic diseases like the flu or cold, childbearing, or medical conditions cured with surgery or reasonable treatment). Mental impairments include mental or psychological conditions listed as disorders by psychiatric and psychological associations. Organic learning disabilities are included. Undesirable personality traits such as quick temper, irresponsibility, obnoxiousness, offensiveness, and irrationality are not impairments. Homosexuality and bisexuality cannot be claimed as impairments. The ADA also specifically excludes current addiction to illegal drugs and a number of sexual and criminological disorders.[38]

The ADA also includes alcoholism as a disability whether or not the person is recovering or a current alcoholic.[39] While such individuals may not be discriminated against and must be treated equally with other employees in regard to discipline, they must follow workplace rules and be able to fulfil all the essential functions of their job with or without reasonable accommodation. If alcoholism affects their work, they are subject to the sanctions of the employer.[40] The ADA's neutral position on alcoholism (as just another disabling condition) is to be contrasted with the position taken by the federal government.

In 1970 Congress passed the Hughes Act, which required agencies to have alcoholism treatment programs for their employees. No person was to be denied or deprived of federal civilian employment solely because of *prior* alcohol abuse or *prior* alcoholism.[41] After the Rehabilitation Act of 1973 was passed, there was some question as to whether alcoholism was covered as a handicap under the act. Under Executive Order 11914, the president asked then HEW to promulgate regulations that would establish standards for determining who are handicapped individuals. The attorney general provided an opinion in 1978 that alcoholics and drug addicts were "handicapped individuals" under the scope of the act. Congress then passed the Anti-Drug Abuse Act of 1986[42] and the Office of Personnel Management set up regulations for alcoholism and drug abuse programs. Under the regulations, whenever a manager or supervisor becomes aware that a federal employee's use of alcohol and/or drugs is contributing to a performance or conduct deficiency, that supervisor is required to refer the employee to a counseling program. If the employee fails to participate in the program or, having participated, the employee fails to bring conduct or performance up to a satisfactory level, the agency can take steps to evaluate the employee accordingly and initiate appropriate performance-based or adverse action.[43] The federal umbrella of tolerance of alcoholics in the workplace has particular limits. Employees in national security agencies and law enforcement agencies who are currently alcoholics or addicts are not guaranteed employment while pursuing a rehabilitative track. The FBI can exercise considerable discretion in discharging agents who may not overcome an alcoholism problem as expeditiously as expected, and the FBI has no obligation to transfer the individual to a job not involving law enforcement (thus keeping that person under the ambit of the Rehabilitation Act).[44]

Candidates for a position who demonstrate they are qualified in spite of a disability may be asked to meet other criteria such as successful completion of an interview process. This raises the issue of mixed motives for denial of a position to an applicant. This emerged in the case of *Pushkin v Regents of Univ. of Colorado,* a Rehabilitation Act case involving a state institution using federal funds.[45] A doctor who suffered from multiple sclerosis was denied admission to a residency program in psychiatry. While acknowledging that he could perform his duties, a screening committee denied him admission because he failed to meet other qualifications: "He was not up to the caliber of other students. The program would be too rigorous for him. He communicated anger to patients. Patients would be put off by his appearance." The court noted that the committee had used these reasons as a blind for rejecting him on the basis of expressions of his disability. The reasons aside, he was denied solely on the basis of his disability.

Once an agency has brought on board a qualified person with a disability, under both the Rehabilitation Act and the ADA, the employer must determine whether or not the individual can perform the essential functions of the position with or without reasonable accommodation. If modifications or adjustments are necessary to enable the person to fulfil job duties, an employer must make such accommodation unless it presents an undue burden for the employer. A number of accommodations may be necessary in the total work experience:

1. making facilities readily accessible and usable by an employee with a disability;
2. providing reserved parking for an employee with a mobility impairment;
3. providing benefits to the disabled employee equal to those offered other employees (access to restrooms, lounges, lunchrooms, social events, etc.);
4. allowing the employee to provide equipment or devices that the employer is not required to provide;
5. permitting use of paid or unpaid leave for treatment or rehabilitation.

These accommodations are generally seen as reasonable burdens to lay on the employer. As the disability becomes closely entwined with the job performance and conventional expectations of productivity, the reasonableness of the accommodation comes more into question. Disabled employees may feel that they are entitled to accommodations that include:

1. being granted part-time or modified work schedules; flex-time; modified examinations, training materials, or policies that allow employee to do tasks at home or through a communications system;
2. being provided with qualified readers, interpreters, or aides;
3. being provided with private work environments within the workplace;
4. being excused from tasks that might aggravate an existing condition;
5. requiring the employer to do extensive renovation or new construction;
6. granting of leave time on demand, allowing for flexible forms of leave.

Hard-and-fast rules cannot be drafted to cover every eventuality because each individual case is different. The EEOC recommended that employers utilize a process to determine what is a reasonable accommodation on a case-by-case basis, a process that involves close consultation with the disabled employee to determine what accommodations are necessary, which one(s) would increase the efficiency of the employee, and what the employee prefers. The employer might offer alternatives. An employer is not, however, required to make a reasonable accommodation if it is an undue hardship on the operation of the business. Accommodations that are unduly costly, extensive, disruptive, or that would fundamentally alter the nature or operation of the business would not be required. In many cases, the issue of retaining an employee and making an accommodation comes down to costs. Additional costs that exceed the salary of the position could certainly be seen as an undue burden. But even here the EEOC suggests mediated settlements such as the employer and employee sharing the costs of special equipment.

The Rehabilitation Act and the ADA requirements are straightforward in respect to common physical disabilities involving vision, hearing, mobility, and dexterity. These can be addressed through technological adjustments and structuring of the workplace. Certain physical/mental conditions push the limits of the obligation of employers to make accommodations. These same conditions also seem to skirt the requirements that an employee with a disability satisfy the qualifications of the position and be able to perform all its essential functions. The conditions that raise particular issues tend to create temporary but periodic job interruptions or disruptions. They include such conditions as insomnia, hypersomnolence, narcolepsy, bipolar mental disorders, apraxia, aggression control disorders, and chronic stress disorders. The issue becomes the degree to which the employer must extend accommodation and tolerate interruption or disruption in the workplace.

One of the pathfinding cases giving guidance in this regard is the Rehabilitation Act case *Southeast Community College v Davis*.[46] In this case a plaintiff who had a very severe hearing disability sought to be admitted to a nursing program that received federal funds, bringing it under the ambit of the Rehabilitation Act. Here the Supreme Court said that an "otherwise qualified person" is one who is able to meet all of a program's requirements in spite of the handicap. To be admitted to or to maintain employment means that a disabled person must meet all essential functions of the position.

An application of *Southeast Community College* is shown in *Matzo v Postmaster-General*.[47] A worker who had been diagnosed for a manic-depressive illness began experiencing emotional problems and began acting erratically and disruptively. She received permission to take leave time for twice-weekly therapy sessions. As her attendance problems increased, the Postal Service required her to report for a fitness of duty examination, a request that was ignored. The agency then moved to remove her formally from the service. The court upheld the dismissal, affirming the rule that a minimal and basic qualification for a job was the ability to report for work and remain on duty for the duration of the workday.

Stress disorders pose particular problems with cases presenting a wide range of circumstances that have to be addressed individually. In *Arneson v Sullivan*[48] a claims representative for the Social Security Administration suffered from the condition of apraxia.[49] He claimed that his errors in work performance were a result of the stress of the work environment. He had originally performed up to expectations when he had a semiprivate work place, but his work deteriorated when he was transferred into a busier environment. The court accepted the employee's arguments and ordered his reinstatement with new training and efforts to provide him a distraction-free environment.

This case is to be contrasted with *Johnson v Shalala*,[50] a case in which a National Institutes of Health (NIH) scientist suffered from a syndrome of disorders including idiopathic narcolepsy, cardiac arrhythmia, and stress disorder. She had also been treated for a malignancy. In her efforts to seek accommodations that would allow her to perform her duties, she requested flexible starting and ending times for work, permission to take naps at work, extended sick leave, advance sick leave, and leave without pay. When the agency did not accede to her specific requests, Johnson resigned, citing intolerable conditions. She then filed a suit alleging that NIH had failed to provide her with accommodations and had constructively discharged her. While a district court found in her favor,[51] the appeals court said that the plaintiff must present evidence that the employer sought to drive her from her position. NIH's efforts, while unsatisfactory, did attempt to address a part of the problem and the agency did assist her in obtaining disability retirement benefits.[52] While this decision negated the claim of a constructive discharge, it left open the question of whether an employee requesting a high degree of accommodation such as Johnson demanded would prevail in a case in which the employer finally took steps to terminate her for unsatisfactory performance.

A similar issue came up in the case of *Walders v Garrett*.[53] The employee in question was an information systems specialist who suffered from chronic fatigue syndrome.[54] Her performance was satisfactory when she was available for work. However, her condition could unpredictably flare at any time and when it did it left her totally debilitated. As a result she experienced a high level of absenteeism. Her agency permitted her to use both annual and sick leave to cover periods of unscheduled absences but charged her as absent without leave (AWOL) for any unscheduled absence for which she lacked accrued leave. The agency took steps to remove her when her AWOL time accumulated to intolerable levels. The court supported her removal for unavailability for full-time duty. The preceding cases carry a common thread of disability-linked absenteeism beyond what the employer can tolerate. The requirement of regular attendance as an essential job function has been held consistently by the courts. Agencies might reinforce their position by stating clearly a regular attendance requirement within a job description. However, passage of the ADA has raised the issue whether there is a different standard for measuring the obligation to provide accommodation from that provided in Rehabilitation Act case law. In the first case to be decided under the ADA in federal court, *EEOC v AIC Security Investigations Ltd.*,[55] a district court in Illinois ruled that ability to perform the functions of a position rather than regular attendance was the primary consideration in determining whether the employer was obligated to provide accommodations. The case involved an executive of a security company who developed lung cancer. Although he was given only six to twelve months to live he continued to work. After increased absences and statements by his physicians that he could not drive, his firm involuntarily retired him. Rather than accept that option, he sued under the ADA, arguing that his productivity was not affected by his condition and the EEOC pressed the case on his behalf. The court addressed the issue of whether the executive was a "qualified individual with a disability":

> To be sure, attendance is necessary to any job, but the degree of such (especially in upper management positions) . . . where a number of tasks are effectively delegated to other employees requires close scrutiny. An executive . . . more than likely handled a number of his business matters by phone. Whether a phone call is made from the office, a car phone, or a home is immaterial. Whether a contract is negotiated in the office or out of the office is immaterial. What is material is that the job gets done.[56]

Mental disabilities carry their own set of complications.[57] Many mental conditions including depression and bipolar disorders can be controlled by medications and various therapies, allowing sufferers to maintain and hold employment without consequences for employee or employer. Some mental conditions may raise an issue of a threat to health and safety of the disabled person or to others such as when the employee may manifest suicidal tendencies. The EEOC in its interpretive guidance manual suggests that employers in evaluating individual cases balance a number of variables, including an assessment of the severity of the potential harm, the likelihood of the harm, and the duration and risk. Such assessments may, however, be tainted by subjective perceptions, generalized fears, or stereotyped notions of "breakdowns." Determination of a direct threat must be based on an objective factual record—something that establishes a pattern of behavior, something that one court has noted demonstrates an appreciable risk of harm or recurrence.[58] Employers also face the problem of dealing with employees whose dangerous tendencies may have root in a mental disorder. A recent court decision found in favor of an employee who challenged his dismissal for bringing a loaded firearm into the workplace. The court determined that the employee's misconduct, the nexus of conduct to a disability, and the actual threat that the employee posed were factual questions to be determined by a jury.[59]

Some symptomatic expressions of mental conditions may preclude accommodation. A qualified individual with a disability must be able to do the essential functions of a position, functions that incorporate behavioral expectations. For instance many positions require contact with the public and polite and civil behaviors. An employee who had been treated for depression notified her employer that she could not tolerate the stresses of contact with the public, particularly the interviewing of difficult clients. The interview function was an essential element of the position and that accommodation does not allow an employee to rewrite the job description.[60] Essential elements of a position may also require a person to confront and cope with stressful situations as would be obvious for law enforcement and rescue personnel.

Accommodations to employees with disabling but controllable mental conditions or mental deficits require sensitivity and good interpersonal skills on the part of the employer. Aloof, arms-length supervision may not work to the advantage of either employee or employer. A worker's self-esteem may be fragile and expectations may need to be communicated in a receptive style. An employer may need to do things like allow time off for therapy sessions and may also need to provide a mentor or job coach to demonstrate and discuss tasks and to provide supervision at the start and end of work periods to help the employee organize activity. Evaluation may pose particular challenges because of the supersensitivity of some individuals. In the case of *Pesterfield v TVA*,[61] an employee diagnosed as having a depressive disorder expressed explosively reactive tendencies when confronted with the slightest hint of rejection and criticism. He charged any criticism as harassment. The court, however, found that the employee's inability to tolerate even the slight hint of criticism was a bar to performing the essential elements of the job.

One disability, HIV infection, and its successor conditions ARC and AIDS have become a particular workplace issue. The scope of the problem is indicated in a survey conducted by the American Management Association in 1994.[62] Of nearly eight hundred managers responding to a survey, 37.5 percent said that they dealt with actual or perceived cases of HIV infection. This represented a 65 percent increase in the incidence of cases over 1991, and the public sector figures may mirror those in the private sector. This disability deserves its own discussion because the disease raises its own questions of coverage under the Rehabilitation Act and ADA:

1. hiring of individuals diagnosed as having AIDS;
2. integrating individuals into the workforce;
3. reasonable accommodations expected of the employer;
4. privacy concerns of the HIV/AIDS employee.

Individuals who have become infected with the HIV virus are disabled persons under both the Rehabilitation Act and the ADA. In 1988 the Department of Justice issued an opinion advising that persons infected with HIV or AIDS were covered by Section 504 of the Rehabilitation Act.[63] The ADA does not explicitly include AIDS in its inventory of disabilities, but a Senate report accompanying the ADA included HIV infection within the meaning of physical and mental impairments.[64]

As previously noted, the Rehabilitation Act and the ADA prohibit medical examinations prior to consideration for employment. Those proscribed exams would include blood tests for HIV. However, the Department of State introduced a test for HIV as part of its requirements for appointment to the Foreign Service. The American Federation of Government Employees challenged the requirement as violating the Fourth Amendment and Section 504 of the Rehabilitation Act.[65] But the court would not overrule the public policy. An HIV-infected officer would not "otherwise be qualified for worldwide duty," given the uncertainty of appropriate medical treatment and the danger of contracting opportunistic infections in many diplomatic postings.

The requirement of a test for HIV has been affirmed in other contexts. In a Rehabilitation Act case, a practical nurse was discharged for refusing to take an HIV test. While the individual was asymptomatic, he lived with a person who had contracted AIDS. The court ruled that a person who refused the test was "not otherwise qualified" for the position.[66] And in the case of a municipality that required HIV tests of firefighters and paramedics, a Fourth Amendment constitutional challenge was rejected in federal court. The court found that the city's interest in providing a safe workforce and its duty to keep its employees free from the risk of contagious disease prevailed over privacy interests.[67]

The Supreme Court has not directly ruled on the relation of HIV infection or AIDS to the Rehabilitation Act or ADA. HIV and AIDS are contagious, and the broader issue is whether a person with a contagious disease can be regarded as disabled and yet be excluded from the workplace because of the contagious nature of the disease. In *Arline v Nassau School Bd.*[68] the Supreme Court addressed the issue of an elementary school teacher dismissed from her position because she had tested positive for tuberculosis. The Court found that the plaintiff was a "disabled person" under Section 504 of the Rehabilitation Act. She had a record of impairment (previous hospitalization) and was the object of prejudiced perceptions of disability. Whether she was otherwise qualified to perform the duties of the position was a factual question that would take into account nature of risk, duration, severity of risk, and the probability that the disease will be transmitted. Following the decision, Congress codified the principle in the 1988 amendments to the Rehabilitation Act,[69] excluding from coverage of the act those who by reason of disease or infection would constitute a direct threat to the safety and health of others.

Given the attention to alleged discrimination against HIV and AIDS-infected individuals, it is surprising to note that there have been few cases brought under the Rehabilitation Act or ADA that challenge rejection of job applicants because of known HIV or AIDS status. An application of *Arline* to HIV/AIDS was taken in *Doe v District of Columbia*.[70] Doe applied for a position of firefighter with the District of Columbia. He successfully passed the written and physical examination and was offered the position. The employer had not tested for or inquired of the applicant whether he had HIV. After the applicant voluntarily declared his HIV status, the offer of employment was withdrawn. The court found that under the guidelines of *Arline*, HIV infection constituted a disability. The court found no difficulty in finding that the applicant was "otherwise qualified," given the fact that he had passed the rigorous physical. The court noted that an asymptomatic HIV-infected person not only did not constitute any direct threat to others, the risk of transmission was so small as to be unmeasurable.

One of the problems of bringing on board a person who is HIV-positive or who has ARC or AIDS is worker reaction. This particular issue also embraces privacy concerns. There is no necessity to notify other employees that an HIV-positive employee is on board unless there is a "need to know," as in the case of supervisors or first aid and safety personnel.[71] It is still unclear whether an employer may provide notification to other employees working in close proximity where there is significant risk of cuts that may entail bleeding. Commentators have generally suggested that employers put into place an education program to inform all workers on the real medical risks of transmission and provide information on preventing the spread of the virus in workplace settings. That would operate to mitigate the irrational fears that might circulate in a workforce. It is also imperative that the employer provide protective equipment and protocols that would prevent accidents of transmission.[72]

The requirements of ensuring the protection of employees from risks of contagion as mandated by the Occupational Health and Safety Act come up against the right of employees to privacy and confidentiality of their medical records. As previously noted, the ADA mandates the confidentiality of medical records. The stigmas attached to HIV status indicate that public identification of an employee as an HIV/AIDS carrier can lead to possible harassment, calumny, and libelous injury for the worker. Employers who intentionally allow these violations of privacy may find themselves not only subject to sanctions for violating the ADA but also subject to civil actions for libel and violation of privacy under common law tort doctrine.[73] Since the decision *U.S. v Westinghouse Electric Corp.*,[74] which recognized that an employee has a very strong constitutionally protected privacy interest in avoiding the disclosure of personal matters such as exist in medical records, courts have granted awards to employees who have been subject to public embarrassment through disclosure of medical information.[75]

Since HIV is a progressive condition that matures into ARC and then AIDS, a point is reached where employees can perform their duties only with accommodation. Employees will manifest increased fatigue, a lower ability to tolerate stress, and an increased need for health services as they succumb to opportunistic diseases. Accommodation for ARC/AIDS employees is no different from that for employees who may suffer from cancer or myasthenia gravis. AIDS advocates have suggested the full range of accommodational alternatives: part-time or modified work schedules, reassignment to vacant positions, job rescheduling, and reducing the strenuous aspects of job duties.

Few courts have addressed the boundaries of reasonable accommodation for HIV/ARC/AIDS employees. In a recent Rehabilitation Act case, *Buckingham v U.S.*,[76] the Ninth Circuit held that transferring an HIV-positive employee from Mississippi to California to allow the employee to have access to more specialized medical care was a reasonable accommodation, particularly because the employer made such job transfers available to his workforce. Transfer of an employee to duties that did not pose a direct threat to others was also upheld in *Bradley v U. of Texas*,[77] another Rehabilitation Act case, in which a surgical assistant who was diagnosed as HIV-positive was transferred to a clerical position—the type of accommodation that employees themselves would be expected to request.

Both the Rehabilitation Act and the ADA have also raised the issue of borderline or "perceived" disabilities. Such an issue arose in the case of an employee with a pulmonary disability who felt that tobacco smoke in the work environment aggravated his condition. The employer initiated a smoking policy that provided smokeless ashtrays and air filtration devices. An effort was also made to segregate smokers from nonsmokers. The employee, however, demanded that the entire building be declared smoke-free. The court noted that reasonable accommodation is what is necessary for an employee to perform the essential elements of the position. The employee was able to perform those essential functions without a totally smoke-free environment.[78] The case may be the forerunner of other similar cases following an EPA report of January 7, 1993, establishing a link between second-hand smoke and cancer.[79] One perceived disability that has received a great deal of attention is that of obesity. Can employers discriminate against overweight persons? While both federal and state laws prohibit discrimination on the basis of handicap or disability, only one state, Michigan, has enacted legislation that prohibits employment discrimination on the basis of weight.[80] Case law involving state law appeared equally divided on this issue.[81] The applicability of federal law was finally addressed in *Cook v State of Rhode Island, Dept. of Mental Health, Retardation, and Hospitals*.[82] An institutional attendant who had a spotless work record made application for reemployment after a voluntary interruption of employment. Her previous employer then concluded that the applicant's obese condition compromised her ability to evacuate patients and rendered her unqualified for the position. When the applicant sued under the Rehabilitation Act, MHRH argued that morbid obesity could never constitute a handicap under the Rehabilitation Act. Both the lower and appellate courts drew a fine line. The courts recognized that the employer had failed to hire the individual solely because of her morbid obesity. Her condition constituted a disability, and she was otherwise qualified to perform the functions of the position. The courts found critical the fact that the plaintiff's obesity was the result of a dysfunctional metabolism, which was an immutable condition (permanent). While the case was brought under the Rehabilitation Act, the court of appeals gleaned some guidance from the ADA and its implementing regulations that directed employers to consider the duration and long-term impact of a condition in defining a disability covered by law.[83] The distinction between physiological and volitional obesity was drawn by the California Supreme Court, which rejected the claim of an overweight person who had been denied a job based on her weight.[84] The state court, interpreting the California Fair Employment and Housing Act (which contained provisions modeled on the federal Rehabilitation Act), cited *Cook* in limiting the reach of the statutes to physiological disorders.[85]

Rehabilitation Act and ADA disability cases may also engender collateral issues of harassment. Federal discrimination laws, which prohibit employment discrimination on grounds of race, national origin, and gender, have been extrapolated to include harassment and hostile environments as discriminatory labor practices. The same may soon be true of laws covering disabled persons. Unthinkable as harassment of disabled persons is, some cases are breaking ground. A case originating at Sonoma State University in California involved a graduate student who suffered from toxic brain syndrome, a condition in which a person is hypersensitive to airborne chemicals such as insecticides or even perfumes.[86] Exposed to an intolerable substance, the student could experience life-threatening seizures. To avoid exposures to our chemical world, the student did not attend most of her classes, relying on tapes and note-takers. Required to be in class for examinations, the student was exposed to fumes and became disoriented. The instructor, losing patience, accused the student of faking a disability. Following that, the student began receiving a series of cruel and demeaning messages and a dead skunk was placed near her locker. The institution moved to conclude a settlement after the student sued for violation of her civil rights. It was noted that the student completed the course and graduated, indicating that she was otherwise qualified to enter and complete the program in which she had enrolled. Authorities for the institution noted that even highly educated staff have to be educated about disabilities and both the legal and moral obligations attendant to accommodation of individuals so affected.

The ADA is a very recent tool in the campaign against discrimination in the workplace. Its effects have still to be assessed. It has become an important vehicle for the ventilation of grievances and a search for remedies. From July 26, 1992, when the ADA went into effect, until June 30, 1994, the EEOC received over 29,270 complaints.[87] While the EEOC has filed only a handful of cases in federal courts, it has been successful in obtaining out-of-court settlements for a large number of claims. The average settlement for a disabled claimant has been $14,930 a claim, a figure higher than the $8,800 settlement for other discrimination claims. The ADA is seen as a fertile spawning ground for new litigation, given the wide range of individual disability and qualification issues, the large population of employees that may fall under its coverage, and the many unresolved questions with a law that gives employers new responsibilities and few bright lines. The interplay of different legislation illustrates the complexity of the issue of disability. There will be a need to reconcile the requirements of the Rehabilitation Act, the ADA, and the Family and Medical Leave Act. Separate legislation dealing with drug and alcohol rehabilitation for federal workers or for state workers under state law must be integrated with the ADA to create coherent agency policies. The ADA extends to state and local subdivisions. Many of the states have begun to craft and adopt their own disability rights statutes. The extent to which part-time workers are to be accommodated has to be reconciled with provisions under the National Labor Relations Act. Public administrators are forewarned that this is one area where constant vigilance and education is expected.

THE FAMILY AND MEDICAL LEAVE ACT

The requirements of the Rehabilitation Act and the ADA have been supplemented by the passage of the Family and Medical Leave Act of 1993 (FMLA), which became effective for employers of 50 or more persons on August 5, 1993.[88] Title II of the act extends such leave entitlements to almost all civil service employees in the federal government. The FMLA entitles an employee of a covered employer to take up to twelve weeks of unpaid leave a year for these family-related events:

1. care of a seriously ill child, spouse or parent;
2. the birth or placement for adoption or foster care of a child (expiring one year after date of birth or adoption);
3. a serious illness of the employee, preventing the performance of functions in his or her position.

If an employer has a paid sick leave plan in place, the employer may choose or require that all accrued paid leave (accumulated sick leave, paid personal leave, paid vacation) be substituted for any part of the twelve weeks the employee is entitled to receive.

The FMLA offers up to twelve weeks of unpaid leave, which may involve intermittent leave. For instance this might entail twenty three-day leaves. However, the disruptive effects of intermittent absences is eased for an employer by the requirement that employees must give thirty days advance notice of need to take FMLA leave although the employer has discretion to waive such advance notice in favor of the employee. Leave to take care of a family member or for the employee's own health condition may be taken when medically necessary.

The FMLA is to be read in conjunction with the Rehabilitation Act and the ADA in terms of discerning employer responsibilities.[89] First, it is noted that the FMLA is not limited to covering employees with disabilities that impair one of life's activities. Any serious health condition that makes the employee unable to perform job duties triggers the act; this includes injuries and mental and physical illnesses.[90]

An employee experiencing a temporary medical emergency would be covered by the FMLA but not the ADA. On the other hand, an employee who tested positive for HIV would be covered under the ADA only because the asymptomatic status does not create a present "serious health condition."

Other differences between the two laws are in the obligation of the employer to accommodate the employee. The FMLA obligates the employer to provide leave if the employee has a serious health condition and it furnishes the employer with no "undue burden" defense. Once the employee exhausts the twelve weeks of medical leave, the ADA would then be triggered to require the employer to provide additional leave, but the employer might refuse to accommodate the employee because it has become an undue burden. There is still the question of whether employers can argue that the first twelve weeks of accommodation made under the FMLA had strained resources to the point where accommodation beyond that point of time becomes an undue burden.[91] The issue is under consideration by the EEOC. Until regulations are drafted it can be assumed that the FMLA twelve-week entitlement is a reasonable accommodation under the ADA. Would this be regarded as a maximum? For instance, an employee with ARC or AIDS might require more than twelve weeks' leave during a year.

CONCLUSION

This chapter focused on age discrimination and the reasonable accomodation provisions that employers are now required to provide under the Americans with Disabilities Act. It also provided an overview of the Family and Medical Leave Act. It is critical that public administrators be able to adapt to the new conditions that family leave, the Age Discrimination Employment Act, and the ADA will bring to the public workplaces of the 1990s.

PUBLIC ADMINISTRATOR CHECKLIST

   1. Does the agency have in place a policy prohibiting discrimination based upon age or disability?
   2. Has the agency examined its promotion policies to ensure they are blind to age or handicap considerations?
   3. Has the agency conducted an evaluation of office space such as meeting rooms to ensure accessibility for disabled employees?
   4. Does the agency have a need for specialized visual or hearing equipment?
   5. What internal appeals mechanism is provided for employees who allege that they have been discriminated against because of disabilities that do not affect ability to perform the essential functions of their position?

6. In conducting preemployment tests, what guarantees are in place that the tests and exams do not include elements of a medical examination (designed to reveal individual's physical or psychological health)?

7. Does the agency have a system in place to ensure that any medical information gathered (post-job offer) is collected and maintained in separate forms and files?

8. Does the agency have in place a policy for sick leave and leave for family emergencies? Does the agency have in place policies that allow for the functions of the absent person to be performed?

9. Does the agency have policies in place that allow for persons who demonstrate temporary disabilities or temporary illnesses to be rehabilitated into the demands and normal performance expectations of their positions by means of lighter work loads, diminished work hours, and other accommodations?

EXAMPLE POLICY: DISCRIMINATION AGAINST THE DISABLED

The 1990 Americans with Disabilities Act(ADA) prohibits employment-related discrimination on the basis of disability. The Forestry Department is an equal employment opportunity employer and does not discriminate on the basis of disability.

The department guarantees that all current and prospective employees who are protected by the provisions of the ADA have a right to a workplace free of discrimination.

The department guarantees that it will make *reasonable accommodation* to all disabled employees provided that the accommodation does not pose an undue hardship on the employer.

Unlawful discrimiation occurs when:

1. a qualified disabled job applicant is denied employment solely on the basis of disability;
2. the employer refuses to make reasonable accommodation to assist in the performance of the employee's duties;
3. promotion, training, salary, benefits, and sanction decisions are made on the basis of disability.

Any employee who is aware of discriminatory employment practices against a disabled employee or prospective employee should immediately notify the supervisor or director.

Any employee found to be intentionally discriminating against a disabled employee or prospective employee will be subject to disciplinary action including dismissal.

Exercises

13.1 Personnel Grievances 4, 8, and 11 in the appendix all deal in some manner with discrimination based on age. Assess the merits of each case and prepare a memorandum outlining your position.

13.2 Personnel Grievance 7 alleges that actions on the part of the employer violate the provisions of the Americans with Disabilities Act. Does the employee have a case?

13.3 A public employer has an employee in a publications department that has begun to miss work because of migraine headaches. The episodes of migraine are unpredictable and when they do occur, the employee may be debilitated and unable to work for three to five days. The agency allows one hundred hours of sick leave a year. The employee has utilized that. The agency also has a leave policy that requires that requests to utilize vacation time be submitted one week in advance for approval by the personnel officer. Because of the interdependence of many positions, the agency feels that it must have advance notice of any absences to prevent disruption of schedules. The agency's policy provides that vacation or personal days off for which the employee gave inadequate notice would be treated as unscheduled leave and could adversely affect an employee's appraisal ratings. In the case of employee D.W.M., he was denied permission to use vacation time as sick leave and was forced to take unpaid leave. He was also denied the option of working ten hours a day and building up a reserve of hours when he was healthy (because this would entail payment of overtime under the FLSA). His next appraisal listed him as "unsatisfactory" as to punctuality and attendance. D.W.M. appeals the rating and now requests that the employer accommodate him under the Family and Medical Leave Act. He requests that the ratings be reconsidered under his entitlements under the FMLA. Discuss this situation.

Notes

1. *Fair Employment Practices* (Washington, D.C.: BNA, Dec. 6, 1993), pp. 141–42.
2. PL 90-202 (1967).
3. See Fair Labor Standards Amendments of 1974 (PL 93-259). It was extended to state and local governments under the Commerce Clause (see affirmation with *E.E.O.C. v. Wyoming*, 460 U.S. 226 (1983)) and under section 5 of the Fourteenth Amendment (see *Johnson v. Ballermine*, 515 F.Supp. 1287 (D., Md. 1981), cert. denied, 455 U.S. 944 (1981).
4. Originally the Act provided for protection against discharge or involuntary retirement until age 65 but this was raised to age 70 under amendments of 1978. Upper-age specifications were removed with the amendments of 1986. (PL 99-592, sec. 6(a), 100 Stat. 3342, 3244 (1986).

5. See Jay W. Waks, "Firms React to Charges of Age Bias in Ads," *National Law Journal*, 7 Mar. 1994, pp. 22–25.
6. For a discussion of this case see Julia Lamber, *Overqualified, Underqualified, or Just Right: Thinking About Age Discrimination and* Taggart v. Time, 58 Brooklyn L Rev 347 (1992).
7. 1990 WL 16956 (S.D. N.Y. Feb. 20, 1990).
8. *Taggart v Time*, 924 F2d 43, 47 (2d Cir 1991).
9. 999 F2d 271 (7th Cir 1993).
10. *Green v Edward J. Bettinger Co.* 608 F.Supp. 35 (E.D. Pa. 1984), affirmed without opinion, 791 F2d 917 (3d Cir 1984), cert. denied, 479 US 1069 (1986).
11. 3 F3d 838 (5th Cir 1993).
12. Ibid. at 850.
13. See Frank J. Cavaliere, *Derogatory Remarks as Evidence of Discrimination Under the Age Discrimination in Employment Act of 1967*, 44 Labor L J 664 (November 1993).
14. 995 F2d 846 (8th Cir 1993).
15. Ibid. at 850.
16. Arthur J. Marinelli, *Age Discrimination and Reductions in Force*, 20 Ohio Northern U L Rev 277 (1993).
17. See *Cooper v Cook Paint and Varnish Co.* 563 F.Supp. 1146 (W.D. Mo. 1983).
18. See for example *Rose v Wells Fargo & Co.*, 902 F2d 1417 (9th Cir 1990).
19. See *Lowe v Commack Union Free School District*, 886 F.2nd. 1364 (2nd Cir. 1989), cert. denied, 110 Sp. Ct. 1470 (1990), which held that discriminatory effect must be demonstrated for the group protected (40+) and not subgroups within that class. Compare with *Barnes v Gen Corp. Inc.*, 896 F2d 1457 (6th Cir 1989), cert. denied, 111 Sp. Ct. 211 (1990), which held that employers violate the ADEA when they favor younger employees over older employees even if younger persons are within the protected class.
20. Daniel Frier, *Age Discrimination and the ADA: How the ADA May be Used to Arm Older Americans Against Age Discrimination By Employers Who Would Otherwise Escape Liability Under the ADEA*, 66 Temple L Rev 173 (1993).
21. For detailed discussion of the points and issues raised in the following sections, see Jean Fitzpatrick Galanos and Stephen H. Price, *Comment: Title I of the Americans With Disabilities Act of 1990: Concepts and Considerations for State and Local Government Employers*, 21 Stetson L Rev 931 (1992); Equal Employment Opportunity Commission, "A Technical Assistance Manual on the Employment Provisions of Title I of the Americans with Disabilities Act," (Washington, D.C.: January 1992).
22. PL 617, 62 Stat. 351., chap. 434 (June 10, 1948). The amendment provided that "no person shall be discriminated in any case because of any physical handicap, in examination, appointment, reappointment, reinstatement, reemployment, promotion, transfer, retransfer, demotion, or removal with respect to any position the duties of which . . . may be efficiently performed by a person with such a handicap."
23. See sec. 504 of the Act (29 U.S.C. sec. 794).
24. Secs. 501 and 503 of the Act (29 U.S.C. secs. 791, 793). Sec. 501(b) states "Each department, agency, and instrumentality (including the U.S. Postal Service. . .)

shall submit to the Civil Service Commission . . . an affirmative action program plan for the hiring, placement, and advancement of handicapped individuals in such department, agency, or instrumentality. Such plan shall include a description of the extent to which and methods whereby the special needs of handicapped employees are met."

25. See 43 Fed. Reg. 12295 (Mar. 24, 1978) codified in 29 C.F.R. sec. 1613.703 and 41 C.F.R. sec. 60-741.
26. See *Gardner v Morris*, 752 F.2nd. 1271, 1280 (8th Cir 1985).
27. ADA, sec. 2: Congressional Findings and Legislative Purpose (42 U.S.C. sec. 12101).
28. Chai Felblum, *Medical Examinations and Inquiries Under the Americans With Disabilities Act: A View From the Inside,* 64 Temple L Rev 521 (1991).
29. While the Rehabilitation Act of 1978 occupied only a page, the Americans with Disabilities Act of 1990 is over fifty pages, a reflection of wholesale incorporation of Sec. 504's regulations into the progeny statute. See Nancy Lee Jones, *Overview and Essential Requirements of the Americans With Disabilities Act,* 64 Temple L Rev 471, 476 (1991).
30. Secs. 705, 706, 707, 709, and 710 of the Civil Rights Act of 1964, codified as 42 U.S.C. secs. 2000e—2000e-17.
31. See 29 C.F.R. 1603.707.
32. General Accounting Office, "Americans With Disabilities Act: Initial Accessibility Good but Important Barriers Remain" (Gaithersburg, Md., 1992).
33. Felblum, "Medical Examinations," pp. 531f.
34. See *Gardner v Morris*, 752 F2d 1271 (8th Cir 1985).
35. See *Barth v Gelb*, 761 F.Supp. 830 (D.C. Cir 1991).
36. See *EEOC Guidance on Medical Exams Under ADA: Pre-Employment Disability Related Inquiries—May 19, 1994,* 2 Emplymt Discrim Rptr 651 (May 25, 1994).
37. See *Annotation: Who is "Qualified" Handicapped Person Protected From Employment Discrimination Under Rehabilitation Act of 1973,* 80 ALR Fed 830 (1986).
38. These include transvestism, transsexualism, pedophilia, exhibitionism, voyeurism, and gender identity disorders not resulting from a physical impairment. Criminological disorders include kleptomania or pyromania. Compulsive gambling is also not covered.
39. H. Rept. 485, 101st Cong., 2d sess. See 1990 *U.S. Code Cong. and Admin. News* 445, 450–451.
40. See Larry Goff, *The Legislative Response to Alcoholism and Drug Addiction in the Americans with Disabilities Act,* 21 J of Psychiatry and the Law 77 (spring 1993) and David K. Fram, *The ADA Rules for Drug and Alcohol Abuse,* 39 Practical Lawyer 35 (Oct. 1993).
41. PL 91-513, 84 Stat. 1236 (Oct. 27, 1970), formally titled "The Comprehensive Alcohol Abuse and Alcoholism Prevention, Treatment and Rehabilitation Act of 1970."
42. Title VI of PL 99-570, 100 Stat. 3207-157 (Oct. 27, 1986), codified as 5 U.S.C. 7361–62.
43. 5 C.F.R. part 792.105 (49 Fed. Reg. 27921 (July 9, 1984) as amended at 50 Fed. Reg. 16692 (Apr. 29, 1985)).

44. See *Butler v Thornburgh*, 900 F2d 871 (8th Cir 1991); and *Little v F.B.I.*, 793 F. Supp. 652 (D. Md. 1992).
45. 658 F2d 1372 (10th Cir 1981).
46. 442 US 397 (1979).
47. 685 F.Supp. 260 (D.C. Cir 1987).
48. 946 F2d 90 (8th Cir 1992), rsg., *Arneson v Heckler*, 879 F2d 393 (8th Cir 1989).
49. Apraxia can be described as "difficulty in bringing ideas together, difficulty in writing or organizing expression, and distractibility" (non-medical definition in *Arneson v. Heckler*, 879 F2d 399 [8th Cir 1989]).
50. 991 F2d 126 (4th Cir 1993).
51. 764 F.Supp. 1053 (D. Md. 1991).
52. NIH did, however, falsify an evaluation to allow her to obtain a disability retirement, a fact that the court did not hold against the agency on the constructive discharge issue.
53. 765 F.Supp. 303 (E.D. Va. 1991).
54. Termed CFIDS or chronic fatigue syndrome or Epstein-Barr virus, it is marked by chronic viral activity, extreme fatigue, and other symptoms. Episodes may completely debilitate patients (make them unable to get out of bed). It appears aggravated by stress.
55. 820 F.Supp. 1060 (N.D. Ill. 1993).
56. Ibid. at 1064.
57. For a thorough discussion see Margaret Hart Edwards, *The ADA and the Employment of Individuals with Mental Disabilities*, 18 Employee Relations L J 347 (winter 1992–1993); Paul F. Mickey Jr. and Maryelena Pardo, *Dealing With Mental Disabilities Under the ADA*, 9 Labor Lawyer 531 (1993); and John M. Casey, *From Agoraphobia to Xenophobia: Phobias and other Anxiety Disorders Under the Americans with Disabilities Act*, 17 Univ Puget Sound L Rev 381 (1994). For a comprehensive exploration of mental health in the workplace, see Donna R. Kemp, *Mental Health in the Workplace* (Westport, Conn.: Greenwood Publishing Group, 1994). For issues involving claims of emotional distress, see James J. McDonald Jr. and Francis Kulick, *Mental and Emotional Injuries in Employment Litigation* (Rockville, Md: BNA Books, 1994).
58. See *Doe v New York University*, 666 F2d 761, 777 (2d Cir 1981). An appreciable risk of harm can be something considerably less than a 50 percent chance. How significantly less is still a question.
59. *Hindman v GTA Data Services*, 3 A.D. (Americans with Disabilities) Cases (BNA) 641 (M.D. Fla. 1994), discussed by Frank C. Morris and Teresa L. Jakubowski "ADA Places Employers of Mentally Ill in a Bind," *National Law Journal* April 17, 1994, pp. C31-33.
60. *Hill v State of Florida Dept. of Health*, 715 F.Supp. 346 (M.D. Fla. 1992). The court found that the plaintiff's requests would have excused her from any contact with the public, would have absolved her from following schedules, and would have permitted her to be disorganized.
61. 941 F2d 437 (6th Cir 1991).
62. The American Management Association membership includes seven thousand

large and mid-sized companies. The survey is reported in *Fair Employment Practices* (Washington, D.C.: BNA, May 9, 1994), p. 53.
63. Department of Justice, *Memorandum on Application of Rehabilitation Act, Sec. 504 to HIV Persons* (Sept. 27, 1988).
64. See S. Rept. 101-116, at 22. The House Conference Report (101-596), which was adopted by the Senate, did not deal with specific contagious diseases but noted that an employee need not accommodate a person who posed a significant risk of harm to others (as distinguished from the Senate Report, which used the term "direct threat") taking into account the magnitude, severity, and likelihood of harm or infection. *1990 U.S. Code Cong. and Admin. News:* Legis. Hist. at 569.
65. *Local 1812 A.F.G.E. v U.S. Dept. of State*, 662 F.Supp. 50 (D.C. Cir 1987).
66. *Leckelt v Bd. of Comm'rs. of Hosp. Dist. 1*, 909 F2d 820 (5th Cir 1990).
67. *Anonymous Fireman v City of Willoughby*, 779 F. Supp. 402 (N.D. Ohio 1991).
68. 480 US 273 (1987).
69. PL 100-630, 102 Stat. 3303 (Nov. 7, 1988), codified as 29 U.S.C. sec. 706(8)(C).
70. 796 F.Supp. 559 (D.C., Cir 1992).
71. The ADA provides for confidentiality of all medical records. See sec. 102(c)(3)(B). Exemptions for supervisors and safety personnel are indicated in sec. 102(c)(3)(B)(ii).
72. See James Monroe Smith, *HIV/AIDS and Workplace Discrimination: Dickens Revisited—It Was the Best of Times. It Was the Worst of Times*, 22 U West Los Angeles L Rev 19 (1991); Debra A. Abbot, *Workplace Exposure to AIDS*, 48 Maryland L Rev 212 (1989); and Jeffrey S. Klein and Lawrence J. Baer, "With More Businesses Having to Accommodate HIV-positive Employees, Companies Need Guidance to Address Federal Disability Laws and Privacy Rights," *National Law Journal*, 9 May 1994, p. B5.
73. See *EEOC Regulations to Implement the Equal Employment Provisions of the ADA*, 29 C.F.R. 1630.14 (1993).
74. 638 F2d 570 (3d Cir 1980).
75. See for example *Miller v Motorola Inc.* 560 N.E.2d 900 (Ill. App. Ct. 1990) where an actionable invasion of privacy was noted because employer disclosed fact that employee had a mastectomy; and *Levias v United Airlines*, 500 N.E.2d 370 (Ohio Ct. App. 1985) where an invasion of privacy claim was sustained where employer had explained his employee's anemia as related to menstrual hemorrhages.
76. 998 F2d 735 (9th Cir 1993). The case was remanded to determine if transfer is in fact a reasonable accommodation.
77. 3 F3d 933 (5th Cir 1993), cert. denied, 114 Sup. Ct. 107 (1994).
78. *Harmer v Virginia Electric and Power Co.*, 831 F.Supp. 1300 (E.D. Va., 1993).
79. Andrew Blum, "Secondhand Smoke Suits May Catch Fire," *National Law Journal*, 1 Mar. 1993, p. A1.
80. *Mich. Comp. Laws Ann.* sec. 37.2101.
81. See *Comment: Employment Discrimination Against Overweight Individuals: Should Obesity be a Protected Classification*, 30 Santa Clara L Rev 951 (1990).
82. 834 F.Supp. 57 (D.R.I, 1993), affirmed with expanded opinion, 10 F.3d 17 (1st Cir 1993).

83. 10 F3d at 25 (1993).
84. *Cassista v Community Foods Inc.*, 22 Cal. Rptr.2d 287 (1993).
85. Ibid. at 296.
86. Scott Jaschik, "A Convoluted Harassment Dispute at Sonoma State U.," *The Chronicle of Higher Education*, 22 June 1994, p. A30.
87. 3 Emplymt. Discrim. Rptr. 128 (Aug. 4, 1994). Also see Brian Bulger, "Impact of the ADA Exceeds Predictions," *National Law Journal*, 28 Feb. 1994, p. S7.
88. PL 103-3, 107 Stat. 7 (Feb. 5, 1993).
89. See Peggy R. Mastroianni and David K. Fram, *The Family and Medical Leave Act and the Americans with Disabilities Act: Areas of Contrast and Overlap*, 9 Labor Lawyer 531 (1993). Also see David Block and Margaret R. Bryant, "After a Year, FMLA Still Provokes Questions," *National Law Journal*, 28 Feb. 1994, p. S12.
90. See Dept. of Labor Interim Rule, 29 C.F.R. 825.115 (58 Fed. Reg. 31,817 (1993)).
91. Ibid. at 557.

14

Appraisal, Discipline, Employer Sanctions

An inescapable part of a personnel administrator's role is to both reward and discipline employees under his or her jurisdiction. Administrators, supervisors, and peer-review groups within public agencies have allocational powers that determine granting of permanent status (or tenure), promotions or the increase of responsibilities, and bonuses. The other side of this coin involves the exercise of deprivational powers in decisions to discipline, demote, or even terminate an individual from employment. These are usually the hardest decisions any administrator may face. This chapter will explore some of the dimensions of this administrative responsibility and attempt to show the balancing of agency interests and the necessities of the service against employee's rights.

Public employees, like private employees, at one time operated under the doctrine of employment at will, which generally gave an employer absolute discretion in terminating the employment of an employee. In 1877 Harris G. Wood, an Albany lawyer, legitimated the concept in a treatise on master-servant relationships. Wood concluded that a general (noncontractual) hiring is an indefinite hiring and is determinable by the will of either party.[1] Wood's rule soon became the general rule in state jurisdictions. It was regarded as an equitable concept because it gave the employer the maximum flexibility to control the workplace through the unfettered power of discharge, and it also gave the employee the freedom to resign and move to more satisfactory employment. However, the application of Wood's rule did away with the whole notion of "unlawful discharge" and opened the door to unabashed abuses of administrative power and discretion.[2]

Employment at will controlled public as well as private employment. The federal government became the first institution to move away from this draconian policy. In the 1960s the Supreme Court recognized that federal employees have constitutional protections in their employment. By limiting removals to those for just cause, the federal government was distinguished from private employers, who have complete freedom of action in dealing with personnel.[3] Civil service provisions also mandated that public employees could be dismissed only for "just cause."[4] Legislation such as the Civil Rights Act of 1964 and the Age Discrimination Employment Act added just-cause provisions. But it still remained relatively easy for federal employers to sanction or dismiss employees. Courts gave agencies broad discretion to make personnel management decisions. Courts limited their review to determining whether an adverse employment decision was reached in accordance with relevant procedural requirements.[5] At the state level, some erosion of the employment at will doctrine occurred with courts and legislatures creating a public policy exception that prohibited employers from discharging employees for refusing to violate criminal statutes at the behest of an employer or for exercising statutory rights or duties.[6] States also moved to recognize two other exceptions to employment at will, the implied contract and the implied covenant of fair dealing. The states have, however, remained cautious in passing legislation that would set standards for just discharge and require that employees be discharged only for good cause and with the benefit of procedures that allow employees to defend themselves. In 1991 the National Conference of Commissioners on Uniform State Laws (NCCUSL) passed a Model Employment Termination Act.[7] This was a model act rather than a uniform act, so it allowed states to tailor their own variants. The heart of the model act lies in Section 3, which requires a reasonable basis for terminating an employee. It does, however, give employers several advantages. Instead of requiring a nexus between conduct and job performance, it only requires that conduct be relevant to job performance or employer concerns. While it allows an employee to regain a position, it fails to provide that an innocent victim of unjust discharge be made whole or that an employer be deterred from repeating his or her actions. It has in fact been criticized as having many shortcomings and in being a "toothless tiger" in standing up for employee rights.[8]

The greatest progress came with the passage of the 1978 Civil Service Reform Act (CSRA).[9] This wide-ranging federal statute covered recruitment and selection of federal workers, prohibitions on discrimination, protection of constitutional and privacy rights of employees, and equitable compensation. It also outlined a long list of prohibited personnel practices including actions relating to removals, suspensions, suspensions of pay, disciplinary or corrective decisions, and performance evaluations.[10] It provided important guidelines for deprivational actions taken as a result of an employee's incompetence or unsatisfactory performance (Section 43) and as a result of employee misconduct (Section 75). Importantly, the procedures put into place by the statute would include genuine fairness requirements, opening up these decisions to greater court scrutiny. These two sections have provided a standard for deprivational actions at the federal level and a model to be applied at the state level. The chapter will first consider the unsatisfactory performance issue and then misconduct issues.

ADVERSE ACTIONS FOR UNSATISFACTORY PERFORMANCE

The 1978 amendments to 5 U.S.C. chap. 43 were intended to give personnel managers more authority to root out incompetence within the ranks of employees. Many managers and personnel officers had complained that procedures in place before 1978 intended to ensure merit and protect employees from arbitrary management actions had become the refuge of incompetent and inefficient employees who were allowed to stay on the work rolls as long as they avoided misconduct.[11] Under the new provisions, adverse employment decisions could be taken in reaction to unacceptable performance. The old dichotomous evaluation system that rated an employee's performance as satisfactory or unsatisfactory was to be replaced with evaluations tied to established standards of performance in all the critical elements of a position. Under Section 43, all federal agencies were to develop performance appraisal systems that provided for periodic appraisals of the job performance of employees, encouraged employee participation in establishing those standards, and directed that the removal or management of employees be based on the results of those performance appraisals. The statute also strengthened notice requirements and involved administrators and supervisors in assisting employees in improving unacceptable performance. They could reassign, reduce in grade, or remove employees who continued to have unacceptable performance only after they had been provided an opportunity to demonstrate acceptable performance.

The section mandates a performance appraisal system to be in place that provides employees a clear notice of the expectations of their position. Performance requirements were to be made known to all employees, every employee was to be currently advised and notified of the performance rating, and every employee receiving less than a satisfactory rating could request a hearing and a decision on the merits of the appealed rating. Courts soon saw the section as containing substantive as well as procedural standards. While agencies had considerable discretion in establishing these standards, those standards had to be reasonable, realistic, and objective. Performance standards could not be vague or nebulous. A standard requiring an employee to "direct work activity and issue orders on what, how, and by whom action should be taken," was found to be inadequate. A grievant was demoted for unacceptable performance because, "(Her) assignments and instructions to staff were hastily made, sometimes misunderstood, and her direction of work activities was occasionally effective."[12] Courts also saw an abuse in discretion where an agency required a compliance examiner to complete 30 audits a year when no one in the regional office at any grade had ever conducted that many examinations;[13] where clerks were required to meet a 99.5 percent efficiency rating in screening, logging, and distributing four hundred to seven hundred pieces of correspondence a month;[14] where an agency established an absolute standard that one substantiated act of discourtesy constituted unsatisfactory performance.[15] Courts also weighed in against "backwards standards."[16] Backwards standards identify faults in regard to critical elements of a job and trigger unsatisfactory evaluations. For instance, such a standard focusing on timeliness would state "provides materials to staff late," or focusing on accuracy would state, "material returned more than once for corrections or repreparation."[17] These kinds of standards fail to inform workers what they must do to maintain acceptable performance. Agency performance standards also had to be approved by the Office of Personnel Management (OPM). Agencies were required to provide documentation of OPM approval or introduce the standards through regulations that were cleared with OPM.[18] Once the agency had its performance standards in place it was allowed to remove or demote employees for unsatisfactory performance. Employees adversely affected under these provisions were given procedural protections and also had a right to appeal a removal or a reduction in grade to the Merit Systems Protections Board.[19]

While an agency is given flexibility in terms of communicating performance standards to workers, agencies must prove by substantial evidence that an employee was made aware of and understood performance standards and critical work requirements at the beginning of the appraisal period that was used for an adverse action against the employee. The communication of standards may be in written instructions, in counseling sessions held with the employee, or in group briefings.[20] Supervisors may give content to written performance standards that embrace individualized expectations by oral communications, or through performance improvement plans, but an agency may not change written performance standards under the guise of giving content to it.[21]

Once an agency determines that an employee is deficient in one or more of the critical elements of the position, the agency may *propose* a reduction in grade or removal action. Any proposed action must be based on unacceptable performance that occurred within a one-year period ending with notice of the proposed action. The agency must also afford remedial opportunities and afford the employee a gamut of protections:[22]

1. 30 days advance written notice indicating how employee has failed to perform critical elements of the position;
2. right to respond orally and in writing;
3. right to representation;

4. right to receive a decision concurred in by supervisor higher in agency than employee proposing action;
5. right to demonstrate improved performance;
6. right to raise medical issues that may have contributed to diminished performance. An agency can then consider accommodation or application for disability if the employee has requisite years of service.

In giving an employee an opportunity to demonstrate improved performance, the agency must prove that it afforded the employee an opportunity to demonstrate acceptable performance *before* the agency's action was taken.[23] Also, if an employee has performed acceptably from the beginning of an opportunity to demonstrate acceptable performance and the employee's performance again becomes unacceptable, the agency is to afford the employee an additional opportunity to demonstrate acceptable performance.[24] A necessary result of these requirements has been to create a Maginot Line against any disciplinary campaign, as illustrated in a newspaper column focusing on attempts to sanction incompetence in the U.S. Postal Service.[25] While the agency discovered numerous employee deficiencies (postal workers who refuse to go out in very cold weather, bags of mail tossed into lobbies of high-rise buildings, mail gathering dust in stations, employees who were persistently inebriated on the job), few workers were disciplined or dismissed. Under postal service regulations, any complaint is followed by a letter of warning with specific expectations as to improvements, followed by thirty days to show improvement. If there is no improvement, then there is a second letter with a thirty-to-sixty-day period to show improvement. This can be accompanied by a suspension of one to two weeks. A third letter provides another sixty-day grace period. Only then can removal be effected and the employee can, of course, appeal.

The new statutory requirements reflect what may be termed a curative style of personnel administration. Employees are to be genuinely counseled and in effect retrained to meet the expectations of the position. The statutes are not specific on the amount of time that is allowed for improvement or on the approaches that may be utilized to achieve such an objective. The reasonableness standard is controlling here. Efforts to obtain improvement should be positive rather than negative or punitive. This was indicated in *Zang v Defense Investigative Service*,[26] in which a demotion of a personnel clerk was not sustained because of the nature of the remedial program.

> Counseling sessions given the [employee] by her supervisor were often disparaging in nature, did not produce guidance or advice on how to improve her work, and were not used to warn her of the possibility of impending or contemplated actions based on her performance. . . . (W)ithin three days of the beginning of [the supervisor's] tenure in that capacity, [he] had judged her incompetent, had begun to assemble a secret, negative record against her designed to support her pre-ordained ultimate demotion, and had thus effectively deprived her of a meaningful opportunity to improve.[27]

One inherent difficulty in the application of the opportunity to improve may occur with employees who have a record of long service. If there are indications of diminished performance, then an employer may run afoul of the Americans with Disabilities Act, which may require the employer to provide some accommodations that would allow the person to function in a satisfactory manner. There is also a fine line in imposing newer, higher standards of performance than were previously called for. In one sense, performance standards should be open to upgrading. At the same time new, higher levels that are unreasonable or a pretext for displacing an employee cannot be imposed. An example of such an unreasonable expectation was made of a scientist of twenty-seven years of service who, at the beginning of her performance improvement period, was given 120 days to submit a high-level research proposal, which the court found was unlike any that she or her colleagues had been required to prepare.[28] Employees cannot be called on to do the impossible in the name of significant improvement.

ADVERSE ACTIONS FOR MISCONDUCT

Federal employers have also had the authority to dismiss employees for misconduct. The basis for such authority was the Lloyd-Lafollette Act of 1912 and the Veterans Preference Act of 1944, which indicated that, unless in the case of excepted service, a federal employee could be removed only for such cause as will promote the efficiency of the service.[29] This open-ended phrase provided employers almost total discretion in sanctioning employees. The Civil Service Commission provided guidelines in 1968 that listed some of the circumstances that might justify removal of a person to promote the efficiency of the service. These included criminal, infamous, dishonest, immoral, or notoriously disgraceful conduct; intentional false statements or deception or fraud in examination or appointment; habitual use of intoxicating beverages to excess; reasonable doubt as to the loyalty of the person involved to the government of the United States; and any legal or other disqualification that makes the individual unfit for service.[30] The last residuary clause allowed administrators to broaden the range of cause for dismissal to such causes as excessive absences, insubordination, disorderly conduct, discourteous behavior, acceptance of favors, disrupting the workplace, lowering morale, emotional instability on the job, and engaging in notoriously disgraceful conduct that would discredit the agency. Preemployment behaviors (sometimes decades old) and off-duty behaviors often provided grounds for dismissals to promote the efficiency of the service.

The movement toward directly "work-related conduct" began with guidelines for evaluating individuals for federal employment published in 1975 by the U.S. Civil Service Commission.[31] While the new guidelines affirmed the provisions of 5 C.F.R. sec. 731.201, the guidelines said disqualification from employment was warranted only when notoriously accompanying conduct can be expected to affect the ability to perform.[32] Several court cases then established that if personal or public misconduct was grounds for dismissal from employment, there had to be a nexus between the misconduct and the efficiency of the service. In *Young v Hampton*,[33] a federal employee was convicted of possession of a controlled substance (off-duty arrest) and served a ninety-day sentence. The government removed him from employment to "promote the efficiency of the service," making a point that his sentence created a ninety-day absence from work. The court found that although Young's off-duty conduct resulted in a felony conviction, there was no showing whatsoever that plaintiff's misconduct impaired functioning at the arsenal or that retention of plaintiff would have any negative effects. While the government claimed a morale problem, the court found that the problem resided in a few employees who unjustifiably objected to what they presumed was a drug seller working in their midst. As to the absenteeism issue, the court found the government's arguments disingenuous. Taking the issue to its logical conclusion, an employer could suspend an employee from the service, then dismiss the employee for being absent from work.[34]

Courts took the nexus test further, declaring that there had to be a vital connection between the misconduct and the efficiency of the service. The determination of a vital nexus was to rest on a rational basis and not on a distortion of facts. In *Phillips v Bergland*,[35] the court reversed the discharge of an employee who had assaulted a fellow employee during a lunch break as a consequence of a private off-duty dispute. While the incident took place on the public employer's property, it took place away from any work area. The court appeared to find the incident did not directly implicate the conditions of employment. If a nexus was to be demonstrated it was to be on the basis of genuine effects, not speculation about employee reactions.

Courts demanded that agencies do more than simply say *ecce nexus*. A vital nexus would be established if the misconduct affected the employee's own work performance, affected other employees' performance on the job, or adversely affected the agency's achievement of goals and responsibilities.

A key to a determination that behaviors impact on the efficiency of the service is a finding that the misconduct goes to the heart of an employee's job responsibilities. Thus an Internal Revenue Service agent who fails to report some of his own income or a postal worker who tampers with the mails would be vulnerable for discharge. Law enforcement employees are held to a more stringent standard of conduct on and off duty, given the expectation that they execute and uphold the law. Certain other conducts like falsification of records, assault at work, theft, insubordination, or disruption of workplace discipline tend to be regarded as sufficiently egregious to impair the efficiency of the service. The federal service appears to uphold severe sanctions when there is a misuse or theft of government property. The Merit System Protection Board has upheld the removal of an employee for attempting to steal two containers of cinnamon. This may appear harsh but the government has a high expectation of integrity in those who control and have custody of its property. Being lenient with petty thieves could promote a culture of theft.[36] The commission of serious felonies, even if off duty, can per se provide the nexus to the efficiency of the service. For instance, a conviction of an employee for manslaughter or conviction for violent criminal conduct casts doubt on the employee's reliability, trustworthiness, and ethical conduct and can diminish public respect for an agency.[37] Determinations become more dicey when the misconduct involves sex offenses or child abuse. In a 1984 case, *Hayes v U.S. Dept. of the Navy*,[38] the court affirmed a Merit System Protection Board decision that upheld the discharge of a civilian technician who had been convicted of assault and abuse of a child. The court found job-relatedness in that the employee had access to housing where children resided. More recent cases involving sex abuse cases and postal workers have upheld removals and indefinite suspensions of employees who were convicted of or admitted such behavior. This may be one area where the egregiousness of the offense reaches out to taint the agency as employer.

Procedural protections for employees subject to adverse employment decisions because of misconduct have also evolved. Originally the procedural protections were limited to those provided under the Lloyd-Lafollette Act. The act required that an employee be given thirty days written notice of the action and charges against the employee and that all material relied upon by the agency be made available to the employee. In addition, the employee was permitted to respond orally in person and was entitled to a full hearing after removal. In *Arnett v Kennedy*[39] in 1974, a federal employee discharged for making false accusations against his superior challenged his discharge and, more specifically, the constitutionality of the process under which he was sanctioned. Alleging both property and liberty interests in his position, Kennedy alleged that the statutory procedures under Lloyd-Lafollette were deficient. Kennedy felt that a trial-type hearing before an impartial agency official should have been invoked prior to removal. The Supreme Court upheld the procedures and the due process afforded Kennedy under Lloyd-Lafollette. But it was a 5-4 decision in which three disparate opinions failed to arrive at a consensus in defining the specific due process guarantees to which a federal employee was entitled.[40] Utilizing a balancing test, Justices Powell and White found that the government's interest in efficient administration and conservation of fiscal resources outweighed an employee's interests in having a full and immediate hearing.[41]

The confusion following *Arnett* was addressed in the CSRA of 1978. The act builds upon Lloyd-Lafollette and establishes a framework for a wide range of possible adverse actions giving administrators flexibility in remedying personnel situations as well as demoting, transferring, or terminating individuals.[42] Supensions are provided as less drastic alternatives. Even with a short suspension (less than fourteen days) an employee is given notice and allowed access to review material that is the basis for suspension. An employee is allowed representation and allowed to file a grievance to contest such suspension. Decisions that call for suspensions of more than fourteen days, furloughs, reduction in pay or grade, or removal also have notice and representation provisions. The employee is given a reasonable time to review the material and to respond. The procedures, however, do not mandate formal hearings with examination of witnesses unless the agency provides for same in its own regulations. Employees are also given opportunity and time to furnish medical documentation that may be in the employee's interests. Importantly, an employee who is designated for removal or suspension shall remain in a duty status in his or her regular position during the advance notice period. If the agency determines that presence of an employee in the workplace may pose a threat to others or jeopardizes legitimate government interests, the agency can follow several options: it can assign the employee to other duties that do not raise the threat; it can allow the employee to take leave or carry the employee in appropriate leave status, or it can place the employee in a paid non-duty status for such time as is necessary to effect the action.

The statute and regulations allow for a "crime" exception to these procedural protections.[43] The thirty-day advance notice may be waived if the agency has reasonable cause to believe that the employee has committed a crime for which a sentence of imprisonment may be imposed. Pending removal, the agency may institute an indefinite suspension. The agency may require the employee to furnish an answer to the proposed action, but it must give the employee at least seven days in which to respond. When circumstances require that an employee be kept away from the work site, the agency may place the employee on nonduty status *with pay* for as long as may be necessary to effect the action. In effect, the statute allows for an application of "innocent until proven guilty" before the deprivational action is taken.

Disciplinary actions involve a balancing of factors, particularly with the commission of off-duty crimes. Whether an employee is to be removed or given a fourteen-, thirty-, or sixty-day suspension is governed by reasonableness standards subject to judicial review. For example, a common decision is how to discipline an employee who has been caught in off-duty shoplifting. Administrators are to take into account a number of elements including: fact of prior or no disciplinary record, length of service with the agency, seriousness of the nature of the offense, profit from the misconduct, and potential for rehabilitation. For instance, a shoplifting incident involving a twenty-three-year employee with no record who picked up a sixteen-dollar item would not merit a removal action as taken by the U.S. Postal Service but would justify a short-term suspension.[44]

The 1978 CSRA provided two separate channels for deprivational actions against employees. The division between Section 43 actions and Section 75 actions is not clear-cut. Employees challenging procedures employed in Section 43 actions found out, however, that invalidation of a Section 43 action did not exclude a Section 75 action ostensibly for performance reasons. In 1985 in *Lovshin v U.S. Department of the Navy*,[45] a civilian engineer was able to demonstrate that a Section 43 action was defective because the agency's performance standards were not in place until after his removal. But the court supported the agency in taking a Section 75 removal action against the employee for performance-based reasons as long as the agency could establish "such cause as will promote the efficiency of the service." The decision would appear to put employees into a Catch-22. However, in the *Lovshin* case, the performance issue was inextricably entangled with malfeasance issues, which can be the basis for Section 75 sanctions.

It is one thing to have in place a process to deal with misconduct in the workplace. Another essential element is to have a code of conduct and responsibilities. This should be comprehensive in covering all those elements of workplace duties and administrative expectations that are illegal, improper, or unethical. There are general principles of conduct that should be made clear to all agency personnel as well as more specific expectations that may attach to the particular function of an agency. A sample listing of code elements follows:

Prohibited Employment Practices

1. using one's public position for private gain;
2. acceptance of or solicitation of favors, gifts, loans, in-kind services, or hospitality;
3. working within a conflict of interest (contracting with one's agency);
4. engaging in nepotistic practices;
5. favoritism or unequal treatment of employees;
6. receipt of private compensation for services to the agency;
7. abuse of authority;
8. disrespect or abuse of employees or creation of a hostile environment for employees (both discriminatory and nondiscriminatory);
9. release of agency or confidential information (including prohibitions under the Privacy Act of 1974);
10. misuse or appropriation of public property;
11. excessive or unexplained absenteeism;
12. alcohol or drug abuse.

In addition, a code of conduct should govern a range of workplace activities that might raise questions of impropriety or "gray behaviors." An agency staffed with professionals should also have clear guidelines on the following issues:

1. limits on off-duty earnings;
2. off-hours teaching and lecturing;
3. research, writing, and publication of material that is agency-related;

4. profit from such publication activity; on-duty/off-duty production of publications;
5. attendance at conferences at agency expense (guided by job-relatedness);
6. exchange of gifts or gratuities between lower and supervisory employees;
7. fraternization between upper-level and lower-level employees;
8. participation in civic activities (generally encouraged but may be limited by competition for time of employee).

The preceding inventory is not exhaustive. However, it points out the necessity of clarifying in advance the boundaries of proper conduct in positions at all levels of an agency.

In addition to the intrinsic procedural protections attached to initiation of adverse personnel actions under Sections 43 and 75, federal regulations also allow for an independent grievance procedure for federal employees. Under 5 C.F.R. sec. 771, an employee may file a grievance applied to any matter of dissatisfaction relating to employment of an employee subject to an agency's management, including any matter on which an employee alleges that coercion, reprisal, or retaliation has been practiced against him or her by filing a grievance. The grievance process is open-ended and details are left to the agencies to work out. Agencies are directed to establish procedures that give employees a reasonable opportunity to present a grievance and receive fair consideration of it. Employees are given assurance of freedom from restraint, interference, and coercion and are allowed representation. A grievance file is established and the grievant has the opportunity to review it at any time. The agency can set up fact-finding procedures, hearings, or other means to address the grievance. The fact finders or hearing officers are not to have been involved in the making or influencing of an adverse decision or be subordinate to such individuals.

The open-ended character of the grievance process could be abused by malcontents who would want to tie up an agency's energies and resources in frivolous and peevish claims. To avert such misuse of the process, federal regulations exclude issues in which an employee is directed to initiate grievances under Section 7121 of Title V of the U.S. Code, which allows for informal mediation or arbitration where the employee is in a collective bargaining contract with the federal employer. It also excludes situations in which an employee may file an appeal to the Merit Systems Protection Board, Office of Personnel Management, or Equal Employment Opportunity Commission. To screen out non-meritorious claims, an agency can cancel or suspend a grievance if a grievant fails to provide sufficient information to identify or verify the grievance or if the grievant fails to define a remedy. Also, a grievance may be cancelled by the agency if an employee uses the grievance to request disciplinary action against another employee. It should be noted that these provisions allowing a federal employee to protect him or herself from arbitrary federal action are safety-net protections that do not rule out other approaches to resolve employee concerns or perceptions of injustice. Agencies are encouraged to establish informal channels for voluntary resolution of disputes, using such means as counseling, negotiation, mediation, or settlement.[46] What is important is the intent behind Section 771, and that is that agencies shall have in place systems that allow for fair, open, responsive, equitable, flexible, expeditious, and uncomplicated resolution of disputes in public employment.

CONCLUSION

In 1958 Paul Van Riper decried the trend toward overprotection of public employees, noting that intervention of courts and new rules of fair play for civil employees were wreaking havoc with flexibility, administrative discretion, and effective administration.[47] This was in an era in which employees had no property interests that might be protected under the due process clause and due process itself was limited to being given a reason for being terminated. The world of public employment has undergone a transformation, not only at the federal level but in state systems that fall under the Fourteenth Amendment due process clause. Congress through the Civil Service Reform Act and the Office of Personnel Management through its regulations have addressed the two substantive areas of personnel management integral to vital functioning of any public agency, performance appraisal and regulation of workplace conduct. Much attention has been given to protection of employee interests. More attention should, however, be directed to the positive effects of compliance with this legislation: having employees who are better informed on expectations of their performance, the greater effiency of workers who know their grievances will be fairly heard, the turnaround of workers who are assisted in improving their performance. While demoting or dismising employees might "promote the efficiency of the service," initiating performance standards, remedial programs, and grievance procedures does as much to "promote the efficiency of the service."

CHECKLIST FOR PERSONNEL ADMINISTRATORS (BASED ON FEDERAL MODEL)

1. Are performance standards established for each position?
2. Are the performance standards for each position tied into the critical elements of the position's function?
3. For professional positions, are performance standards tied to goals and functions of the agency? How are performance standards operationalized for peoples' skills, policy implementation, legal compliance?
4. Are performance standards published in an employee policy manual or handbook?

5. What employee input is solicited in the drafting of performance standards?

6. Do performance standards allow for flexibility (flextime, variable schedules or deadlines) while achieving agency goals and functions?

7. Are performance standards expressed in terms of positive achievement-oriented expectations (as against "backwards" standards)?

8. Are new employees given notice in person of performance standards? How is content given to the standards? Are examples of acceptable work provided to employees?

9. Are timetables in place for performance evaluations? Is the evaluation period for a regular period (e.g., a year)?

10. Is there provision for maintaining an objective record of all instances of both good and sub-standard performance for all employees?

11. Is there a notice and response policy in effect for unfavorable performance evaluations?

12. What policies are in place to allow employees to improve their performance? Are there improvement plans for employees placed on probation?

13. What techniques (counseling, mentoring, peer or team training) are available to help employees improve their performance?

14. Does the organization have in place a code of conduct for employees and officers of the agency?

15. Is the code of conduct sufficiently specific that a reasonable person would have adequate notice of what would be regarded as improper, unethical, illegal?

16. Is there a process in place to record and verify any allegations of misconduct (to establish that a pattern of misconduct may be developing)?

17. For misconduct situations, is there a formal hearing process that gives employees adequate notice, opportunity to review their file, opportunity and time to respond, representation, fact-finding by a neutral fact finder, and decision by an official who is not making the charges?

18. Are procedures in place to transfer an employee to other duties or to suspend an employee from duties (with or without pay) pending final determination of adverse action?

19. If the agency workforce is organized through a public employees' union, what is the role of union representatives or employee defenders in any grievance or complaint process?

20. Is the agency tied into an extra-agency appeals process (like a state-wide employee grievance board)?

21. Does the agency have an informal grievance process that allows for simple and expeditious address of employee complaints and concerns and that allows for accommodation, negotiation, mediation, or arbitration of issues? Does the agency have a means of ensuring that any settlements will be equitable in regard to the full workforce of the agency?

Exercises

14.1 An agency supervisor is required to make a biennial review of all his employees. The agency has a personnel evaluation process and performance review system analogous to that for federal civil servants. Looking over the file of an employee, the supervisor notes the employee has shown a continual slide in performance. Anecdotal information presented to him indicates the employee is having some personal problems that affect his work. He calls in the employee and informs him that his performance measures show him declining in efficiency and productivity. The supervisor informs the employee that he will be given a period in which to improve and that he will be reevaluated after sixty days. He tells the employee, "I'm going to give you sixty days to shape up. I want you to get your files in order, to clear up your backlog, to complete that report that was due last week, and to improve your accuracy on your reports. In addition, I'd like you to do something about your appearance. You're beginning to look like a mess. Now, I'm going to be generous and lighten the workload we've been sending you. But if you don't improve, you may get one final notice in sixty days. My advice to you is when the going gets tough, the tough get going." Critique this attempt to correct a deteriorating incidence of employee performance. What did the supevisor neglect to do?

14.2 A public agency supervisor discovers that an employee has engaged in a series of actions that can be interpreted as misconduct. An investigation has revealed the following:

1. The employee has used supplies for personal communications.
2. The employee has inserted a number of personal files into her office computer. Those files are protected from discovery by personal passwords.
3. The employee has taken some equipment meant to be salvaged and given it to a local charity.
4. The employee has made personal phone calls on her office phone at a cost of several hundred dollars.

When confronted with the evidence of these actions, the employee professes that she was never given adequate notice of what was prohibited by agency rules and policies. The agency has a handbook on proper activities but the prohibitions are written in general terms, "Employees are not to use agency equipment or supplies for personal use." She contends that she was neither explicitly told what was forbidden nor orally instructed. What might have been done to provide clearer notice to personnel of improper activities? What kind of discipline might be appropriate here? Would counseling and restitution be a proper response or has a pattern of misconduct been indicated that would merit more severe sanctions?

14.3 A state agency of natural resources has a problem employee. The permanent employee, a mechanic in the agency motor pool, has within the past year been credited with the following actions:

1. He wrecked a vehicle after he lost control and careened off a forest road.
2. He stopped into a bar during his lunch break and had several beers. This occurred several times while on duty.
3. He had taken vehicles into town for personal use.
4. He had a sexual harassment complaint lodged against him by a female employee.
5. He had an altercation with his supervisor and cursed and reviled him in his presence.
6. He had the highest failure rate for the vehicles he repaired.

After the employee was given reprimands and three separate notices of misconduct and poor performance, his supervisors decided to initiate termination proceedings. He retaliated with an unjust discharge claim. He alleged that the agency failed to provide him with safe vehicles to drive, that the agency entrapped him under the sexual harassment charge, that the agency was engaged in a conspiracy to oust him as indicated by the fact that his file contained only negative references and no references to his heroic and tireless efforts during a recent forest fire. He claimed that supervisors were overheard unprofessionaly referring to him as a "goofus." How can agencies deal with the increasing cry of "I'm a victim" by disgruntled employees?

NOTES

1. Horace G. Wood, *Master and Servant* (Albany, N.Y.: John Parsons Publishers, 1886), sec. 134, p. 271.
2. See Lawrence Blade, *Employment at Will vs. Individual Freedom: On Limiting the Abusive Exercise of Employer Power,* 67 Columbia L Rev 1404 (1967).
3. See *Cafeteria Workers Local 473 v McElroy,* 367 US 886, 897 (1961).
4. *Note, Protecting At-Will Employees Against Wrongful Discharge: The Duty to Terminate Only in Good Faith,* 93 Harvard L Rev 1816 (1980).
5. See for example *Kandall v U.S.,* 186 Ct. Cl. 900 (1969); *Wathen v U.S.,* 527 F2d 1191, 208 Ct. Cl. 342 (1975), cert. denied, 429 US 821 (1976). Even as late as 1981, the role of the federal courts was *strictly* limited to reviewing whether an employment decision was not arbitrary or capricious, reached in accordance with relevant procedural requirements, and did not otherwise violate the Constitution. *Yacavone v Bolger,* 645 F2d 1028 (D.C. Cir 1981), cert. denied, 454 US 844 (1981).
6. See *Note, Limiting the Right to Terminate at Will: Have the Courts Forgotten the Employer,* 35 Vanderbilt L Rev 201 (1982).
7. Reprinted in 9a Lab Rel Rep. (BNA) 21 (Aug. 8, 1991).
8. For a discussion of the Model Employment Termination Act, see Kenneth A. Sprang, *Beware the Toothless Tiger: A Critique of the Model Employment Termination Act,* 43 American U L Rev 849 (spring 1994).
9. Civil Service Reform Act of 1978, PL 95-454, 92 Stat. 1111 (codified in scattered sections of 5 U.S.C., 15 U.S.C., 28 U.S.C., 38 U.S.C., 39 U.S.C., and 42 U.S.C.).

10. For the legislative history and purpose of the 1978 amendments (PL 96-251), see *1978 U.S. Code Cong. and Admin. News* 496.
11. See S. Rept. 969, 95th Cong., 2d sess, 3,40, reprinted in *1978 U.S. Code Cong. and Admin. News*, 2723,2725,2762.
12. *Wilson v Department of Health and Human Services*, 770 F2d 1048 (D.C. Cir 1985), (revsg. 25 M.S.P.R. 681 (1985)).
13. *Rocheleau v S.E.C*, 29 M.S.P.R. 193 (1985), aff'd, 802 F2d 469 (1985).
14. *Walker v Dept. of Treasury*, M.S.P.R. 227 (1985).
15. *Callaway v Dept. of Army*, 23 M.S.P.R. 592 (1984).
16. See *Note, Challenges to Performance Appraisals of Federal Employees Under the Civil Service Reform Act of 1978*, 38 S Dak L Rev 341 (1993), 353–55. The term "backwards standards" was first articulated in *Eibel v Department of the Navy*, 857 F2d 1439, 1441–42 (D.C. Cir 1988).
17. See *Burnett v Department of Health and Human Services*, 51 M.S.P.R. 615 (1991).
18. See *Chennault v Department of the Navy*, 796 F2d 465 (Fed. Cir 1986).
19. 5 U.S.C. sec. 7701.
20. *Papritz v Dept. of Justice*, 31 M.S.P.R. 495 (1986).
21. *Williams v Dept. of Health and Human Services*, 30 M.S.P.R. 217 (1986).
22. 5 C.F.R. sec. 432. See 54 Fed. Reg. 26179 (June 21, 1989), as amended 57 Fed. Reg. 10125 (Mar. 24, 1992), 57 Fed. Reg. 20042 (May 11, 1992), 58 Fed. Reg. 13192 (Mar. 10, 1993), and 58 Fed. Reg. 65533 (Dec. 15, 1993).
23. *Gormley v Dept. of Navy*, 43 M.S.P.R. 330 (1990).
24. 5 C.F.R. sec. 432.105(a)(2).
25. Mike Royko, "Chicago Postal Workers Don't Deliver Customer Service," syndicated column, Mar. 17, 1994.
26. 26 M.S.P.R. 155 (1985).
27. Ibid. at *4.
28. *Stone v Department of Health and Human Services*, 38 M.S.P.R. 634 (1988).
29. Codified at 5 U.S.C. sec. 7513(a).
30. 5 C.F.R. sec. 731.201 (1968).
31. The guidelines appeared to be a response to two judicial decisions that overturned dismissals of federal employees because there was no connection between immoral conduct or personality traits (homosexuality) and employees' performance on the job. *Schlegel v U.S.*, 416 F2d 1372 (D.C. Cir 1969), cert. denied, 397 US 1039 (1970); *Norton v Macy*, 417 F2d 1161 (CT. Cl. 1969).
32. U.S. Civil Service Commission, 731-3 (July 3, 1975). In a coda to the new guidelines, the Commission enjoined commissions or agencies in finding a person unavailable for federal employment solely because person is a homosexual or has engaged in homosexual acts. (See chap. 10.)
33. 568 F2d 1253 (7th Cir 1977).
34. A court of appeals rejected a similar federal employer claim in *Abrams v U.S. Department of the Navy*, 714 F2d 1232 (3d Cir 1983).
35. 586 F2d 1007 (4th Cir 1978).
36. See *Underwood v Department of Defense*, 53 M.S.P.R. 355 (1992).

37. See *Brown v Department of Treasury,* 34 M.S.P.R. 132 (1987).
38. 727 F2d 1535 (Fed. Cir 1984).
39. 416 US 134(1974).
40. *Note, Current Procedures for Adverse Action Against Civil Service Employees Do not Violate the Due Process Clause,* 23 U Kan L Rev 206 (1974).
41. Ibid., p. 212. The government had an interest in keeping a disruptive employee away from other workers, it faced the costs of extensive hearings, and it would be required to provide full salaries to employees who would eventually be discharged. The interest of the employee was temporary loss of income pending possible vindication.
42. 5 U.S.C. secs. 7504, 7514, 7543; 5 C.F.R. sec. 752.101-406.
43. 5 U.S.C. sec. 7513(b); 5 C.F.R. sec. 752.404(d)(1).
44. *Hawkins v U.S. Postal Service,* 35 M.S.P.R. 549 (1987).
45. 767 F2d 826 (Fed. Cir 1985).
46. 5 C.F.R. sec. 771.202.
47. Paul P. Van Riper, *History of the United States Civil Service* (Evanston, Ill.; Row Peterson, 1958), pp. 527-29.

15

Future Issues in Personnel

INTRODUCTION

Forecasting the future is tricky business at best. It involves projection premised upon a series of current events and prediction of how actors on the agenda will react and alter their behaviors in response to these events. As we have discovered throughout this book, the actors on the public personnel agenda are diverse and the myriad of issues confronting them seriously complicates our ability to predict future outcomes accurately. With this caveat in mind, this chapter provides an overview of seven macro-level issues that we believe will impact public personnel management well into the next century—resource constraints, workforce diversity, labor-management relations, role of the courts, employee benefits, technological development, and human resource development.

The overarching framework for discussing future personnel issues is Vice President Gore's *Report of the National Performance Review*. This evaluation of how the federal government provides services to the public is the cornerstone for government reform in general and public personnel in particular. Moreover, many of the recommendations contained in the report are consistent with the Republican majority's commitment to change in the "Contract With America."

The report calls for fundamental change in the way government conducts its business. It focuses on quality and customer satisfaction and proposes that public employees be empowered to be more productive and to seek innovative and cost-effective ways to conduct the public's business. It calls for partnerships between labor and management, between national and subnational governments, and between citizens and their government. The report challenges the president and Congress to implement its recommendations and to transform government from a group of rule-bound bureaucracies into results-oriented entities geared to customer satisfaction through the delivery of quality services. The future of public personnel is clearly linked to the success of reform initiatives such as this report.

RESOURCES

Most practitioners and scholars of public administration agree that public sector financial resources will continue to be tight. Governments at all levels have cut back on their commitments to fund programs and this general retrenchment has been accompanied by a reluctance on the part of the American people to pay additional taxes. As this trend continues, there are many implications for public personnel management; in many instances the ramifications are obvious.

First, employment opportunities in many government sectors are likely to decline. This is particularly the case for middle-management positions. This will not only mean fewer jobs for young people seeking entry-level positions, it also does not bode well for existing employees seeking promotion to the next managerial rank. This does not mean, however, that there will be no growth in public employment. Individuals with professional qualifications in areas such as computers and financial management will continue to be in demand. But in the aggregate sense there will be fewer jobs in the more traditional generic management and administrative positions.

Second, resource constraints dictate that public servants will continue to see wages and benefits erode when adjusted for inflation, and the gap between government and private sector wages and benefits will continue to widen. Many public employers, particularly at the state and local level, are cutting back on employer premiums paid into benefit plans, forcing employees to pay a growing proportion of their incomes toward supporting existing health care and retirement packages.

Third, the bleak budget picture will continue to impact negatively the ability to initiate new programs in the area of human resource management such as those discussed in module 3. One obvious example is in the area of training. As workers' skills rapidly become obsolete, massive investments will be required to retrain these employees so they can continue to be productive. The situation presents a Catch-22. The United States needs to invest in programs such as training in order to remain competitive in the face of globalization, but there appears to be little concrete action by political leadership to implement long-term plans to address the problem because of a lack of resources.

Finally, resource constraints will continue to pressure governments to use alternative delivery strategies to provide programs and services to clients in the most cost-effective and productive manner. Privatization and the growth of non-profit organizations will continue. As Don Kettl points out; "Privatization" became the administrative buzzword of the 1980s and is destined to reshape public administration into the next century."[1] Privatization is attractive to politicians because in service delivery areas, salaries and benefits can account for up to 75 percent of an agency's total budget. Outright divestiture of public programs to the private sector, on the surface at least, gives the appearance that the program is being delivered more efficiently even though in reality this may not be the case. The public, of course, wants to hear that taxpayers' dollars are being used in the most efficient manner possible. Moreover, a precedent exists whereby several public sector agencies currently rely heavily upon the private sector to deliver public programs and with a fair degree of success. Defense Department procurement and Medicare are two examples. President Reagan's famous Grace Commission proposed massive privatization as a means to control a federal bureaucracy that was perceived by many as the root of all government problems.[2] The Reagan administration went further in mandating that all public services be assessed to determine if they should be provided by government or by the private sector.

Those who oppose privatization claim that the business model is not always more efficient than government-delivered services. They further contend that employee morale has been seriously damaged by this fixation on privatization, and some union leaders see it as a government plot to break powerful public sector unions, especially at the local government level. What is more interesting for human resource managers of the future, however, is that privatization will dictate that public personnel practices will continue to transcend government boundaries and be applied in the private sector. Currently, federal regulations dictate that private sector firms conducting business with the federal government and employing a specified number of employees must file affirmative action plans. In addition, private employers must now allow unpaid maternity leave. The door is open for further regulations mandating merit personnel practices, screening contract awards to avoid blatant patronage, and so forth. This is interesting because one thing that privatization is supposed to accomplish is to reduce government red tape. In reality, however, the need to ensure that private deliverers of public services adhere to some sort of public and ethical standards in the area of personnel may ultimately result in more rules and regulations, not less.

Restructuring and the elimination of outdated programs is a major reform initiative proposed by the National Performance Review. It specifically identifies consolidation and elimination of field offices in such federal agencies as Agriculture, Housing and Urban Development, Energy, and the U.S. Army Corps of Engineers, to name a few. The report also recommends termination of several federal programs in areas such as price support programs for certain agricultural products and various federal training and education programs.

On the positive side, this restructuring is intended to eliminate waste and provide better quality of services to the client. On the negative side, elimination of programs and the reduction in the numbers of field offices mean less jobs for individuals seeking public sector employment. The report estimates that a total of 252,000 jobs will be lost but the government will save a total of $108 billion.[3]

WORKFORCE DIVERSITY

The changing composition of the public workforce is a phenomenon that is only in its infancy. As more women, members of the disabled community, and people of color seek public employment, agencies will be forced to adapt to the changing organizational culture that new membership will foster. The National Performance Review notes that "[o]ur increasingly diverse workforce struggles to manage child care, elder care, family emergencies, and other personal commitments, while working conditions become ever more important."[4]

Issues such as diversity training, for example, are hot topics in the academic literature. Academic journals such as *Public Administration Review* now devote entire sections to the subject.[5]

Rubaii-Barrett and Beck argue that the changing demographics of the public sector will ultimately necessitate that traditional theories of leadership and supervision be supplanted by management approaches that are sensitive to the culture and ethnicity of the workforce.[6] Their study showed that Mexican workers differed markedly from their white counterparts when it came to job satisfaction and motivation. In other words, because of a difference in culture, Mexican workers express different preferences than other groups that are employed in the same task environment. Supervisors must be trained to be sensitive to the organization's cultures if they are to maintain a productive and motivated workforce. *Cultures* is used here to reflect the belief that organizations often possess a plurality of cultural preferences, depending upon both the agency mission and its ethnic composition.

There is also another dimension to cultural diversity—the changing composition of senior management. Current trends indicate that more women and minorities will move up the hierarchy into senior management positions, shattering barriers that historically have reserved the senior executive ranks for white males only.

The National Performance Review indicates that balancing work and nonwork obligations will pose many challenges for future managers. Romzek notes that successful managers will need to recognize the link between the two if they are to recruit and retain employees.[7] The traditional manner in which work is structured will have to change to accommodate dual-career families, elder care, and changing technology. Many agencies currently provide on-site child care facilities to accommodate dual-career couples with small children. Others have developed flextime plans that allow employees to schedule their work outside of the traditional 9 A.M.–5 P.M. model. Finally, technological advances permit many employees to work at home by linking the home work-station to the office via computer or FAX.

LABOR-MANAGEMENT RELATIONS

Chapter 6 provided an overview of the differences between the private and public sectors in the area of labor-management relations. As the public sector continues to professionalize, the traditional role of unions is likely to change. More and more middle managers are entering graduate programs in public administration and personnel management, hoping to complete their degrees on a part-time basis. With the advent of interactive video networks, campuses can "beam" their graduate courses to almost any location in the country. These professional managers normally belong to some association rather than a union—the American Society for Public Administration and the International Personnel Management Association are examples.

There may also be some transformation in the current process of collective bargaining, particularly at the federal level. The present system is much too rigid and the process is anything but coequal. Employees will likely be given greater input into determining workplace issues that need to be coordinated with management, and the right to strike could possibly be extended to some federal agencies.

Richard Kearney emphasizes four core areas in which change is likely to occur in public sector labor-management relations.[8] The first is fiscal crisis and retrenchment. Unions did quite well during the 1960s and early 1970s as membership grew and federal grants-in-aid payments to state and local governments increased dramatically. During that time, because resources were plentiful, unions were successful in negotiating lucrative wage and benefit packages for their members. Federal government retrenchment in the early 1980s severely impacted public sector unions and membership declined. Kearney's second core area concerns public opinion. Numerous surveys show that Americans hold unions in low esteem. These negative feelings are exacerbated when a public sector union goes on strike and is perceived by many as holding the public ransom. Ethics scandals among the leadership in both private and public sector unions has also fueled this negativism. Turning public opinion around is going to present a difficult challenge for future union leaders.

The third core area, the changing nature of the workforce, presents yet another dilemma for the continued viability of public sector unions. Kearney writes:

Unions have yet to define their role in accommodating the socially diverse Workforce 2000. Their organizational health and well being depends largely on how they respond to the new sets of employment issues associated with demographic and sociocultural changes in the labor force. To remain viable organizations, unions must convince the new breed of workers that they can effectively represent their interests and serve their employment-related needs.[9]

The final core element concerns increased labor-management cooperation. The traditional adversarial model will eventually be supplanted by a move toward increased cooperation between workers and management. Kearney predicts a growth in labor-management committees, quality circles, and total quality management groups where all members of the organization work in concert to increase employee motivation and productivity and provide a better product or service to the client. Vice President Gore calls upon senior federal executives to provide the leadership that is required in empowering employees, building team environments, and focusing on customer satisfaction.[10] The National Performance Review calls for labor and management to form partnerships and to work together to build a quality workforce.

ROLE OF THE COURTS

Module 4 of this book emphasized the point that it is no longer acceptable for public managers to lack knowledge of the legal/constitutional aspects of personnel. The courts will continue to play an important role in determining the constitutionality of personnel policies. The issues such as sexual harassment, preemployment testing, affirmative action, discrimination, and so forth raised in the previous chapters will undoubtedly continue to dominate public personnel. One area that could prove more troublesome than most for public managers concerns some privacy issues that are now beginning to emerge. The changes in technology that allow managers to monitor electronic mail and install workplace surveillance systems may help promote efficiency but they also raise serious questions about employees' rights to privacy. It is certain that many more court cases will be heard over the next several years as judges attempt to establish guidelines for employers and to protect the privacy rights of employees. A second and even more complex privacy issue of the future concerns genetic testing. Medical science continues to develop rather sophisticated scientific tests that can determine the genetic composition and DNA blueprint of each and every employee in an organization. These genetic blueprints, in turn, can be utilized to determine the probability that a particular employee may contract a certain type of cancer, whether the individual has homosexual tendencies, and even whether the person is a probable alcoholic. There may a compelling need on the part of an employer to use such tests. However, it becomes immediately apparent that these types of tests could easily be used to discriminate against employees. It will be interesting to observe how the courts will balance the employer's rights with the reasonable privacy expectations of employees.

BENEFITS

The standard manner in which agencies provide employee benefits is already changing and this process will definitely continue. This is in part driven by cost and in part by a change in demand as the composition of both the workforce and the family change. Bruce and Reed refer to this phenomenon as the work-family dichotomy.[11] Traditional benefit plans typically included some provision for retirement benefits, perhaps health care benefits, annual vacation, and so forth. Typically, all employees were treated similarly, irrespective of need.

This traditional approach to the provision of employee benefits is rapidly changing. As more women enter the workforce and as more families have double wage earners, increasing pressure is being brought to bear to provide benefits such as child-care and elder-care services. Some agencies have adopted cafeteria-type benefit plans allowing employees to choose the package that best suits their particular needs. Obviously a single individual without children would have no need for child care. A related issue concerns part-time employees. Many employers hire temporary workers to avoid paying benefits.

TECHNOLOGY

It is an understatement that technology will continue to have a dramatic impact in the area of personnel. In addition to the remarkable advances in genetic testing mentioned above, government agencies will be driven to invest in new technology to improve service delivery and to reduce costs. Although the government does tend to lag behind the private sector in investment in new technology(except for Defense and NASA), most government employees have computers and all offices now have electronic mail, desktop publishing, and tele-conferencing capabilities. Senior managers can now communicate directly through electronic media to most employees even at district and regional offices several thousand miles away.

The National Performance Review advocates utilizing technology to "reengineer" the manner in which public services are delivered. This "electronic government," as it is called, will ultimately be able to deliver benefits to individuals electronically and to market government databases to businesses. This information explosion both provides a positive benefit in the form of increases in productivity and can also make thousands of jobs obsolete and in fact completely alter our traditional notion of bureaucratic organizations.

Consider the ramifications for human resource managers that improved technology brings. New technology has prompted many private firms to downsize especially in the middle-management ranks in order to remain competitive. Computer networks allow a single manager to direct and monitor the activities of scores of subordinates. Improved air traffic control technology at the nation's airports provides safer skies for the traveling public and also reduces the need to maintain the existing numbers of air traffic controllers. In the future, as more and more Americans own computers with electronic and voice mail capabilities, the number of jobs in the U.S. Postal Service will decline dramatically because there will be little need to hand-deliver mail door-to-door except in exceptional circumstances. A large component of the types of design services traditionally supplied by architects, engineers, and planners is now provided by technicians trained in the use of computer-assisted design.

Dealing with the positive aspects of improved technology may prove to be easier for the manager of the future than coping with its dysfunctions. Retraining technologically obsolete personnel will be expensive and time-consuming. Coping with the change in interpersonal roles that new technology brings will fundamentally alter the culture of public sector agencies. Indeed, it may dehumanize them. Arie Halachmi writes:

> One dysfunctional aspect of the new technology is that it facilitates the separation of authority from responsibility by enabling all employees to ignore the formal structure of the organization. . . . Through electronic information networks, an employee may be able to handle diverse and more complicated tasks without the need to solicit help or advice from a supervisor. However, in the process, the employee may unwittingly use values, considerations, and priorities that are important. . . .[12]

HUMAN RESOURCE DEVELOPMENT

As has been said several times throughout this book, most Americans would argue that government does some things well but there is certainly room for improvement in a number of areas. As module 3 made clear, if government is ultimately to work better, more time and resources need to be devoted to personnel programs that lead to a more qualified, competent workforce in general and to training and professional development programs in particular. Considerable lip service is paid to improving the capacity of the civil service, yet rarely are commitments seen toward improvements that are sustained over long periods of time. Politicians talk about the need to allocate resources to the training and professional development of employees, they recite the principles of total quality management, and they proclaim that they will strive to make government more efficient and responsive to the American people. The problem, of course, is that moving from political rhetoric to the implementation of programs requires massive infusions of money. This does not rest well with the public because new programs mean increased taxes, reductions in other programs, or some combination of the two. Government agencies will come under increasing pressure to improve the quality of services delivered to the public and, in so doing, to design and implement human resource development policies at all levels in the organization.

The 1993 National Performance Review addressed these human resource development issues. Although some of the recommendations contained in the report have been successfully implemented, others have not. If the way government services are delivered is to be changed and if personnel management at the national level is to be improved, Congress and the president need to continue with these reforms.

AN EPILOGUE FOR PUBLIC MANAGERS

At the beginning of this book we made a rather bold claim that managing human resources in a public sector environment is a dynamic process. Moreover, we argued that those who contend that personnel is boring and simply involves the clerical function of filling out forms do this subfield of public administration a great disservice. We hope that the book has prompted you to think more critically about some of the issues—technical, human, and legal—that will affect those who currently or in the future will pursue public sector careers. Your ability to succeed as a manager to a large degree relates to your ability to motivate and manage people. Part of this process involves developing and facilitating an atmosphere of trust, cooperation, and teamwork. Accomplishing this goal requires you to take the human resource management dimension seriously. Remembering that people are the most important asset to any organization is a good place to start.

Notes

1. Donald F. Kettl, "Privatization: Implications for the Public Work Force," in *Public Personnel Management: Current Concerns—Future Challenges*, ed. Carolyn Ban and Norma M. Riccucci (New York: Longman, 1991), pp. 254–64.
2. President's Private Sector Survey on Cost Control, *A Report to the President* (Washington, D.C.: Government Printing Office, 1984).
3. Al Gore, *From Red Tape to Results: Creating a Government That Works Better and Costs Less: Report of the National Performance Review* (Washington, D.C.: U.S. Government Printing Office, 1993), p. iii.
4. Ibid., p. 84.
5. For example, see the four articles in *Public Administration Review* 54, no. 3 (May/June 1994), pp. 265–90, under the section entitled "Diversity."
6. Nadia Rubaii-Barrett and Ann C. Beck, "Minorities in the Majority: Implications for Managing Cultural Diversity," *Public Personnel Management* 22, no. 4 (winter 1993).

7. Barbara S. Romzek, "Balancing Work and Nonwork Obligations," in *Public Personnel Management: Current Concerns—Future Challenges,* pp. 227–39.
8. See Richard C. Kearney, *Labor Relations in the Public Sector,* 2d ed. (New York: Marcel Dekker, Inc., 1992), chap. 9.
9. Ibid., p. 416.
10. Al Gore, "The New Job of the Federal Executive," *Public Administration Review* 54, no. 4 (July/August, 1994).
11. Willa Bruce and Christine Reed, "Preparing Supervisors for the Future Work Force: The Dual-Income Couple and the Work-Family Dichotomy," *Public Administration Review* 54, no. 1 (January/February 1994).
12. See Arie Halachmi, "Information Technology, Human Resource Management, and Productivity," in *Public Personnel Management; Current Concerns—Future Challenges,* pp. 240–53.

APPENDIX

Personnel Law Grievances

The following section includes twelve hypothetical grievances involving issues presented in the legal module. These typical grievances can be the basis for student discussion or for mock hearings. In a mock hearing students will assume the role of the grievant(s) and the defendants, who may be the employer, supervisor, or fellow employee. Other students may assume the role of a litigant's counsel or an employee union representative. Students will also constitute the grievance board (three to five members) and receive testimony and arguments from each side. A hearing would be conducted according to rules drawn beforehand for entertaining evidence and cross-examination. The grievance board can then establish facts and arrive at a reasoned decision. These grievances provide issues within a generalized juridical framework. This framework can be altered to reflect variations in state laws and policies, procedures, and manuals of actual agencies.

Decisions of grievance boards or committees should extend to:

1. issue of whether a grievance exists in fact and whether applicable laws were violated;

2. issue of whether employment decisions were made under proper authority and within range of legitimate discretion;

3. issue of whether the grievant was given a measure of due process commensurate with the deprivation involved, to include proper notice, full hearing, and ample opportunity to defend one's employment interests;

4. issue of whether constitutional conditions are implicated;
5. issue of whether administrative or public interests override employee interests;
6. issues of remedies or sanctions that are an appropriate response to the grievance;
7. issues of changes needed in procedures and policies to prevent or avert future grievances.

PERSONNEL GRIEVANCE 1

DeMontreville v. Human Services Center

This is a grievance of Auguste DeMontreville against the State Human Services Center alleging discrimination in employment. The specific complaint lists several alleged incidents of racial discrimination affecting the terms, conditions, and privileges of employment. The complainant brings his grievance before a State Personnel Board Grievance Committee. If the complainant is not satisfied with the determinations and remedies of this board, he professes to file suit against the state in federal court, alleging violations of both the Civil Rights Act and the equal protections clause of the U.S. Constitution.

Auguste DeMontreville, a member of the Chippewa Band of Turtle Lake Indian Reservation, was hired as a "youth counselor" to work with young people on chemical or alcohol abuse problems. He had completed a degree in Indian Studies and had received an addiction counselor's license from the State Human Services Center in 1991. In 1993 when the state legislated a licensing program through an addiction counselor's board the licenses of previous counselors were affirmed under a grandfather provision (which still required continuing education for renewal). The State Human Services Center then initiated a program to hire more counselors who could deal with a minority clientele. DeMontreville and a Mr. Grayhorse were hired onto the staff of the Alcohol and Substance Abuse Division of the Human Services Agency.

At the conclusion of the year, DeMontreville was given a performance appraisal that could be summarized as "borderline satisfactory." He was also informed of a number of deficiencies at the end of another year. In effect, he was put on probation. Also, he was not included among the department members given a 4 percent raise in salary. Neither was Grayhorse given a raise. This was explained in terms of a policy decision to give the raise only to those workers who had completed their full two-year probationary period. The deficiencies noted included the following:

1. DeMontreville had not taken sufficient steps to upgrade his certification in a program of continuing education of his addiction counseling.

2. DeMontreville had failed to convey a properly professional image to clients. He had worn inappropriate hair styles, preferred casual dress, and had generally presented an image of strong Native American identity. While DeMontreville had been hired to work with a particular constituency, he was also expected to work with other youth as well. At least half his case assignments were with white youth. It was felt his work with these clients was adversely affected by his dress and grooming practices.

3. DeMontreville had put family and community demands above the job responsibilities of his position. On three occasions he took time off to attend family funerals or deal with crises in an extended family. He also took time off to spend three days at an Indian powwow. Under the personnel rules of the agency, a person can take time with notice, using sick leave or compensatory time. DeMontreville had utilized seven days of sick leave for these absences and was an additional three days in arrears in terms of work time.

4. DeMontreville had problems in communicating with fellow workers. A particular chill in work relations had arisen between DeMontreville and the other addiction counselors.

DeMontreville contests the evaluation and the omission of himself and his coworker from the raises given all other members of the office. He also counters with complaints of his own.

1. He contends that the decision not to give raises to him and Grayhorse as "probationary employees" is a pretense for discriminating against them on racial grounds.

2. He contends that negative evaluations have strong racist overtones and the complaints are invalid. He was hired to provide a certain access to a constituency of clients that had resisted services. In order to gain access it was vital that one demonstrate a common identity with those clients. His credibility and efficacy as a counselor are enhanced through his visibility in the Native American community and his social activities in that community.

3. He contends that the chill in relations with co-workers stems from their racist remarks and attitudes. When he was first hired, a number of his coworkers called him "Chief." When he protested, they said, "Hey, lighten up. We only meant it to be friendly. After all, 'Auguste' is not a common name." To demonstrate their racist orientation, however, he notes their characterization of his Native American clients as "bucks," "buckskins," "twine-heads," "string-hairs," "peace-pipe smokers" (marijuana smokers) and "kickapoo joy-juicers." His attempts to educate his coworkers on sensitivity about such matters actually strained relations. In fact, he questioned their professionalism in terms of their patronizing and deprecatory attitudes toward substance abusers in general.

4. He contends that the dress and grooming rules they have imposed on him make it more difficult for him to fulfill his duties in the Native American community and represent a distinct effort to rob him of his cultural identity.

5. He finally indicates that the consideration of his leaves should have no bearing on his evaluation. No issue was made of any other employee's use of time-off privileges. He also contends that the questioning of his attendance of a powwow involves an intrusion into his free exercise of religion.

DeMontreville asks for a reevaluation of his first year by outside evaluators. He also asks that his salary be adjusted to include the raises given all members of the department with the exception of himself and Grayhorse. He also asks for an investigation of racial attitudes of department employees.

How would a grievance board approach this case?

PERSONNEL GRIEVANCE 2

Aquarius v. Department of Psychology, Ivy Cliffs State College

This is a grievance filed by Leo Aquarius challenging a decision by the department, upheld by the administration, to terminate his tenured employment at the college. He alleges that his termination involved invasion of privacy, violation of professional standards, denial of due process, and violation of his academic freedoms.

Dr. Aquarius was hired to teach psychology at Ivy Cliffs State College, and after seven years he received a tenured appointment. A few years after that he underwent a personal and professional change in identity and direction ("midlife crisis"). He discovered that his discipline as he had practiced it was sterile and unfulfilling. He considered most of what he had been taught was little more than "bovine excreta." He began to explore and profess what he termed creative psychic frameworks and to build his teaching around these exploratory frameworks.

The circumstances of the grievance emerge from the following facts. Aquarius was absent by illness on a day on which students in one of his classes were scheduled to return papers he had assigned. As students dropped off the papers at the office they were put on a side table and a fellow colleague noted that a number of papers turned in by the students involved some very bizarre subjects. He wondered "What is going on in this class?" and alerted the chair. The chair then arranged some appointments with students in Aquarius's classes and also arranged for some students to attend Aquarius's classes and report back to the chair.

The reports confirmed that Aquarius's teaching was quite unconventional. He used the text as a syllabus of errors, using the material to launch his own theories and ideas. Thus a reference to "dreams" became the occasion for a discussion of "dreams as consciousness bosons." His course content involved such topics as Wilhelm Reich and his orgone box; spirit-channeling; neuropolitics—powerpush or powerpull; reincarnation and revisualization; reinfantalization—playing out one's childhood dreams; the grammar of relationships—personality types fitting into social networks—psychological identity as subjects, objects, verbs: transitive or intransitive, regular or irregular, adjectives, or adverbs.

It was clear that Aquarius had substituted a mix of popular psychology, cultist attractions, pseudoscience, and creative fantasy for the accepted body of knowledge in the field. The department also received information about extracurricular contacts between Aquarius and his students. He would have groups of his students come to his home for "an introduction to the Elysian mysteries." From reports it was determined that at these gatherings or parties, Aquarius and his students would engage in bizarre rituals that Aquarius said were long-lost rituals engaged in by ancient Greeks and Romans to achieve mental well-being. From reports the rituals involved seminudity, massages, essential oils, and hypnotic exercises. Some students claimed that they had to join in these "Elysian mysteries" in order to be favored with good grades in his classes.

Faculty members are given regular three-year departmental evaluations. While Aquarius's regular peer evaluation was scheduled a year hence, the department chair called for an immediate evaluation of his performance. Aquarius was given ten days notice of a hearing and given notice of charges of "unprofessional teaching" and "unprofessional conduct involving students," charges that support a termination for cause in the college handbook.

At the hearing Aquarius defended his teaching and approach, noting that his teaching was creative, innovative, and stimulating. He defended his ideas, stating that they were protected expressions of his academic freedom. As to their unconventional nature, he noted his ideas were no more startling and radical than those made by Freud at the turn of the century. He was simply ahead of his time. And if he was later proved wrong, so what? After all, a great deal of Freudian theory is now questionable in terms of scientific validity. What was so sacred about traditional psychology?

He defended his social contacts with students, noting that nothing in any way illegal ever occurred at those gatherings. He did not, however, volunteer to describe what did occur because that would mean revealing the Elysian mysteries, which bind all participants with an unbreakable oath of secrecy.

The department then voted to terminate Aquarius's employment at the conclusion of the current semester. It noted that while the academic community has a great toleration and acceptance of idiosyncrasy, Aquarius had abandoned what is known as the core of the field for totally untested, unverified, and unvalidated course material. It also said that the pattern of social contacts posed an irrefutable risk of favoritism toward students who followed him and a risk of discrimination against those who did not participate. The one-year notification requirement for termination was waived in light of a termination for cause.

The president of Ivy Cliffs affirmed the decision not to renew his contract for the succeeding year. An appeal of that decision was then filed with a college-level faculty grievance committee. Aquarius contends:

1. He was illegally terminated for exercise of his academic freedoms as protected under the First Amendment to the Constitution.

2. He was illegally terminated for exercising rights of association (with students), rights of association bound with discussions of ideas and exchange of knowledge protected under the First Amendment.

3. He was terminated with the use of illegal procedures and denied due process. An unscheduled ad hoc evaluation gives faculty members no notice of pending threats to their employment. No attempt was made by the department to provide for an informational exchange and informal resolution of the issues. The procedure was confrontational from its outset and really indicated a prejudgment on the part of the department to rid itself of an unconventional faculty member.

4. The termination involved gross violations of privacy that tainted the entire proceeding. By looking at the stack of papers, another faculty member intruded into the faculty/student academic relationship to determine what might be going on in his classes. The chair had not taken the opportunity to learn from him what he was teaching but had planted student spies in his classes. It was customary in the departmental peer evaluation procedures to obtain permission from a faculty member to sit in on classes as an observer. The inquiry into the extracurricular contacts with students had also violated the social privacy of the students. The only information on those gatherings was irrelevant to the competency concerns.

5. The termination involved a failure of notice in terms of the department's expectations of teaching objectives and aims. There had been no effort on the part of the department to establish rules of conformity in teaching, even as to the basic courses.

If the department had expected him to conform to some nebulous and unarticulated "subject matter core," it should have spelled this out in detail.

6. The ad hoc evaluation did not follow the balanced character of the standard departmental and peer evaluations as it did not give proper weight, in fact any weight, to student evaluations considered in any such standard evaluations. In fact, Aquarius had the highest student evaluations of any member of the seven-member department.

Aquarius asks that the termination decision be reversed on grounds that it was illegal, improper, and insupportable.

How would a grievance board address this case?

PERSONNEL GRIEVANCE 3

Derianne Smith v. Statistical Service Bureau

This is an action by Derianne Smith contesting decisions regarding her employment. She contends that her employment at the Statistical Service Bureau was marked by a pattern of sexual harassment, making it impossible to fulfil her duties. Upon registering her complaints, the bureau ordered a transfer to a branch office some seventy miles away. The bureau defended the transfer as a budgetary necessity and noted that it was also an accommodation to her complaints. She claims that this particular "accommodation" amounts to "constructive discharge" because the transfer is so onerous and burdensome that a reasonable administrator would see it as presenting the employee no remedy or choice. The bureau responds that the transfer did not involve any loss of prestige, loss in benefits, or significant change in working conditions or duties. She asks for remedies that address her complaints, including transfer of the person who sexually harassed her.

In registering her complaints, she notes the following actions or activities that adversely affected working conditions:

1. A generally sexist atmosphere in which women were exposed to sexist, demeaning, and harassing actions. She cites a Valentine's Day contest in which the male members of the bureau voted for "the sweetheart of the bureau." The winner of this congeniality contest was taken out to dinner at an expensive restaurant by the three top officers of the bureau (two males and one female). In connection with Valentine's Day, the bureau director sent a box of expensive chocolates and a valentine to all the female employees. She particularly resented the fact that many of the cards referred to the women in such saccharine and fatuous terms as "sweetie pie," "muffin," "honey," and "sugarplum," terms never applied to males. She had also received a birthday card that had a picture of different pies, "Apple Pie—Cherry Pie—Pumpkin Pie." She opened the card to find a little mirror with the statement "Sweetie Pie. Happy Birthday, Derianne."

2. She also cites the distribution and sale of some offensive t-shirts. One featured a female and the logo, "Statisticians Fool Around With Figures," and another said "When it Comes to Women, Statisticians Will Use Any Means."

3. She also cites the failure of the bureau to deal with a persistent admirer. The admirer, a male employee, made several attempts to invite her to lunch and to arrange a date with her, which she declined. He then began to leave memo slips on her desk with messages that could be regarded as crush notes. When he was asked not to use office communications, he began to phone her and mail her long, passionate communications ("How intense are the sparks that we strike on each other. How can we fall into the soft sweet embrace of twilight to sleep in the down of night to await the dawn?") Offended by these attentions, she complained to the director, who laughed off the matter and said, "As long as he doesn't slobber over your desk and does it on his own time, it's not our problem."

4. When she began to complain about the atmosphere and the failure of the bureau to transfer the admiring employee, she was called in and told that the bureau found a solution, her transfer to another office of the Statistical Research Bureau some seventy miles away. She said that the transfer was a sham—a constructive discharge to get her out of the organization. Such a move would mean disruption of her life, necessary sale of her home in a soft real estate market, and disruption of the life of her dependent son who was finally in a satisfactory day-care facility. She contends that it represents an impossible choice and asks why the male employee was not given a transfer. She also states that the decision to offer her a transfer was made after it became known that she was keeping a file of her observation of harassing and sexist practices and incidents. Thus it was an act of retaliation against employment rights activity.

The bureau contends that Smith's complaints were genuinely trivial. The bureau does not see the behaviors as demeaning, rude, coarse, or sexually threatening. In fact, it regards "perquisites" extended to female employees as complimentary and signs of appreciation for good work performance. At no time was there any situation where women in the bureau had to respond to male demands to continue employment or get favorable job treatment. As to the amorous activities of the admirer, those took place outside the work environment.

Smith responds that while the activities complained about did not directly affect her economic well-being or the terms of her employment, a "hostile and offensive" working environment was engendered, nurtured, condoned, and maintained. It also did not matter whether the administrators of the bureau considered this unoffensive and unobjectionable. This type of harassment must be viewed from the standpoint of what a "reasonable woman"—not the prototypical man—would find offensive. The "sweetheart" contests had the effect of differentiating the female workforce within the bureau and differentiating it in a way that set it off and apart from a workforce that is perceived in terms of its productivity, efficiency, or administrative ability.

Smith asks for a cancellation of the transfer order, that positive steps be taken to deal with her "harasser," and elimination all elements of a hostile work environment from the bureau.

How would a grievance board address this case?

PERSONNEL GRIEVANCE 4

Vance Agentry v. Nodak Highway Department

This is an appeal from a discharge of a fifty-seven-year-old employee of the Nodak Highway Department. Mr. Agentry was a shop steward responsible for the buildings, yard, repair facilities, and tools of a regional highway shop. He was discharged for failing to meet work performance standards. Cited in the required (biennial) evaluation of classified employees was loss of efficiency, lower productivity, lack of job commitment, ineffective communication with supervisor or peers, and negligence.

Under rules for public personnel, employees may be discharged "for cause" for a variety of reasons: criminal behavior, disruptive or destructive behavior, alcohol or drug abuse affecting job performance, or insubordination. Employees are also evaluated every two years for their prior two years of job performance. If the employee does not meet job standards, he is informed of his deficiencies and counseled as to improvement. If satisfactory improvement is not shown within six months, that person may be discharged.

Agentry had a record of twenty-three years of employment with the highway department. He had excellent performance reviews for twenty-one of those years. He was particularly noted for his scrupulous maintenance standards, his neatness, and diligent care of facilities and equipment. His shop and yard were impeccable—a model display of polished objects arranged in the most orderly manner. Two incidents contributed to a change of attitude and work habits. He expected to be named chief shop steward in 1991 and was beaten out by a younger, less experienced applicant. He was thus denied what would have been a 15 percent increase in salary. Also in 1993 the state electorate referred a number of revenue measures passed by the legislature and, as a consequence, raises scheduled for state employees were canceled for the coming year and budgets of all public agencies were reduced. After that other workers heard him say, "I'm not going to break my back or work my fingers to the bone for this state." Conversations indicated a change of attitude inclining toward malaise, bitterness, and passive resistance. From that time forward, performance declined. He would perform only the most necessary maintenance. Equipment and tools that he once regarded as repairable were designated as salvage. His salvage entries tripled over the next two years. The shop environment became less orderly. When the new chief steward directed Agentry to change the floor plan of the shop, Agentry resisted saying that it would be a waste of effort and would not promote efficiency. In the end he moved two work tables. The supervising chief steward rated Agentry's performance as "minimally adequate—just enough to get by. Agentry lacks initiative—seems burned out." To Agentry's face, he said, "You're so much dead wood."

Agentry was called in on several occasions and informed that better performance was expected. His biennial evaluation was reported to him, and the chief steward informed him that improvement was expected and said that "We haven't decided what to do with you, but you should be aware of the consequences if the next report does not show improvement. And that is going to be in six months." During this period, one year after the referral, the state discovered that revenues were higher than expected and restored the money available for state employee raises. In the allocation of those raises, the district division allocated the raises on the basis of merit evaluations and Agentry was given only a minimal $50-a-month increase while several colleagues received raises two to three times that amount. This increased Agentry's bitterness. He began to avoid the supervisor and began to effect a "slowdown" of work projects. At the end of six months, Agentry was called in for a formal evaluation hearing and asked to explain his record and the fact that he had a backlog of a dozen work orders. He claimed that the supervisor was harassing him and that he was doing his best. The chief supervisor found his explanations unsatisfactory. He also ruled that Agentry had demonstrated sufficient negligence to merit discharge. Negligence was indicated in a variety of ways. Agentry allowed disappointment over his failure to be promoted affect his attitude toward supervisors in the last two years of employment, and he failed to heed a number of warnings that his job was in jeopardy. He was then issued a certificate of discharge.

Agentry appeals the termination decision to the Highway Department Employees Grievance Board. He alleges that his discharge is illegal, unjustified, and insupportable.

1. He alleges that his job performance meets all requirements. He indicates that his performance in the preceding two years was compared to his past performance, which was beyond job requirements and beyond expectations. The previous record was based on voluntary and uncompensated overtime, on work that was not specified as required. The attention he gave to the appearance of the shop and yard was a plus that he contributed. When he at last realized that employees were neither compensated nor appreciated for this dedication, he decided to do only that work that was necessary, a level of performance he maintains he met and that reflects the norms set by other workers.

2. He contends that the demands made upon him by the new supervisor represented a deliberate attempt to trap him in some deficiencies. The demands often made no sense, would have resulted in unnecessary expenditures, and were an outlet for arbitrary exercises in authority (e.g., the floor plan demand). The repeated disciplinary calls of the chief steward simply added work stress. Agentry noted that the chief steward did not in any way involve himself in the labor of these tasks as Agentry himself had when he had been the acting chief steward.

3. He contends that the termination procedure was insufficient in terms of giving him notice of possible termination. He was not given sufficient warning of actual termination. Such ambiguous comments as "We don't know what to do with you" did not provide clear notice. Termination procedures should require both a clear oral statement that one is on final probation and that one will be terminated by a certain date if changes do not occur and a written notification. The chief steward should have known that Agentry's twenty-one years of adequate service would create a presumption of job security on his part and that warnings would need to be clear and unambiguous to override such perceptions.

4. He also contends that the termination is illegal under the Age Discrimination in Employment Act (29 U.S.C. 621, et seq.), which protects persons over forty years of age from employer consideration of the age of a claimant in determining if an employee is to be retained or discharged. He contends that his age was a determinative factor in his dismissal. When the chief steward made remarks in the record that the employee was "burnt out" and is "outmoded in his thinking" and stated to his face that he was "dead wood," he expressed code words that indicated a prejudice against senior workers.

Agentry asks for reinstatement into his position. How would a grievance board address this case?

PERSONNEL GRIEVANCE 5

Darin Puffington et al. v. Nodak Tax Department

This grievance involves complaints and request for redress and remedies for a group of smoking employees who feel they have been adversely affected by regulations prohibiting smoking within their workplace and subjected to discrimination as a result.

The state personnel board issued a directive that indicated that "all state agencies, divisions, and bureaus shall within six months of the effective date of this directive establish and implement written rules governing smoking and nonsmoking in the workplace. The rules shall be readily available for viewing by the employees and may include the designation of smoking and nonsmoking areas. In any dispute arising under rules and policies, the rights of the nonsmoker shall be given precedence."

The tax department then issued a set of rules that in effect banned any smoking in the work areas, halls, restrooms, and storage rooms. Workers were allowed fifteen-minute work breaks in the morning and afternoon; thus, the only choice for smokers was to spend their work breaks outdoors in order to smoke.

The complainants filed a grievance with the Tax Department Employee Grievance Committee contesting the legality and fairness of the regulations.

1. They contend that the rules of the department went beyond the original directive, which governs "smoking" in departments and designation of "smoking areas" as well as non–smoking areas. They contend that the directive implicitly requires departments to balance the rights of smokers and nonsmokers.
2. They contend that the department should utilize the least onerous approach to accommodate the "smoke-free" environment policy. Examples of "balancing" policies involve physical barriers or buffer zones between smokers and nonsmokers. Specifically, they request a special room to which they can retire during their breaks for smoking. Such an accommodation would keep the "work areas" smoke-free as well as meet the policy objective that protects nonsmokers and those particularly sensitive to secondhand smoke.
3. They contend that the present option (smoking outdoors) exposes the smoker to health hazards. One employee contends she contracted a severe case of bronchitis because of the necessity of smoking in weather that was –16 degrees with a 20-mile-per-hour wind (–38 degree windchill). Another worker contends he must smoke in order to counteract his tendency to narcolepsy (suddenly falling asleep).
4. They contend that the present rules subject them to discriminatory treatment and opprobrious conduct by other employees. As they smoke their cigarettes outside building entrances, they feel that they are regarded as "outcasts." They receive looks and glances that remind them of the treatment accorded panhandlers. As persons who are disabled through an addiction, they endure discrimination as handicapped persons.
5. They contend that the rules depress worker morale to the point where efficiency of operations is threatened.

The tax commissioner contends that it was necessary to ban smoking totally from the premises of the agency. The policy indicates that disputes shall be resolved in favor of nonsmokers. At particular issue are the concerns of people who are allergic to tobacco smoke. Setting aside a room for smoking would not solve the issue. In fact, such a room would provide such a heavy concentration of smoke that opening of doors or passing by the room would trigger unfavorable reactions.

Budgetary restrictions prevent the department from establishing a second employee lounge and equipping it with a ventilation system. In any case, smokers are not in any way a protected class under the equal protections clause.

How would a grievance board address this case?

PERSONNEL GRIEVANCE 6

Hassleschmitt v. Minnedota State Tax Department

This grievance involves an appeal to the dismissal of Mr. Hassleschmitt from the position of staff attorney at the Minnedota State Tax Department. Hassleschmitt is a tax attorney and he was dismissed for violating an agency rule that prevents agency attorneys from engaging in private legal practice. The relevant provision in the agency handbook states "Attorneys in the employ of the Tax Department shall not engage in the private practice of law. Nor shall any attorney become involved in any activity which represents a conflict of interest with his duties and responsibilities at the Tax Department."

Hassleschmitt was a member of the Blessed Assembly Evangelical Church. He volunteered to serve as an unofficial advisor to his church, giving advice on legal matters. Among the matters on which he provided legal advice was purchase of church property. He also was a member of the board of trustees for the Blessed Assembly Foundation, which provides financial support for the church, its school, and its youth camp. As a member he provided advice to individuals who sought to bequeath property or monies to the church or who would purchase insurance policies listing the foundation as the beneficiary. He provided these services to his church and to church members free of any charge. He considered this a matter of tithing his talents and, in fact, the precepts of his religion indicate a strong responsibility to tithe. None of this activity was done during hours of employment. It was done during evening hours and Saturdays. Any encounters with persons seeking information and advice took place in an office in the church.

Hassleschmitt's activities came to the attention of his superiors at his agency in a roundabout way. An audit of a state taxpayer, Mr. Jenerous, revealed that the taxpayer had listed as a deduction on his tax return a charitable deduction of a motorboat to the Blessed Assembly Youth Camp. An audit revealed that in the transfer of title, Hassleschmitt had signed as a representative of the Blessed Assembly Foundation in taking title of the property. Further inquiry revealed the fact that Jenerous continued to use the boat on Crystal Lake, the site of the youth camp.

His superior then called Hassleschmitt into his office and inquired about the matter. Hassleschmitt indicated that he had played a role in the transfer but that it was as a trustee of his church's foundation and not as a lawyer. He admitted advising Jenerous that he could use his boat but only in conjunction with youth camp activities. For instance, he could pilot the boat with church youth on board, instruct camp personnel on piloting the boat safely, or use the boat in conjunction with maintenance of the craft. In the course of the inquiry,. Hasselschmitt's broader activities in this regard came to light. The superior then gave Hasselschmitt notice of intended termination.

After receipt of notice of intent to terminate, a hearing was held ten days later.

Hassleschmitt argued that his activities were in no way in conflict with his duties. He expressed the view that he did not engage in the practice of law per se. Irrespective of that, a department hearing board voted to terminate his employment immediately.

Hassleschmitt appealed his termination. He argued as follows:

1. The activities in which he engaged did not constitute legal representations. It is true that he served in various advisory and official positions in his church but his role was that of a financial advisor. He noted that before he obtained his law degree he had completed a management accountancy degree.
2. The proffering of advice to his church did not constitute practice of law. The proffering of advice to the church member represented only good commonsense advice, which he incidentally noted was not taken. There was no attorney/client relationship between himself and Jenerous.
3. Any conflict of interest on a tax matter can be addressed by a simple recusal (if for instance he had been put in a position of working on the Jenerous case).
4. He also contended that the termination was an infringement of his rights of free exercise of religion. Under the free exercise clause, he is permitted during off-duty hours to serve his church as the demands of his religion and his conscience allow. In effect, he is being harshly penalized for his religious activity, which had no impact on the activities of his agency. He also contends that his termination involves a violation of his rights of association under the First Amendment.

The agency contended that:

1. However disingenuous Hassleschmitt's arguments are, there is no denying that his advisory activities represent the type of activities that lawyers engage in and that there is an inextricable merger of legal, accounting, and financial planning activities. Estate planning is regarded as a branch of legal activity.
2. However Hassleschmitt's activities might be regarded as standing apart from agency concerns, the point remains that his volunteer activity involved charitable contributions that bear upon tax liabilities of the state's taxpayers. Conflicts of interest would present themselves. What if the audit of Jenerous had by draw come under the supervision of Hassleschmitt?

How would a grievance board address this case?

PERSONNEL GRIEVANCE 7

Paula Astrupp v. State Environmental Control Agency

This is a grievance filed by Paula Astrupp contending that she was fired as a paralegal worker in the State Environmental Control Agency legal department on grounds prohibited by the Americans With Disabilities Act of 1990.

Astrupp was hired provisionally as a paralegal worker to assist in the research and preparation of briefs, orders, and legal matters in which the agency was involved. Astrupp was known to have a weight problem. She had a weight of 290 pounds on a 5'4" frame. After a six-month probationary period, she was told that she would not be employed as a nonprobationary employee. Among the reasons given for her termination were the following:

1. Continued problems in terms of providing a workstation that was not inconvenient and cramped. Unavailability of proper equipment and furniture to accommodate the employee. Permanent employment would diminish work efficiency.
2. Inability of the employee to use the library stacks for legal research. The library stacks are placed fourteen inches apart. In addition to inability of the employee to use the library stacks, employee would also be unable in that position to shelve and reshelve library materials, take care of looseleaf updates of library materials, and prepare library materials for binding.
3. Inability of the employee to use the photocopying machine located within a closet.
4. Disruptive work attitudes. She was particularly cited for verbal outbursts on at least three occasions. It was noted that her outbursts were over comments by coworkers that could be termed trivial. The conclusion is that the probationary employee lacks maturity and has probable psychological problems that would interfere with the performance of her duties.

Astrupp contends that:

1. No efforts were made to accommodate her particular handicap. Her computer workstation could have undergone some minor adjustments to provide her with a more comfortable work environment.
2. The agency could easily make adaptations that would provide her with an appropriate work environment. Space exists to move the stacks twenty inches apart. The photocopy machine could easily be moved out of the closet. The argument of an inability to accommodate is a pretext for discrimination against a person because of an obese handicapped condition.
3. In response to the issue of her outbursts, she notes that she simply registered a defense against remarks by other workers that were discriminatory in tone and content against overweight persons. She notes that snide comments and jokes were made about her lunch choices, her eating habits, and her clothes. She considered these harassing remarks. She said that she simply indicated her chagrin at what she termed intolerant and unprofessional behavior on the part of educated employees. She also resented the fact that she was known around the office as "Two Chins" and "Roly-Poly" and after the incidents as "Rowdy Powdy." Thus, her negative evaluation was based on her complaints against harassment.
4. She also notes that the reasons given for failure to complete the probationary period successfully made no reference to poor work performance, inadequate knowledge, or inefficiency. She indicated that she was constantly told that her research was outstanding, that her brief drafting preparation skills were excellent, that legal papers and correspondence that she prepared never had to be rewritten and needed few revisions or editing. The lack of negative information on job skills and performance would indicate that the reasons given are simply pretextual to a discriminatory decision directed against a person with an accommodatable handicap.

How would a grievance board address this case?

PERSONNEL GRIEVANCE 8

Marvella Laws v. State Audit Commission

This is an action in which Marvella Laws claims that she has been unlawfully demoted from her position as assistant to the director of administration of the State Auditing Commission. She was demoted from her position to the position of administrative records director. She contends that this particular demotion not only involved a reduction in salary of $6,000 a year but also a removal from any policymaking responsibilities. In effect she is now nothing more than a glorified file clerk. Laws is forty-eight years old, and she contends that the demotion was motivated by age and sex discrimination.

Laws is a twenty-year employee with the agency. The director of administration handles issues like payroll for the agency, travel funds, internal personnel issues, drafting the agency's budget, and computer services. As assistant to the director, Laws had responsibility for payroll and travel funds. When a new director, who was thirty-two years old, arrived on the scene in 1992, she contends that the agency engaged in a plan to replace older, long-time employees, and replace them with younger employees. The computer systems for the agency were vastly upgraded and not only auditors but also management personnel were required to upgrade their computer skills. Just as soon as one system of software was installed, another upgrade was introduced. Older employees were required to attend training sessions that were intense, total-immersion sessions structured to upgrade the work skills within two working days. The director of administration published a policy that indicated that all workers were required to attend these sessions and that promotion was dependent upon being current in skills. Failure to attend those sessions was grounds for transfer, reassignment, or demotion.

Laws contends that after these policy changes, older workers tended to get most of the negative reviews and criticism. In terms of salary schedules, the agency also said that no credit for over ten years' experience would be given. As the director of administration indicated, "Ten years of experience is as valuable as twenty years, because the first ten years are obsolete." She also notes that older employees were encouraged to resign through the mechanism of a severance payment of six months of wages. She noted that in 1992 there were sixteen employees in the agency over the age of forty-five. There are now four.

In terms of her own situation, Laws began to experience increasing conflict with the director. They disagreed over the computer updating training sessions, Ms. Laws feeling that the intense, concentrated training sessions put pressure on older employees that was difficult to overcome. She preferred incremental training whereby new procedures or software would be introduced on a step-by-step basis over a period of two weeks. She disagreed with the director rejecting out of hand all her original drafts on a policy. She herself received negative reviews of her work, including comments that she "was out of date," "tended to defend out-of-date systems," and "tended to be over-lenient in terms of leave policies, especially in favor of women employees." In respect to the latter comment, it was noted that the director overruled Laws on eight occasions, ruling that absence of women employees should be recorded as vacation leave or personal no-paid leave rather than as sick leave.

These pressures caused Laws extreme distress and aggravated her physical problems. She had arthritis and a bronchial condition and this led to an extended leave of absence of several weeks. In fact, she used all her sick leave and paid vacation leave in recovery. When she returned, she found out that the director had mandated a new software program for her payroll and had installed it. The training sessions had been held in her absence, and the director indicated he would not bring in the software experts for another training session. He pointed to the three-pound manual and simply said, "If you don't know the ropes within one week, I'm going to have to transfer you. Your job description now reads proficiency with Abacus."

A week later when she said she had not mastered the system she was informed that her assistant director's position was open and that she was being reclassified as director of administrative records. When she stated that she would prefer to resign and do so under the severance arrangements provided to several older male employees, she was told she was not being severed, so the six-month severance would not be available.

She asked for reinstatement in her old position, contending that the actions of the agency constituted both age and sex discrimination. The agency contends that all the personnel actions were prefectly legitimate management actions.

How would a grievance committee address this case?

PERSONNEL GRIEVANCE 9

Cartierre v. Oxley, Director of Sunshine Center

This grievance originates with Ms. Clariette Cartierre, an occupational therapist at the Sunshine Center who claims she has been the victim of sexual and religious discrimination in a selection process to fill key supervisory positions in the state Human Services Department's Sunshine Center. The department maintains an extensive system of group homes for persons suffering developmental and physical disabilities in order to provide them with a least-restrictive environment. The Sunshine Center is a centralized facility that allows for temporary transfer of residents at the group homes to a center where they can, for a period of one to six weeks, get diagnostic services, rehabilitation services, or additional training and education to reinforce their living skills.

Five years ago, the state hired Dr. Oxley as director. Oxley is a physician who has specialized in development disabilities. His premedical training was obtained at Graham Elder University, a denominational university of the Church of the Second Coming. The denomination has a strong mission in dealing with humanity's disadvantaged, and its university has established departments in sensory impairment, disability counseling, occupational and physical therapy, and health administration that have won accreditation and are renowned nationally.

Over the next five years, Oxley instituted several innovative programs and also took steps to recruit a supervisory staff that embodied his innovative approaches. As the supervisory staff retired or resigned because of policy differences, candidates were recruited on an open-application process. The first four vacancies were filled with applicants who had been colleagues or former students of Oxley at Graham Elder or Taylor Medical School. All were members of the Church of the Second Coming. When the position for head of the occupational therapy division at Sunshine Center opened, Cartierre applied. She had ten years experience working at the center and was interim supervisor during the search. She was in the process of completing a master's degree in health administration from Bison University. Her evaluations over the past five years were all superior. The occupational therapy position was filled with a male who had a degree in occupational therapy from Graham Elder University.

Cartierre filed a grievance with the state's Equal Employment Opportunity Commission, contending that she had been the victim of employment discrimination grounded on sex and religion. She makes the point that she is a member of a protected class, that she applied for a position for which she was qualified, that she was rejected, and that the position was held open and filled with an applicant of lesser qualifications who was not a member of her protected class. She also charges religious discrimination in hiring practices in that for the five administrative positions open at the center, a member of the Church of the Second Coming was chosen in every case.

Oxley rebuts the notion that either sex or religion were factors in final selection. He contends that in every case he chose the most qualified individuals for the position. He also contends that he was hired to implement innovative and effective programs for clients who were developmentally disabled. His programmatic approaches were shared by those finally selected, individuals who he admits were once coworkers or protégés but were particularly fitted to be on a team that would harmoniously address the problems of this clientele group. All the individuals chosen were professionals with whom the director had some acquaintance and good knowledge of their skills and potential. Also, the director was conducting ongoing research at the facility and it was important to recruit individuals who were familiar with his research protocols. Finally, Oxley contends that Cartierre was not selected because his appointment was predicated on implementing a new approach and changes at the center. Cartierre, in spite of her experience, simply was a part of the old system with no background in the changes being instituted. Cartierre can point to no instances where statements were overtly made favoring a person because of religious background or downgrading an employee because of gender.

Cartierre claims that these reasons are simply a pretext that cover a pattern of discrimination. The pattern is clear. Of the five administrative positions to be filled, all were filled with males and all were filled with persons who were known to be members of the director's church. The statistical probability of that given the 120 applicants with 9 applicants being Graham Elder graduates is approximately 2 in 100,000. The applicant file contains a number of female applicants with qualifications at least equal to those of the males selected. In the case of Cartierre's rejection, experience became a liability. As to evidence indicating favoritism toward employees on account of their religion, Cartierre notes that the inner clique of supervisors and two employees of the same denomination's membership engage in an informal range of social activities such as Boy Scout activities, bird-watching, and backpacking, with no invitation to participate in this informal networking ever extended to other employees.

Cartierre finally claims that the recruitment of employees and the administration of the Sunshine Center have been the subject of nepotistic practices—not in the sense of favors extended exclusively to blood or marital relatives—but favors extended exclusively to friends and those already known to the director.

How would a grievance board approach this case?

PERSONNEL GRIEVANCE 10

Piney Greenbusch v. Superior State Forestry Department

This grievance is brought by Piney Greenbusch, a forestry scientist employed by the Superior State Forestry Department. On three separate occasions he applied for a departmental class I position (a classification that covers division chiefs and assistant division chiefs and district and assistants to district directors). A division chief heads a central functional division such as Research and Ecology, Fire Control and Suppression, Pest and Insect Control, Economic Utilization, Tree Breeding and Reforestation, Roads and Facilities, and Public Relations. A district director is an administrative position with full administrative responsibility for the management of a particular forest area that may range from twenty-four to two hundred square miles. Three years ago the department created the position of assistant to the district director, opening up ten new positions in the department's ten districts. Greenbusch applied for three positions of assistant to the district director for three of the districts. A competitive hiring process resulted in other applicants being chosen for the three positions. One of the positions was filled by an African American, one by a white woman, and one by a Native American woman. Greenbusch contends that the Forestry Department has embarked on a program of reverse discrimination under the cover of a voluntary affirmative action program. Greenbusch contends that not only did the department select people with lesser qualifications than his own, the department has in the previous three years made a practice of preferring minorities and women, filling nine of ten positions with them. He also charges that the department has failed to fill these managerial positions with persons who have background in vital areas of forestry management. He notes that none of the three assistant district directors hired have a background in fire control, a vital department responsibility. That happens to be one area in which Greenbusch has experience and expertise. Four years earlier, the department had drafted a voluntary affirmative action program. Even without a self-analysis, the department demonstrated that it was an exclusive white-male domain, with all of its class I administrators being white males. A self-analysis revealed that the agency culture not only ignored any suggestion that it might recruit minorities but it also expressed a degree of hostility toward the possibility of integrating women into its high-level positions. Class I positions were almost exclusively recruited from the forestry scientific staff.

The director of the department was committed to changing the situation and implemented a voluntary affirmative action plan aimed at increasing the representation of minorities and women in class I positions as well as in the department at large. He was able to obtain increased appropriations from the legislature to promote diversity in the agency. Each district director was to be provided with a director's assistant. In addition, the department increased the number of paid internships to be made available for students seeking entry-level jobs. These internships would allow more minorities and women to be recruited into the agency's entry-level positions.

The affirmative action plan contained the following components:

1. job service advertisements that would encourage minorities and women to apply for positions;

2. a goal of placing minorities and women into vacancies as soon as qualified candidates are available;

3. a relaxation of experience criteria for hiring an assistant to the director positions and other selected positions. Experience over three years would no longer be counted as a factor in hiring. A reliance upon experience factors would rule out any progress on affirmative action at upper levels given the paucity of applicants in protected classes with experience.
4. opening of assistant to the director positions to individuals who were qualified in fields other than forestry. Positions would be open to persons having degrees in business administration, public administration, forestry, and the biological sciences.
5. minority and women candidates would receive a "first on the list consideration" in terms of the top five persons making a final list (filling of all vacancies).
6. in the final interview stage, members of the interviewing panel are to indicate objective reasons for either preferring or rejecting a candidate in writing. The other members of the panel are then to react to those comments on the record.
7. implementation of a mentoring system for assistant directors. The assistant directors would work with the director and first-line supervisors in the planning and implementation of the department's activities. During the three-year probationary program for assistant directors, the assistant would have opportunity to participate in management or administration of all programs being conducted in the district.

Mr. Greenbusch contends that the creation of the new assistant district director positions and the affirmative action program were not coincidental. While the assistant director positions are ostensibly open to all applicants irrespective of race, ethnic origin, or gender, the process of filling the positions has not been neutral or even tied to qualifications or merit. The process has in practice been as exclusive and discriminatory as the task force program declared unconstitutional in *Bakke*. Male applicants for the assistant district director positions are made to participate in a charade. He contends that the cumulative preferential mechanisms have operated to make selection of a person on the basis of protected status determinative. Not only have minorities and women been given a competitive edge, but the qualifications for the positions have been downgraded to allow more applicants of the protected classes to compete.

He also contends that the persons chosen over himself in the three hirings in which he participated had a much weaker profile in forestry knowledge and skills. In addition, the final selection panel went over a past performance evaluation that listed strengths and weaknesses of each candidate. His own evaluation showed a great many strengths and no weaknesses. In some cases, the evaluation for the other candidates simply said "Insufficient information available" to compare strengths and weaknesses.

He also contends that the record of deliberations following the interview revealed a tendency of the panel to favor women and minorities as a prophylactic response to the avoidance of discrimination suits. A number of panel members, in indicating their reason for choice of a candidate, responded "Candidate would assist department in meeting its affirmative action goals." When a panel member voted against the hiring of the African-American candidate, who had previously worked for the Georgia Forestry Department, the panel member said, "It's unlikely this candidate will stay or work out in our frigid climate. He'll freeze his posterior and be gone." Other panel members then rebutted his reasoning, noting that the objecting panel member was voicing a prejudiced and stereotypical attitude. One panel member stated, "If we reject him and that is on the record as a reason, we will have our posteriors in a sling and he will have cause to sue." Greenbusch concludes that the whole hiring process was marked by an apprehension over possible discrimination suits by minority or female candidates rejected for the positions. The objectivity of the hiring process was tainted.

The Forestry Department defends itself against any charge of reverse discrimination. The assistant director positions were created as a means of diversifying the demographic profile of managers and high-level administrators and in overcoming the effects of decades of neglect and discrimination. The hiring process is open to all and white male applicants are not inhibited from applying or being chosen. One of the new assistant directors is a male. Had Greenbusch viewed the position he applied for in proper perspective, he would have noted that it is a position developed to provide an applicant with familiarization and training to serve ultimately in high-level supervisory positions in the department. It is a position that involves mentoring of new employees. It is analogous to a residency in the professions. Mentoring allows new employees to compensate for lack of experience and service in the department. One of the reasons Greenbusch was not hired was that he is, in effect, overqualified. His experience and evaluations would indicate that he would be an appropriate candidate for a district director were one of those positions to open. It is also noted that he is particularly qualified to apply for the division chief positions. Very specific field qualifications are critical to these positions. While an assistant to the director represents a class I position, because occupants will carry out managerial tasks, it is not an associate director's position in which that official could take responsibility for tasks entrusted to the director.

The department also notes that the addition of the ten assistant district director positions has not displaced any managerial personnel in the department. The department also notes that the impact on its staffing is minimal. The department has sixty-four class I positions on its rolls. The addition of ten new positions providing the first rung of a career track for minorities and women is an incremental change in the personnel pattern that is not threatening to members of the majority presently occupying class I positions.

How would a grievance board deal with the Greenbusch case?

PERSONNEL GRIEVANCE 11

Marcus Madison, Eldon Oregonne, et al. v. State Department of Educational Assistance

This grievance is filed by Mr. Madison, Mr. Oregonne, and four other male supervisory and administrative employees who were discharged from their positions after a restructuring of the department, which eliminated their positions. The ages of the six individuals were sixty-two, fifty-eight, fifty-seven, fifty-five, fifty-five, and forty-six.

All personnel were employed in the State Department of Educational Assistance, which provides support services to local school districts. It provides support services of special education and for children with special needs, in curricular development and materials, in architectural and technical services, in professional development, in school health, in counseling and clinical services, in educational equality programs (affirmative action), and in contract services (which allow school districts to buy supplies through a central purchasing office in order to save through large-volume purchases). The department is headed by a director appointed by the governor. The director has been customarily given the authority to hire his eight division administrators. These eight division administrators are assisted by deputies who happen to be career civil servants. The six persons bringing this grievance were discharged when a restructuring eliminated their positions. The legislature, facing a financial crisis, was forced to cut appropriations for the department by 15 percent. In a statement of intent attached to the appropriation, the legislature directed the department to cut administrative costs before cutting aid or services directed to local school districts. The director indicated that the central office would need to cut its budget by some 25 percent. He indicated that the deputy division positions would be eliminated for six of the eight divisions within the department. The only divisions to retain a deputy would be those of architectural and technical services, which was filled by an architect (age thirty-eight) who specialized in the rare field of school architecture, and special education and children with special needs, which was filled by a special education needs specialist (age thirty-five). Under the restructuring, the director of each division would assume the tasks and responsibility for the deputies. In addition, each division head would reduce his support staff by 10 percent. Reductions would be conditioned on a review of the essential nature of the positions and possible redundancy in positions. The Department of Educational Assistance reduced its staff by eight, reducing its janitorial complement of three by two and its clerical staff by six. Of these eight individuals, the two janitors were sixty-two and sixty-three and were eligible to retire under the state personnel retirement system (at a slightly diminished level of reimbursement from those who retire at sixty-five). Of the six clerical workers, three were over forty and three were under forty. Employees whose positions are eliminated are given preference in a transfer to vacancies within the state personnel system, but the entire system was facing cutbacks and none of the persons released was able to transfer immediately to other positions.

The deputies were also given the option of transferring to a different department if vacancies were open, a rather symbolic option because most of them were true specialists, or of filling a lower position in their division at a cut in salary. The final result of this retrenchment was to place the burden of reducing positions on older career workers who had provided continuity and stability through different changes of administration.

Mr. Madison and his fellow grievants contend that the agency has violated the provisions prohibiting discrimination in employment on the basis of age. They contend that the reduction in force was oriented to save the agency funds by the elimination of positions held by older personnel whose salaries are several steps above that of other personnel in the various divisions. They also find the reduction in force a pretext for elimination of staff members on political grounds in that the career specialists would not support the same priorities or policy preferences of the political appointees of a new administration.

The six senior employees also contend that the reduction in force blatantly targeted the older deputies. Not all deputy positions were eliminated. Two were retained but by people under forty. Inclusion of at least one employee in a reduction of force who is not in the protected age group of the Age Discrimination in Employment Act (ADEA) may negate inference that age was a factor in terminations. That is not indicated here: the Administrator of Educational Assistance chose to eliminate all deputy positions occupied by employees over forty and retain those under forty.

The six senior employees contend that one approach to the reduction in force would have been to eliminate the position of deputy as a political appointment and to move the experienced and specialist deputies into positions of division chiefs. They also note that in transferring the responsibilities of the deputy onto the division chiefs, the administrator along with the director of central personnel allowed for an upgrade in salary of $8,000 a year for the division chiefs. Thus the objective of fiscal savings was really a pretext for the discharge of the older career employees.

Eldon Oregonne, sixty-two, was the deputy when he was given notice that his position was being eliminated. He is eligible to retire under the state personnel retirement system. He contends that this is an involuntary and forced retirement that violates the ADEA.

The state contends that the discharge of the older employees is only a consequence of a necessary restructuring and reduction in force. There is no intent to discriminate on the basis of age where the objective is to eliminate positions. The reduction in force focused on positions, not individuals or the characteristics of those occupying those positions.

While six of the eight deputy positions were eliminated, the elimination of positions was conditioned on a review of the functional necessity for the positions. The deputy positions that were retained possessed specialized skill requirements that could not be sacrificed even in the face of financial exigencies.

The reduction in force eliminated mid-level management positions that were policymaking positions. Agencies have much more leeway in changing or eliminating personnel in policymaking positions than in changing personnel who may implement policy. The traditional staffing of the deputy positions with career employees actually provided an impediment to the policymaking function of the agency and to the leadership of the agency under its appointed director. The reduction in force eliminates the structural impediment to efficient administration.

A reduction in force must be looked at in its totality; when one includes the lower-level positions eliminated with the middle-management positions, there is a reduction of force including both younger and older workers.

While appointed division chiefs received an increase in salary, that does not negate the objective of saving labor costs as a motivation behind reduction in force. On balance, the savings realized from elimination of deputy positions far outweigh the reasonable adjustments made to the salaries of division heads. The agency also was legislatively mandated to put a priority on reducing administrative costs, a mandate that invites a reduction in middle-management positions.

The ultimate issue is whether age was a factor in decisions to terminate an employee and whether the age of the employee made a difference in whether he was to be retained or discharged. A review of this reduction in force indicates that financial, administrative, and policy interests were the driving considerations in this effort.

How would a grievance board address this case?

PERSONNEL GRIEVANCE 12

Derri Sipple v. Boris Peddwhiskey

This is a grievance filed by Derri Sipple, an information management specialist in the Department of Policy Development, State Human Services, against her immediate superior, Boris Peddwhiskey, for threatened retaliation against her for filing a sexual harassment complaint against him. She asks that Peddwhiskey be separated from any appraisals and evaluations as to her performance in the department and that evaluation be undertaken by a grievance committee, one member to be a representative of the public employees union. The department resists this request, feeling that this completely undermines the authority chain within the department and takes away from administrators the powers of performance appraisal.

Sipple, a permanent state employee, transferred into the department from another office. Her job description involved analyzing surveys and managing data information. She got off on a wrong start with her supervisor. While he was away on a field trip, the department received new computers and Sipple transferred the files. She reorganized and renamed the files and deleted several hundred files of surveys that were over five years old and had not been utilized. When Peddwhiskey returned he was understandably upset and was about to take steps to immediately terminate her. In his outburst he asked whether she was having a "periodic cleaning frenzy." Sipple prevailed on him to give her a chance to rectify her actions. Working day and night for a week she was able to restore the files and set up an indexing system that was superior to the idiosyncratic system then in place. Peddwhiskey was impressed. He indicated he was wrong about her capabilities and praised her. Then he said, "We are going to have to work together as a team. We need to know each other better." Then putting his hand on her shoulder he invited her out to lunch, "Some nice place like LeBoueffs." Sipple seemed taken aback and declined.

Two days later Peddwhiskey was called into the office of his superior, Dante Cozzomacho, who informed him that Sipple had come into his office to file a complaint of sexual harassment against him. She related the incidents, the original outburst, and the invitation to lunch, which she interpreted by his speech, manner, gaze, and incident of touching to be a polite but "unwelcome" sexual advance. Peddwhiskey thought the allegations ridiculous. Cozzomacho then advised Peddwhiskey to be very careful, to extend no social overtures, and to do nothing that might be misinterpreted.

When Peddwhiskey next encountered Sipple, he could not contain himself. He said, "Let's get something straight. I know your game. You filed that complaint just to protect your job status in this department. Well, we're going to work together but it's going to be strictly business. And I'm going to watch you, day in and day out. Just like a top sergeant. Any mistakes, anything that's not strictly to Hoyle will be noted in your personnel file. You want cold objectivity. You'll get cold objectivity."

The next day, Cozzomacho received a formal complaint from Sipple that Peddwhiskey had threatened retaliation against her, that he was singling her out for scrutiny that was not extended to other employees, and that the sole reason for this was her filing of the harassment complaint. She feels that her appraisal will be tainted by any participation by Mr. Peddwhiskey. She asks for a grievance committee to be convened and that it act on her complaint and provide the following remedies: that she be allowed to insert rebuttal material to counter the material in her file on the computer files transfer; that her evaluation be assigned to a different administrator and that her her final assessment be discussed and made by a committee to which she can name one member (as in the case of an ad hoc grievance committee); and that a public employees union representative be present at these deliberations.

How would a grievance committee handle these questions?

Glossary

Achievements review: A system of review between an employee and a supervisor that utilizes interactive, collaborative processes and highlights accomplishments.

Adverse action: An employment decision that results in a loss or change in condition or terms of employment (disadvantageous) to an employee.

Adverse employment: A situation in a work environment whereby an employee is denied the benefits of a position (such as a raise in pay, a promotion, etc.) for a discriminatory reason (age, gender, race, etc.).

Adverse impact: Another term for *disparate impact* that alludes to a group suffering a discriminatory effect from an employment practice. This concept has been established by the *Uniform Guidelines* and it occurs if women and other minorities are not hired at a rate of at least 80 percent of the best-achieving group.

Affirmative action: A plan or program to restructure a workforce to provide for greater representation of qualified members of groups that have been the victims of past discrimination by employers.

Assessment center: An appraisal approach that requires employees to participate in activities that are similar to those they might be expected to do in an actual job.

Balancing tests: A weighing of factors supporting institutional interests against those that an individual may assert as a personal or a legally protected right.

Behaviorally Anchored Rating Scale (BARS) method: Variants on standard rating scales, in which the various scale levels are anchored with behavioral descriptions directly applicable to jobs being evaluated.

GLOSSARY 323

Bona Fide Occupational Qualification (BFOQ): A defense to an allegation that an employer discriminates in job assignments or job restrictions. The defense asserts that an employee attribute (e.g., gender) is a necessary element for the performance of the functions of the job.

Burden of proof: The obligation placed upon a party in an employment claim of persuading a trier of fact that discrimination has occurred.

Bureaucracy: A term devised by Max Weber to describe a pyramidal, hierarchical organization that has a highly structured chain of command and a distinct division of labor and that utilizes professionals with unique specialized abilities.

Business extension: The recognition of exclusive proprietary interests of an organization in the use of its properties and space.

Cafeteria plans: A benefit plan in which employees have a choice as to the benefits they receive, usually within some dollar limit. Most frequently a core benefit package can be augmented by employee selections of various elective programs.

Career development: An organization's plan to assure that people with proper qualifications and experience are available to fill positions when needed.

Career planning: Employees define career goals and outline plans to achieve them. Designed to further education and diversify training of employees and to enhance job performance.

Central tendency bias: An evaluation error in which employees are incorrectly rated near the average or the middle.

Collective bargaining: The performance of the mutual obligation of the employer and a representative of the employees to meet at reasonable times and confer in good faith with respect to wages, hours, and other terms and conditions of employment, or the negotiation of an agreement, or any question arising thereunder, and the execution of a written contract incorporating any agreement reached if requested by either party, but such obligation does not compel either party to agree to a proposal or require the making of a concession.

Compelling state interests: Governmental objectives that are advanced to override individual assertion of rights and to justify the placement of a burden on the exercise or assertion of an individual's legal rights.

Compressed work scheduling: Arranging work hours in order for employees to fulfil work obligations in fewer days. For example, an employee may work four ten-hour days in one work week rather than the standard eight-hour five-day week.

Constructive discharge: A resignation from a position because of intolerable conditions in the workplace as imposed or tolerated by an employer. This is treated by the courts as a discharge.

Contract With America: A campaign contract drawn up in 1994 and signed by incumbent and prospective Republican members of the U.S. House of Representatives that calls for broad-based reductions in the size of the federal government, tax breaks (capital gains and middle-class relief), a balanced budget amendment to the Constitution, and reform of the institutional structure of Congress.

Critical element: Performance evaluation technique requiring written documentation of employee's highly favorable and highly unfavorable work behavior. Rates workers on their performance of critical tasks.

Disparate impact: An application of selection criteria that results in a disproportionate selection of persons belonging to a protected class as compared to groups not included in the protected group. Individuals in a protected class are statistically underrepresented as a result.

Disparate treatment: An employer treating members of a protected class differently to their disadvantage with respect to other employees. An employer taking an adverse action against an employee for impermissible reasons (race, color, national origin, religion, gender, or handicap status).

Diversity: In relation to employment, a balanced, fair, and equitable proportion of ethnic, racial, and gender groups among a workforce.

Due process: The proceedings that, in the full interests of fairness, government owes persons deprived by government of a life, liberty, or property interest. See U.S. Constitution, fifth amendment, and fourteenth amendment, section 1.

Efficiency of the service: The orderly and efficient conduct of agency operations. Employee actions that disrupt or interfere with the conduct of operations may not be tolerated.

Employee development: Programs and efforts aimed at developing an employee's self-esteem, educational boundaries, and challenging internal behavioral boundaries.

Essentiality: A term used to define the nature of a particular government service. Any government body that performs a function that is necessary to public order and maintenance (such as police, fire fighting, sanitation, etc.) is deemed essential.

Exclusive recognition: A term used in labor/management relations whereby the employer will recognize only the union as the representative of all employees (both union and nonunion).

Expectation of privacy: An expectation that employers will not intrude or concern themselves with elements of personal life unrelated to job performance.

Factor classification system: A job evaluation technique in which evaluators make decisions on separate specific factors of the job.

Flextime: The practice of permitting employees to choose their own working hours.

Free exercise: The right of an employee to hold religious beliefs and to express his/her religious conscience without being penalized for it.

Glass ceiling: A subtle barrier between women and minorities and the highest job categories.

Hostile environment harassment: Conduct or surroundings created by or permitted by an employer that are offensive or abusive to a reasonable person.

Job-relatedness: Factors applied in personnel decisions that are limited to a measurement or prediction of job performance and job expectations.

Knowledge, Skills, and Ability (KSA): Criteria used by a rater in evaluating a prospective or current employee on potential or actual job performance.

Labor-management relations: A general term used to characterize and describe the relationships that exist between an employer and the employees.

Leadership and executive development: Programs and efforts established by an organization to develop executives as leaders and to help direct and motivate promising, productive employees onto a path toward supervisory, leadership positions.

Merit: A personnel system that bases recruitment, promotions, and rewards strictly on the basis of qualifications and performance.

Mixed motive: A motivation for taking a personnel action that includes both permissible and impermissible reasons (including employee activities protected by law).

National Performance Review: A commission established by President Bill Clinton and chaired by Vice President Al Gore to examine how to create a more efficient and productive federal government. The commission published its recommendations in *Creating A Government That Works Better and Costs Less.*

Nexus test: Requirement that an employer can apply sanctions to an employee only if conduct shows a relationship to job performance or the efficiency of the service.

On-the-spot hiring: A recruiting tool used by select government agencies where college graduates who meet specific criteria are given offers of employment immediately after the interview.

Patronage: A personnel system in which employment, benefits, promotions, and rewards are distributed on the basis of personal favoritism, "quid-pro-quo" arrangements, kinship, etc. and not on the basis of past performance or merit.

Pay banding: Combining different job classifications into smaller divisions or bands designed to increase flexibility. Also used as a recruiting device where pay scales for a given position are collapsed to create a more competitive and attractive starting salary.

Performance appraisal: An attempt to align employees and their task outcomes with employer expectations through individual evaluation.

Performance management: Any system or established set of criteria used to evaluate an employee and to guide that employee toward better future performance.

Performance planning: The phase of performance management when supervisor and employee establish job-related goals and objectives as well as performance standards for the next year.

Point factor method: A quantitative job evaluation technique in which numerical points are assigned to specific job components. These values are totaled to determine a quantitative assessment of a job's worth.

Politics/administration dichotomy: A phrase first utilized by Woodrow Wilson in his classic treatise on public administration "The Study of Administration," *Political Science Quarterly,* June 1887, in which he argued for the separation of politics from the administration of the public bureaucracy in order to facilitate a more efficient and equitable operation.

POSDCORB (Planning, **O**rganizing, **S**taffing, **D**irecting, **CO**ordinating, **R**eporting, **B**udgeting): Developed by Frederick Taylor and the scientific management movement, it was intended to provide the "one best way" to successful public administration.

Prima facie case: Presentation of evidence or demonstration of a particular set of facts that can persuade one that discrimination is more likely than not to have occurred in employment. The demonstration establishes the fact of discrimination, which stands until rebutted (contradicted).

Privatization: Government initiatives to divest itself of certain programs and functions and turn them over to private-sector administration. It is theorized that by doing so, the functions would be more efficiently administered and delivered.

Protected class: A class of persons identified in the law as being protected against discriminatory action. Statutes have identified race, color, religion, gender, national origin, handicap or disabled status, marital status, and sexual orientation as categories meriting protection.

Quality Oriented Position Management Systems (QOPMS): A system that is oriented towards quality improvement and the training and professional development of employees. Various criteria (e.g., critical tasks) are used to guide improvement.

Quid pro quo sexual harassment: Inducing a person to acquiesce or tolerate an unwelcome behavior of a sexual nature as a requirement for obtaining or retaining a condition or term of employment.

Reasonable person standard: A test of conduct or injury based on an evaluation by a disinterested average person asking the question "Is it reasonable to conclude this?"

Reasonable woman test: A test of conduct or injury to a woman based on an evaluation by a disinterested average person of the same sex asking the question "Is it reasonable to conclude this?"

Reengineering: A term devised by Vice President Al Gore's National Performance Review as an all-encompassing term for recommendations for reform of the federal government ("reinventing government").

Religious establishment: Actions by public personnel or instrumentalities that endorse, support, promote, and encourage religion or convey a message of symbolic union between church and state.

Retaliation: An adverse action by an employer against an employee taken after an employee has exercised a right or filed a complaint.

Reverse discrimination: Personnel actions and decisions that may operate to benefit members of a protected class and have the effect of disfavoring or displacing members of an unprotected group.

Rotational assignments: Short-term work assignments outside an employee's normal work routine; used to expand that employee's knowledge, skills, and understanding of the larger organization work environment.

Rule of three: The process whereby the personnel department forwards the names of the top three qualified candidates to the agency. The agency can then select one of those three for employment.

Scientific management: A body of organizational theory founded by Frederick Taylor that attempted to use scientific, quantifiable measures of job performance and overall productivity and efficiency to evaluate success.

Spoils system: A form of patronage that was particularly linked to the administration of Andrew Jackson, wherein employment, rewards, promotions, and contracts were awarded on the basis of "connections" rather than merit.

Standard operating procedures (SOPs): Rules and guidelines (written and unwritten, explicit or implicit) that exist in any organization and that serve to direct the day-to-day operations and performance of employees and employers.

Technological innovation: A phrase used to describe the new developments in science and technology that may impact on an employer and employees in terms of the tools and skills needed to remain current and competitive with respect to such developments industry-wide.

Training: The process of instructing people in the "how-to" and "what-for" of a particular task or assignment in an effort to make them proficient in the skills necessary to perform their job satisfactorily.

Traits approach: A method of employee evaluation that identifies key personality characteristics or traits necessary for good and effective leadership.

Undue hardship: Costs associated with accommodations to an employee's work needs that override any benefits that the employer will realize from the employment of persons seeking such accommodations.

Unity of command: A principle of management whereby each employee has only one direct supervisor.

Variable due process: The provision of procedural safeguards for an employee in proportion to the severity of the deprivation imposed on the employee. The more severe the penalty imposed on the employee, the broader the scope of procedural safeguards (also known as "Goss" principle).

Whistle-blowing: When an employee identifies practiced waste, fraud, mismanagement, or abuse to superiors, political officials, the press, or the public.

Bibliography

1992 Federal Personnel Journal. Washington, D.C.: Key Publications, 1992.
1995 Federal Personnel Guide. Washington, D.C.: Key Communications, 1995.
Aaron, Benjamin. "The Future of Collective Bargaining in the Public Sector." In *Public Sector Bargaining.* 2d ed. Edited by Benjamin Aaron, Joyce M. Najita, and James L. Stern. Washington, D.C.: The Bureau of National Affairs, Inc., 1988.
Abbot, Debra A. *Workplace Exposure to AIDS,* 48 Maryland L Rev 212 (1989).
Allegretti, Joseph G. *Sexual Harassment of Female Employees by Co-workers: A Theory of Liability,* 15 Creighton L Rev 437 (1981-1982).
American Law Institute. *Restatement of the Law.* In *Torts,* 2d.ed., (1981).
Annotation: Employer's Enforcement of Dress or Grooming Policy As Unlawful Employment Practice Under Sec. 703(a) of Civil Rights Act of 1964 (42 U.S.C. 2000e-2(a)) 27 ALR Fed 274 (1976).
Annotation: *Who is "Qualified" Handicapped Person Protected From Employment Discrimination Under Rehabilitation Act of 1973,* 80 ALR Fed 830 (1986).
Appleby, Paul. "Government is Different." In *Classics of Public Administration,* 3d ed. Edited by Jay M. Shafritz and Albert C. Hyde. Pacific Grove, Calif.: Brooks Cole, 1992.
Argyris, Chris. *Integrating the Individual and the Organization.* New Brunswick, N.J.: Transaction Publishers, 1990.
Aron, Martin W. *Whistleblowers, Insubordination, and Employee's Rights of Free Speech,* 43 Labor L J 211 (April 1992).
Aronson, A.H. *State and Local Personnel Administration: Biography of an Idea.* United States Civil Service Commission. Washington, D.C.: U.S. Government Printing Office, 1974.
Aronson, Sidney H. *States and Kinship in the Higher Civil Service: Standards of Selection in*

the Administrations of John Adams, Thomas Jefferson, and Andrew Jackson. Cambridge, Mass.: Harvard University Press, 1964.

Bach, Tracy L. *Gender Stereotyping in Employment Discrimination: Finding a Balance of Evidence and Causation Under Title VII,* 77 Minn L Rev 1251 (1993).

Balfour, Danny L. "Impact of Agency Investment in the Implementation of Performance Appraisal." *Public Personnel Management* 21, no. 1 (spring 1992).

Baptiste, Brad. "Race Norming, Validity Generalization, and Employment Testing," forthcoming chapter in *Handbook of Public Personnel Administration.* Edited by Jack Rabin et al. New York: Marcel Dekker, 1994.

Bardwick, Judith M. *Danger in the Comfort Zone.* New York: American Management Association, 1991.

Barnard, Chester I. *The Functions of the Executive.* Cambridge, Mass.: Harvard University Press, 1938.

Barnett, Tim, Winston N. McVea Jr., and Patricia A. Lanier. *An Overview of the Family and Medical Leave Act of 1993,* 44 Labor L J 429 (July 1993).

Bejarano, Patricia J. *Labor Pains: The Rights of Pregnant Employees,* 43 Labor L J 780 (Dec. 1992).

Bellone, Carl J., and George Fredrick Goerl. "Reconciling Public Entrepreneurship and Democracy." *Public Administration Review* 52, no. 2 (March/April 1992).

Belton, Robert. *The Civil Rights Act of 1991 and the Future of Affirmative Action: A Preliminary Assessment,* 41 DePaul L Rev 1085 (1992).

Bennis, Warren G., Kenneth D. Benne, and Robert Chin. *The Planning of Change.* 4th ed. New York: Holt, Rinehart & Winston, 1985.

Blade, Lawrence. *Employment at Will vs. Individual Freedom: On Limiting the Abusive Exercise of Employer Power,* 67 Columbia L Rev 1404 (1967).

Block, David, and Margaret R. Bryan. "After a Year, FMLA Still Provokes Questions," *National L. J.,* 28 Feb. 1994.

Blum, Andrew. "Secondhand Smoke Suits May Catch Fire," *National L. J.,* 1 Mar. 1993.

Boehmer, Robert G. *Artificial Monitoring and Surveillance of Employees: The Fine Line Dividing the Prudently Managed Enterprise From the Modern Sweatshop,* 41 DePaul L Rev 739 (1992).

Bolles, Richard N. *The Three Boxes of Life.* Berkeley, Calif.: Ten Speed Press, 1981.

Bolt, James F. *Executive Development: A Strategy for Corporate Competitiveness.* New York: Harper & Row, 1989.

Bowers, Mollie H. *What Labor and Management Need to Know About Workplace Smoking Cases,* 43 Labor L J 40 (Jan. 1992).

Bruce, Willa, and Christine Reed. "Preparing Supervisors for the Future Work Force: The Dual-Income Couple and the Work-Family Dichotomy." *Public Administration Review* 54, no. 1 (January/February 1994).

Bulger, Brian. "Impact of the ADA Exceeds Predictions," *National L. J.,* 28 Feb. 1994.

Byrne, John A., "The Craze for Consultants." *Business Week,* 25 July 1994.

Casey, John M., *From Agoraphobia to Xenophobia: Phobias and Other Anxiety Disorders Under the Americans with Disabilities Act,* 17 Puget Sound L Rev 381 (1994).

Cavaliere, Frank J. *Derogatory Remarks as Evidence of Discrimination Under the Age Discrimination in Employment Act of 1967,* 44 Labor L J 664 (November 1993).

Cayer, N. Joseph. *Managing Human Resources: An Introduction to Public Personnel Administration.* New York: St. Martin's Press, 1980.

———. *Public Personnel Administration in the United States.* 2d ed. New York: St. Martin's, 1986.

Clark, Miriam B., and Frank H. Freeman. *Leadership Education 1990: A Source Book.* West Orange, N.J.: Leadership Library of America, Inc., 1990.

Clayton, Susan D. "Remedies for Discrimination: Race, Sex and Affirmative Action." *Behavioral Science and the Law* 10 (1992).

Cleary, Martha. *Sufficiency of Defendant's Nondiscriminatory Reason to Rebut Inference of Sex*

Discrimination in Promotion or Demotion of Employee as Violation of Title VII of Civil Rights Act of 1964, 111 ALR Fed 1 (1993).
Coleman, Charles J. *Managing Labor Relations in the Public Sector.* San Francisco: Jossey-Bass Publishers, 1990.
Comment: *Employment Discrimination Against Overweight Individuals: Should Obesity be a Protected Classification*, 30 Santa Clara L Rev 951 (1990).
Coshan, Margaret. "An EAP Can be Part of the Solution." *Canadian Business Review* 19, no. 2 (summer 1992).
Covey, Stephen R. *Principle Centered Leadership.* New York: Simon & Schuster, 1990.
Cozzetto, Don. "The Officer Fitness Report as a Performance Appraisal Tool." *Public Personnel Management* 19, no. 3 (fall 1990).
Crenson, Matthew A. *The Federal Machine: Beginnings of Bureaucracy in Jacksonian America.* Baltimore: The Johns Hopkins University Press, 1975.
Crosby, Philip. *Quality is Free.* New York: New American Library, 1979.
Cutrera, Terri A. *Computer Networks, Libel and the First Amendment*, 12 Computer L J 555 (Dec. 1992).
Dahl, Robert A. "The Science of Public Administration: Three Problems." *Public Administration Review* 7 (1947).
Dahlstrom, W. Grant, and Leona Dahlstrom, *Basic Readings on the M.M.P.I.: A New Selection on Personality Measurement.* Minneapolis: University of Minnesota Press, 1978.
DeLapa, Judith A. "Job Descriptions that Work." *Personnel Journal* 68, no. 6 (June 1989).
Delatte, Ann Perkins. "Eight Guidelines for Successful Diversity Training." *Training* 30 (Jan. 1993).
Deming, W. Edwards. *The New Economy for Industry, Government, and Education.* Cambridge, Mass.: MIT, Center for Advanced Engineering Study, 1993.
———. *Out of the Crisis.* Cambridge, Mass.: MIT, Center for Advanced Engineering Study, 1982.
DiIulio Jr., John J., Gerald Garvey, and Donald F. Kettl, *Improving Government Performance: An Owner's Manual.* Washington, D.C.: Brookings Institution, 1993.
Edwards, Margaret Hart. *The ADA and the Employment of Individuals with Mental Disabilities*, 18 Employee Relations L J 347 (winter 1992–1993).
EEOC Guidance on Medical Exams Under ADA: Pre-Employment Disability Related Injuries. The Employment Discrimination Reporter 651, 25 May 1994 (Washington, D.C.: Bureau of National Affairs).
Epstein, Cynthia Fuchs. *Women in Law.* Urbana: University of Illinois Press, 1993.
Epstein, Richard A. *Forbidden Grounds: The Case Against Race Discrimination Laws.* Cambridge, Mass.: Harvard University Press, 1992.
Equal Employment Opportunity Commission. *A Technical Assistance Manual on the Employment Provisions of Title I of the Americans with Disabilities Act.* Washington, D.C.: Jan. 1992.
Essary, Melissa A. *The Dismantling of McDonnell Douglas v. Green: The High Court Muddies the Evidentiary Waters in Circumstantial Evidence Cases*, 21 Pepperdine L Rev 385 (1994).
Fair Employment Practices. Washington, D.C.: BNA, May 9, 1994.
Fair Employment Practices. Washington, D.C.: BNA, Dec. 6, 1993.
Federal Personnel Guide. Washington, D.C.: Key Communications Group, 1993.
Felblum, Chai. *Medical Examinations and Inquiries Under the Americans With Disabilities Act: A View From the Inside*, 64 Temple L Rev 521 (1991).
Finding a "Manifest Imbalance": The Case for a Unified Statistical Model for Voluntary Affirmative Action Under Title VII, 87 Mich L Rev 1987 (1989).
Fontaine, Valerie A. "Cultivating a Diverse Work Force: Firms' Profiles Need to Reflect Reality," *National L. J.*, 10 Jan. 1994.

Fram, David K. *The ADA Rules for Drug and Alcohol Abuse,* 39 Practical Lawyer 35 (Oct. 1993).
Freed, Mayer G. *Suits to Remedy Discrimination in Government Employment—The Immunity Problem,* 5 Columbia Human Rights Review 383 (1973).
Freedman, Anne. *Patronage: An American Tradition.* Chicago: Nelson-Hall Publishers, 1994.
Frier, Daniel. *Age Discrimination and the ADA: How the ADA May be Used to Arm Older Americans Against Age Discrimination By Employers Who Would Otherwise Escape Liability Under the ADEA,* 66 Temple L Rev 173 (1993).
Galanos, Jean Fitzpatrick, and Stephen H. Price. *Comment: Title I of the Americans With Disabilities Act of 1990: Concepts and Considerations for State and Local Government Employers,* 21 Stetson L Rev 931 (1992).
Garner, Donald W. *Protecting Job Opportunities of Smokers: Fair Treatment for the New Minority,* 23 Seton Hall L Rev 417 (1993).
General Accounting Office. *Americans With Disabilities Act: Initial Accessibility Good but Important Barriers Remain.* Gaithersburg, Md.: 1992.
Gilbert, C. Ronald. "Human Resource Management Practices to Improve Quality: A Case of Human Resource Management Intervention in Government." *Human Resource Management* 30 no. 2 (summer 1991).
Gilbert, Jonathon. *Computer Bulletin Board Operator Liability for User Misuse,* 54 Fordham L Rev 439 (Dec. 1985).
Goff, J. Larry. *The Legislative Response to Alcoholism and Drug Addiction in the Americans with Disabilities Act, 1993,* 21 J of Law and Psychiatry 77 (spring 1993).
Goodman, Janice. "Sexual Harassment Laws Face Lax Enforcement," *National L. J.,* 11 Jan. 1993.
Goodnow, Frank J. *Politics and Administration: A Study In Government.* New York: Russel and Russel, 1900.
Goodsell, Charles T. *The Case for Bureaucracy: A Public Administration Polemic.* 3d ed. Chatham, N.J.: Prentice-Hall, 1994.
Gore, Al. *From Red Tape to Results: Creating a Government That Works Better and Costs Less: Report of the National Performance Review.* Washington, D.C.: U.S. Government Printing Office, 1993.
———. "The New Job of the Federal Executive." *Public Administration Review* 54, no. 4 (July/August 1994).
Graglia, Lino A. *Racial Preferences, Quotas, and the Civil Rights Act of 1991,* 41 DePaul L Rev 1117 (1992).
Gray, John A. *Preferential Affirmative Action in Employment,* 43 Labor L J 23 (Jan. 1992).
Guinn, Kathleen. "Performance Management: Not Just an Annual Appraisal." *Training* (Aug. 1987).
Gulick, Luther, and Lyndall Urwick, eds. *Papers on the Science of Administration.* New York: Institute of Public Administration, 1937.
Guy, Mary E. *Professionals in Organizations: Debunking a Myth.* New York: Praeger, 1985.
Halachmi, Arie. "Information Technology, Human Resource Management, and Productivity." In *Public Personnel Management: Current Concerns—Future Challenges,* edited by Carolyn Ban and Norma M. Riccucci. New York: Longman, 1991.
Hale, Mary M., and Rita Mae Kelly. *Gender, Bureaucracy, and Democracy.* New York: Greenwood Press, 1989.
Hames, David S., and Nickie Dierson. *The Common Law Right to Privacy: Another Incursion into Employers' Rights to Manage Their Employees?* 42 Labor L J 757 (Nov. 1991).
Hammer, Michael, and James Champy. *Reengineering the Corporation: A Manifesto for Business Revolution.* New York: Harper Collins, 1993.
Hanson, Heather L. *The Fourth Amendment in the Workplace: Are We Really Being Reasonable,* 79 Virginia L Rev 243 (1993).
Hays, Steven W., and Richard C. Kearney. "Employee Discipline and Removal: Coping

With Job Security." In *Public Personnel Administration: Problems and Prospects.* 2d ed. Englewood Cliffs, N.J.: Prentice-Hall, 1990.

———. "State Personnel Directors and the Dilemmas of Workforce 2000: A Survey." *Public Administration Review* 52, no. 4 (July/August 1992).

Herzberg, Frederick, Bernard Mausner, and Barbara Synderman. *The Motivation to Work.* New York: Wiley, 1959.

Hickman, Craig R., and Michael A. Silva. *Creating Excellence: Managing Corporate Culture, Strategy and Change in the New Age.* New York: Penguin Books, 1984.

Hill Jr., Marvin, and Emily Delacenserie. *Procrustean Beds and Draconian Choices: Lifestyle Regulations and Officious Intermeddlers—Bosses, Workers, Courts, and Labor Arbitrators,* 57 Missouri L Rev 51 (1992).

Hoogenboom, Ari. *Outlawing the Spoils: A History of the Civil Service Reform Movement 1865–1883.* Urbana: University of Illinois Press, 1961.

Hotzman, Jonathon. *Applicant Testing for Drug Use. A Policy and Legal Inquiry,* 33 Wm & Mary L Rev 47 (1991).

Hoyman, Michele, and Ronda Robinson. "Interpreting the New Sexual Harassment Guidelines." *Personnel Journal* (Dec. 1980).

Hyde, Albert C. "Rescuing Quality Measurement from TQM." *The Bureaucrat* 19 (winter 1991).

Imundo Jr., Louis V. *Some Comparisons Between Public Sector and Private Sector Collective Bargaining,* 24 Labor L J 810 (1973).

Jaschik, Scott. "A Convoluted Harassment Dispute at Sonoma State U.," *The Chronicle of Higher Education,* 22 June 1944.

Jones, Nancy Lee. *Overview and Essential Requirements of the Americans With Disabilities Act,* 64 Temple L Rev 471 (1991).

Juran, Joseph. *Juran on Leadership for Quality.* New York: Free Press, 1989.

Justice Department. *Memorandum on Application of Rehabilitation Act, Sec. 504 to HIV Persons.* (Sept. 27, 1988).

Kaplan, Robert E., Wilfred H. Drath, and Joan R. Kofodinos. "High Hurdles: The Challenge of Executive Self Development." *The Academy of Management Executive* 1, no. 3 (1987).

Kaufman, Herbert. "The Growth of the Federal Personnel System: A Profile of the Federal Civil Service. In *The Federal Government Service.* 2d ed. Edited by Wallace S. Sayre. Englewood Cliffs, N.J.: Prentice-Hall, Inc., 1965.

Kearney, Richard C. *Labor Relations in the Public Sector.* 2d ed. New York: Marcel Dekker, Inc., 1992.

Kearney, Richard C., and Steven W. Hays. "Labor-Management Relations and Participative Decision Making: Toward a New Paradigm." *Public Administration Review* 54, no. 1 (January/February 1994).

Kemp, Donna R. *Mental Health in the Workplace.* Westport, Conn.: Greenwood Publishing Group, 1994.

Kettl, Donald F. "Privatization: Implications for the Public Work Force." In *Public Personnel Management: Current Concerns—Future Challenges.* Edited by Carolyn Ban and Norma M. Riccucci. New York: Longman, 1991.

Kingsley, J. Donald. *Representative Bureaucracy.* Yellow Springs, Ohio: Antioch Press, 1944.

Kirrane, Diane. "EAPS: Dawning of a New Age." *Human Resources Magazine* 25, no. 1 (January 1990).

Klein, Jeffrey S., and Lawrence J. Baer. "With More Businesses Having to Accommodate HIV-positive Employees, Companies Need Guidance to Address Federal Disability Laws and Privacy Rights," *National L. J.,* 9 May 1994.

Koch, Cora S. "Rights Act Reshapes Remedies," *National L. J.,* 30 Mar. 1992.

Kotter, John P. *The General Managers.* New York: Free Press, 1982.

Krislov, Samuel. *Representative Bureaucracy.* Englewood Cliffs, N.J.: Prentice-Hall, 1972.

Laguzza, Ross P. "Assessing Attitudes and Beliefs: Employment Cases Stir Jurors' Emotions," *National L. J.*, 28 June 1993.
Lamber, Julia. *Overqualified, Underqualified, or Just Right: Thinking About Age Discrimination and* Taggart v. Time, 58 Brooklyn L Rev 347 (1992).
Lassem, Ronnie. *Development Management: Principles of Holistic Business*. Colchester: Basil Blackwell, 1990.
Lombardo, Michael M., and Robert W. Eichinger. "Preventing Derailment: What to Do Before It's Too Late." *Application Report*. Greensboro, N.C.: Center for Creative Leadership, 1989.
Loundry, David. *E-Law: Legal Issues Affecting Computer Information Systems and System Operator Liability*, 12 *Computer L J* 101 (Dec. 1993).
Lovrich Jr., Nicholas P. "Performance Appraisal." In *Public Personnel Administration: Problems and Prospects*. 2d ed. Edited by Steven W. Hays and Richard C. Kearney. Englewood Cliffs, N.J.: Prentice-Hall, 1990.
Lundquist, Laura A. *Weighing the Factors of Drug Testing for Fourth Amendment Balancing*, 60 The George Washington L Rev 1151 (1992).
Macdonald, Charles R. *MBO Can Work!: How to Manage by Contract*. New York: McGraw-Hill, 1982.
Macneil, Neil, and Harold W. Mietz. *The Hoover Report 1953–1955: What it Means to You as Citizen and Taxpayer*. New York: The Macmillan Company, 1956.
Major, Michael J. "Employee Assistance Programs: An Idea Whose Time has Come." *Modern Office Technology* 35, no. 3 (March 1990).
Marcosson, Samuel A. *Harassment on the Basis of Sexual Orientation: A Claim of Sex Discrimination Under Title VII*, 81 Georgetown L J 1 (1992).
Marinelli, Arthur J. *Age Discrimination and Reductions in Force*, Ohio Northern U L Rev 277 (1993).
Maroney, Bernard Patrick, and M. Ronald Buckley. "Does Research in Performance Appraisal Influence the Practice of Performance Appraisal? Regretfully Not!" *Public Personnel Management* 21, no. 2 (summer 1992).
Marx, Gary T. "The Case of the Omniscient Organization." *Harvard Business Review* (Mar./Apr. 1990).
Marzotto, Toni. "The Crisis in Pay: Reform or Fragmentation?" In *Public Personnel Management: Current Concerns—Future Challenges*. Edited by Carolyn Ban and Norma M. Riccucci. New York: Longman, 1991.
Maslow, Abraham H. "A Theory of Human Motivation." *Psychological Review* 50 (July 1943).
Mastroianni, Peggy R., and David K. Fram. *The Family and Medical Leave Act and the Americans with Disabilities Act: Areas of Contrast and Overlap*, 9 Labor Lawyer 531 (1993).
McAllister, Bill. "Atlanta's VA Hospital: A Top-Level Conspiracy of Silence: Blatant Sexual Harassment Persisted for Years," *Washington Post Weekly Edition*, 15–21 Mar. 1993.
McCall, Morgan W., and Michael M. Lombardo. "Off the Track: Why and How Successful Executives Get Derailed." *Technical Report #21*. Greensboro, N.C.: Center for Creative Leadership, 1993.
McDonald Jr., James J., and Francis Kulick. *Mental and Emotional Injuries in Employment Litigation*. Rockville, Md.: BNA Books, 1994.
McGee, Bill. "EAP Evolution: Employee Assistance Programs Provide Stress 'Safety Valve.'" *Denver Business Journal* 44, no. 50 (August 27, 1993).
McGregor, Douglas. "The Human Side of Enterprise." *Management Review*, November 1957.
———. *The Human Side of Enterprise: Twenty-fifth Anniversary Printing*. New York: McGraw-Hill, 1985.

———. "An Uneasy Look at Performance Appraisal." *Harvard Business Review* (Sept./Oct. 1972).

Mezey, Susan Gluck. *In Pursuit of Equality: Women, Public Policy, and the Federal Courts.* New York: St. Martins Press, 1992.

Michaels, Lawrence, and Adam Levin. "Courts Are Divided on Drug Tests," *National L. J.* 24 Oct 1994.

Mickey Jr., Paul F., and Maryelena Pardo, *Dealing With Mental Disabilities Under the ADA,* 9 Labor Lawyer 531 (1993).

Mintzberg, Henry. *The Nature of Managerial Work.* New York: Harper & Row, 1973.

Mobley, Michael, and Tamara Payne. "Backlash: The Challenge to Diversity Training." *Training and Development* 46 (Dec. 1992).

Moe, Ronald C. "The 'Reinventing Government' Exercise: Misinterpreting the Problem, Misjudging the Consequences." *Public Administration Review* 54, no. 2 (Mar./Apr. 1994).

Morin, Richard. "Bringing Sexual Harassment Out Where Everyone Can See It." *Washington Post Weekly Edition,* 21–27 Oct. 1991.

———. "Think Twice Before You Say Another Word: A Poll Shows the Definition of Sexual Harassment is Changing," *Washington Post Weekly Edition,* 28 Dec. 1992–3 Jan. 1993.

Moore, John. "Possibly One 'Thou Shalt Not' Too Many," *National L. J.,* 21 May 1994.

Morris, Frank, C., and Teresa L. Jakubowski. "ADA Places Employers of Mentally Ill in a Bind," *National L. J.,* 17 April 1994.

Morrison, Ann M. *The New Leaders: Guidelines on Leadership Diversity in America.* San Francisco: Jossey Bass, 1992.

Morrison, Ann M., Randall P. White, and Ellen Van Velsor. *Breaking the Glass Ceiling: Can Women Reach the Top of America's Largest Corporations?* Reading, Mass.: Addison Wesley, 1982.

Nadler, Leonard, and Zeace Nadler. *Developing Human Resources.* San Francisco: Jossey Bass, 1991.

Naff, Katherine C. "Labor-Management Relations and Privatization: A Federal Perspective." *Public Administration Review* 51, no. 1 (Jan./Feb. 1991).

Nalbandian, John. "Performance Appraisal: If Only People Were Not Involved." *Public Administration Review* 41, no. 3 (May–June 1981).

National Institute for Occupational Safety and Health. *Fatal Injuries to Workers in the United States, 1980-1989.* Washington, D.C.: 1993.

Nesbit, Murray B. *Labor Relations in the Federal Government Service.* Washington, D.C.: The Bureau of National Affairs, Inc., 1976.

New Economy for Industry, Government, and Education. Cambridge, Mass.: MIT, Center for Advanced Engineering Study, 1993.

Note: Challenges to Performance Appraisals of Federal Employees Under the Civil Service Reform Act of 1978, 38 S Dak L Rev 341 (1993).

Note: Constitutional Status of Sexual Orientation: Homosexuality as a Suspect Classification, 98 Harvard L Rev 1285 (April 1985).

Note: Current Procedures for Adverse Actions Against Civil Service Employees Do Not Violate Due Process Clause, 23 U Kan L Rev 206 (1974).

Note: Developments in the Law—Sexual Orientation and the Law, 102 Harvard L Rev 1509 (May 1989).

Note: Limiting the Right to Terminate at Will: Have the Courts Forgotten the Employer, 35 Vanderbilt L Rev 201 (1982).

Note: Protecting At-Will Employees Against Wrongful Discharge: The Duty to Terminate Only in Good Faith, 93 Harvard L Rev 1816 (1980).

Osborne, David, and Ted Gaebler. *Reinventing Government: How the Entrepreneurial Spirit is Transforming the Public Sector.* Reading, Mass.: Addison Wesley, 1992.

Perrow, Charles. *Complex Organizations: A Critical Essay.* 2d ed. New York: Random House, 1979.

Perry, Ronald W., and N. Joseph Cayer, "Evaluating Employee Assistance Programs: Concerns and Strategies for Public Employers." *Public Personnel Management* 21, no. 3 (fall 1992).
Peters, Thomas J., and Robert H. Waterman Jr. *In Search of Excellence*. New York: Harper and Row, 1982.
Petro, Sylvestor. *Sovereignty and Compulsory Public-Sector Bargaining*, 10 Wake Forest L Rev 25 (March 1974).
Piskulich, John Patrick. *Collective Bargaining in State and Local Government*. New York: Praeger, 1992.
Plevan, Bettina B. "Harassment Gets Taken Seriously," *National L. J.,* 30 Mar. 1992.
Pollitt, Daniel H. *Racial Discrimination in Employment: Proposals for Corrective Action*, 13 Buffalo L Rev 59 (1963).
Preer, Robert M. *Reasonable Accommodation of Religious Practice: The Conflict Between the Courts and EEOC,* 15 Employee Relations L J 67 (summer 1989).
President's Private Sector Survey on Cost Control, *A Report to the President*. Washington, D.C.: Government Printing Office, 1984.
Priest, Dana. "When the Enforcer Commits the Sexual Harrassment: Federal Agencies Often Don't Discipline Their Wrongdoers," *Washington Post Weekly Edition,* 9–15 Dec. 1991.
Public Administration Review. "Diversity." Vol. 54, no. 3 (May/June 1994).
Public Service Research Council. *Public Sector Bargaining and Strikes.* 6th ed. Vienna, Va.: The Public Service Research Council, 1982.
Pynes, Joan E., and Joan M. Lafferty. *Local Government Labor Relations: A Guide for Public Administrators.* Westport, Conn.: Quorum Books, 1993.
Pynes, Joan, and H. John Bernardin. "Mechanical vs Consensus-Derived Assessment Center Ratings: A Comparison of Job Performance Validities." *Public Personnel Management* 21, no. 1 (spring 1992).
Rabin, Jack, Thomas Vocino, W. Bartley Hildreth, and Gerald J. Miller. *Handbook of Public Sector Labor Relations.* New York: Marcel Dekker, Inc., 1994.
Reasonable Woman Standard, The: Preventing Sexual Harassment in the Work-place, 18 William Mitchell L Rev 795 (1992).
Reese, Laura A., and Karen E. Lindenberg. "Staff Perceptions of Sexual Harassment Policy: Content and Recommendations." Paper delivered at the 1993 Annual Meeting of the American Political Science Association, Sept. 1993.
Reich, Robert B. *The Work of Nations.* New York: Vintage, 1991.
Reid, P.T. "Racism and Sexism: Comparison and Conflicts." In *Eliminating Racism: Profiles in Controversy.* Edited by P.A. Katz and D.A. Taylor. New York: Plenum, 1988.
Report to the President and the Congress of the United States by the U.S. Merit Systems Protection Board. *Attracting and Selecting Quality Applicants for Federal Employment: A Report Concerning Significant Actions of the Office of Personnel Management.* April 1990.
Report to the President and the Congress of the United States by the U.S. Merit Systems Protections Board. *Attracting Quality Graduates to the Federal Government: A View of College Recruiting.* June 1988.
Report to the President and the Congress of the United States by the U.S. Merit Systems Protection Board. *A Question of Equity: Women and the Glass Ceiling in the Federal Government.* Oct. 1992.
Report to the President and the Congress of the United States by the U.S. Merit Systems Protection Board. *Balancing Work Responsibilities and Family Needs: The Federal Civil Service Response.* Nov. 1991.
Report to the President and the Congress of the United States by the U.S. Merit Systems Protection Board. *Federal Personnel Offices: Time For Change?* Aug. 1993.
Rice, Mitchell F., and Brad Baptiste. "Race Norming, Validity Generalization, and Employment Testing." In *Handbook of Public Personnel Administration.* Edited by Jack Rabin et al. New York: Marcel Dekker, 1995.

Rivera, Rhonda R. *Queer* Law: Sexual Orientation Law in the Mid-Eighties*, 10 Dayton L Rev 481 (1985).
Roche, George. *America by the Throat: The Stranglehold of American Bureaucracy.* Hillsdale, Mich.: Hillsdale College Press, 1985.
Rohr, John A. *To Run A Constitution: The Legitimacy of the Administrative State.* Lawrence: University of Kansas Press, 1986.
Romzek, Barbara S. "Balancing Work and Nonwork Obligations." In *Public Personnel Management: Current Concerns—Future Challenges.* Edited by Carolyn Ban and Norma M. Riccucci. New York: Longman, 1991.
Roumell Jr., George T. *The Impact of Free Speech on Arbitrable Review of Discipline in the Public Sector,* 3 Detroit College of L Rev 807 (1992).
Rubaii-Barrett, Nadia, and Ann C. Beck. "Minorities in the Majority: Implications for Managing Cultural Diversity." *Public Personnel Management* 22, no. 4 (winter 1993).
Ryan, James E. *Smith and the Religious Freedom Restoration Act: An Iconoclastic Assessment,* 78 Virginia L Rev 1407 (Sept. 1992)
Sackett, Paul R., Laura Burris, and Christine Callahan. "Integrity Testing for Personnel Selection: An Update." *Personnel Psychology* 42 (1989).
Samborn, Randall. "Love Becomes a Labor Law Issue," *National L. J.,* 14 Feb. 1994.
Sarrazin, Robbin T. *Defamation in the Employment Setting,* 29 Tennessee Bar J 18 (May/June 1993).
Savage, David C. "Thomas Urged Reagan Administration to Toughen Stand Against Harassment," *Minneapolis Star Tribune,* 10 Oct. 1991.
Scholtes, Peter R. *The Team Handbook.* Madison, Wis.: Joiner Associates, 1992.
"Section 131, Job Discrimination," 45A Am Jur 2d 189.
Seidman, Harold, and Robert Gilmour. *Politics, Position, and Power.* 4th ed. New York: Oxford University Press, 1986.
Selznick, Phillip. *Leadership in Administration.* New York: Harper & Row, 1957.
Senge, Peter M. *The Fifth Discipline: The Art and Practice of the Learning Organization.* New York: Doubleday, 1990.
Shafritz, Jay M., Albert C. Hyde, and David H. Rosenbloom. *Personnel Management in Government: Politics and Process.* New York: Marcel Dekker, Inc., 1986.
Siegal, Gilbert B., and James R. Marshall. "The Use of PC Software in Teaching Public Personnel Administration." *Public Personnel Management* 20, no. 1 (spring 1991).
Simon, Herbert A. *Administrative Behavior: The New Science of Management Decision.* New York: Harper and Row, 1960.
———. "The Proverbs of Administration." *Public Administration Review* 6 (winter 1946).
Singer, Craig D. *Conduct and Belief: Public Employees' First Amendment Rights to Free Expression and Political Affiliation,* 59 U of Chicago L Rev 897 (1992).
Smith, Brian N. "The Effects of Job Description Content on Job Evaluation Judgements." *Journal of Applied Psychology* 25, no. 3 (June 1990).
Smith, D. Gordon. *Beyond "Public Concern": New Free Speech Standards for Public Employees,* 57 U of Chicago L Rev 249 (1990).
Smith, James Monroe. *HIV/AIDS and Workplace Discrimination: Dickens Revisited—It Was the Best of Times. It Was the Worst of Times,* 22 U West Los Angeles L Rev 19 (1991).
"Smithsonian Campus on the Mall." Washington, D.C.,: The Smithsonian Institution, fall 1994.
Snyder, Richard C. "To Improve Innovation, Manage Corporate Culture." In *The Planning of Change.* Edited by Bennis, Benne, & Chin. New York: Holt, Rinehart & Winston, 1985.
Sprang, Kenneth, A. *Beware the Toothless Tiger: A Critique of the Model Employment Termination Act,* 43 American U L Rev 849 (spring 1994).

Stacey, Donald R. *Subjective Criteria in Employment Decisions Under Title VII*, 10 Georgia L Rev 737 (1976).
Stahl, O. Glenn. *Public Personnel Administration*. 8th ed. New York: Harper & Row, 1983.
Starr, Tama. "So Sue Me Already: In the Age of Hyperfairness, a Business Owner Swims through Litigious Waters," *Washington Post National Weekly Edition*, 19–25 April 1993.
Stephan, Eric, Gordon E. Mills, R. Wayne Pace, and Lenny Ralphs. "HRD in the Fortune 500: A Survey." *Training & Development Journal* (Jan. 1988).
Swisher, Kara. "Diversity Training: Learning from Past Mistakes," *Washington Post National Weekly Edition*, 13–19 Feb. 1995.
Swiss, James E. "Adapting Total Quality Management (TQM) to Government." *Public Administration Review* 52, no. 4 (July/Aug. 1992).
Szymanski, A. "Racism and Sexism as Functional Substitutes in the Labor Market." *Sociological Quarterly* 17 (1976).
Taylor, Frederick W. *The Principles of Scientific Management*. 1911. Reprint, New York: W.W. Norton, 1967.
Thomas, Jeff. "White Male Backlash in the Workplace," *Colorado Springs Gazette Telegraph*, 2 Jan. 1994.
Tichy, Noel M., and Mary A. Devanna. *The Transformational Leader*. New York: Wiley Press, 1986.
Tipple, Terence J. "Executive Development Programs: A Framework for Coherence." Ph.D. diss., Virginia Tech, 1992.
Traynor, Michael. "Computer E-Mail Privacy Issues Unresolved," *National L. J.*, 31 Jan. 1994.
Underfuffler, Laura S. *Discrimination on the Basis of Religion: An Examination of Attempted Value Neutrality in Employment*, 30 Wm & Mary L Rev 581 (1989).
U.S. General Accounting Office, *A Management Concern: How to Deal with the Nonproductive Federal Employee*. Washington, D.C.: U.S. Government Printing Office, 1978.
U.S. Office of Personnel Management. *Civil Service 2000: Policies for the Future*. Washington, D.C.: 1988.
U.S. Office of Personnel Management. *Demographic Profile of the Federal Workforce* (PSO-OWI-5). 1992.
U.S. Office of Personnel Management. *Federal Total Quality Handbooks*. Vols. 1, 2, 3. June 1990.
U.S. Office of Personnel Management. *Presidential Management Intern Program*. 1993.
Urofsky, Melvin I. *A Conflict of Rights: The Supreme Court and Affirmative Action*. New York: Chas. Scribners, 1991.
Van Alstyne, William. *Demise of the Right-Privilege Distinction in Constitutional Law*, 81 Harvard L Rev 1439 (1968).
Van Riper, Paul P. *History of the United States Civil Service*. Evanston, Ill.: Row, Peterson and Company, 1958.
Volcker Commission Report. *Leadership for America: Rebuilding the Public Service*. Lexington, Mass.: Heath & Company, 1989.
Waks, Jay W. "Firms React to Charges of Age Bias in Ads," *National L. J.*, 7 Mar. 1994.
Waldo, Dwight. *The Administrative State: A Study of the Political Theory of American Public Administration*. New York: The Ronald Press, 1948.
Wallach, Eric J., and Alyse L. Jacobson. "'Reasonable Woman' Test Catches On," *National L. J.*, 6 July 1992.
Walton, Mary. *The Deming Method*. New York: Praeger, 1986.
"Wearing of Religious Garb by Public School Teachers," 60 ALR 2d 300 (1958).
Weber, Max. "Bureaucracy." In *From Max Weber: Essays in Sociology*. Edited by H. Gerth and C. Wright Mills. Oxford: Oxford University Press, 1946.

Whalen, Charles, and Barbara Whalen. *The Longest Debate: A Legislative History of the Civil Rights Act.* New York: Mentor Books, 1985.
White, Leonard D. *The Federalists.* New York: The Macmillan Company, 1948.
———. *Introduction to the Study of Public Administration.* New York: Macmillan Publishing Company, 1926.
———. *The Jeffersonians: A Study in Administrative History.* New York: The Macmillan Company, 1951.
———. "Strikes in the Public Service." *Public Personnel Review* 10, no. 1 (Jan. 1949).
Wildavsky, Aaron. *The New Politics of the Budgetary Process.* New York: Harper Collins Publishers, 1992.
Wilson, Woodrow. "The Study of Administration." *Political Science Quarterly* 2 (June 1887).
Woll, Peter. *American Bureaucracy.* 2d ed. New York: W.W. Norton & Company, 1977.
Wood, Horace G. *Master and Servant.* Albany, N.Y.: John Parsons Publishers, 1886.

Case Citations

Abrams v U.S. Department of the Navy, 714 F2d 1219 (3rd Cir 1983).
Accord, AFGE v Cavazos, 721 F.Supp. 1361 (D.C. Cir 1989).
AFGE v Barr, 794 F.Supp. 1466 (N.D. Calif. 1992).
AFGE v Cheney, 754 F.Supp. 1409 (N.D. Calif. 1990).
AFGE Local 1533 v Cheney, 754 F.Supp. 1409 (N.D. Calif. 1990).
AFGE v Skinner, 885 F2d 884 (D.C. Cir 1989), cert. denied, 495 US 923 (1990).
Albemarle Paper Co. v Moody, 422 US 405 (1975).
Alverado v Wash. Public Power Supply System, 759 P2d 427 (Wash. 1988).
American Federation of Government Employees, Council 33 v Barr, 794 F.Supp. 1466 (N. Calif. 1992)
American Federation of Government Employees, Local 1533 v Cheney, 754 F.Supp. 1409 (N.D. Calif. 1990).
Anderson v Bessemer City, North Carolina, 470 US 564 (1985).
Andrews v City of Philadelphia, 895 F2d 1469 (3d Cir 1990).
Anonymous Fireman v City of Willoughby, 779 F.Supp. 402 (N.D. Ohio 1991).
Ansonia Board of Education v Philbrook, 479 US 60 (1986).
Arline v Nassau School Board, 480 US 273 (1987).
Arneson v Sullivan, 946 F2d 90 (8th Cir 1992).
Arnett v Kennedy, 416 US 134 (1974).
Bailey v Richardson, 182 F2d 46 (D.C. Cir 1950), aff'd by an equally divided court, 341 US 918 (1951).
Barbano v Madison County, 922 F2d 139 (2d Cir 1990).
Barnes v Costle, 561 F2d 983 (D.C. Cir 1977).
Barnes v Gen Corp. Inc., 896 F2d 1457 (6th Cir 1989), cert. denied, 111 Sup.Ct. 211 (1990).

Barrett v Omaha National Bank, 726 F2d 424 (8th Cir 1984).
Barth v Gelb, 761 F.Supp. 830 (D.C. Cir 1991).
benMiriam v Office of Personnel Management, 647 F.Supp. 84 (M.D. N.C. 1986).
Bertoncini v City of Providence, 767 F.Supp. 1194 (D. R.I. 1991).
Bibbs v Block, 778 F2d 1318 (8th Cir 1985).
Birnbaum v Trussell, 371 F2d 672 (2d Cir 1966).
Bluestein v Skinner, 908 F2d 451 (9th Cir 1990).
Board of Regents v Roth, 408 US 564 (1972).
Bourke v Nissan Motor Corp. in U.S.A., B068705 (Cal. App., 2d Dist., Div. 4 (July 26, 1933)).
Bowen v Roy, 476 US 693 (1986).
Bradley v U. of Texas, 3 F3d 933 (5th Cir 1993), cert. denied 114 Sup.Ct. 107 (1994).
Bratton v City of Detroit, 704 F2d 878 (6th Cir 1983), cert. denied, 464 US 1040 (1984).
Brener v Diagnostic Center Hospital, 671 F2d 141 (5th Cir 1982).
Briggs v North Muskegon Police Dept., 563 F.Supp. 585 (W.D. Mich. 1983).
Brooms v Regal Tube, 830 F2d 1554 (11th Cir 1987).
Bross v Smith, 608 N.E.2d 1175 (Ohio App. 12 Dist., 1992), cert. denied by U.S. Supreme Court, 124 L.Ed.2d 251 (1993).
Brown v Department of Treasury, 34 M.S.P.R. 132 (1987).
Brown v Polk County, Iowa, 37 F3d 404 (8th Cir 1994).
Bruhwiler v U. of Tennessee, 859 F2d 419 (6th Cir 1988).
Buckingham v U.S., 998 F2d 735 (9th Cir 1993).
Bundy v Jackson, 641 F2d 934 (D.C. Cir 1981).
Burnett v Department of Health and Human Services, 51 M.S.P.R. 615 (1991).
Burns v McGregor Electronic Industries, 955 F2d 559 (8th Cir 1993), on remand, 807 F.Supp. 506 (N.D. Ia., 1992), revs'd, 989 F2d 959 (8th Cir 1993).
Bushey v N.Y. St. Civ. Serv. Com'n., 733 F2d 220 (2d Cir 1984).
Butler v Thornburgh, 900 F2d 871 (8th Cir 1991).
Butta v Anne Arundel County, 473 F.Supp. 83 (D. Md. 1979).
Buxton v City of Plant City, Florida, 871 F2d 1037 (11th Cir 1989).
Cafeteria Workers Local 473 v McElroy, 367 US 886 (1961).
California Federal Savings and Loan v Guerra, 479 US 272 (1987).
Callaway v Department of Army, 23 M.S.P.R. 592 (1984).
Carreno v I.B.E.W., 54 F.E.P.C. 81 (D. C. Kans. 1990).
Cassista v Community Foods Inc., 22 Cal. Rptr.2d 287 (1993).
Castaneda v Partida, 430 US 482 (1977).
Catherine Tanks v Greater Cleveland Regional Transit Authority, 930 F2d 475 (6th Cir 1991).
Chennault v U.S. Department of the Navy, 796 F2d 465 (Fed. Cir. 1986).
Chicago Firefighters v Washington, 736 F.Supp. 923 (N.D. Ill. 1990).
City of Richmond v Crosen, 488 US 469 (1989).
Cleveland Board of Ed. v LaFleur, 414 US 632 (1974).
Cleveland Board of Ed. v Loudermill, 470 US 532 (1985).
Connecticut v Teal, 457 US 440 (1982).
Connelly v Newman, 753 F.Supp. 293 (N.D. Calif. 1990).
Connick v Myers, 461 US 138 (1983).
Cook v State of Rhode Island, Dept. of Mental Health, Retardation and Hospitals, 834 F.Supp. 57 (D. R.I. 1993), affirmed with expanded opinion, 10 F3d 17 (1st Cir 1993).
Cooper v Cook Paint and Varnish Co., 563 F.Supp. 1146 (W.D. Mo. 1983).
Cooper v Eugene School District, 723 P2d 298 (Oreg. 1986), cert. denied, 480 US 942 (1986).
Crawford v Western Electric, 614 F2d 1300 (5th Cir 1980).
Cummings v Walsh Construction Co., 561 F.Supp. 972 (D. Ga. 1983).
Curle v Ward, 389 N.E.2d 1070 (N.Y. 1979).

CASE CITATIONS 341

Dew v Halaby, 317 F2d 582 (D.C. Cir 1963).
Diaz v Pan American World Airways, 442 F2d 385 (5th Cir 1971).
Dillan v Frank, 1992 Daily Lab. Rptr., No. 17 (6th Cir, Jan. 27, 1992).
Doe v District of Columbia, 796 F.Supp. 559 (D.C. Cir 1992).
Doe v New York University, 666 F2d 761 (2d Cir 1981).
Dothard v Rawlinson, 433 US 321 (1977).
Drinkwater v Union Carbide Corp., 56 F.E.P.C. 483 (1990).
E.E.O.C. v Alton Packaging, 981 F2d 920 (11th Cir 1990).
E.E.O.C. v AIC Security Investigation LTT., 820 F.Supp. 1060 (N.D. Ill. 1993).
E.E.O.C. v LA. Dept. of Social Services, 63 F.E.P.C. 161 (E.D. La. 1993).
E.E.O.C. v Pacific Press Pub. Assn., 676 F2d 1272 (9th Cir 1982).
E.E.O.C. v Wyoming, 460 US 226 (1983).
E. N. Bridgeport Guard Inc. v Members of Bridgeport Civil Service Comm., 482 F2d 1333 (2d Cir 1973), cert. denied, 421 US 991 (1975).
Egger v Phillips, 710 F2d 292 (7th Cir 1983).
Eibel v U.S. Department of the Navy, 857 F2d 1439 (D.C. Cir 1988).
Ellison v Brady, 924 F2d 872 (9th Cir 1991).
Employment Division v Smith, 494 US 872 (1990).
Ezold v Wolf, Block, Schorr, and Solis-Cohen, 751 F.Supp. 1175 (E.D. Pa. 1990).
Fountain v Safeway Stores 555 F2d 753 (9th Cir 1977).
Frontiero v Richardson, 411 US 677 (1973).
Fugate v Phoenix Civil Service Bd., 791 F2d 736 (9th Cir 1986).
Garcia v Elf Atochem North America, 28 F3d 446 (5th Cir 1994).
Gardner v Morris, 752 F2d 1271 (D.C. Cir 1985).
Gay Law Students Ass'n. v Pacific Telephone and Telegraph Co., 595 P2d 592 (Calif. 1979).
Geduldig v Aiello, 417 US 484 (1974).
Georgia Ass'n. of Educators v Harris, 749 F.Supp. 1110 (N.D. Ga. 1990).
General Electric Co. v Gilbert, 429 US 125 (1976).
Givhan v Western Consolidated School District, 439 US 410 (1979).
Goldman v Weinberger, 475 US 503 (1986).
Goluszek v Smith, 697 F.Supp. 1452 (N. Ill. 1988).
Gomez v Texas Dept. of Mental Health, 794 F2d 1018 (5th Cir 1986).
Gormley v Department of Navy, 43 M.S.P.R. 330 (1990).
Goss v Lopez, 419 US 565 (1975).
Green v Edward J. Bettinger Co., 608 F.Supp. 35 (E.D. Pa. 1984), affirmed without opinion, 791 F2d 917 (3d Cir 1984), cert. denied, 479 US 1069 (1986).
Greene v McElroy, 360 US 474 (1959).
Griggs v Duke Power Co., 401 US 424 (1971).
Griswold v Connecticut, 381 US 479 (1965).
Grussendorf v City of Oklahoma City, 816 F2d 539 (10th Cir 1987).
Guardians Assoc. of NY City Police Dep't. v Civil Service Commission of City of New York, 630 F2d 79 (2d Cir 1980), cert. denied, 432 US 940 (1981).
Hammon v Barry, 606 F.Supp. 1082 (D.C. Cir 1987), rev'd, 813 F2d 412 (D.C. Cir 1987), reh. denied, 826 F2d 73 (D.C. Cir 1987), cert. denied, *Barry v U.S.* 486 US 1035 (1988), vacated, 841 F2d 426 (D.C. Cir 1988).
Harmer v Virginia Electric and Power Co., 831 F.Supp. 1300 (E.D. Va. 1993).
Harmon v Thornburgh, 878 F2d 484 (D.C. Cir 1989).
Harris v Forklift Systems, 126 L.Ed.2d 295 (1993), 114 Sup.Ct. 367 (1993).
Hartness v Bush, 919 F2d 170 (D.C. Cir 1990), cert. denied, 111 Sup. Ct. 2829 (1991).
Hazlewood High School v U.S., 433 US 299 (1977).
Hayes v Department of Navy, 727 F2d 1535 (Fed Cir 1984).
Henson v City of Dundee, 682 F2d 897 (11th Cir 1982).
Hicks v St. Mary's Honor Center, 756 F.Supp. 1250 (1993).
High Tech Gays v Defense Indus. Sec. Clear. Off., 895 F2d 563 (9th Cir 1990).

High Tech Gays v Defense Indus. Sec. Clear. Off., 668 F.Supp. 1361 (C.D. Calif. 1987).
Hill v Seaboard Coast Line R. Co., 885 F2d 804 (11th Cir 1989).
Hill v State of Florida Dept. of Health, 715 F.Supp. 346 (M.D. Fla. 1992).
Hindman v GTA Services, 3A.D. Cases 641 (M.D. Fla, 1994) BNA
Hopkins v Baltimore Gas and Electric Co., (C. Md.), No. H-934167 (Dec. 28, 1994).
Hustler Magazine v Falwell, 485 US 46 (1988).
Immigration and Naturalization Service v Federal Labor Relations Authority and American Federation of Government Employees, AFL-CIO, 855 F2d 1454 (9th Cir 1988).
Interlekofer v Turnage, 973 F2d 773 (9th Cir 1992).
International Brotherhood of Electrical Workers, Local 1245 v Skinner, 913 F2d 1454 (9th Cir 1990).
Int'l Brotherhood of Teamsters v Dept. of Transportation, 932 F2d 1292 (9th Cir 1991).
International Brotherhood of Teamsters, Chauffeurs, Western Conference of Teamsters v Department of Transportation, 932 F2d 1292 (9th Cir 1991).
International Union of Flight Attendants v FAA, 908 F2d 451 (9th Cir 1990).
Jackson v Howell, 577 F.Supp. 47 (W.D. Mich. 1983).
Jacobs v Kuenes, 541 F2d 233 (9th Cir 1976).
Johnson v Ballermine, 515 F.Supp. 1287 (D. Md. 1981), cert. denied, 455 US 944 (1981).
Johnson v Bunny Bread Company, 646 F2d 1250 (8th Cir 1981.)
Johnson v Shalala, 764 F.Supp. 1053 (D. Md. 1991).
Johnson v Shalala, 991 F2d 126 (4th Cir 1993).
Johnson v Transportation Agency of Santa Clara County, 480 US 616 (1987).
Joint Anti-Fascist Refugee Committee v McGrath, 341 US 123 (1951).
Jones v. Rivers, 722 F.Supp. 771 (D.C. Cir 1989).
Jurgensen v. Fairfax County, Va., 745 F2d 868 (4th Cir 1984).
Kandall v U.S., 186 Ct. Cl. 900 (1969).
Katz v U.S., 389 US 347 (1967).
Kelley v Johnson, 425 US 139 (1976).
Kettell v Johnson & Johnson, 337 F.Supp. 892 (D. Ark. 1971).
King v Trans World Airlines, 738 F2d 255 (8th Cir 1984).
Knott v Missouri Pacific R.R., 527 F2d 1249 (8th Cir 1975).
Kukla and Kukla v Village of Antioch, 647 F.Supp. 799 (N.D. Ill. 1986).
Kyriazi v Western Electric Co., 461 F.Supp. 894 (D. N.J. 1978).
La Riviere v E.E.O.C., 682 F2d 1275 (9th Cir 1982).
Lawrence v Mars Inc., 955 F2d 902 (4th Cir 1992).
Leckelt v Bd. of Comm'rs. of Hosp. Dist. 1, 909 F2d 820 (5th Cir 1990).
Ledoux v Dist. of Columbia, 820 F2d 1293 (D.C. Cir 1987), reh. gr., 833 F2d 368 (D.C. Cir 1987), vac., 841 F2d 400 (D.C. Cir 1988).
Leggett v First Interstate Bank of Oregon, 739 F2d 1083 (9th Cir 1987).
Levias v United Airlines, 500 N.E.2d 370 (Ohio Ct. App. 1985).
Little v F.B.I., 793 F.Supp. 652 (D. Md. 1992).
Local 1812 A.F.G.E. v U.S. Dept. of State, 662 F.Supp. 50 (D.C.Cir 1987).
Local 93, Int. Assoc. of Firefighters A.F.L.-C.I.O. v E.E.O.C., 478 US 501 (1986).
Local 28 of Sheet Metal Workers v E.E.O.C., 478 US 412 (1986).
Lovshin v U.S. Department of the Navy, 767 F2d 826 (Fed Cir 1985).
Lowe v Commack Union Free School District, 886 F2d 1364 (2nd Cir 1989), cert. denied, *Maciarello and Rowell v City of Lancaster*, 122 L.Ed.2d 356 (1990).
Maciarello v Sumner, 973 F2d 295 (4th Cir 1992), cert. denied, *Maciarello and Powell v City of Lancaster*, 122 L.Ed.2d 356 (1993).
Matzo v Postmaster-General, 685 F.Supp. 260 (D.C. Cir 1987).
Mayor v Educational Quality League, 415 US 605 (1974).
McAuliffe v Mayor of Bedford, 155 Mass 216 (1882).
McDonald v Santa Fe Trail Transportation Co., 427 US 273 (1976).
McDonnell-Douglas Corporation v Green, 411 US 792 (1973).

CASE CITATIONS 343

McKenna v Fargo, 451 F.Supp. 1355 (D. N.J. 1978).
Meritor Savings Bank v Vinson, 477 US 57 (1986).
Mekss v Wyoming Girl's School, 813 P2d 185 (Wyo. 1991).
Michael M. v Sonoma County, 480 US 616 (1981).
Milkovich v Lorain Journal Co., 497 US 1 (1990).
Miller v Bank of America, 418 F.Supp. 233 (N.D. Calif. 1976).
Miller v Motorola Inc., 560 N.E.2d 900 (Ill. App. Ct. 1990).
Monroe v Pape, 365 US 167 (1961).
Moulton v Iowa Employment Security Commission, 34 N.W.2d 21 (1948).
Mount Healthy City Board of Education v Doyle, 429 US 274 (1977).
Munford v James T. Barnes and Co., 441 F.Supp. 459 (E.D. Mich. 1977).
National Federation of Federal Employees v Greenberg, 789 F.Supp. 430 (D.C. Cir 1993), vac., 983 F2d 286 (D.C. Cir 1993).
National Treasury Employees Union v Von Raab, 489 US 656 (1989).
National Treasury Employees Union v Yeutter, Sec. Agric., 733 F.Supp. 403, 918 F2d 968 (D.C. Cir 1990).
New York v Wal-Mart Stores, NY Sup. Ct., App. Div. 70609 (Jan. 1, 1994).
New York Times v Sullivan, 376 US 254 (1964).
Norton v Macy, 417 F2d 1161 (Ct. Cl. 1969).
O'Connor v Ortega, 480 US 709 (1987).
Odum v Frank, 3 F3d 838 (5th Cir 1993).
Officers for Justice v Civil Service Commission of the City and County of San Francisco, 979 F2d 721 (9th Cir 1992).
Padula v Webster, 822 F2d 97 (D.C. Cir 1987).
Palmer v Baker, 905 F2d 1544 (D.C. Cir 1990).
Palmer v Schultz, 616 F.Supp. 1540 (D.C. Cir 1985), 815 F2d 84 (D.C. Cir 1987).
Papritz v Department of Justice, 31 M.S.P.R. 495 (1986).
Parker v Baltimore & O. R. Co. 652 F2d 1012 (D.C. Cir 1981).
Partington v Broyhill Furniture, 999 F2d 269 (7th Cir 1993).
Payton v New York, 445 US 573 (1980).
People v Otto, 9 Cal. Rptr. 2d 596 (1992).
Perez v F.B.I., 714 F.Supp. 1414 (W. Tex. 1989).
Perry v Sinderman, 408 US 593 (1972).
Pesterfield v TVA, 941 F2d 437 (6th Cir 1991).
Phillips v Bergland, 586 F2d 1007 (4th Cir 1978).
Philbrook v Ansonia School Board, 757 F2d 476 (2d Cir 1986).
Pickering v Board of Education, 391 US 563 (1968).
Potter v Murray City, 585 F.Supp. 1126 (D. Utah 1984), 760 F2d 1065 (10th Cir 1985).
Price-Waterhouse v Hopkins, 490 US 228 (1989), 737 F.Supp. 1202 (D.C. Cir 1990).
Pushkin v Regents of U. of Colorado, 658 F2d 1372 (10th Cir 1981).
Rabidue v Osceola Refining Co., 805 F2d 611 (6th Cir 1986).
Rankin v McPhereson, 483 US 378 (1987).
Regents of U. of California v Bakke, 438 US 265 (1978).
Reynolds v U.S., 98 US (8 Otto) 145 (1878).
Rocheleau v S.E.C., 29 M.S.P.R. 193 (1985), affd. without opinion, 802 F2d 469 (1985).
Rogers v E.E.O.C., 454 F2d 234 (5th Cir 1971).
Rose v Wells Fargo & Co., 902 F2d 1417 (9th Cir 1990).
St. Mary's Honor Center v Hicks, 125 L.Ed.2d 407, 113 S.Ct. 2742 (1993).
Saxton v American Telephone & Telegraph, 10 F3d 526 (7th Cir 1993).
Schlegel v U.S., 416 F2d 1372 (D.C. Cir 1969), cert. denied, 397 US 1039 (1970).
Scott v Sears Roebuck, 798 F2d 210 (7th Cir 1986).
Segar, et al. v Civiletti, 508 F.Supp. 690 (D.C. Cir 1981).
Shawgo v Spradlin, 701 F2d 470 (5th Cir 1983), cert. denied, 464 US 965 (1983).
Sherbert v Verner, 374 US 398 (1963).

Shoars v Epson America, SWC 112749 (St. of Appeals for 2nd Dist. Calif.–L.A. (June 1994)), unpublished decision.
Singer v U.S. Civil Service Comm., 530 F2d 247 (9th Cir 1976).
Skinner v Railway Labor Executives Assoc., 489 US 602 (1989).
Smith v Maryland, 442 US 735 (1979).
Soroka v Dayton-Hudson, 1 Cal. 2d 77 (1992).
Southeast Community College v Davis, 442 US 397 (1979).
Stern v Teamsters "General" Local Union No. 200, 626 F.Supp. 1043 (E.D. Wis. 1986).
Stone v Department of Health and Human Services, 38 M.S.P.R. 634 (1988).
Swentek v USAir, 830 F2d 552 (4th Cir 1987).
Swift v U.S., 649 F.Supp. 596 (D.C. Cir 1986).
Taggart v Time, 924 F2d 43 (2d Cir 1991).
Texas Dept. of Community Affairs v Burdine 450 US 248 (1981).
Thorne v City of El Segundo, 726 F2d 459 (9th Cir 1983), cert. denied, 469 US 979 (1984).
Toledo v Nobel Sysco, 651 F.Supp. 483 (D. N.Mex. 1986).
Tomkins v Public Service Electric and Gas Co., 422 F2d 553 (D. N.J. 1976).
Tomkins v Public Service Electric and Gas Co., 568 F2d 1044 (3d Cir 1977).
Torres v Wisc. Dept. of Health and Social Services, 859 F2d 1523 (7th Cir 1988).
Trans-World Airlines v Hardison, 432 US 63 (1977).
Underwood v Department of Defense, 53 M.S.P.R. 355 (1992).
United Public Workers v Mitchell, 330 US 75 (1947).
U.S. v Hazelwood High School, 534 F2d 805 (8th Cir 1970).
U.S. v Orito, 413 US 139 (1973).
U.S. v Takela, 923 F2d 665 (9th Cir 1991).
U.S. v Westinghouse Electric Corporation, 638 F2d 570 (3d Cir 1980).
United Steelworkers of America v Weber, 443 US 193 (1979).
Valdez v Mercy Hospital, 961 F2d 1401 (8th Cir 1992).
Wade v Mississippi Cooperative Extension Service, 528 F2d 508 (5th Cir 1976), on remand, 424 F.Supp. 1242 (5th Cir 1976).
Walders v Garrett, 765 F.Supp. 303 (E.D. Va. 1991).
Walker v AT & T Technologies, 995 F2d 846 (8th Cir 1993).
Walker v Department of Treasury, 28 M.S.P.R. 227 (1985).
Wards Cove Packing Co. v Antonio, 490 US 642 (1989).
Warner v Graham, 675 F.Supp. 1171 (D. N.Dak. 1985).
Washington, et al. v Davis, 426 US 229 (1976).
Waters v Churchill, 511 US ___, (1994), 128 L.Ed.2d 686, 144 S.Ct. 1878 (1993).
Wathen v U.S., 527 F2d 1191, 208 Ct. Cl. 342 (1975), cert. denied, 429 US 821 (1976).
Watkins v L. M. Berry & Co., 704 F2d 583 (11th Cir 1983).
Watkins v U.S. Army, 847 F2d 1329 (9th Cir 1988), 875 F2d 699 (9th Cir 1989).
Weiss v U.S., 595 F.Supp. 1050 (E.D. Va. 1984).
Williams v Department of Health and Human Services, 38 M.S.P.R. 217 (1986).
Williams v Saxbe, 413 F.Supp. 654 (D.C. Cir 1976).
Willner v Thornburgh, 928 F2d 1185 (D.C. Cir 1991).
Wilson v Department of Health and Human Services, 770 F2d 1048 (D.C. Cir 1985).
Wilson v Southwest Airlines, 517 F.Supp. 292 (N.D. Tex. 1981).
Wilson v U.S. West Communications, 860 F.Supp. 665 (D. Neb. 1994).
Wood v Strickland, 420 US 308 (1975).
Wygant v Jackson Bd. of Educ. 476 US 267 (1986).
Yacavone v Bolger, 645 F2d 1028 (D.C. Cir 1981), cert. denied, 454 US 844 (1981).
Young v Hampton, 568 F2d 1253 (7th Cir 1977).
Zaken v Boerer, 964 F2d 1319 (2d Cir 1992).
Zang v Defense Investigative Service, 26 M.S.P.R. 155 (1985).

Index

affirmative action 7, 194, 201, 225
  beneficiaries (female), 227
  diversity training, 210
  four-fifths rule, 203, 214
  future of, 210–211
  gender discrimination, 225–227
  ladder of actions, 201
  policy (example) 213
  prophylactic measures, 201, 203, 208
  promotion process, 209
  protected status as a plus, 205, 225–226
  quotas, use of, 201–202
  race-norming, 203–205
  standards and guidelines, 202, 206, 213
  voluntary plans, 205–208, 226
age-based discrimination, 246–250
  burden of proof, 249
  compulsory retirement, 247–248
  EEOC role, 246
  pre-textual terminations, 247–250
  tied to reductions in force, 249–250
Age Discrimination in Employment Act (ADEA), 246–250
alcoholics. *See* disability and handicapped discrimination
Americans with Disabilities Act of 1990, 250–256, 260, 264
Anti-Drug Abuse Act of 1986, 254

appraisal of employees. *See* performance management
alternative work scheduling (AWS), 63
  compressed work scheduling, 63
  flextime, 63
Architectural Barriers Act, 250

Behaviorally Anchored Rating System (BARS), 77–79
Brownlow Commission Report of 1937, 21
Budget and Impoundment Act of 1974, 5
bureaucracy
  neutrality of, 5–6
  separation of powers, 4–5
bureaucrats
  appointees, 9–10
  careerists, 9–10
  neutrality of, 5–6
  rights of, 5–6
  senior executives, 8, 22
Bush, George, 10

Civil Rights Act of 1866, 193
Civil Rights Act of 1871
  suits under Sections 1981,1983,1985, 193, 196, 200
Civil Rights Act of 1964, 149, 194–198, 219, 236
  See also Title VII

345

Civil Rights Act of 1972, 149, 194, 220
Civil Rights Act of 1991, 204–205, 222, 233, 249
Civil Service Act of 1871, 193
Civil Service Reform Act of 1978, 274–278, 280–281
  amendments of 1989, 146
  Section 43 actions, 275–278
  Section 75 actions, 278–282
classification, 51–62
Clinton, William (Bill), 26–27
college recruitment
  on-the-spot hiring, 67
  pay banding, 66
  Presidential Management Internship (PMI), 67
Commission on Organization of the Executive Branch of Government. *See* Hoover Commission
Constitution of the United States 140, 194
  role of the U.S. Senate, 5
  separation of powers, 4

Deming, Edward. *See* total quality management
disability and handicapped discrimination
  and absenteeism, 257–258
  and alcoholism, 253–254
  capital expenditures, 251
  definition of disability, 253–254
  and the EEOC, 251, 255, 258, 263
  employment questioning, 166–167, 252–253
  harassment of disabled persons, 263
  HIV infection, 259–262
  mental disability, 258–259
  obesity as a disability, 262–263
  perceived disabilities, 262
  policy (example), 266
  stress disability, 256–257
  and Title VII, 251
  workplace accommodation, 255–256
discipline of employees, 281–282
disparate treatment, 195–197
diversity in work force, 7–8, 209, 226, 293–294
drug and alcohol abuse
  policy (example), 185–187
drug testing, 6–7, 177–181
  and Fourth Amendment rights, 176–177
  and law enforcement employment, 178–180
  on-duty vs. off-duty, 279
  protocols and standards for, 181
  use in sensitive positions, 180, 185–187
due process
  and the Constitution, 140–141
  and liberty interests, 142
  procedural, 140–142, 275–277, 280–281
  and property interests, 141

efficiency
  of the service, 278, 282
  standard operating procedures, 19–21
  use of classifications, 51–62
e-mail surveillance, 182
employee benefits
  cafeteria plans, 66
  and child care, 63–66
employee assistance programs (EAPs), 87–88
employee discipline, 86–87, 281
  procedures, 280–281
employee grievances, 139, 283
  See also labor management relations
Employee Polygraph Protection Act, 167–168
employment at will doctrine, 140, 273–274
Equal Employment Opportunity Commission, 173, 194–195, 198–199, 228–230, 234–236, 251, 255–256, 258, 263, 283
  and affirmative action, 206–207
  Uniform Guidelines on Employee Selection Procedures, 205
Equal Pay Act of 1963, 219
ethical standards, publication of, 282–283
examinations for employment, 164–167, 196–197, 251–253
  job–related questioning, 164–167, 197, 224, 251–253
  physical, 251–253
  polygraph, 167–168
  psychological, 164–167, 253
executive development
  career planning, 133
  continuing education, 134–135
  definition of, 121–122
  growth of, 122
  instruments used in, 123–129
  leadership, 123–129
  rotational assignments, 134

Fair Employment Practices Committee, 194
Family and Medical Leave Act of 1993, 264–265
Federal Labor Relations Authority (FLRA), 93

Garfield, James
  assassination by Charles Guiteau, 17–18
gender discrimination, 219–238
  affirmative action, 225–227
  bona fide occupational qualification (BFOQ), 220–221
  differential treatment, 221
  disparate impact practices, 223–224
  equal protections doctrine, 226
  "glass ceiling," 224
  harassment (*see* sexual harassment)
  mentoring, 225
  mixed-motive actions, 221–223

INDEX 347

gender discrimination (*continued*)
  stereotyping, 221–222, 224–225
  and Title VII, 219, 226
Goodnow, Frank, 19
Gore, Al
  Creating Government That Works Better &
  Costs Less, 30, 33–37
  National Performance Review, 2, 8, 33–38,
  290, 298
grievance procedures for employees, 88,
  283
handicapped discrimination. *See* disability
  and handicapped discrimination
HIV infection
  as a disability, 259–262
  incidence in workplace, 259
  worker reactions, 261
  workplace accommodation, 261–262
Holmes, Oliver Wendell, 140
homosexuals
  Civil Service Commission guidelines on
  employment, 172
  having disability, 253
  entitled to equal protection, 170–171
  harassment of, by, 172–173
  in the military, 171
  sensitive and security positions, 171–172
Hoover Commission, 22
Hughes Act of 1970, 254
human resource development
  definition of, 113–115
  development, 108–13
  education, 115
  external human resource professionals,
  116–117
  future development of, 118–119
  internal human resource professionals,
  116
  key issues in, 117–118
  roles of employees, 116
  roles of supervisors, 116

Jackson, Andrew
  creation of the "spoils system," 16–17
Jefferson, Thomas, 15
judicial system
  role in public administration 6–7,
  295–296

Kennedy, John F.
  Executive Order 10988 (collective bargaining), 93
Keynesian economics, 22

labor management relations (LMR)
  arguments against public sector unionization, 94
  collective bargaining, 96–100
  future issues in, 101–104
  historical development of unions, 92–94
  private vs. public sector, 95–96

labor management relations (*continued*)
  role of unions, 102–103
  striking, 100–101
Leadership. *See* executive development
Leadership Development Program (LDP),
  131–132
Leadership for a Democratic Society (LDS),
  132–133
Lloyd-Lafollette Act, 278, 280
Malek, Fred
  Federal Political Personnel Model (the Malek
  Manual), 5
mental disabilities. *See* disability and handicapped discrimination
Merit Systems Protection Board, 146, 276
misconduct
  prohibited employment practices, 282
Model Employment Termination Act, 274
National Performance Review
  summary of recommendations, 30–31,
  33–38
  See also Gore, Al
Nixon, Richard
  Executive Order 11478 (affirmative action), 206
  Executive Order 11914 (handicapped status), 254

Occupational Health and Safety Act, 175,
  261
Office of Personnel Management, 276
organization culture, 110–111, 113–115,
  127–128
patronage, 16–17
pay systems
  Foreign Service Schedule, 65
  General Services Schedule (GS), 64
  Geographic Adjustment Schedule, 64, 65
Pendleton Act of 1883, 18–19
performance management
  achievement review, 82–86
  appraisal of employees, 82–86, 275–276
  "backwards standards," 276
  managing performance, 81–86
  performance planning, 80–81
  problems with appraisal technique, 77–80
  problems with the rater, 76–77
  traditional style, 75–76
personal behavior and habits
  dress and grooming, 173–174
  dress codes, 174
  public notoriety, 172, 278–279
  smoking, 175–176
personnel administration
  concept of unity of command, 5
  tensions in, 4–10
political appointees, 9
politics/administration dichotomy. *See* Wilson, Woodrow

POSDCORB (acronym)
  definition, 21–22
  development of, 21–23
position classification
  factor classification system, 51–62
position descriptions
  critical tasks, 48–50
  examples, 48–50, 68–71
  knowledge, skills, and abilities (KSA), 50–51
  performance standards, 47
  quality-oriented position management system (QOPMS), 47–51
  traditional style, 46–47
position management, 45–71
Pregnancy Discrimination Act, 237–238
President's Committee on Equal Employment Opportunity, 194
President's Private Sector Survey on Cost Control (Grace Commission), 25
privacy, 164–192
  and background checks, 165–167
  due process protection, 164
  job-related questioning and examinations, 165–167, 251–253, 261
  Ninth Amendment, 164
  off-duty behaviors, 169
  polygraph examinations, 167
  relationships, 168–169
  tort actions, 170
  See also surveillance in the workplace
privatization
  of the public sector, 8–9, 24–25
  and Ronald Reagan, 8–9, 24–25
public bureaucracy. *See* bureaucrats
racial discrimination, 193–218
  burden of proof, 195–197
  disparate impact, 196–198
  disparate treatment (intentional discrimination), 194–196, 199
  EEOC guidelines, 195, 202–203
  systematic intentional discrimination, 198
  and testing, 197, 204
  and Title VII, 194–198
racial harassment
  adverse action, 198–199
  EEOC regulations, 202, 206–207
  retaliatory discharge, 199–200
  and Title VII, 198
  in the workplace, 198–200
Reagan, Ronald
  Executive Order 12564 (drug testing), 178
recruitment of employees. *See* college recruitment
reduction in force (RIF), 249–250
reengineering
  definition of, 40–41
  elements to, 41–42

reengineering (*continued*)
  future issues in, 43
  technology and, 42–43
  worker roles in, 42
reform in government
  history of, 13–27, 30–43
  private sector models, 24–25
Rehabilitation Act of 1973, 250–256, 260, 262–264
  1988 amendments, 259
relationships in the workplace
  exploitive, 172–173, 229–230
  fraternization, 169
  marriage, 168
religion in the workplace, 148–154
  constitutional protection, 148
  definition of discrimination under Title VII, 149
  and drug use, 153–154
  establishment clause violations, 151–153
  harassment, 152–153
  reasonable accommodation of, 149–150
  retaliation, 151–153
Religious Freedom Restoration Act of 1993, 153–154
representative bureaucracy, 14, 183, 201
  in Canada (example), 7–8
  use of demographics, 7–8
retaliatory discharge, 146, 150–153, 199–200, 228
reverse discrimination
  burden of proof, 200
  Civil Rights Act of 1871, Sec. 1981, 1983, 200
  and Title VII, 200
RIF (reduction in force), 249
search and seizure
  concept of reasonable search, 176
  and the Fourth Amendment, 176–177
  mixed private and employer property, 177
  in the workplace, 176–177
Senior Managers in Government (SMG) Program, 129–130
Senior Executive Service, 9
sex-linked discrimination, 235–238
  due process, 236
  judicial standards, 236–237
  maternity leave, 236–238
  Pregnancy Discrimination Act, 237
  Title VII, 236
sexual harassment
  damages in, 233–234
  and the EEOC, 228
  employer responsibility, 234–235
  hostile work environment, 229
  judicial standards for, 228–230
  quid pro quo harassment, 228
  policy (example), 239

sexual harassment (*continued*)
  psychological impact of, 232–233
  reasonable woman standard, 231–232
  retaliation 228–229
  and supervisors, 230–231
  and Title VII, 228
smoking. *See* personal behavior and habits
speech in the workplace
  balancing tests, 143–145
  defamation and libel, 147
  due process protection, 141
  and the First Amendment, 143–148
  symbolic expression, 145–146
  See also whistleblowing
surveillance in the workplace
  Federal Wiretap Act, 182
  methods used, 182–183
  and privacy interests, 181–182
  technological surveillance, 181–183
Taylor, Frederick
  model of scientific management, 19–21, 46
  testimony to the U.S. House of Representatives, 19
  specialization and standardization, 20
  technology and technological innovation, 42, 296–297
Tenure of Office Act (1867), 17
termination of employees
  "crime exception," 280
  and procedural due process, 276–277, 280–282

Title VII of Civil Rights Act of 1964, 139, 172, 174, 193–200, 202–203, 206, 220, 222, 227–228, 233–237, 246, 251
total quality management (TQM)
  definition of, 38
  elements to, 38–39
  role in government, 39–40
unions and unionization. *See* labor management relations
U.S. Civil Service Commission Guidelines, 172, 278–279
U.S. Congress
  efforts in public bureaucracy reform, 4–5
Van Riper, Paul, 14–15, 18, 284
Van Alstyne, William, 141
veterans preference, 13–15, 278
Volker Commission Task Force, 66–67
Weber, Max
  model of bureaucracy, 20–21
whistleblowing
  matters of public concern, 144–146
  statutory protection, 146
White, Leonard D., 20
Wood, Harris G., 273
workforce composition, 7–8, 293–294
Wilson, Woodrow
  politics/administration dichotomy, 5